...tions

PEOPLE

Bassett

The Beauty Manifesto

Children of Killers

Cloud Busting

Frank & Ferdinand

Gap

Gargantua

Shooting Truth

Those Legs

Too Fast

with an introduction by

ANTHONY BANKS

Bloomsbury Methu...
An imprint of Bloomsbur...

B L O O M S ...

LONDON · OXFORD · NEW YORK · NEW DELHI · ...

Bloomsbury Methuen Drama

An imprint of Bloomsbury Publishing Plc

Imprint previously known as Methuen Drama

50 Bedford Square	1385 Broadway
London	New York
WC1B 3DP	NY 10018
UK	USA

www.bloomsbury.com

BLOOMSBURY, METHUEN DRAMA and the Diana logo are trademarks of Bloomsbury Publishing Plc

This collection first published in 2011 by Bloomsbury Methuen Drama
Reprinted 2012, 2013, 2015, 2017

Frank & Ferdinand © Samuel Adamson 2011
Gap © Alia Bano 2011
Cloud Busting © Helen Blakeman 2011
Those Legs © Noel Clarke 2011
Shooting Truth © Molly Davies 2011
Bassett © James Graham 2011
Gargantua © Carl Grose 2011
Children of Killers © Katori Hall 2011
The Beauty Manifesto © Nell Leyshon 2011
Too Fast © Douglas Maxwell 2011

Introduction © Methuen Drama 2011
Resource material © Anthony Banks/National Theatre 2011

British Library Cataloguing-in-Publication Data
A catalogue record for this book is available from the British Library.

ISBN: PB: 978-1-4081-3179-4
ePDF: 978-1-4081-4569-2
ePub: 978-1-4081-4568-5

Library of Congress Cataloging-in-Publication Data
A catalog record for this book is available from the Library of Congress.

Series: Play Anthologies

Typeset by Country Setting, Kingsdown, Kent
Printed and bound in Great Britain

Contents

Introduction

The National Theatre launched Connections in 1995 to commission exciting, contemporary, adventurous plays for young actors to perform. Each festival year around two hundred young companies take on the imaginative and practical challenge of staging these new plays and sharing their work with other young theatre companies in their region. And each year we publish the plays, this year for the first time in partnership with Methuen Drama, to give other schools and youth theatre companies their chance to bring these new works to the stage.

The ten plays in the 2011 *Connections* edition offer a huge variety of stories and styles to inspire young actors and creative teams. The playwrights have worked with young people across the country and beyond – from the Shetland Isles to Devon, from Wiltshire to Manhattan – to create plays which respond to the imaginations, ideas and concerns of young people.

With each play we also publish a set of notes for rehearsal and production. These are drawn straight from the National Theatre's workshops, which give directors the chance to explore the world of the play with its writer. We offer these as an insight into the writer's ideas for the play, and as a starting point for your own exploration and staging.

We hope you enjoy reading the plays in this 2011 *Connections* anthology; and still more, that you will find opportunities to get them on their feet – in the classroom, in your youth theatre group, in your local theatre. For more information, please visit www.nationaltheatre.org.uk/connections

Frank & Ferdinand
CAST SIZE 6 *leading, and ensemble of as many as possible*
AGE SUITABILITY 13–19

Samuel Adamson is from Australia, and has lived in London for the last twenty years. He has written many plays for the National Theatre. While working on his last play, *Mrs Affleck* – a re-imagining of an Ibsen play called *Little Eyolf*, which contains a rat-catcher character – Samuel found himself investigating the various versions of the Pied Piper story, which had its origins in medieval Germany.

A village in a war-ravaged country wakes to find that one hundred and thirty children have vanished. Only four are left: Otto, Aloysius, Sarah and Flora. Interviewed by a Military Inquiry, each child tells the events of the night before. But their accounts seem to differ. Who is the elusive Sebastian and why does the Inquiry's depiction of him keep changing from delinquent to charmer and back again? What's real, and what's fairy tale? *Frank & Ferdinand* is a short, satirical mystery about the suppression of truth, the making of myths, and how we see what we want to see, not what's there.

Gap
CAST SIZE 17
AGE SUITABILITY 15–19

Alia Bano is from Birmingham. She recently spent several weeks travelling around Brazil, where she spent some time in a youth hostel near Copacabana Beach, Rio de Janeiro. The people she met on the beach and in the hostel inspired the characters and stories in her play. *Gap* refers to the enormous poverty gap Alia became aware of between the gap-year westerners who were out there for a limited period, and the young Brazilians who ran the beach and the hostel.

Twenty-four hours in an exotic country with a medley of fifteen characters all brought together by their choice of hostel. Jay wants to rule the roost, Hailey wants Jay, Kat wants social change and Dee just wants to make a living. *Gap* follows these diverse personalities from the beach to the dorm and finally to the bar to see what has brought them here, how they embrace their first steps into independence and how they respond to each other.

Cloud Busting
CAST SIZE 10m, 6f
AGE SUITABILITY 13–15

Helen Blakeman is from Liverpool, and her play *Cloud Busting* was inspired by Malorie Blackman's novel of the same title. Featuring a cast of typical Year Eights, and set in and around a typical school, it's a play for younger actors about making up poems and the highs and lows of first friendships.

When Sam wakes up, he fully believes today will be just another ordinary day – but that's before Mr Mackie tells class 8M to write a poem about someone they care about. Unexpectedly, Sam volunteers to write about Davey . . . Davey was Sam's friend – not that Sam wanted anyone to know that. While the cool girls in the class thought Davey was well cute in a sad-dog sort of way, the tough boys – Alex and his crew – just saw Davey as different. Davey liked to dance. Davey liked to look at the clouds and see the shapes they made. Davey liked looking at the world in a different way to everybody else. But no matter how much Sam liked being with Davey, he always denied their friendship. Then one day, Alex's bullying goes a step too far . . . But will Sam step in to help his friend? It's not the ordinary day Sam thought it was going to be.

Those Legs
CAST SIZE 3m, 3f
AGE SUITABILITY 15–19

Noel Clarke is from London and is an actor, director and screenwriter. He is well known for playing Mickey Smith in *Doctor Who* on television, and created the hit films *Kidulthood* and *Adulthood*. *Those Legs* is his debut as a theatre writer.

Georgia, Aaron and Leon have been friends since they were kids. Now they're young adults, in their first jobs, and sharing a house in the city with newcomer Lana. It's been two years since the accident in which Georgia lost the use of her legs and she's doing her best to adjust, but her boyfriend and friends find the change testing. An intense, psychological drama that presents the precarious nature of friendship and young love in startling close-up.

Shooting Truth
CAST SIZE 8m, 8f
AGE SUITABILITY 13–19

Molly Davies is from Norfolk, and developed her idea and carried out her research for her play *Shooting Truth* with a group of young people from Norfolk at the Garage Theatre in Norwich.

Deep in the woods near an abandoned village, a group of students is about to shoot the story of the youngest-ever witch – and Alice feels she's finally found a role. In the same woods, four centuries earlier, a gang of teenagers gather, fearful and intrigued to have found a witch in their midst – and Freya thinks at last she has some power. Past and present collide in an unsettling tale of witchcraft, film-making and practical jokes gone wrong.

Bassett
CAST SIZE 14
AGE SUITABILITY 15–19

James Graham is from Mansfield, and he travelled to Wootton Bassett School in Wiltshire to research his play *Bassett*. He was intrigued to find out what the young people in the town thought of the regular repatriation ceremonies from nearby RAF Lyneham, and what they knew of the events of 9/11, which most of them are too young to remember.

The setting is a 'Citizenship' classroom at Wootton Bassett School, and the supply teacher has gone a bit nuts, doing a runner and locking the pupils in. That's bad enough, but tensions are higher today than normal, on a day when only yards from their confinement a repatriation of fallen British soldiers is happening along the high street – as it has over a hundred times before through this quiet Wiltshire town. And this one is more personal than most . . . Dean needs the toilet, Aimee needs a coffee, Amid needs to pray, and Leo – well, Leo really, really wants to be at the repat, and is determined to escape. As factions form and secrets are revealed, maybe he's not the only one who'll want to get away. *Bassett* is a pacy, funny and exhausting look at young people who have inherited a world at war; who, as they grow older, are starting to ask questions about these conflicts, their country, and themselves.

Gargantua
CAST SIZE 15 *main parts and various choruses*
AGE SUITABILITY 13–16

Carl Grose has written for and performed in many productions by acclaimed theatre company Kneehigh, whose stories are often based on mythological tales and performed in a physically inventive, rough and very ready style. Their production of Cornish legend *Tristan and Yseult* was a big hit at the National a few years ago. For inspiration for this play, Carl read sixteenth-century writer François Rabelais's enormous series of five novels, *Gargantua and Pantagruel*, a satirical and often grotesque comedy about the lives of two giants, a father and son.

Mr and Mrs Mungus have just had a baby. Unfortunately, it isn't the bouncing blue-eyed boy they were hoping for. After a two-year pregnancy, Mini Mungus has birthed a monster – one with an accelerated growth rate and an insatiable appetite for anything that moves (including joggers). But when a gaggle of sinister military scientists intent on cloning an army of giant babies extract little Hugh's DNA, he breaks his chains and escapes. The world can only watch in horror as he embarks on learning how to walk – and on rampant destruction. Who will stop this freak of nature? Who will decide his tragic fate? And who, more importantly, will change his nappy? *Gargantua* is an absurd comedy that combines the epic with the domestic, high concept with low comedy, and the grotesque with the heartfelt.

Children of Killers
CAST SIZE 3m, 3f, *plus chorus of ghosts*
AGE SUITABILITY 15–19

Katori Hall is from Memphis, Tennessee, in the USA. She became well known to British audiences when her play *The Mountaintop* won the Olivier Award for Best New Play in 2010. For her Connections play, Katori decided to travel to Rwanda, where she interviewed teenagers and their families who witnessed first-hand the genocide of 1994. The play she wrote as a result of her research, *Children of Killers*, was workshopped with All Stars Youth Onstage, an extraordinary group of young actors, at the Castillo Theatre on 42nd Street in New York City.

The president of Rwanda is releasing the killers. Years after the Tutsi genocide, the perpetrators begin to trickle back into the countryside to be reunited with their villages. A trio of friends, born during the genocide's bloody aftermath, prepare to meet the men who gave them life. But as the homecoming day draws closer the young men are haunted by the sins of their fathers. Who can you become when violence is your inheritance?

The Beauty Manifesto

CAST SIZE 10 *plus ensemble*

AGE SUITABILITY 13–19

Nell Leyshon is from Somerset and has written many plays with rural settings for stage and radio. In 2010 she became the first woman to write a play for the Globe Theatre on Bankside in London. Before writing *The Beauty Manifesto*, Nell developed her idea with an inclusive group of sixteen young people from across Devon, who spent their half-term holiday working with her at TR2, which is Plymouth Theatre Royal's Production and Education Centre. The play she has written, although set in an imagined expressionist landscape, is a political one, and is based on detailed research about the canny methods used by marketing organisations which influence the views and aspirations of young people.

The world of *The Beauty Manifesto* is one of extreme physical conformity, where teenagers celebrate their sixteenth birthdays with cosmetic surgery. Jasmine and her sister Chloe are ambassadors for the manifesto and their father is the chief cosmetic surgeon. It is Silas's birthday and the time has come for his transformation. The problem is, Silas can think for himself and believes the manifesto is designed to make teenagers so unhappy about their bodies that they accept they need change. *The Beauty Manifesto* explores living in a world of airbrushed images and perfect bodies, and questions contemporary ideas of beauty.

Too Fast

CAST SIZE 8f, 4m

AGE SUITABILITY 13–19

Douglas Maxwell is one of Scotland's leading playwrights. His award-winning plays have been performed all over the UK and throughout the world. His Connections play *Too Fast* is inspired by memories of his own childhood, and was workshopped with Scottish Youth Theatre in Glasgow, and in a real church on the Shetland Islands, with Shetland Youth Theatre.

Sensation Nation is a vocal group founded and led by the unstoppable DD. Her grand plan is for the group to storm next year's *Britain's Got Talent*. But first they need a gig, and more importantly a heartbreaking back-story that will win them votes later on down the line. So she's booked them in to sing at a funeral. And not just any funeral either. Sensation Nation is to sing at the funeral of Ali Monroe, an older girl from their school who was killed in a car crash. *Too Fast* is an ensemble comedy with a strong emotional heart and a huge theatrical reveal in the final scene.

*

The themes you will find in these plays are both typically teenage and universally recognisable: ambition, dashed hopes, fear and confidence, loyalty and betrayal. The plays embrace a huge range of sources and contexts for their inspiration; they plunder classics and imagine the future. We look forward to seeing them brought to life by young actors across the country during the Connections 2011 season, and hope they will continue to be performed by teenagers everywhere for years to come.

Anthony Banks,
National Theatre, January 2011

Acknowledgements

The National Theatre would like to thank the writers, directors, partner theatres, the groups of young people who helped develop the scripts, all the Connections companies and Ruth Little, script advisor.

Samuel Adamson

Frank & Ferdinand

Characters

Gendarme, *either gender, any age*

133 Children:
Otto
Sebastian
Um-Aloysius
Flora
Sarah
The Rest, *as many actors as possible (two is OK, four is fine, six is satisfactory, ten is great, twenty is splendid, 128 is perfect)*

Costumes
School uniforms will do it.

Set
Could just be chairs, with actors sitting in or around the playing space, leaving their chairs and returning to them as required.

Music
There is some Bach in Scene Five. Other music, of any kind, can be used elsewhere. Feel free to compose music for the chant in Scene Two.

Captions of some kind – projections, banners – to indicate the days as specified at the top of each scene.

A slash (/) suggests the place where dialogue can overlap.

Swearing: there is a little. It can be cut.

Scene One

Caption: WEDNESDAY MORNING.

Gendarme, *with documents. Enter* **Otto**. *He is disabled.*

Gendarme Good morning. I'm record-keeper with the Gendarmerie. Name?

Otto Otto.

Gendarme Are you in your right mind?

Otto Yes.

Gendarme What's the date?

Otto Mayor Hoffman says it's the End of Time. He's climbed the bell tower of the town hall; he's pleading to God to bring them home.

Gendarme Where do we live? I said, where do we live, Hopalong?

Otto Sorry . . . it's just with everyone crying so much, I can't hear myself think. Is Sarah still here?

Gendarme The blind girl?

Otto Yeah.

Gendarme She didn't see anything, makes my job a breeze. Tell me, Otto: is she indigenous?

Otto Sarah? Yes.

Gendarme One of us? No drop of Colonist blood?

Otto (*shakes head*) Could I have some water? I'm a bit upset.

Gendarme Of course. One hundred and twenty-nine children have gone missing, but you need a moment because your legs are knackered. If I didn't have a job to do, I'd throw your crutches into the canal, you little punk.

Otto I'm upset about my missing friends, not my legs.

Gendarme Where were you last night?

Otto   By the woodsman's hut.

Gendarme   What time?

Otto   Two a.m.

Gendarme   You often loiter in the forest?

Otto   I was following instructions.

Gendarme   And the missing?

Otto   They'd left by the time I arrived. Sebastian took them.

Gendarme   Who's he?

Otto   Sebastian Schmidts.

Gendarme (*looks at records*)   On the list? You're saying he's responsible for the disappearance of one hundred and twenty-nine children, including himself – but you didn't see it?

Otto   I was meant to, so I might as well have.

Gendarme   'Might as well have.' I like it. So what happened, he spirited them away?

Otto   No, he talked them into it.

Gendarme (*writes*)   'Spirited away', excellent –

Otto   That's not what I said, I said he talked them into it –

Gendarme   It says here *you* said they were spirited away.

Otto   No, Sebastian talked them into going to the war, / so –

Gendarme   What's in your / pocket?

Otto   – 'mobilised' / is the word –

Gendarme   What's *moving in your pocket*?

A moment, then **Otto** *produces a rat.*

Gendarme   Otto, Otto, Otto. Got a name?

Otto   Abraham.

Gendarme Abraham?

Otto Yes. Because he's the daddy.

Gendarme The daddy?

Otto I didn't mean to . . . It just happened . . . Can I get a lawyer?

Gendarme Let me guess. Once, there lived a rat. And another. A teenage boy put them together, gave them some privacy and bob's your uncle, the whole shire was positively swarming.

Otto That's a bit of an exaggeration –

Gendarme I'll decide the exaggerations. Have you been a naughty vermin-breeder?

Otto It wasn't me.

Gendarme Are you the sicko behind the plague?

Otto No . . . Sebastian is! Sebastian Schmidts brought the plague on us!

Scene Two

Caption: THE NIGHT BEFORE.

130 **Children** *marching, two-by-two, at night. At the head of the column are* **Sebastian** *and* **Um-Aloysius**. **Sebastian** *leads a musical chant.*

Sebastian Tomorrow belongs to the Plains –

The Rest Tomorrow belongs to the Plains!

Sebastian Trounce the Hills –

The Rest Trounce the Hills!

Sebastian Glory to the Plains –

The Rest Glory to the Plains!

Sebastian   Kill the Hills –

The Rest   Kill the Hills –

The singing drops to a whisper but continues underneath. **Um-Aloysius**'s *speech is peppered with hesitant, stutter-like 'um's (though often they drop away). The text offers suggestions, but where he ums is up to the actor.*

Um-Aloysius   Um, Sebastian –

Sebastian   Infantry, Um-Aloysius!

Um-Aloysius   Um –

Sebastian   Feel the earth –

Um-Aloysius   Can't, my toes have, um, frost-bite –

Sebastian   – smell that air!

Um-Aloysius   Can't, my nostrils are, um, iced over –

Sebastian   Find your balls: this is the night of our lives.

Um-Aloysius   And our deaths?

Sebastian   Cheer up, we won't bleed, the Colonists will.

Um-Aloysius   But, um, does the army really need *us* to help with that? Can't they do it without *us*?

Sebastian *holds up his hand and the marching/whisper-singing stops.*

Sebastian   A story. Before Dad was murdered, he gave me his axe.

He resumes marching; **The Rest** *follow suit; whisper-singing resumes.*

When the handle split, I replaced it. When the blade was past sharpening, I replaced *that*; now blade *and* handle are new – it's the same axe, just stronger and sharper.

A moment, then **Um-Aloysius** *laughs at him.*

Um-Aloysius   Um, as your brother, and because, um, *(points ahead)* the Grim Reaper's round that bend licking his chops, I have to say, Sebastian: what a pile of purple-coloured cock. Cock.

Sebastian *holds up his hand, marching/chanting stops.*

Sebastian   They all said, 'Leave the fairy at home' – Ferdinand, Max, Julius. But we're Schmidts. Don't disgrace me.

Marching/whisper-chanting resumes.

Um-Aloysius   It's just . . . I used to be a fan of this string trio from the North Shire. The violinist and violist were old mates, so the cellist quit when she realised they were never going to give her the time of day; so, um, they got a *new* cellist, but then the violinist and violist decided actually they hated each other, and after a game of rock-paper-scissors, the violinist was sent packing, and the violist found, um, a new violinist; then the new violinist started having it off with the new cellist; so the violist flounced off, and then a *new* violist replaced *her*, so the new *cellist* was the oldest member! And they have the audacity to keep playing when no one original is left – and they're nowhere near as 'strong'. So, um, I know it's frigging sub-zero out here and a bit hard to fire up the old rhetoric – but believe me, brother, it's not Dad's axe if Dad never touched it, and it's not indisputably a stronger axe either! I'm scared shitless, I'm tired, I'm not going to salivate over any shaggy-dog yarn like it was Shakespeare; all our lives I've done that; I've finished your homework, paid your debts, washed the skidmarks out of your boxers; I've helped you seduce beautiful girls; and now I'm about to be killed in action having not even *seen* a pair of *breasts*, Sebastian, when you've seen – and I've no doubt manipulated – millions! So, um, I think I'll use what's left of my life to say 'The Tale of Father's Axe' is whopping great *bollocks*: we're not the army's 'fresh blood', or 'new blade': we're a bunch of untrained, gullible schoolchildren – and this is suicide!

Sebastian *stops; marching stops.*

Sebastian   I wasn't born to plant lead into Colonists' skulls. But since those cave-dwellers raped Katherine Osterhagen, put the Ritter family on the streets, murdered our father in cold blood, tell me, Aloysius, what's the point of string trios . . . or even breasts . . . Who gives a damn about the snow . . . What fucking relevance Shakespeare, Bach – anything on earth that isn't vengeance?

Um-Aloysius   Sebastian –

Sebastian   We were called.

Um-Aloysius   Were we? I never heard anyone except *you* tell us we / had to do this!

Sebastian   The Elders called us, now march! (*Resumes.*)

Um-Aloysius   But, / Sebastian –

Sebastian   Do you want to be court-martialled?!

Um-Aloysius (*laughs*)   You don't have the authority / to –

Sebastian (*roars*)   I was *given the authority*.

Marching.

Um-Aloysius   Um, Mum needs me on the till in the hardware shop, she can't do percentages; she can't reach the hooks and doorknobs on the top shelf . . .

Marching.

Um, I'm the only person in the whole village who reads Middle Dutch. Someone has to finish translating the constitutional documents in the library . . .

Marching.

Um, I forgot my coat.

He stops marching, forcing **Sebastian**, *and thereby* **The Rest**, *to do the same.*

Um-Aloysius   Sebastian, I, um, forgot my coat.

Sebastian *resumes marching, quickens pace.* **Um-Aloysius** *cries, struggles to keep up.*

Um-Aloysius   Sebastian . . .

Marching. **Um-Aloysius** *cries.*

Sebastian   See the sky above the Hills?

Um-Aloysius   Yeah . . .

Sebastian   It's ours.

Um-Aloysius   Even the sky belongs to us? We've enlisted to safeguard the, um, bloody *sky* from Hillsmen? I don't think you think that! We had all the learning Dad could afford, we're so much smarter than that!

Sebastian (*points*)   Dad's eyes. Grandfather's. See them? *See them, Aloysius?*

Um-Aloysius   Yeah.

Sebastian   What do you see?

Um-Aloysius   Pride in you. Contempt for me. I'm, um, an insect. I'm, um, not worth the turd on your boot. I, um, forgot my coat.

He steps out of the marching. **Sebastian** *marches onwards with the 128 children.*

Um-Aloysius   Caroline . . . ? Hilda . . . ? Um, Sophie? Sophie, don't go! Um, Frank? Max? Stephan? Stephan? Sebastian!

But they have all marched on.

Scene Three

Caption: THE SAME NIGHT. *Then another:* AN HOUR LATER.

Flora, *on her own. She looks about. She hears something and hides. Enter* **Sarah**. *She is blind. She finds and feels some marker, which tells her this is the right place.*

Sarah (*to herself*)   The woodsman's hut. (*Pauses, senses someone, smiles.*) I'm here, Sebastian. (*Touches her Braille watch.*) You're never late, I can hear you.

Flora *comes out silently.*

Sarah   Whenever I think of you now, I hear your cello. The Bach you played me wraps itself round me like warm wind – no, don't speak. We're mobilising; your battalion; it's time! God, you're the pinnacle, Sebastian. But it doesn't mean you're not a teeny bit wicked, does it? There's a scratch on your shiny boot. A button's undone. You're a miracle – everything you've said to bring us to now is miraculous – but you're also a rascal, and a white liar, and more sensitive than you let on to Ferdinand and Julius and the rest, and I love that I know that about you now, you clever music-maker miracle; touch me before they get here, that's why you asked me to meet you early isn't it, let me touch your soft . . . (*about to say 'hair'; now close to* **Flora**.) Flora?

Flora *runs off.*

Sarah   Flora, you snoop! Flora!

She exits, pursuing **Flora**. *Enter* **Otto**, *holding a compass, a sack slung over his shoulder. Things are moving inside the sack.*

Otto   Sebastian? (*Looks at the compass, satisfied; puts it away, waits a moment; looks at his watch.*) Sebastian?

He looks about, hums. **Flora** *appears, not from the direction she exited.* **Otto** *starts.*

Otto   Flora? Jesus! What are you doing here? Go home.

Flora *shakes her head.*

Otto   You have to, someone'll see you!

Flora *shakes her head.*

Otto   I'm sorry but he doesn't want you. You know why.

Flora *shakes her head.*

Otto   You do. Go! (*Doubts himself.*) It is *Tuesday* night, isn't it?

Flora *nods.*

Otto   I've got this right?

Flora *shakes her head.*

Otto   I have, you're not meant to be here, this isn't your mission, you know that.

Flora *shakes her head.*

Otto   Take a hike, Flora. Bugger off!

Flora *runs off the way she came.* **Otto** *looks at his watch nervously, impatiently.*

Otto   Come on, come on, come on . . .

Re-enter **Sarah**, *from the direction she exited.* **Otto** *stares at her, surprised, confused.*

Sarah   Who's there? Who is it! Sebastian? Flora?

Otto   Sarah, why are you here?

Sarah   Otto, you worm! Did you see Flora?

Otto   Flora? No.

Sarah   She was definitely . . . Why are you here? You're not coming with us, you're a cripple.

Otto   You're not coming with us, you're blind!

Sarah   Oh, you always do this –

Otto   What? –

Sarah   Poke about where you're not wanted!

Otto   Er, pot kettle black, Sarah! I followed my instructions –

Sarah   What / instructions – ?

Otto   – and you still haven't told me why *you're* / here.

Sarah   You must have seen Flora!

Otto   Why would Flora come?!

Sarah   You've got it wrong. Go home to Mummy – what's that noise?

Beat.

Otto   Distressed lady rats.

Sarah   Excuse me?

Otto   Well . . . you know how there's been a few pests about the village lately –

Sarah   A plague –

Otto   Not a *plague*, it's not as if, if you could see, you'd see an *infestation*, though you would see *some*, and, well, that *could* be my fault. So I've rounded up as many females as I could and put them in this sack, because Sebastian said that to get to the recruitment camp to swell the army to annihilate the Colonists to safeguard our territories to be the supreme race, we cross the river: and I'm going to drop them from the bridge. Don't stress, it's humane, I've put rocks in, it'll sink quick, they won't feel a thing, bless them. (*Looks inside.*)

Sarah   A sack full of female rats, you dirty hobbling noxious *maggot*?!

Otto   I'm not noxious.

Sarah   Go home, snake!

Otto   But this is it. (*Points.*) The woodsman's hut: the compass doesn't lie!

Sarah   You're being left behind!

Otto   No, you are, he told me!

Sarah   *You* are, he told *me*!

Otto   Shut up, he gave me a secret message to meet him here early –

Sarah   No, he didn't –

Otto   I followed orders, now where is he?

Re-enter **Flora**, *and* **Otto** *snaps against his nature:*

Otto   Flora, piss off! D'you think we'd take the daughter of Colonists to kill Colonists? He detests you, you freeloader, you bloodsucker, you nasty little cave-dwelling immigrant wog!

Sarah   I knew it was you, Flora.

Scathingly, to **Otto**, **Flora** *puts her fingers to her eyes, then points to* **Sarah**; *then points to* **Otto***'s crutches, caricatures him.*

Sarah   What's she saying? (*To* **Flora**.) Say something!

Beat.

Otto   Two a.m. here, Sarah? Sarah, you too? Yes or no?

Sarah   Yes, but he couldn't have told *you* to come / early –

Otto   It's five past, Sebastian's never late.

A moment. A noise as someone approaches.

Sarah   Who's there?

Enter **Um-Aloysius**. **Sarah** *and* **Otto** *are thrilled and relieved to see him.*

Otto   Um-Aloysius?

Sarah   Um-Aloysius!

Otto   Oh, mate, thank you, / thank you – !

Sarah   You see, Otto! –

Otto   Um-Aloysius, me old / mucker – !

Sarah   Thank God, where's Sebastian – ?

Otto   Compadre – !

Sarah   Is he OK? –

Um-Aloysius   Um –

Sarah   You've got a message? – I came as instructed, where is he?!

Otto   *She* wasn't instructed, *I* was / instructed, pal –

Sarah   If you're here, where are the others?! Stephan? Caroline? Max?

Um-Aloysius   Um –

Otto   Amigo –

Sarah   Where do we / go?

Otto   Dude –

Sarah   Um-Aloysius?

Otto   Let's march, buddy, make Molotov cocktails, kill the Hills, glory to the Plains!

Beat. **Um-Aloysius** *starts to leave.*

Otto   Where are you going?

Um-Aloysius   Um, bed.

Sarah   But tonight our bed's on the ground. In trees, in trenches, till with our help the army's shown the Hillsmen that if they colonise here, they're killed here. Only then will our *beds* be safe.

Um-Aloysius   Flora –

Sarah   But you have to have a message! What does Sebastian want me to do?

Otto   *Me* to do?

Um-Aloysius   Sebastian and the rest left for the recruitment camp two hours ago. The real rendezvous was three miles from here.

He looks at **Flora**. *She begins to cry.*

Sarah   No . . . no . . .

Um-Aloysius   They know where they're going, Sarah. (*To* **Otto**.) Um, they can walk through mud. (*Re* **Flora**.) They're all native Plains.

Otto   Oh, you mean they're not blind, mute or spaz?!

Beat.

So what are *you* doing here, Um-Aloysius? You're as normal and pure as white bread. Even if he called you a fairy, he still wanted *you* next to him!

Um-Aloysius   Um, I forgot my coat.

Otto   What?

Um-Aloysius   I, um, forgot my coat. (*Starts to leave again.*)

Sarah   Um, no; um, *no*, he wouldn't have done this to me –

Um-Aloysius   I'm going home, Sarah; um, let me take you –

Sarah   Um, no, 'Um'-Aloysius, don't 'um-let-me-take-you-home' me. In fact don't 'um' at all, you don't need to 'um', you could say what you're thinking, it's just your brother's so much more eloquent and charming, so you put on dandy clothes and um um um um um / um um um um . . .

Otto   Yeah, who gives a rat's arse about second fiddle Um-Aloysius when his superhero brother Sebastian 'Field Marshal' Schmidts is in town!

Um-Aloysius *suddenly rounds on him, pushes him.* **Otto** *retreats but answers back.*

Otto   Don't come any nearer . . . bullying the handicapped, I don't know how you sleep at night . . . I'll tell the Elders . . . ! I'll tell the Gendarmerie . . . ! I'll tell Mayor Hoffman . . . ! (*Holds up sack.*) One more step and these ravenous bitches will chow down on you like you were cheese!

Um-Aloysius *grabs the sack, looks in, recoils / screams, slams the sack on the ground over and over, roaring. They all stare.*

Otto   Well. That was one way of doing it. (*Caresses sack*). I'm sorry . . .

Um-Aloysius   You've been had, Sarah.

Sarah   No . . .

Um-Aloysius   I'm sorry. (*Makes to leave.*)

Otto   He's a deserter! A traitor! We're off to fight with our comrades, you coward!

Um-Aloysius (*turns on him*)   Wake up, Otto, they're mincemeat by now, they're *dead*.

Beat.

You'll never see Sebastian or Julius or Abel or Hilda or Sascha or Ferdinand or Adelaide or Stephan or Gertrude or Wolf or Gretel or Thora or Ernst or Winifred or Abby or Leopold or Caroline or Lotte or Finn or Marie or Sophie or Karl or Agatha or Suzanne or Veronica or Frank or any of them ever again.

Otto   Yes, we will! They'll walk up the High Street as heroes while everyone showers white feathers over you, you chicken . . . you sissy . . . !

Um-Aloysius *leaves.* **Flora** *cries.*

Sarah   No . . . Sebastian! No!

Scene Four

Caption: WEDNESDAY MORNING.

Gendarme *and* **Sarah**.

Gendarme   My name? What an impertinent question.

Sarah   But how do I address you?

Gendarme   Forget etiquette, just tell me the facts.

Sarah   I wish every one of my friends dead. Fact.

Gendarme   Now, Sarah, why demonise one hundred and twenty-nine innocents?

Sarah   Fine, one hundred and twenty-eight can live; the bastard one hundred and twenty-ninth can fry!

Gendarme   Who's that?

Sarah   The ringleader!

Gendarme   Who's that?

Sarah   Sebastian Schmidts!

She stamps her feet furiously, then begins to cry.

Gendarme   Take your time, you have two seconds, would you like a sherbet lemon?

The **Gendarme** *offers a sweet.* **Sarah** *shakes her head.*
Gendarme *refers to notes.*

Gendarme   Sebastian Schmidts? Ah yes. The dumb one called him 'legendary' . . . 'Floppy hair, killer smile'.

Sarah   Flora spoke?

Gendarme   No, Flora's mute.

Sarah   Then how – ?

Gendarme (*turns page*)   The lame one said he bred rats.

Sarah   What – ?

Gendarme (*turns page*)   Another claimed he was the devil. You side with them, obviously?

Sarah (*shocked*)   No . . . no, who said / that?

Gendarme   But you just wished him dead. He made you cry.

Sarah   Yes . . . but . . . it's because I've just realised something. Is he alive? Please tell me he's alive.

Gendarme   No evidence to the contrary.

Sarah (*wave of relief; laughs; pulls herself together*)   It's just, you
see . . . over the past month, Sebastian's been . . . 'Field
Marshal Schmidts', glorious commander of our battalion, and
I've just realised he knew he'd be put in his place out on the
front by the sergeants and so on! Underneath the swagger
he's fragile. It's hard to explain, but I see into him. To
everyone else he has to strut about, but with me, he can be
different . . . I truly know him, but then he gets threatened,
because men have strange egos. And out on the front, he's
just a boy, isn't he? A private – and he didn't want me to see
that! But he's alive, that's all that matters, and I forgive him!

She laughs; the **Gendarme** *laughs but keeps laughing.*

Sarah   What?

Gendarme   Field Marshal? Private? What are you on
about?

Sarah   The war.

Beat.

The Elders called for a battalion of young fighters. The Plains
Army needed us to take up arms for a particular engagement
last night.

Beat.

Gendarme   Most of your fellow pupils have vanished.
We're trying to establish why, and you have the nerve to
fairy-story me?

Sarah   Fairy story . . . ? Fairy story's not a verb.

Gendarme   I'll decide the verbs. A 'battalion'?

Sarah   But . . . but you know where they went. You know.

Gendarme   We know nothing! That's why Mayor
Hoffman's on the bell tower, crying his eyes out. It's why I'm
interviewing you.

Sarah   But you just told me Sebastian was safe.

Gendarme   No: that I have no evidence to the contrary.

Sarah   But they left for the recruitment camp.

Gendarme   What 'recruitment camp'?

Sarah   The army recruitment camp north of the river.

Gendarme   The army doesn't have a recruitment camp north of the river.

Sarah   It does, I was on my way there!

Gendarme   Then why are you here?

Sarah   Sebastian gave me the wrong time.

Gendarme   The wrong time?

Sarah   He said two, but they left at two-thirty –

Gendarme   Two-thirty?

Sarah   I mean midnight, but they were *meant* to leave at two-thirty –

Gendarme   Oh, Sarah, Sarah, please.

Sarah   But people-in-the-know know they were going!

Gendarme   What people?

Sarah   The Gendarmerie!

Gendarme   That's *me*! Good Lord, you think you can pull a fast one on me! I'm Lieutenant Pencil-Pusher, you delinquent newt, I can outrun a fox and outwit a big brown bear.

Sarah   I want to see my grandmother –

Gendarme   Not in the vicinity.

Sarah   Ask Otto, or, or, or Flora!

Gendarme   She's a *mute*!

Sarah   You're trying to confuse me –

Gendarme   Sarah, the missing children were – what? – *conscripted*? I've never heard anything so despicable.

Sarah   But – / but –

Gendarme (*back to notes*)   Now, the mute one described your ringleader as 'charming, like a rough diamond'. The timid one said he was 'pure evil, with the charm of a rattlesnake' – and claimed he's a murderer.

Sarah   Um-Aloysius?

Gendarme   What you said about self-doubt and ego? Smart. All big talkers eventually come a cropper. They don't ultimately like it that we stand and fall on the strengths and weaknesses of others. There's only one truly non-collaborative act . . .

Sarah   You're not saying . . . He didn't *kill* them . . . you can't think that . . . Um-Aloysius is crazy, he's jealous, don't trust him! And *he's* the murderer, he smashed-in the heads of a hundred rats!

Gendarme   When?

Sarah   Last night at the woodsman's hut.

Gendarme   It was a right little orgy at the woodsman's hut.

Sarah   Listen to Flora: she spoke the truth!

Gendarme   A Colonist, the truth? Now I'm getting angry. Are you a collaborator?

Sarah (*shakes head, increasingly distressed*)   Of course not . . .

Gendarme   You're covering for this ringleader of yours.

Sarah   He was a good man, they went to the war to save our village before it dies, please let me see my grandmother . . . !

Gendarme   Tell me about the rape.

Sarah   What?

Gendarme   Tell me all you know about Sebastian Schmidts's rape of Katherine Osterhagen.

Beat.

Sarah   No . . . no . . .

Gendarme   'No'? You refuse to give testimony?

Sarah   A Colonist raped Katherine Osterhagen. Everyone knows that. A Colonist raped Katherine Osterhagen . . .

Gendarme   Sarah, I'm marking your statements 'unreliable' because you're in love.

Sarah   Please, I –

Gendarme   You know, this is the Inquiry, not the Inquisition! It's all right to say, 'I don't know what happened'! If you don't know, then you don't know! That's OK!

Sarah   But this isn't right . . . he loved music . . . he, he played cello . . . Does that sound evil to you?

Gendarme   Oh, now you're being silly. Sebastian Schmidts is or was many things, but he never blew an instrument – 'cept his own trumpet.

Sarah   Cello.

Gendarme   The boy didn't have a musical bone in his body.

Sarah   Stop it!

Gendarme   You're hysterical: the files don't mention *cellos*!

Sarah   He played it like an angel –

Gendarme   What did you see between the hours of eleven p.m. and three a.m., as regards Sebastian Schmidts or any other missing child? Answer the question.

Sarah   But . . . but . . . but where did they go if they didn't go there?

Gendarme   You saw *nothing*, did you? You were abandoned at some woodsman's hut concentration camp for deformities and cave-dwellers – and to make sense of it, you spin this ludicrous tale –

Sarah   No – !

Gendarme   *Do you know, beyond doubt, where they went?*

Beat. **Sarah** *shakes her head.*

Gendarme   Speak up.

Sarah   No.

Gendarme (*writes, then laughs*)   One hundred and twenty-eight people below legal age led to war! One might as well say they followed a fiddle player down a rabbit hole!

Sarah   He played cello.

Gendarme   Yes, but a cello's preposterous so I calibrated my narrative; call it a violin and suspension of disbelief is possible whilst essential truth remains.

Sarah   A violin down a rabbit hole is still stupid . . .

Gendarme   Fine: call it a flute.

Sarah   A flute . . . ?

Gendarme   *Voilà!* – A flute, or better yet a recorder. Yes, he blew on his fife and, enchanted, the children followed him to – (*mocks*) 'a recruitment camp', you wag! (*Writes.*) We'll have your testimony made up in Braille. Wait outside that door – no, that one – no, that one. I'll need to re-interview you. No, door four, left, left, that's it: join the rat-freak; in fact, send him back in; his story doesn't hold water at *all* now that I have yours.

Scene Five

Caption: MONDAY MORNING.

Sarah, *holding satchel. She touches her watch. Throughout this scene – which is at school somewhere, a corridor or the playground –* **The**

Rest *walk or drift by, intermittently, singly, in pairs or groups, holding books, etc., on their way to lessons, rehearsals, P.E. So, the conversation wavers between 'private' and 'public'.*

Sarah   Five, four, three, two . . . two . . .

Enter **Sebastian***, holding schoolbooks.*

Sebastian   Sarah.

Sarah   Sebastian! Hello. Morning.

Sebastian   I missed you.

Sarah   You did?

Sebastian   The longest weekend, I couldn't stop thinking about you. Now it's five minutes till double maths, I bloody hate Mondays.

Sarah   We should be grateful for maths.

Sebastian   Why?

Sarah   Because it's normal. Sometimes I dream about a chain of normal things, one after the other . . . then the gunfire wakes me up.

Beat.

Twenty-nine and a half hours till we leave.

Sebastian   Yeah. (*Leads her away from passing students. Sotto voce.*) I want you to meet me earlier tomorrow night, Sarah. Two a.m. By the woodsman's hut.

Sarah   Why?

Sebastian   Don't tell anyone, but I'm nervous. I'll need you.

Sarah (*laughs, gives in to her attraction to him*)   What colour are your eyes?

Sebastian   Blue.

Sarah   I knew it, like sky and ink.

Sebastian   No. More the colour of my thoughts when I think about the state of the village . . . of you only being able to dream about normal things . . .

Sarah   But they'll become reality, you're seeing to that: the whole school's signing up.

Sebastian   The more people who know, the harder this is.

Sarah   But you can trust us, we know it's the only way; when I think of everything going to the dogs –

Sebastian   Of Katherine Osterhagen raped by a cave-dweller on her way home –

Sarah   Of your father murdered –

Sebastian   Of them opening a prayer room right in the High Street –

Sarah   And the rats. All the rats. (*Has her hand out, touches him.*) There isn't a crease in your shirt.

Sebastian   Slaves ironed it for me.

She laughs. Beat.

Sarah . . . will you listen to my speech for tomorrow night?

Sarah   *The* speech? Now? Your Agincourt speech?!

Sebastian   My what?

Sarah   Your Henry the Fifth, your crowning speech!

Sebastian   Oh. Yeah. I'd appreciate your thoughts.

Sarah (*laughs*)   Of course!

He moves her. She takes the opportunity to touch him some more; his face, hair. He positions himself.

I'm listening.

Sebastian   'From this moment, our beds are on the ground, in the trees, down a trench till with our help the army's driven the Colonists out and Hillsmen see that to settle here's to die here – ' (*Points.*) Then I point.

Sarah Towards the Hills?

Sebastian No: to Flora.

Sarah Flora?

Sebastian That troglodyte will follow us, but she ain't coming.

Sarah She was born here, Sebastian.

Sebastian Her father put the Ritters out of business. She turns up, I tell her she has a choice: return to her side of the border – or take a bullet, Colonist scum.

Beat.

'The Elders made the plea direct to me to enlist you. Every second village is sending young fighters, the time's now, we want our / livelihoods, our land – '

Sarah It's perfect.

Sebastian I haven't finished. 'We want our livelihoods, our land; this sacred earth has been / contaminated by – '

Sarah (*snaps or scoffs at him*) Why don't you say that if the cave-dwellers colonise here they're killed here, then you get some racist alliteration, which is always charming.

Beat.

Sebastian Sarcasm?

Sarah God, I'm beginning to think we'd follow you no matter what the twaddle: 'The fewer men the greater share of honour!' 'What we do tonight, the rest of the country will do tomorrow!' 'Many a mickle makes a muckle!'

Sebastian 'Many a mickle makes a muckle'?

Sarah 'On the first of March, the crows begin to search!' 'It's a sin to steal a pin, St Crispin!'

She is now upset, angry. Beat.

Sebastian   Who do you think you are, making fun of me?

Sarah   I don't mean to –

Sebastian   You don't have a clue how hard this is – what are you, a collaborator?

Sarah   No – !

Sebastian   Out of every single person in this school, I chose you to show who I really am, and you're the only person who makes me doubt myself!

Sarah   It's just –

During this: one of the passers-by is **Um-Aloysius**. *He is holding schoolbooks and a cello. As well as his school uniform, he wears a colourful silk scarf, the only student to do so. He stops at the sight of them.*

Sarah   – it's just . . . if we had peace, Sebastian . . . I wonder what colours I'd see with you. If all we had was the normal things I long for, just sky and school and music, like in stories, then who would you be? Sometimes I wonder if we even know what we're fighting for. Forget it, I'm sorry; it's all in your speech, of course I know; you're a miracle, and I'll be there, I feel our country rotting, I know you're right, you're right.

She makes to leave. **Sebastian** *puts up his hand to indicate to* **Um-Aloysius**, *'Stop. Be quiet. Take your cello out of the case.' And* **Um-Aloysius** *obeys.*

Sebastian   Sarah!

Sarah *stops.*

Sebastian   I want to play for you.

Sarah (*confused*)   What?

Sebastian   Play. Music.

Beat.

Sarah   You?

Sebastian   Yes. Me.

Sarah   Really?

Sebastian   I have my cello.

Sarah   You play?

Sebastian   There are a million things you don't know about me, Sarah. I hate how you underestimate me. Yes, I play. I play. And when the cave-dwellers leave and there's peace I'll show you colours you don't even know about.

Some others gather. **Sebastian** *puts a finger to his mouth: 'Be quiet.' Then, to* **Um-Aloysius**, *his finger held out like a gun:*

Sebastian   So yes?

Sarah   Yes.

Um-Aloysius *plays from a Bach Cello Suite (perhaps the prelude of No. 3, or No. 6, or – a more obvious choice – No. 1) stunningly. (It's fine if the actor mimes this – but the story should be that he can play, beautifully.) More people gather, everyone but* **Otto** *and* **Flora** *– 131* **Children**. *As a group they are instructed silently by* **Sebastian** *to stay silent so that* **Sarah** *doesn't sense them. Many are moved by* **Um-Aloysius**'s *playing, none more so than* **Sarah**, *who of course doesn't see any of them. Once or twice,* **Sebastian** *mimics* **Um-Aloysius**, *air-celloing. A few of* **The Rest** *smirk silently at this.* **Sebastian** *is like the conductor of them all. If the production has lighting, then perhaps the state changes, perhaps, in tableaux, the main characters are variously picked out.*

Sarah   Maestro.

Sebastian *guides her hand to the cello.* **Um-Aloysius** *is close to* **Sarah** *as she caresses it.*

Sebastian   You think I don't know that we're fighting for this, Sarah?

Sarah *shakes her head. Most of* **The Rest** *realise what has happened; some silently mock* **Um-Aloysius***. A school bell breaks this moment, but none of* **The Rest** *leave.*

Sarah   Thank you. I'm sorry.

The Rest *break up a bit. Some exit.*

Sebastian   See you in class, I have to take my cello to the music room. (*Sotto.*) Don't forget what I said about meeting early tomorrow night. Woodsman's hut.

Sarah   Thank you, Sebastian . . .

She exits. Others follow silently. A few remain.

Sebastian   Get the message out. No one tells Otto or Sarah where or when. It's the Elders' express wish. Only the strong.

Student One   That was brilliant.

Student Two (*taunts*)   Um, um, um Aloysius.

Student Three   Dithers and ums, makes up for it by wearing his lurid scarves.

Sebastian   Yeah . . . my brother's a pretty boy, all right.

Student Four   Oh, he's more than that.

Student Five   He's a peacock.

Student Six   He's a queen.

Student One (*fairy-tale bow*)   Her Majesty.

Student Two   Silk's the only thing that gets her through the day.

Student Three   We're leaving him behind, too?

Sebastian   No. He's up for it.

Student Four   The fairy?

Sebastian   He's up for it, Ferdinand! Aren't you . . . Queen Aloysius? (*To* **The Rest**.) Those cave-dwellers murdered our father.

Student Five   And mine –

Student Six   When I think of Katherine Osterhagen raped –

Student One   A meeting house in our bakery?

Sebastian   And the rats, all the rats. Tomorrow. Midnight.

Everyone leaves, except **Sebastian** *and* **Um-Aloysius**. *They stare at each other.* **Sebastian** *makes to leave.*

Um-Aloysius   What's happened to you?

Sebastian   Put the cello in the attic.

Um-Aloysius   What did they do to you?

Sebastian   I'm a patriot. And you'll march next to me, for our father, and never question me again.

He pulls the scarf off **Um-Aloysius** *and stuffs it into one of* **Um-Aloysius**'s *pockets. Enter* **Otto**, *running late.*

Sebastian   Otto!

Otto   Sebastian!

Sebastian *whispers in his ear.* **Otto** *nods.*

Otto   Yes, Sebastian. Yes, Sebastian.

Sebastian   Maths, quick march.

Otto   Yes, Sebastian.

He exits. **Flora** *runs on, breathlessly, carrying schoolbooks.*

Sebastian   Flora?! – No, don't speak. Why are you always running late? No, don't speak. I said, don't. Get to your lesson, you don't want to end up an illiterate cave-dweller – oh, you already are! And don't speak!

Flora *runs off.* **Sebastian** *exits after her.* **Um-Aloysius** *is left on his own.*

Scene Six

Caption: WEDNESDAY MORNING.

Gendarme *and* **Um-Aloysius**. **Um-Aloysius** *is worked-up, feverish.*

Um-Aloysius   Um.

Gendarme   Um?

Um-Aloysius   Um, one day some Elders came to our shop and took him to the storeroom for two hours, and the moral is, speak to Elders, you die – and that's all I have to say.

Gendarme   Die?

Um-Aloysius   On the front!

Gendarme   How many more times, we're in a ceasefire!

Um-Aloysius   No, we're losing, you needed us and that's all I have to say!

Gendarme (*at records*)   The lame boy alleges you're a weakling and a sissy.

Um-Aloysius   Please let me go.

Gendarme   You know, it's all right to say you don't know what happened, Aloysius.

Um-Aloysius (*screams*)   But I do know! Jesus! This is like talking to him, you're just like that *devil*!

Gendarme   Why do you hate your brother so much?

Um-Aloysius   I don't!

Beat.

There's this girl at school . . . She was pretty, but she was teased for always being late, and her uniform that never fitted; her accent. She retreated so far into herself she isn't there any more. That's a true story. My brother killed that girl.

Gendarme   Sebastian murdered someone?

Um-Aloysius   Metaphorically, absolutely.

Gendarme   I don't deal in metaphors.

Um-Aloysius   Yes you do! He bullied her so much she stopped speaking, and that's the same as murder . . .

Gendarme   Sonny, you need a dictionary. Flora is *alive*, she's through that door sucking a sherbet lemon. The missing children are my concern: what happened to *them*?

Um-Aloysius   I told you, *you keep denying it*! *Fine*: no frigging children's battalion!

Gendarme   Not that *you* saw; you saw nothing because you 'forgot your coat'!

Um-Aloysius   No, I came back for Sarah!

Gendarme   I beg your pardon?

Beat.

You love the blind one? You do realise she has eyes only for your brother?

Beat.

What's in your pocket?

Um-Aloysius   What?

Gendarme   That thing, what is it? Is it a scarf?

Um-Aloysius   Um . . . yes.

Gendarme   That isn't regulation. Why do you have a scarf?

Um-Aloysius   It . . . it isn't mine.

Gendarme   Whose then?

Beat.

Um-Aloysius   Sebastian's.

Gendarme   Oh? Why do you have it?

Um-Aloysius   He dropped it. In the forest.

Gendarme (*writes*)   Near the cave?

Um-Aloysius   There's no cave in the forest.

Gendarme   Then pray tell where do the hermits defecate? So your brother wore scarves?

Beat.

Um-Aloysius   Like a queen.

Gendarme   Oh?

Um-Aloysius   Like, um, a queeny fop. Like a pretty-boy dandy fop with lollipops. Like a narcissistic self-loving rattlesnake with a penchant for –

Gendarme   Penchant – ?

Um-Aloysius   – for lurid things.

Gendarme (*writes*)   I'm loving these words. 'Lurid'. So Sebastian was like a strutting red and yellow – what?

Um-Aloysius   Peacock.

Gendarme   Good, like a multi-coloured bird?

Um-Aloysius   Um, yeah, attracted to shiny vain things –

Gendarme   Like a magpie?

Um-Aloysius   Yeah, like a murdering pleasure-seeking power-hungry evil lusty magpie –

Gendarme   Pied, like a magpie?

Um-Aloysius   – attracted to shiny lurid things and shiny shallow things were lured by him, weak, effeminate things, girly blind musical Bach-loving things, like an addictive gaudy killer Shakespearean music-making maestro magpie.

Beat.

And he wore a white feather.

Beat.

Gendarme   You may go.

The **Gendarme** *writes.* **Um-Aloysius** *makes to leave. He turns back.*

Um-Aloysius   There's no ceasefire. You tell me what happened. He's my brother . . . and he was good . . .

Gendarme   So he's *not* an evil lusty magpie-devil in a scarf?

Um-Aloysius   He worked hard, put food on our table, supported our mother, kept the shop afloat –

Gendarme   Yes, by stealing from the Ritter family to pay your father's gambling debts.

Um-Aloysius   That's a lie. Liar!

Gendarme   Oh, he kept that from you? Did he never mention that your father raped Katherine Osterhagen, either?

Um-Aloysius   No . . . not true . . .

Gendarme   'True', you little schmuck?! I'll tell you what's true. Everyone has a debt to society and it was time for the Schmidts to pay theirs. *That's* the truth – but you, lucky boy, 'forgot your coat'! Last night the Colonists suffered colossal losses and, invigorated by fresh cub blood, we were victorious, no casualties, all participating soldiers accounted for: that's also true. Also, your mother's a drunk and your father was a sexual pest. Finally, though, here's the *recorded* truth. (*Holds up records.*) Aloysius Schmidts didn't know what happened to his poor brother and friends, but in the forest by the cave did see an alluring stranger with a feather in his hat. Correct? Good. Now send the mute one back in, and take a leaf from her book whilst you're at it: there are more eloquent people in the world than you; just don't speak, Aloysius, let Bach do your talking for you, and you'll always have a pleasant little life in our pleasant little land.

Scene Seven

Caption: THE NIGHT BEFORE.

Sebastian *is addressing 130 assembling marcher* **Children**, *including* **Um-Aloysius**. *Perhaps he uses a loud-hailer.* **Flora** *is on the periphery.*

Sebastian   What we do tonight, the rest of the country will do tomorrow!

Whistles, hand-clapping, cheers: 'Colonists out!'

Many a mickle makes a muckle!

Whistles, hand-clapping, cheers: 'Colonists out!'

On the first of March, the crows begin to search!

By now they're marching, **Sebastian** *and* **Um-Aloysius** *at the head of the column.*

Sebastian (*sings*)   Tomorrow belongs to the Plains –

The Rest   Tomorrow belongs to the Plains!

Sebastian   Trounce the Hills –

The Rest   Trounce the Hills!

Sebastian   Glory to the Plains –

The Rest   Glory to the Plains!

Sebastian   Kill the Hills –

The Rest   Kill the Hills –

The march, where in Scene Two it had been theatrical somehow – in one place, in order to meet the demands of the scene – now moves realistically, through the theatre, through the audience, out of a door, whatever is possible to take everybody (including **Um-Aloysius**) *away.* **Flora** *is pushed to the ground by the marching* **Children**, *and left behind.*

Scene Eight

Caption: WEDNESDAY MORNING.

Gendarme *and* **Flora**.

Gendarme   Flora. Tell me what you saw. Cat got your tongue? All right. Once upon a time . . .

Scene Nine

Caption: WEDNESDAY MORNING. *Then another:* AND EVER AFTER.

Sarah, **Otto** *and* **Um-Aloysius**, *waiting, on chairs in a row.* **Um-Aloysius** *is rocking or fidgeting obsessively.*

Sarah   I miss Ferdinand.

Um-Aloysius   Shhh.

Otto   How long's she been in there?

Sarah   Hours.

Beat.

Listen. Mayor Hoffman's still crying on the bell tower.

Otto   Mayor Hoffman's a noddy.

Um-Aloysius   Shhh.

Sarah   You're so right, Otto, I don't believe that routine for a second.

Um-Aloysius   Shh, Sarah, shh.

Silence.

Sarah   I miss Suzanne.

Silence.

Otto   I miss Veronica.

Otto/Sarah (*together*)   Gertrude.

Sarah   Caroline.

Otto   I miss Julius.

Sarah   Yes, and Stephan.

Otto   Abel.

Sarah   Ferdinand.

Otto   Gretel.

Sarah   Wolf.

Otto   Willie.

Sarah   Thora.

Otto   Max.

Sarah/Otto/Um-Aloysius (*together*)   Adelaide.

Otto   Frank.

Sarah   Ernst.

Otto   Hilda.

Sarah   Josefine.

Otto   Julius.

Sarah/Um-Aloysius (*together*)   Sascha.

Otto   Ferdinand.

Sarah   Lotte.

Otto   Marie.

Sarah   Abby.

Otto/Sarah/Um-Aloysius (*together*)   Leopold.

Otto   Frank.

Sarah   Frank. (*Calls.*) Frank! Frank!

Um-Aloysius   Shhh.

Sarah   But, Um-Aloysius, where are they?

Um-Aloysius   There was a flash flood, they were washed away.

Sarah   Oh, really? How do you know? Where you there?

Um-Aloysius   Not relevant.

Sarah   Did you see?

Um-Aloysius   Did you?

Sarah   Take me to the site of this so-called flash flood!

Um-Aloysius   Sure, once I've decided where it is, I will. Now just be quiet, shut up!

Enter **Flora**. *She sits next to them in the row. They look at her.*

Otto   Does he [*or* she] want to see me again?

Flora *shakes her head.*

Sarah   Me?

Flora *shakes her head. Silence.* **Sarah** *cries.*

Sarah   I heard you play, Aloysius, of course I did. I'm so so so so sorry.

Otto   Don't cry, Sarah. Don't cry . . . because Um-Aloysius is wrong. It wasn't a flood. It was more that the children heard someone tell them that down the river, life is sweeter.

Sarah   Yes! Who?

Otto   Well . . . someone . . . this boy . . . no, this kind man. He had a certain . . . *je ne sais quoi*.

Beat.

Sarah   Go on, Otto. So they went down the river, what happened then?

Silence. And then **Flora** *talks. The other children don't react to this.*

Flora   Once upon a time, a certain village was overrun with rats, and a mysterious man appeared, wearing a scarf, or was it a coat, of several colours, and he claimed to be a rat-catcher, and he promised that for a certain sum he would rid the town of the rats. And the Mayor agreed, and from his pocket the boy, that is man, produced a recorder, or perhaps a pipe, I don't remember, and when he played the rats followed him into the river, where they drowned. Now rat-free, the Mayor of the town, or city, in New Zealand, or Palestine, or was it China, decided not to pay the piper, and the piper left angry, but on the twenty-sixth of June, or twenty-second of July, you decide, he returned, now dressed even more colourfully, with a lurid cummerbund, or was it scarf, or a white feather in his hat or moreover a black-and-white feather, which caused him to be called pied. And he played his pipe, and this time children followed and disappeared into a cave in the flattened hills that used to exist where the church now stands, that's the truth, ask the Elders.

Beat.

One hundred and twenty-nine children were lost that day or was it night, though some say some were left behind. They say a blind girl was not able to show where they went but that she'd heard a violin, or recorder, or pipe. A lame boy was not able to say where they'd gone as he couldn't keep up, and some say to compensate he told lies that bred like so many mice. A shy boy claimed he knew where they went, because he went halfway, but his timidity had made him scared of the hills, so he came back for a torch, or was it his coat, and by the time he'd got it, they'd vanished, and when the Mayor and parents pressed him for the truth, the shy boy dithered and ummed so much they tired of him.

The bell rings. **Sarah**, **Otto** *and* **Um-Aloysius** *collect their schoolbooks and leave.*

Flora   A mute girl saw everything, but as she was mute and illiterate, her story went with her to her grave.

A gunshot. She doesn't move or react, except to put a hand to her chest. As she removes it, blood is there.

And the moral is, don't talk to strangers, keep promises and pay your debts, and many cheerful songs have been written to memorialise the lost children, and the village is now pure and happy and somewhat rich and even tourists on visitors passes come to see the cave which has been constructed at the end of the High Street, and they recite the poems and sing the songs and watch the plays and photograph the statue outside the delicious bakery of the colourful piper smiling his come-hither smile, the end.

Frank & Ferdinand

*Notes on rehearsal and staging, drawn from workshops
with the writer held at the National Theatre, November 2010*

The Idea Behind the Play

Frank & Ferdinand was written by Samuel Adamson for
Connections 2011. The idea for the story came while Samuel
was working on a new adaptation of *Little Eyolf* by Ibsen for
the National Theatre. This play tells the story of a young boy
who, after an accident, becomes paralysed, and his parents,
who blame themselves, are torn apart by guilt and are unable
to give him the love he needs to be happy. The family is visited
by 'the rat wife', a woman capable of enchanting rodents into
following her into the sea, where they drown. The boy hears
of this story and is amazed. Seizing the opportunity to escape,
he follows the rat wife down to the sea and is drowned. There
is something of the Pied Piper legend in this story and Samuel
became interested in telling his own version of the story.

The Legend of the Pied Piper

In 1284, while the town of Hamelin was suffering from a rat
infestation, a man dressed in pied clothing appeared, claiming
to be a rat-catcher. He promised the townsmen a solution for
their problem with the rats. The townsmen in turn promised
to pay him for the removal of the rats. The man accepted,
and played a musical pipe to lure the rats with a song into the
river, where all of them drowned. Despite his success, the
people reneged on their promise and refused to pay the rat-
catcher the full amount of money. The man left the town
angrily, but vowed to return some time later, seeking revenge.

One day, while the inhabitants were in church, he played his
pipe yet again, this time attracting the children of Hamelin.
One hundred and thirty boys and girls followed him out of the
town, where they were lured into a cave and never seen again.
Depending on the version, three children remained behind.

One of the children was lame and could not follow quickly enough, the second was deaf and followed the other children out of curiosity, and the last was blind and unable to see where they were going. When the villagers came out of the church, these three children informed them of what had happened.

There are many versions, variations and interpretations, depending on where you look. Some are more violent and say the Pied Piper was a child-killer, some celebrate the Pied Piper as a magical and wonderful man, while others declare the story is a cover-up to hide events in a corrupt society. It was this last version that grabbed Samuel's imagination and provided the starting point for *Frank & Ferdinand*, where the children who were left behind are given a chance to tell their stories.

Some Themes in the Play

- The construction of myths, legends and fairy tales. How do we feel when we are told a fairy tale? Every fairy tale has a darkness, and the 'happy ever after' is not always the one that children want to hear.

- Friendship, loyalty and betrayal.

- Brotherly love, which can so easily turn into resentment and bitterness.

- The truth and the construction/distortion of fact. What is 'the truth'? What makes something true? Is there such a thing as an 'objective reality'?

- Memory and perception. Different people remember the same event differently.

- Reputation.

- Justice.

- Power, and the abuse of power.

- Revenge.

- Responsibility and blame.

- Individuality and difference.
- Public and private behaviour – what you choose to show about yourself and what you hide.
- Trust.

At its most complex, it is a story about the construction of fact, the distortion of reality, the terrifying lengths people can go to cover up the truth. At its simplest, it is a tale of the schoolyard, of the cool kids and the not-so-cool kids: of those who effortlessly 'fit in', and those who are branded too different to matter. It is about young people working out who they are and how they can live in the world.

The Title

Frank and Ferdinand are the names of two of the children that have gone missing. They are no more or less important than any of the others who are named in the play, but simply names on a list. By randomly picking these two names, it implies a sense of people we don't know, an anonymity; the names mean nothing and their stories are genuinely forgotten. Frank and Ferdinand have been wiped out by official history.

Style and Setting

The style of the play is definitely not naturalistic. It should be played truthfully, but to treat it as pure naturalism is reductive. Be bold, think big, think visually, theatrically, rhythmically. This is a fairy tale, a myth, a legend, a story, so create your own world in which you think the story can best be told.

The source of this particular story is a German fairy tale, which influences the tone of the story, and there are clues in the text and in the characters' names as to when and where it might be set, but nothing is made specific. It is up to you to make those decisions. It could be timeless and placeless. It could be set in a specific time and place. It could be anachronistic.

Characters

It is important that you see all the children in this story as
victims – even Sebastian. They all try in their own way to tell
their story, but a powerful society prevents them from doing
so. These children are all essentially good, but not perfect.
They are flawed and are not above betraying each other.

It is also vital to understand that all the children tell the truth
at various points in the story, even Sebastian. The moments
when they lie, or withhold the truth, are as a result of being
manipulated, or entrapped by the Gendarme, or overwhelmed
by their own emotions. Sometimes they lie to get back at their
friends, to hurt someone who has hurt them, or because they
are afraid of telling anyone how they really feel. Whether they
lie deliberately, or accidentally in the heat of the moment,
these lies are then used against them by the Gendarme to
undermine each other. Unbeknownst to the children, their
lies mean that they inadvertently contribute to the creation
of the myth.

SEBASTIAN

Sebastian has been convinced by the Elders to carry out their
orders. How did they manage this? What is the underlying
strategy of the town's leaders? What do they have over him?
Does Sebastian believe what he says to Um-Aloysius, Sarah
and the other children? Is he terrified of what might happen
to him if he doesn't obey? Is he a confident, cocky, ambitious
young man whose natural charisma and charm is taken
advantage of by the Elders, who see him as a pawn in their
game? How much does Sebastian know/understand what he
is doing? How much does he believe in it? What does he really
feel about Sarah? And his brother?

GENDARME

Is he/she genuinely evil? Or simply carrying out orders? Is
he/she aware of the consequence of his/her actions? The
scenes with the Gendarme are important in rooting the non-
linear time frame of the play, so it is important to keep the
Gendarme the same throughout. Each child is interviewed by
the Gendarme on the same morning, so a sense of relentless

interrogation is crucial. He/she represents an arm of the State, a paper-shuffling individual who is also the face of the Elders and the Adult World. He/she is a figure representative of – and also wields – extreme power. The children are misled, manipulated, cajoled, blackmailed, charmed and emotionally divided by the Gendarme. Therefore he/she is a very powerful character.

UM-ALOYSIUS

Called a 'fairy' and a 'pretty boy' by his brother and by his schoolmates, Um-Aloysius is shy, but knows who he is and who he wants to be perhaps better than his brother. Despite being more culturally aware, more individual, more sensitive, more talented than Sebastian, he is often in his brother's shadow, and at the butt of his jokes. He plays the cello beautifully and his stutter seems to disappear whenever he is passionate about something. As the stage directions say, the text offers suggestions as to where he 'ums', but this is something that the actor playing him needs to own.

It is vital to pay attention to what Um-Aloysius has to say in every scene he is in. You can tell when he is speaking the legitimate truth and when his words are an act of revenge, and both are revealing in terms of what we learn about Sebastian's character. He obviously loves Sebastian because he is his brother but, mixed in with this, there is huge resentment and bitterness, which drive him to say things that are hugely damaging to him and his brother's future.

SARAH

Sarah is blind, and her other senses are therefore heightened. She is intelligent and, while she has strong feelings for Sebastian, she can see through him and questions him more directly than anybody else. Despite knowing on some level that he is capable of messing her around, she chooses to trample on her doubts and follow him. What is it that makes her do this? How aware is she of possible oppressive forces in the town and country? Is she afraid of things more powerful than Sebastian? What might she lose if she spoke up more publicly in the way she does to Sebastian?

One challenge in playing this character is getting to grips with acting as if you were blind. Perhaps exercises for the actor are helpful – for example, being blindfolded and asked to complete simple tasks, or to make simple journeys around the room, might help with the physical sensation of not being able to see. When one sense is taken away, the other senses have to work harder. What does she rely on if she cannot see? How does she make sense of her environment?

When playing the scenes, don't let your eyes lead you. If you cannot see, perhaps it is what you can hear that determines where you move, or where you look. Try not to make direct eye-contact with the other person in the scene. It might help to focus just about their eyes. Always make sure your eyes are focused on something and not darting about. Try not to use your peripheral vision – only focus on what you see in your direct line of vision.

OTTO
Otto might have a bit of a crush on Sarah, and definitely has a fondness for rats. He has been accused of causing an infestation of rats in the town – something about which he feels a tremendous amount of guilt, even though he is not entirely sure it was his fault. What does this guilt say about the town he lives in? When he accuses Sebastian of starting the plague, what has he understood about Sebastian as ringleader and the prices ringleaders sometimes have to pay? While he might not be as intelligent as Sarah, he is smart enough to know that there are lines he mustn't cross. The dialogue reveals that he uses crutches, but the reason why is not made explicit.

FLORA
A mystery. Um-Aloysius reveals that Sebastian might have bullied her so much that she became too scared to talk, but we have nothing but his words to prove this is true. She is a colonist's daughter, which according to some makes her part of the enemy, and so deserving to be badly treated. She witnesses more than she should, and as a result knows more than the others. Which makes her a threat. Her lack of voice is taken advantage of by the Gendarme, who sees this as an

easy way to tell his/her version of the story, regardless of what the truth actually is, because Flora is not in a position to disagree. Flora, it seems, might have the actual truth, and might be the only one who knows it, but she is unable to speak the truth, so it dies with her.

THE REST
Depending on your cast size, the rest might be a few, several, or a great many. And it is up to you how you make that work. Whatever the size, The Rest have the potential to offer further rich and exciting visual and physical moments to the scenes that they are in.

Music

The story is that Um-Aloysius can play the cello beautifully. You can feel free to achieve this any way you like. If you happen to have a talented young cellist playing the part of Um-Aloysius, that's brilliant. It would not be impossible to substitute the cello for another instrument, if it is an instrument that the actor can play to a high level. However, bear in mind that the cello was chosen for particular reasons and any change could be problematic for the text.

In choosing your section of Bach to play, you are encouraged to be bold and explore, using around two minutes of music. It is worth it and you will have earned it.

Storytelling: Some Hints for Rehearsal

- This play is all about storytelling. In each interview with the children, their particular version of events reveals parts of the Pied Piper story. Therefore, the story of the story being created needs careful consideration. Find a way to keep track (either just for you as a company or for the audience as well) of when the children lie or manipulate the truth, and how the units of the story are created as a result. Perhaps there is a way of highlighting or marking moments when the story is being constructed?

- The story that is told by Flora in the final scene puts together all these pieces, and becomes the reconstructed 'truth' that will now be told for ever more. A hint to whoever plays Flora: keep that final speech simple. The words are so powerful and need little else except an attention to the rhythm of each thought. Take your time. This is what the whole play has been building towards.

- Pay close attention to the time and place of each scene. The chronology and timeline of events will be crucial in the understanding and unravelling of events.

- Do not be afraid of making decisions about what happened. In fact, if you don't make decisions, it will be to the detriment of the production. The play just won't work. So make some rules. Decide what version you want to tell. Be bold and courageous in your choices. And once you have made them, stick to them. Trust in your own version. It is worth taking the time at the beginning to talk about possibilities and to discuss, question, analyse. However you arrive at your version, make sure everyone knows what it is, so you can be sure that everyone is telling the same story.

- Don't get too bogged down in these discussions, however. Too much talking will get everyone lost and confused. Keep the discoveries happening through action and on your feet.

- In every scene, work out the given circumstances. What do you know? What are the facts, the things which are not negotiable? What, literally, is going on?

- For every character in every scene, the actor should ask: 'What do I want and how do I get it?' Keep the answers simple and playable.

- Keep telling yourself the story of the play. For every scene, give yourself a checklist of the following:

  Have I established the facts?

  Are the choices we have made interesting enough?

  Are the stakes right?

Are we telling the story in the clearest possible way?

Are we telling the right story?

- Think about the relationships, where the power lies, who has status, how the power shifts in every scene.

- What are the stakes in every scene? (What does each person stand to gain and what do they stand to lose?) The higher the stakes, the more dramatically interesting the scene.

- Think about the public and the private. When characters are speaking to each other, who else is listening? How might this affect how they say the lines? How different are they in public to how they appear in private? What can you learn about them from this?

- Because the scenes do not play out in chronological order, think about what has happened directly before each scene in the real timeline. If you know what has just happened to your character, then it will inform how you behave in the scene.

Words

It might be helpful to think of the text as a musical score. Every word matters and is there for a reason. Be attentive to the slashes, italics and phrasing of each sentence. They are there for a reason and tell you something about how the line should be said. While the stage directions can be interpreted as you see fit, the words are sacred.

Don't be daunted by the large chunks of text. Don't rush it. Take your time, accept it is a long speech and don't worry about it. Give time to each thought. Pay close attention to the rhythm within the speeches. Hit every single word and don't apologise for any of them.

Learn the words as early as possible. Only once you are familiar with the words, are you really free to explore the characters and bring them to life.

In Scene Seven, these amended stage directions might be helpful in understanding Flora's journey throughout the play:

At the beginning of the scene:
Sebastian *is addressing 130 assembling marcher children, including* **Um-Aloysius**. *Perhaps he uses a loud hailer.* **Flora** IS PRESENT, ON THE PERIPHERY.

At the end of the scene:
The march, where in Scene Two it had been theatrical somehow, in one place in order to meet the demands of the scene, now moves realistically, through the theatre, through the audience, out a door, whatever is possible to take everybody (including **Um-Aloysius**) *away.* **Flora** IS PUSHED TO THE GROUND BY THE MARCHING CHILDREN AND LEFT BEHIND.

Staging

Don't leap ahead in the staging. Make sure everyone understands what is going on and what each character wants and what they are doing in every scene before anything else. Less might be more. What is most important is the clarity of storytelling. Start with nothing but the actors saying words and if you find you need more to help you tell the story, then go for it. When staging things like 130 children marching in Scene Two, for example, consider powerful visual formations and consider when and how they chant, as it might not be necessary for the chanting to underscore all the dialogue.

The stage directions show Samuel's intentions, but are by no means prescriptive. They offer clues, suggestions, starting points, but are not answers in themselves.

The Rape of Katherine Osterhagen

How significant is the rape in the story? It might be useful to think of this event as a myth in itself – nobody really knows who raped Katherine Osterhagen, but the rape is used as a tool to manipulate people. The truth of what actually happened has been lost, but people use it to their own ends.

Conclusion

The play is challenging and ambiguous. The words require careful and thorough investigation. The challenge is to make every beat of the story clear, and to stick to your guns in terms of what you think is happening. Be true to the language, trust your instincts and don't underestimate how many clues lie in the words themselves. If you find yourself being tied up in knots trying to work out what it's all about, go back to the basics: don't get caught up in over-analysis. Remember that at its root, this is a simple story about relationships: love, friendship, loyalty, stuff that everyone knows about on some level.

From a workshop led by Angus Jackson,
with notes by Kate Budgen

Alia Bano

Gap

Characters

Tim
Ginge
Tiny
Pothead

Jay
Matt
Dean

Hailey
Amy

Mike
Poppy
Kat
Dee
Al, *Dee's supervisor*

Sam
Bronte

Rob
Tony

Scene One

THE BEACH — *late morning.*

'Holiday' by Dizzee Rascal plays. Lights up, people dancing and drinking. They all begin to walk offstage, leaving **Tim** *and* **Ginge** *on-stage. They are lying on the beach, sunbathing.* **Ginge** *is covered and wearing a hat.* **Tim** *is dressed more appropriately.* **Ginge** *is applying suntan lotion to* **Tim**'s *back.*

Ginge   It's fucking hot.

Tim   Scorching.

Ginge   Boiling. It's too hot.

Tim   Take off some clothes then.

Ginge   I'll burn.

Tim *turns round and hands the lotion to* **Ginge**.

Ginge   I'm ginger.

Tim   I've never noticed.

In the distance, a young male voice can be heard shouting.

Tiny   Beer, ice-cold beer, nuts, ice cream.

Ginge   I'm thirsty.

Tim   The ocean's just there.

Ginge   I can't drink that.

Tim   It's water.

Ginge   It's salty.

Tim   Must be all those people christening it.

Ginge   You're so dim, Tim. Gonna get a drink.

Tim   We're brassed. Shall we trek back to the hostel?

Ginge   I'll be shrivelled up like a prune by then. How much we got?

They begin counting cash.

Tim   Just over seventy.

Ginge   For the whole week!

Tim *nods.*

Ginge   You're fucking me. We're going to have to dip in the cash for the following week.

Tim   We won't have enough for the rest of the month.

Beat.

Ginge   Better see if the hostel will let us work to stay there.

Tim   I didn't come round the world to skiv like a (*beat*) skivvy. I might have another hundred in my account before the overdraft goes nuclear.

Ginge   My credit card's nearly maxed.

Tiny   Beer, nice cold beer.

Tim (*imitating Homer Simpson*)   Beer, beer, beer.

Tiny *approaches as if he has heard them. He is a teenager aged thirteen or fourteen.*

Tiny   Ice creams, drinks. Beers, ice-cold beers.

Ginge *hesitates, he's almost tempted but knows they are low on cash.*

Ginge   We're good, thanks.

Tiny   I got everything.

He starts bringing out cans of beer.

Tiny   English beer.

Tim   How much?

Tiny   Five.

Tim   Five.

Ginge   We can get it cheaper in town.

Tiny   Not get this in the shop.

Enter **Pothead**.

Pothead   Hey, bros. Good night?

Tim   Yeah man!

Ginge   You?

Pothead   Always, bro, always.

Ginge   Thanks for sharing your stash last night.

Tim   It was good shit. Smoked like a dream.

Pothead   Thank this man. (*He pats* **Tiny** *on the back.*)

Tim   Him?

Pothead   He's the best.

Ginge   He's just a kid. How old is he? Twelve?

Pothead   They grow up fast round here. He does good shit. He'll get you whatever you want.

Pothead *speaks to* **Tiny** *in a foreign language and* **Tiny** *gets out some roll-ups.* **Pothead** *lights one and gives the boys a puff of the roll-up.* **Tiny** *looks round nervously.*

Tiny   Marijuana, pills . . .

Tim   How much for some weed?

Tiny   How much you want?

Ginge   We're good, man. Thanks.

Tim *and* **Ginge** *look at each other.*

Tim   We don't have any money.

Pothead   He'll do you a good price, won't you, Tiny?

Tiny *nods.*

Pothead   These are my amigos, you look after them. Well, take it easy, fellas, I'm off to chill at the café, I'll come check you later.

Tim/Ginge Later.

Beat as **Tim** *and* **Ginge** *look at each other.*

Tim What you saying, Ginge? I could do with a good smoke.

Ginge Me too, but I think we have to pass.

Tim We're sorry, kid.

Tiny *begins to leave.*

Ginge Hang on, kid, one minute.

He pulls **Tim** *to one side.*

Ginge Listen to this, we pool our dough together, buy a stash and we go to a few parties and we sell it.

Tim I don't know.

Ginge We're gonna make a killing.

Tim A killing, how?

Ginge How much are people willing to pay for good shit round here?

Tim A lot.

Ginge We could mix it with tobacco to make some more.

Tim Good idea.

Ginge No working for the rest of the month.

Tim We haven't got enough dough on us to buy a load.

Ginge I'll max the card, you explode that overdraft.

Tim I don't know.

Ginge We'll make the money and we'll drop it back in the bank. And we'll have extra so it'll be party time again. It's a plan.

Tim OK, plan.

Tim *and* **Ginge** *turn back to* **Tiny**.

Ginge   How much can we get for four hundred?

Tiny   Come.

Blackout.

Scene Two

Matt *and* **Dean** *are walking along the beach.* **Dean** *has a football which he is playing with. He passes it to* **Matt**, *who misses it and runs after it limply.*

Dean   Come on, Matty!

Matt *passes it back.*

Dean   Pathetic!

Matt   I'm fucked, man, I need more sleep.

Dean *picks up the ball and puts an arm round* **Matt**.

Dean   You need the exercise. You need to stop looking so yellow if you wanna try with the ladies. You haven't even hit one on the scoreboard.

Matt   Haven't seen anyone I like.

Dean   There's hundreds of babes around, you must be blind.

Matt   You seen my sunnies?

Dean   Nah, mate!

Matt   Had them yesterday, seem to have disappeared.

Dean   Did you have them after we left the beach last night?

Matt   Think so.

Dean   You should keep an eye on your stuff, that Brummie bloke's wallet was picked while he was walking on the beach.

Some kid knocked into him and he thought nothing of it until he needed to pay for something and . . .

Matt   Damn. (*Beat.*) I definitely had them in the dorm after we came back.

Dean   Someone probably nicked them there.

Matt   They're my favourite. They cost a packet too.

Dean   You guys wanted to stay in a dorm with twelve people.

Matt   It was Jay's idea.

Dean   You're his lapdog.

Silence.

Matt   This way we get the real experience.

Dean   I say we move into a hotel.

Matt   We're all right where we are.

Dean   Until you leave something else out and it disappears. Those lockers are crap.

Matt   And we know everyone now.

Dean   I tried my key in a few of the other lockers and guess what? It opens the door to a couple of others.

Matt   No way.

Dean   I say we move round the corner. We can hang at the hostel in the evening. That way we get nice beds, clean showers.

Matt   What about the dough? I've got enough till the end of the trip if I budget, and Jay's struggling.

Dean   Bank of my mum and your dad.

Matt   I already withdrew last week, I can't ask for a few weeks.

Dean   My dear old mum, then. She'll gladly cover it.

Matt   Let's see if Jay's up for it.

Dean   But you're up for it in theory, right?

Matt *hesitates.*

Dean   Matty boy.

Matt   Maybe . . . Yeah, OK in theory.

Dean   Great. Let's find him – he'll be around here somewhere.

Blackout.

Scene Three

Jay *sits in a deckchair, relaxing. The spotlight moves to two girls talking a short distance away from him.*

Hailey   Should I go –

Amy   Talk to him, sure.

Hailey   But I'm –

Amy   Scared. Just do it.

Hailey   I'm really nervous.

Amy   You shagged him, Hail, how hard can it be to talk to him?

Hailey *stares at her.*

Hailey   Fine.

*She fixes her sarong and walks towards **Jay**. She looks at him and smiles. He ignores her. She flicks her hair and coughs, but nothing.*

Hailey   Hey, Jay. Hey.

She realises he's wearing his earphones, and removes one.

Hailey   Hey, Jay.

Jay   Hailey.

Hailey   Thought you were ignoring me.

Jay   I'd never do that, not to you.

Hailey *takes this as invitation to sit on the edge of his deckchair.*

Hailey   Didn't see you last night?

Jay   I was around.

Hailey   Did you have a good night?

Jay   Could have been better.

Hailey *reads her own ending into this: 'if you were there'.*

Hailey   I was fucked out my head.

Jay   Me too.

Hailey   Is that a scratch?

She goes to lift his sunglasses lovingly.

Jay   Don't.

Hailey   Sorry.

Silence as **Hailey** *struggles to say something. She tries to make the atmosphere lighter.* **Matt** *and* **Dean** *approach from a distance.*

Hailey   Your mate was really funny.

Jay   Yeah, guess so. When he's drunk.

Hailey   He's such a lightweight.

Jay   Dean can take his drink.

Hailey   No, Matt. He was falling all over the place. What you doing today?

Jay   Not sure.

Hailey   It's the tour, you coming?

Jay   Did it yesterday.

Hailey   That sucks.

Jay   Yeah.

Hailey   Hey, Matt, Dean.

Matt   Hailey.

Dean   Hi.

Hailey   You stopped puking?

Matt   God, did you see me?

Hailey   The whole dorm did.

Matt   Fuck. Sorry.

Hailey *shrugs as if the puking is normal, not a big deal.*

Hailey   I better go. See you in the bar later?

Matt/Dean   Sure.

Hailey   Jay?

Jay   It's a date.

She exits, almost skipping offstage.

Dean   She's got it bad.

Jay   Yep.

Dean   Thought you weren't interested in her any more?

Matt   She's quite pretty.

Jay   Been there, done that, on to greener pastures.

Matt   You just gave her the come-on?

Jay   Always good to have a back-up, Matty boy.

Dean   When did you start collecting back-ups? Is this because you didn't come back with anyone last night?

Jay   Night off.

Dean   Or you're losing your touch.

Jay   Unlikely.

Dean   Could have gone there with Hailey?

Jay   She's a bit clingy and easy, ruins my flow.

Dean   Can't escape anyone in the hostel?

Jay   But I'll get on it tonight.

Matt   That's like a girl for every night we've been here.

Jay   We're on holiday.

Dean   Matt and I were thinking –

Jay   Yeah, let's fuck the tour, chill on the beach, play some footie.

He gets up and begins to put his top on.

What took you ladies so long?

Matt   Had to change my bed sheets.

Jay   Again?

Matt   Can't sleep on puke.

Jay   How many times they charged you for changing your sheets?

Dean   Every single night.

Jay   They're minting it off you.

Matt   It's only a few quid.

Dean   But we wouldn't have to worry about that shit if we stayed in a hotel.

Matt   You wearing my sunnies?

Jay   What?

Dean   We were thinking –

Matt   Pass them over.

He goes for the glasses, **Jay** *stops him.*

Jay   My head's thumping, is it cool if I wear them for the day?

Matt   Yeah sure, you OK?

Jay   Yeah.

Matt   Look, keep them. I'll wear my Ray-Bans. Shall we get some aspirin?

Jay   Nah, I'll be OK.

Dean   Jay, we were thinking we should move on to that hotel.

Jay   That'll cost twice as much.

Dean   Mum's gonna send me a wad over.

Jay   Lucky you.

Dean   It'll cover the cost for all of us.

Jay   The hostel is where the party's at.

Dean   But we could chill there, come back and sleep in luxury.

Jay   We're fine where we are. Whoever heard of people staying in hotels on their gap year? This way we get the authentic experience and save pounds.

Dean   Matt's with me on this one.

Jay   What you saying, Matty boy?

Beat.

Matt   The hostel's fun.

Jay   Exactly.

Dean *looks at* **Matt**.

Matt   But I do think Dean has a point, we could spend a few days in a hotel and then in the next place go back to –

Jay   Matty boy, do you think there'll be as much access to chicks in that hotel? These girls are on heat and you have yet to extinguish one of their fires. You've got unfinished business; you need to get laid before this holiday's out. Don't you?

Beat.

Matt   Yeah, I guess.

Dean   Matt!

Matt *shrugs as if to say sorry.*

Jay   It's decided, Dean, we're staying put. Matt's got unfinished business and so have I.

Blackout.

Scene Four

Beach bar, early afternoon.

Sexy Boy plays for a few seconds as we watch **Dee** *sweeping up and cleaning up the bar. It's the mess from last night.* **Al** *is counting the float in the till. In this conversation,* **Poppy** *and* **Mike** *should approach and take a seat at a table.*

Al   You nearly finished? We've got five minutes before opening.

Dee   In a bit.

Al   As long as it's all gone before the boss gets here.

Dee   When she coming?

Al   Afternoon, to do the accounts and talk about the show. Serve those customers, I'm going to go get some more beers.

Poppy   This is the life. I think I could live here.

Mike   You probably wouldn't love it as much if you did.

Poppy   No depressing stuff. I'm on holiday.

Mike   Sorry.

Poppy   And today, so are you.

Beat.

Poppy   You still feeling guilty?

Mike   Maybe I should have gone in to work.

Poppy   Everyone's entitled to a sickie now and again.

Mike   Yeah, but –

Poppy   You'll be helping out soon enough. For the moment, just relax and . . .

She goes to kiss him. He kisses her. **Dee** *spots this as she walks towards them.* **Mike** *registers her, looks guilty and embarrassed.*

Poppy (*beat*)   I've wanted to do that all morning.

She goes to kiss him again.

Mike   Not here.

Poppy   There's no one around.

She kisses him again.

Dee   Excuse me.

Poppy   Yes.

Dee   What would you like to drink?

Poppy   We'll have two vodka and Cokes.

Dee *is meant to leave, but she doesn't.*

Poppy   That's all.

Mike   Thanks, Dee.

Dee   OK, Mr Mike.

Mike   What's with the 'Mr Mike'?

Dee   Kat not with you?

Mike   She's at the centre.

Dee   Tell her I said hello.

She goes back behind to the bar. She should bring the drinks over and leave them before **Kat** *enters the scene.*

Poppy   How do you know her?

Mike   Her brother used to be in the project the centre runs.

Poppy   Who's Kat?

Mike   A workmate.

Poppy   Do you know any quiet scenic spots around here?

Mike   A few.

Poppy   Shall we go explore them?

Mike   Maybe I should go in to work, and after we can . . .

Poppy   I'm leaving soon.

Mike   I know.

Poppy   It'd just be a few hours out of your time here.

Mike *hesitates.*

Poppy   I'm not looking for anything serious. I'm here for the next three days and I want to have some fun with you. I know I'm being forward but I haven't got time to play around. I like you and I think you like me too. Unless I've read the situation wrong, just say, it's fine. I'll leave you alone and . . .

She gets up to leave.

Mike   No, no, don't go. I do like you, but . . .

Poppy   But?

Beat.

Mike   But nothing. Let's go explore those scenic spots.

He goes to kiss her, but as they find their flow **Kat** *walks into the bar and stops in shock – which she quickly masks just before* **Mike** *registers her presence. When he does he breaks away from* **Poppy**.

Poppy   These are definitely gonna be three great days to remember.

She notices **Kat**.

Kat   Sorry.

Mike   No, I'm sorry.

Poppy   Don't be silly, Mikey; I'm sure she's seen enough people making out here.

Mike   We work together.

Poppy   Oh.

Kat   It's fine, Mikey. I got your text, thought you weren't feeling well.

Mike   I was feeling a bit queasy this morning.

Poppy   I convinced him to come out and get some fresh air.

Kat   It's the kid's trip tomorrow, are you going to be well enough to make it? Or should I tell them we need someone else – [to come along instead?]

Mike   I'll be there.

Poppy   A trip?

Mike   We're taking the kids go-karting.

Poppy   How lovely. Can I come?

Kat   It's project workers only.

Poppy   Mikey?

Kat   They don't allow plus-ones.

Mike   We could ask Dee – say she's thinking of volunteering.

Kat   Is she?

Mike   No, but –

Kat   The project barely has any money as it is.

Mike   I know.

Poppy   I'll get my ticket. I love the thrill of the speed, we went on the tour of the *favelas* and we had to get up there on these motorcycle taxis – no helmets, nothing, and the guys just sped all the way up. It was amazing!

Kat   You went on the shanty town tour?

Poppy   Haven't you been?

Kat   No.

Poppy   It's great. I recommend it – not just for the bikes, you get to see how the people live, go into their homes.

Kat   You paid to go on a tour of poverty?

Poppy   No, I went to get an insight into how people survive in the slums.

Kat   Did you take loads of pictures?

Poppy   Yes, a few.

Kat   Great mementos, which you can show to all your friends.

Poppy   I don't see what your objection is – they offered a service and I took it.

Kat   It's a bit gratuitous.

Poppy   It brings in money for the people there.

Kat   Really?

Poppy   The tour guide said the money from the tickets goes to the community.

Mike   She does have a point.

Kat   We both know whose hands that money goes into.

Poppy   Everyone bought paintings and souvenirs from the workshop.

Kat   How nice.

Mike   Kat, we know the boys rely on that cash from the paintings.

Kat   It's just a conscience-easer for the tourists, so they can feel better for snooping around and feel like they've helped.

Poppy   It'd probably be harder for them if there were no tourists.

Kat   It'd be a lot easier if our economic system didn't screw them over.

Poppy   As interesting as this is, I think we should head back, we don't want you getting too ill.

Mike   Give me a sec.

Poppy   Sure, I'll be over there.

She kisses **Mike**, *but he doesn't really respond.* **Poppy** *doesn't notice.*

Mike   About this morning –

Kat   What about it?

Mike   I needed a break.

Kat   I thought you cared about the kids, the project?

Mike   I do.

Kat   I'm gonna head back.

Mike   I'll come with you.

Kat   They'll just send you back. You might as well take the day off and enjoy the company of your friend.

Mike   About Poppy –

Kat   I can see what's going on between you.

Mike   Kat, listen –

Kat   She's waiting for you and I better go.

Mike   Kat.

Kat *leaves before her emotions overrun.* **Mike** *watches her as she heads towards the bar. He goes after* **Poppy**. **Dee** *stops* **Kat**.

Dee   Kat, are you OK?

Kat   I'm OK, Dee.

Dee   You sure?

Kat   Yeah.

Dee   You're going to come see me dance tonight?

Kat   Tonight?

Dee   In the bar. (*Beat.*) I would like if you were there.

Kat   Of course I'll be there.

Dee   Mr Mike, he'll come too?

Kat   I don't know, Dee. Can I have a vodka and lemonade?

Dee   A drink so early? This is not like you?

She pours her a drink.

Kat   How much?

Dee   Nothing.

Kat   You'll get in trouble.

Dee   I said nada.

Kat   What about Al?

Dee   What he does not know, does no harm.

Kat   You sure?

Dee *nods.*

Kat   Thanks.

She sits humming to herself.

Dee   Don't worry about the air-cell.

Kat   What?

Dee   The air-cell, the girl he was with now.

Kat *laughs.*

Kat   I think you mean air-head.

Dee (*laughs*)   She is nothing, nada, you come and make up in the bar tonight.

Tiny *walks in.*

Kat   Tiny!

Tiny   Miss Kat.

Kat   How are you?

Tiny   I is good.

Kat   I am fine.

Tiny   I am fine.

Kat   I haven't seen you for a while.

Tiny   I work now.

Kat   I know. Do you like it?

Tiny *nods.*

Tiny   It's OK.

Kat   We all miss you at the centre.

Tiny   The centre was nice. I still practise my English.

Kat   That's good. (*Beat.*) How about I come round on Saturday so we can keep practising your English? Would you like that, Tiny?

Tiny *nods.*

Kat   Great, I'll see you then.

Dee   Al is getting more beers, he'll give you some out back.

Tiny   Bye, Miss Kat.

Kat   See you Saturday, Tiny.

Dee   You don't have to –

Kat   I want to, Dee. It might mean later he can go back to school –

Dee   This will not happen. Father sent him to work, this way it will mean Ella and Jimmy will be able to finish school.

Kat   He's a good kid. I'm gonna miss him.

Dee   We'll miss you also when you leave.

Kat   I might stay here longer.

Dee   Really?

Kat   Go home next year.

Dee   This is wonderful. When you go home maybe I visit you.

Kat   Yes, I'd love that.

Dee   I go when you and Mr Mike marry.

Kat   We're just friends.

Dee   By then I will have saved enough –

Kat   We're just friends.

Dee   You don't like him?

Kat   You have more customers. I'll see you tonight.

Dee *nods and gets back to work.*

Blackout.

Scene Five

The dorms, early evening.

A split stage. The audience can see into both of the dorms.

'Boys Will be Boys' in the backgound. In stylised movements, the boys all get dressed, doing up their hair, putting on their clothes, face-cream. **Ginge** *and* **Tim** *walk in, offer them a smoke. The scene should begin here. We should see* **Jay** *walking to the dorms half-dressed, showered. As he approaches, a girl sees him and walks into the dorm. A couple of girls watch his back, and giggle in excitement before returning to their dorm.*

The girls will be getting ready – their flow more fluid, almost as if they are dancing a waltz. Make-up and magazines should be passed round.

Boys' dorm.

Ginge   This is good shit.

Tim   Good shit!

Ginge   Probably the best shit in the world.

Dean   Pass it.

Tim *hesitates.*

Dean   You guys selling the stuff or smoking it?

Ginge   Tim, pass it.

Tim *hands it over.* **Dean** *takes a puff.*

Dean   Yeah, it's good shit. (*Beat.*) Matt?

Matt *hesitates.*

Dean   Don't be a pussy.

Matt *takes a few puffs – as many as he deems socially acceptable – before passing it to* **Jay**.

Dean   Finish it.

Jay *enters, still wearing his sunglasses.*

Jay   Is that the smell of –

Dean   Want some?

Jay   Sure.

Matt *passes it over gratefully.* **Jay** *puffs it and finishes it.*

Jay   Good shit!

Tim   How much you want?

Dean   We'll probably be good with beer.

Ginge   We'll knock off twenty.

Beat.

Dean   Give us an eighth.

Tim   We got pills.

The guys don't seem interested.

Ginge   We'll do you a good deal on those, too.

Dean   Lads?

Matt   Not after what happened to me the last time.

Jay   Matty's right, forget it, we don't want to risk trekking him to the hospital here – plus they fuck me up too much the day after. I'm good with this bad boy.

Dean   I'll take a couple for me. How much for all that?

Tim   That'll be –

Ginge   That'll be –

Almost of if they are reading each other's minds.

Tim/Ginge   Forty.

Dean *pays* **Tim** *and* **Ginge**.

Dean   Great doing business with you.

Ginge   If you want any more or know anyone else who does . . .

Jay   We'll head them in your directions.

Girls' dorm.

Sam, **Amy** *and* **Hailey** *are getting ready. They do not see* **Kat** *is sleeping in her bed.*

Amy   How long we got?

Hailey   A couple of –

Amy   – hours.

Sam   Fuck.

She begins chucking clothes out of her backpack.

Hailey   Do you have any deodorant? We seem to have run out.

Sam   Yeah.

She chucks Impulse at them.

Hailey   Oh wow, I haven't used this since –

Amy   – we were fourteen.

Beat.

Sam   I hate it, but my mum chucked it into my bag.

Amy   Mums!

Hailey   Let's make sure we make happy hour.

Sam   I brought a bottle of vodka, if you guys want to share.

Hailey   That's really –

Amy   – sweet of you.

Sam   We can start drinking while we get ready. Save gas.

She pulls out a bottle of vodka and mixers.

Hailey   We gotta hide it if any –

Hailey/Amy   – of the staff come round.

Sam   Cool. (*She takes a swig of the bottle.*)

Hailey   I want to wear something hot and tight.

Amy   Isn't that what you're offering Jay?

We should see **Kat** *visibly shudder under her blanket at* **Jay**'*s name.*

Hailey   You're sick.

Amy   But truthful.

Boys' dorm.

Dean   You're gonna wear your sunnies?

Jay   Yeah.

Dean   There's no sun.

Jay   And?

Dean   It looks crap.

Jay   It's stylish. What do you think, Matt?

Dean   You look like a twat.

Jay *turns to* **Matt** *as if to ask whether he agrees.*

Matt   Maybe a little twattish.

Jay   I'll just wear your Rays, they'll match. Pass them.

Matt *gets sunnies out of his backpack.* **Jay** *walks out.*

Dean   Where you going?

Jay   To take a leak. That OK with you guys?

Two guys with backpacks roll in to stop the action.

Rob   Hey, guys.

Dean   Hey.

Matt   You just arrive?

Rob   Yeah.

Tony   Which beds are free?

Matt   Those. (*Points to beds.*) You guys from the West Country?

Rob   Yeah.

Tony   Anywhere good to go tonight?

Dean   The party's in the bar tonight.

Rob   Great.

Tony   Let's shower and get ready.

They exit, but as they do so **Jay** *strolls back in. He knocks into* **Tony***, and the sunglasses drop off.*

Tony   Sorry, mate.

Jay *is sporting a scratch and bruise around his left eye. He quickly puts the glasses on again, hoping the other two guys haven't noticed.*

Dean   How the fuck did you get that?

Jay   What?

Dean   That shiner.

Matt   What happened?

Dean   You look like a one-eyed panda.

Matt   Who did it?

Jay   Drunken scrap last night, you should see the other guy.

Dean   You should have said last night.

Jay   You were way too pissed, I handled it.

Dean   What the fuck happened?

Girls' dorm.

Bronte *walks in.*

Bronte   You seen Kat?

Hailey   Who's –

Amy   Kat?

Bronte *walks to* **Kat***'s bed and pulls her blanket off.* **Kat** *is underneath it.*

Kat   I'll come up for the dance and that's it?

Sam   Shit, babe, we didn't see you there?

Bronte   Come up now.

Kat   I'm working off a migraine.

Bronte   I've got paracetamol somewhere.

The girls realise who she is talking to, and as if she has just come to life they begin persuading her.

Hailey   Tonight's gonna –

Amy   – be buzzing. There's a local dance show.

Kat   I can't take much more of this tourist crap.

Bronte   You promised Dee.

Kat   I'll be there.

Bronte   She said you might need cheering up because of Mike.

Kat   She told you?

Bronte   Yeah. (*Beat.*) You OK?

Kat   Yeah.

Bronte   Kat.

Kat   I just need to be alone.

Bronte   Don't give him – or her – the satisfaction. They're up there; it'll look weird if you make a cameo appearance.

Silence.

I'm not taking no for an answer.

Kat   I want to be fresh for the trip tomorrow.

Bronte   Let Mike take care of that. Why you letting him have all the fun? If you stay up here, he's gonna know he's got to you. (*Beat.*) *Kat!*

Kat   OK, I'm coming. I don't want to give him the satisfaction. I'm gonna go over to his dorm and give him the keys in case I drink too much – he can set up in the morning tomorrow.

Bronte   You go, girl.

Kat *exits girls' dorm and heads towards the boys' dorm.*

Boys' dorm.

Jay   Some new guy that walked in last night.

Dean   And?

Jay   The usual.

Beat. The guys want more of an explanation.

He got upset because some bird that he fancied had the hots for me. Starting mouthing off, pushing and shoving. I told him to take a running jump, he punched me, I forgot to duck. Like lightning I punched him twice, once to the left then twice, I was going for a third when his friend begged me to stop. By that time it was too late, I punched him.

Dean   All this in the bar? Why is no one talking about –

Jay   Outside, we were getting some air.

Dean   We'll get him tonight, show him he can't –

Jay   He's long gone, checked out this morning.

Dean   That must have been one beating you gave him.

Jay   That was yesterday, let's get on with today.

Dean   So who's the prey tonight?

Matt *heads for the door and as he opens it nearly bumps into* **Kat**.

Matt   *Sorry.*

Kat   Sorry.

Kat *addresses herself only to* **Dean** *and* **Matt**. *It's as if* **Jay** *doesn't exist.*

Kat   I was just wondering if Mike was around?

Dean   Mike?

Kat   Yeah.

Jay   He's the charity dude.

Dean   He went out to get a drink with that posh broad, Poppy.

Jay   Rainbow.

Matt   Honey blossom.

The boys crack up.

Jay   They're probably in the bar.

Kat *walks out.*

Dean   That girl just blanked you.

Jay   She didn't.

Dean   Was she the one you were chatting up last night?

Jay   I wasn't chatting –

Dean   Yeah, I remember, you were speaking to her – that's why Matty and I went to the bar.

Jay   I was just asking her something.

Dean   You only ever speak to girls to chat them up – isn't that true, Matty boy?

Matt   It's true.

Jay   She's not my type, too much like a bloke.

Dean   Losing your touch, Jay.

Jay   No, I'm not.

Dean   You might as well been the invisible man.

Jay   I could have her if I wanted to.

Dean   I bet you a hundred, she'll say no.

Matt   This is silly. Jay always gets the –

Jay   It's a sure bet, you sure you want to be a loser?

Dean   I'll give you three hundred.

Jay   Three hundred?

Dean   Three hundred if you win!

Jay (*scornfully, of the local currency*)   Three hundred, that's nothing.

Dean   Pounds.

Jay   Pounds?

Dean   You know I'm good for it.

Matt   Dean!

Beat.

Jay   It'll be like taking money from a baby. It's too easy. Forget it.

Dean   You scared?

Jay   You're on. Be prepared to hand Mummy's wad over.

Blackout.

Scene Six

The bar, evening.

Repetition of first scene, groups of people dancing and having fun. The bar is buzzing. **Dee** *and* **Al** *are behind the counter;* **Dee** *is in a local costume;* **Hailey** *and* **Amy** *are at the bar;* **Poppy** *and* **Mike** *are dancing;* **Poppy** *is making a bit of a show of herself;* **Ginge** *and* **Tim** *are circulating the crowd.* **Pothead** *enters.*

Pothead   Party. Party.

Rob *and* **Tony** *finish having a conversation with* **Tiny** *and walk towards the bar.*

Tony   It's a bit quiet in here.

Rob   It'll pick up.

Tony   Hope so.

Rob   With a couple of these it will do.

He holds up a bag of pills.

Tony   Yeah, let's get a drink.

They walk over to the bar.

Dee   What can I get you?

Rob   Jägerbombs.

Dee *lines them up. They down them.*

Tony   Whoo!

Rob   I'm buzzing. Another round and shall we take one –

Tony *notices* **Hailey** *and* **Amy**.

Tony   Later, let's get some beers. Would you ladies like a drink?

Hailey   We're good –

Amy   Thanks.

Tony   You sure?

Amy   Well, if you're offering, I'll have a vodka and Coke.

Jay, **Dean** and **Matt** *enter.* **Hailey** *spots them and walks over.*

Tony   Is your friend sure she doesn't want [a drink] –

Amy   She's fine.

Hailey   Oh my God, Jay, are you OK? What happened to you?

Jay   Nothing.

Dean   He had a fight with the invisible man.

Hailey   You poor thing.

Jay   The other guy got it worse.

Hailey   You're so brave.

Jay   I'm gonna get a drink.

He walks off.

Hailey   Wait, I'll come –

She looks at **Dean***, who shrugs as if to say sorry. She begins to walk back to* **Amy***. Meanwhile* **Tiny** *walks past* **Kat** *and* **Bronte** *just as* **Bronte** *spots* **Jay** *approaching.*

Kat   Tiny! What you doing here?

Tiny   Hello, Miss.

Kat   You come to see Dee dance?

A beat of hesitation.

Tiny   Yes. I see Dee.

Kat   Me too.

Tiny   I must go now and speak Dee.

Kat   OK, but come sit with me when she dances.

Tiny   OK, Miss.

Kat   Poor kid, I wish he didn't have to –

Bronte   Save the world later. Good-looking guy approaching.

Kat (*wearily*)   Oh God.

Bronte   He fucking hot.

Kat   He's a slag.

Bronte   The hot ones usually are.

Kat   I'm not interested.

Bronte   Just flirt with him, have an ego-boost. Trust me, it'll make Mike jealous. I'm gonna make myself scarce.

Kat   Bronte!

Jay   Hey. How are you?

Kat   I'm not interested.

Jay   I just want to say –

Kat   If you don't move out of my way, I'll punch you again so you can have a matching set.

Jay *takes one step back.*

Jay   And I'm sure it'd pack a punch like the last one.

Kat   What do you want?

Jay   Forgiveness. (*Beat.*) I could blame the fact that I had too much to drink last night but that wouldn't excuse what a dick I was.

Kat   Yeah, you were.

Jay   I'm not usually such an asshole, I read the signals wrong.

Kat   Yeah, you did.

Jay   I think it was great that you whacked some sense into me.

Beat.

Kat I hate to admit it, but I think that my bangle did that.

Jay A worthy opponent always chooses good armour.

Kat *smiles at him.* **Mike** *comes over.*

Mike Are you OK?

Kat What?

Mike Is this guy hassling you?

Kat I can handle myself.

Jay *stands and watches.*

Mike Kat?

Poppy *begins to walk over.*

Kat I think your girlfriend's missing you.

Mike She's not my girl –

Kat Could have fooled me.

Mike Look, Kat –

Kat Before I forget, here are the keys, I'm gonna get in just before the trip. You can set up. I'm gonna have some fun.

Poppy Is everything OK?

Kat Great. Jay was just going to get us a drink, weren't you?

Jay Yeah, of course.

Mike *watches as* **Kat** *walks off.* **Poppy** *takes him back to the dance floor. Throughout this scene* **Mike** *should keep an eye on* **Kat** *and her movements.*

Jay Who was that guy?

Kat I seem to have a knack of attracting assholes.

Jay Seemed like he's interested.

Silence.

Could see why he would be.

Kat   I think I'm gonna head on to bed.

Jay   What about the drink?

Kat   It's fine. You're forgiven.

Jay   Look, I know you're not interested in me, but I know a thing or two about guys. The minute your mate thinks you're interested in someone else, he's gonna think he's lost you. I bet he's only with that girl because he's trying to make you jealous. Why not give him a taste of his own medicine?

Kat   Thanks, but –

Jay   I took you for a fighter, not some sappy girl who –

Kat   I'm not a sap. (*Beat.*) I'll have a vodka and lemonade.

Jay   I'll be right back.

He heads to the bar where he meets **Dean**.

Jay   JD and Coke, and a vodka and lemonade.

Dean   Don't know why you're bothering with the drink. You might as well cough up the dough now.

Jay   You're the one who'll be coughing up.

Dean   You're gonna lose. Everyone knows she has the hots for that geezer. (*Beat.*) Look, she's making eyes at him now.

Jay   The night's still young.

Dean   Give it up, mate. That's one bird you'll never get.

Jay   I'll bet you five hundred quid she's mine.

Matt   Jay, you're being stupid.

Dean   Matt's right, that's way too much mon—

Jay   You scared?

Dean   No.

Jay   Then?

Dean   That's a lot of money, that's all.

Jay   Why you worried? Your mum's got you covered.

Matt   Jay.

Dean   When I win we move out of here.

Jay   When I win no more crying about where we're staying and what I say goes.

Dean   Deal.

Jay   Deal. I'm off to work my magic.

Matt   Why the hell did you push him?

Dean   I didn't.

Matt   You know he can't afford that.

Dean   Then he shouldn't pretend to be the big man.

Matt   I'm gonna let him calm down and then tell him the whole bet's off.

Jay *walks through the crowd. He sees* **Ginge** *and heads towards him,* **Hailey** *stops him.*

Hailey   I've been looking for you –

Jay   Not now, Hailey. Ginge can I have a word?

Ginge   Yeah.

Hailey *watches* **Jay** *walk off with* **Ginge**. **Amy** *comes up.*

Hailey   I can't believe he's blanked me all night and he had –

Amy   – the bad taste to flirt with that boring centre worker.

Hailey   Yeah, he's a –

Amy   – knob with no taste. Forget him. Those lads have been getting Sam and me drinks all night and one of them is way hotter than Jay.

Hailey   Seems like Sam likes him.

Amy   You don't owe her anything. We've only just met her here, plus he's kept asking about you in the first place. She can find her own man.

Hailey *looks over at* **Jay** *and then at* **Rob**, **Tony** *and* **Sam**.

Hailey   Yeah, let's go.

Jay (*as* **Ginge** *reaches into his pocket*)   Thanks, mate.

Ginge   Enjoy.

Ginge *walks off.* **Jay** *stands in a corner and puts a couple of pills in* **Kat**'*s drink.* **Matt** *is walking towards him and sees* **Jay** *drop the pills in from a distance.* **Matt** *walks up behind* **Jay**.

Jay   Your ugly mug made me jump.

Matt   Were you speaking to Ginge?

Jay   Just saying hello.

Matt   Thought you might be getting more smokes.

Jay   Nah, he was trying to persuade me, but I don't want to get too mashed up, I have a bet to win.

Matt   The bet's off. Dean and I decided we should just chill.

Jay   Was that your idea or Dean's?

Matt   This is getting too serious.

Jay   The bet's off when Dean admits he's lost. I'll catch you later.

Matt   Look, just give me that drink and let's have a lad's night.

Jay   Give me that drink back.

Matt   Why?

Jay   (a) It's for Kat.

Matt   Get her another. I'm thirsty.

Jay   (b) It's a girly drink and you'll look gay.

He tries to grab the drink off **Matt** *but fails.*

Jay   Stop being a twat.

Matt   What's your problem? We'll get her another.

Jay   I'll buy you another.

Beat.

Matt   Have you spiked it?

Jay   What? Don't be stupid.

Matt   Then let me drink it.

Jay   Matty boy, what's got into you? I don't need you freaking out on me. The girl and I are gonna have a drink. When I win the bet, you and I will go out paragliding while Dean watches. You and me, mate! Now let me work my magic. You know all I need is the Jay charm, to get my way with any girl.

Matt   I know.

Jay   Then Matty boy –

He strokes **Matt**'s *cheek.*

Jay   – be a good boy and move out my way.

Matt *enjoys his touch for a second and almost unwillingly brushes his hand away.*

Matt   I saw you dropping pills in that glass.

Jay   You're wrong.

Matt   Then let me drink it.

Matt *begins to take a sip. He takes another.* **Jay** *takes the drink out of his hand.*

Jay   Stop.

Matt   I was hoping I was wrong.

Jay   You are! The reason I didn't want you drinking any more –

Matt   Just admit it.

He pulls **Jay** *against the wall and aggressively checks his pockets, finds the pills, chucks them across the floor.*

Matt   What were you gonna do? Rape her to win five hundred quid?

Jay   No.

Matt   You're sick.

Jay   Matt.

Matt   Shut up.

Matt *begins to walk off.*

Jay   Wait. OK. Look, I wasn't gonna do anything, I was just going to take her back to the dorm, let Dean see her in my bed and let him think something had happened. That's it.

He goes to touch him, **Matt** *moves away.*

Matt   I don't believe you'd do that, all that, just for a stupid bet, for your stupid ego. When Dean finds out he's gonna think you're a joke too.

Dean *approaches.*

Jay   Don't say anything to him. (*Beat.*) Please. Please, Matt.

Beat as **Jay** *and* **Matt** *look at each other.* **Dean** *approaches.*

Dean   What's going on?

Jay   Nothing.

Dean   What's with the pills everywhere?

Beat.

Matt   We've decided to move into the hotel tonight.

Dean   What? Really? How?

Matt   The bet's off. Jay agrees it was a stupid idea.

Dean   Jay?

Matt   And that he's been behaving like a dick about it.
Haven't you, Jay?

Beat.

Now he's put his ego to one side, I think we should forget the
bet and move out.

Dean   Jay?

Jay   Matt's right. I've been a dick. I should have listened
when you guys said you wanted to move.

Dean   That's cool, man. Let's go live in some luxury.

Beat.

Pothead   Dudes, you dropped your pills.

Matt   They're not ours.

Pothead   Shame, I've been trying to score all night, thought
you might be able help.

Dean   The ginger lad and his mate may be able to help you.

Pothead   Thanks, guys. See you later.

Dean   Yeah, see you later. Let's go pack.

Matt, **Dean** and **Jay** *leave the bar. We follow* **Pothead** *as he
signals to* **Tiny** *and hands him the pills. They walk towards* **Ginge**
and **Tim**.

Pothead   Hey, fellas, how you doing?

Tim   Yeah, good, thanks.

Pothead   This little fella wants a word with you.

Tiny   You selling my drugs?

Ginge   No, we haven't.

Tiny   I give you good price because you his friend.

Tim   Look –

Tiny   Only I sell here.

Ginge   Hey, calm down.

Tiny   This is trouble for you and me.

Tim   We don't want no trouble.

Pothead   I can't believe you let me down, fellas.

Ginge   We didn't –

Pothead   The proof's in his hands. Tiny, show them.

Tiny *reveals the pills in his hand just as* **Kat** *comes along.*

Kat   Tiny, Dee's about to go on –

She sees the pills in his hands. She takes **Tiny***'s hand.*

Kat   What are these?

Tiny   Nothing, Miss Kat.

Kat   Tiny, I can't believe you're doing this. You know this is wrong, dangerous. Are you guys involved in this?

Pothead   This has nothing to do with me. The little guy was offering a service and I was just getting a few happy pills for me and my mate. It's between these three fellas right here.

Pothead *walks away.*

Tiny   Please leave, Miss Kat. This between three of us.

Kat   Come with me, Tiny.

Tiny   Miss. Kat.

Tiny *moves his hand away,* **Kat** *struggles to hold it, the pills fall from his hand.* **Tiny** *and* **Kat** *watch the pills fall, and see* **Al** *has spotted them. They begin to pick up the pills but are not fast enough.*

Al   What are these?

Kat   Nothing.

Al   Whose are they? Are they yours?

Tiny   No.

Kat   They're mine.

Al   Where did you get them?

Kat   I bought them . . . I bought them outside the centre.

Al   You're a bad liar, Kat. Lads?

Beat.

Ginge   We have nothing to do with this.

Tim   He sold us the drugs.

Al   Is this true? (*Beat.*) Tiny!

Silence.

Come with me.

Kat   Please, Al, he's just a kid.

Al   He's old enough, he knows the risk. I'll lose my job if I don't. I'll need you lads as witnesses.

Kat   What's gonna happen to him?

Al   What always happens.

Kat *looks manically around as* **Al** *and the three guys exit the bar. She begins to look through the crowd till she stumbles upon* **Mike***.*

Mike   Are you OK?

Kat   Have you seen Dee?

Mike   She's just by the bar.

Kat *rushes past* **Mike***.*

Kat   Dee.

Dee   Kat, sit over there and you will see the dance.

Kat   I need to speak to you.

Dee   Not now, I have to dance for –

She rubs her fingers together in the sign for money.

Kat   It's urgent!

Dee   It can wait.

Kat   It's Tiny. Al's caught him selling drugs.

Dee   How? This can't be, he's always careful.

Kat   You knew, Dee, you knew he was selling and you let him?

Dee   We needed the money. I thought he'd be safe to sell here late at night. How did Al find out?

Kat   I tried to get Tiny to come and in the struggle, I don't know, the pills dropped and Al saw –

Dee   Why did you do that?

Kat   I was trying to help. I wanted to make Tiny see –

Dee   Help? This is your idea of help.

Kat   You need to talk to Al, he might listen to you.

Dee   You understand nothing. I cannot talk to him, if he thinks I know, I lose my job. I cannot help Tiny.

Kat   He'll be arrested and that means –

Dee   I know.

Mike *interrupts the conversation.*

Mike   Dee, you're needed onstage.

The music for **Dee***'s dance begins to play.*

Mike   That's your cue.

Kat   I'll sort it out, Dee, I promise.

Dee *walks zombie-like to her position in the centre of the dance floor which has now been cleared for her.*

Mike   What's happened?

Kat   Tiny's going to be arrested and it's all my fault.

Mike   What? Why?

Kat   He was selling drugs and . . . I have to persuade Al not to call the police.

Mike   Al's as straight as they come.

Kat   I have to persuade him that Tiny had no choice, and if he calls them his future will be –

Mike   Maybe you should stay out of it. It's not your fault – you didn't make him start selling.

Kat   You don't understand. I have to help him.

Mike   This isn't your world, Kat, you can't fix everything.

Kat   I have to try.

Kat *leaves the bar,* **Mike** *hesitates, not knowing whether to stay with* **Poppy** *or follow* **Kat***. He decides to follow* **Kat** *and runs after her.*

Dee *steps out into the centre of the dance floor and begins to dance,* **Hailey, Amy, Sam, Rob, Tony, Poppy** *and* **Pothead** *watch.*

Gap

*Notes on rehearsal and staging, drawn from workshops
with the writer held at the National Theatre, November 2010*

Alia Bano explains where her idea for the play came from:

'I went to Rio about three years ago and stayed in a hostel for two weeks. Everyone else staying at the hostel was younger than me. After a week I started to watch the people closely, and saw the "cliques" they brought with them from their different homes. I watched alliances being formed. There were the "rich kids", the "socially conscious kids", the "kids just on holiday". But they were all bored and ended up just wanting to have a party. I'd hear these kids complaining "I'm so poor" while there were native kids all around them working. I thought about the way we take holidays, escaping our world but not taking notice of the world around us. Which is what we do every day. A gap year used to be a useful thing, but seeing these kids it seems it's become a status thing.

'Returning to the UK I workshopped the play with some teenage actors at the National Theatre Studio and they gave me the title, saying they felt it suggested the gap between two worlds while still referencing the term "gap year".

'I would like the audience to gain a sense that there is a darker element to us having fun, and when we are travelling we may need to be more socially conscious. We can return home, but the people we leave behind can't escape, that's their world. That's why I ended the play with the girl dancing – she has to dance because she needs the money. That final image is really important.'

Where is the Play Set?

The idea came from Alia's experiences in Brazil, but it could be India, or any country where the sentence for selling drugs is severe. For the people that live there, the consequences are lethal.

Things that Really Matter when Staging the Play

There are two important things.

- Making sure the eighteen characters aren't painted with the same brush so there isn't just one generic tone.

- How expressive we can be in telling this story. Capturing the mood at the same time as listening to the characters. Where does the focus need to be and when?

Creating Each Character's Back-story

Making the characters individuals is vital. We need to get under the skin of these characters and find out exactly what turmoil is going on. Help the actors to find their character's 'wants' and 'objectives'. A starting point in finding the different layers of a character is to get your actors to prepare four lists.

List 1: the facts about their character
These facts are things that we know are concrete in the play, where there is no doubt. An example if you were playing Tiny could be that 'I have a sister called Dee'.

List 2: things their character says about themselves
Encourage the actors to be specific and quote whole dialogue rather than writing 'I generally say . . . '

List 3: things other people say about my character

List 4: things my character says about other people

This gets the actors to use the script and stops generalisation. It's useful to get them to read their lists out – it starts a conversation. It's useful to hear what other characters say about your character. It gets the answers coming from the actors. The director's job is to facilitate the discovery of character.

With a large cast don't read all of the lists out all at once, as you will exhaust their use; spread them out over a few rehearsals.

Developing Character in Rehearsal

At the beginning of rehearsals, ask the actors to think about three things:

I: YOUR MIND PRINT

It's the thing about your character that you are afraid is actually true – e.g., a brilliant scientist might actually think he is stupid, so his inner dialogue might be 'I am stupid'. This inner dialogue is what drives him to learn to be clever.

A boxer's inner dialogue might be 'I'm a coward', which propels him to fight.

You might explore this at the start of rehearsals and never refer to it again, but it's a trigger that might unlock something for an actor. It's a way to encourage an actor to work out his character's vulnerability.

As you rehearse and discover new things about the play, the actor may find he/she changes the mind print.

The mind print can be used as a rehearsal exercise; get the actors to play a scene with someone whispering their mind print in their ear. You can also impose a mind print on a character to see if it reveals any insights.

2: YOUR SHAME VENT

The thing you did once that you're most ashamed about but never told anyone.

This helps unlock character and provokes the actor into giving themselves a back-story.

The more detail the better. Even if an actor only has one line in the play they still need to represent a three-dimensional character.

3: YOUR DAY OF RECKONING

Your last breath on earth – who would you spend it with, your mother or your father? You can't choose both!

This is all about encouraging the actors to think about their back-story. There is no right or wrong; the actors just need to know what they have chosen and why.

Status

Explore the status of all eighteen characters. What is their real status and what is the status they try to project to people around them?

Characters

GINGE AND TIM

Ginge is more intelligent than Tim. They are two small-time boys who have come to explore the world. Life back home is boring. Ginge and Tim are using their own money. Ginge bails Tim out and Tim goes along with whatever Ginge says. They want to be part of the scene, but are not worried about what people think. They are just glad to be away from home. Are they aware that they behave like a double act? They haven't thought of the consequences of what they do. Back home a bit of weed isn't such a big thing. The actors should play them totally sincerely, otherwise they won't be funny.

POTHEAD

He wants to be there. He didn't plan to do this. He came for a gap year thinking he would return home. Has he found himself? Or is he as oblivious as he was when he arrived? He fell into the situation, needed some money, and found he was good at it. There is now no question of going home, he's having a good time, and he knows that if anything goes wrong it's not his neck on the line, it's Tiny who will get the trouble. He's not far-sighted – he takes each day as it comes. He is happy where he is and doesn't feel the need to raise his status. He is a middle man; if he messed up he would probably just move to another country. Home is a last resort.

TINY

Tiny is Pothead's drug mule. He is thirteen or fourteen years old. He is the younger brother to Dee. He has other siblings and lives in a shanty town. In his dad's mind Tiny is now a man and it's time for him to give up education and start earning money. He is a big fish – the popular kid – and among the locals he has more money than the other kids, so he gets economic status.

MATT AND DEAN
They are probably sharp dressers. Could be Essex boys or
Hooray Henrys – designer-label kids or public schoolboys with
money. Both ways of portraying these two characters would
work, and it's best to make a clear choice about them.

HAILEY
She is fairly insecure. In order to be popular she feels she
needs to sell herself. She is seventeen or eighteen years old.
She wants someone to care for her. She could come from
anywhere.

AMY
She is part of this world. She is best friends with Hailey. Amy
knows what she wants and where she is going. Hailey is more
naive than Amy.

JAY
What are his insecurities? What drives him to sleep with lots of
women? What does it mean for Jay to win the bet? The one
girl who says 'no' fuels an anger in him. Is he used to getting
what he wants? He is charismatic not just in looks. Matt and
Dean are more affluent, but Jay has high status with them
because he gets the girls. Pulling girls is what he is good at.
Dean is potential competition: he gets the girls but not so
often. He has money to back him up, and Jay doesn't. His
friendship with Matt is important to him. He is aware Matt
responds to him differently from Dean but he is not necessarily
aware Matt is gay.

AL
Al is older, in his late twenties. He is a local. Wherever you
decide to set the production, the native characters need to
represent this with their accents. In scenes like the Beach Bar
it helps us to understand that these characters are from
different worlds.

DEE
Dee is twenty or twenty-one years old. Tiny is her baby
brother. She wants a good life. She has a job. She aspires to
more, but is realistic and knows she won't get more. The

dancing she does in the bar isn't seedy, it's the cultural dance. She still lives at home and that is where her wages go. In the final scene it would be good if she was in the traditional costume of wherever you choose to set the play.

POPPY
She is an attractive, eighteen-year-old blonde – what used to be called a 'Sloane Ranger' type. Her family have money. She wants Mike, but she is a realistic female – she knows she likes him but if he says no, she won't be heartbroken. She knows her own mind: what she says about the tour is as truthful as Kat's comments. It's for the audience to decide who is right.

MIKE
He had an aspiration to go out and save the world, but having been here for six months he's discovered it's not as easy as he had hoped it would be. He's found that he can't make a big change so he's not so passionate about it any more. The reality is, 'It's not quite what I signed up for.'

SAM
She is the new girl. Travelling by herself, she is at the beginning of her journey round the world.

TONY AND ROB
They don't have to be from the West Country – they could be Australian. They represent a mirror image of Ginge and Tim, but they are genuinely nice. They want to date rather than sleep with girls. It's the cycle beginning again.

BRONTE
She works with Mike and Kat, and has done for maybe three months, but she is new to the girls at the hostel. She is happy with who she is, and balances work and social life better than Kat or Mike. She is Kat's support.

It's useful to notice how quickly connections forge between the characters. None of them have known each other that long, yet they behave like old friends. Don't undersell this – it's typical behaviour for young people in this kind of situation.

Time Frame

Before the play proper begins, the audience should walk into a sense of massive exhilaration, a good time – this is a party that everyone wants to be at. A good time is being had. The play is written in a twenty-four-hour cycle:

- A party
- Morning after
- Lunchtime
- Getting ready for a party
- A party

Design

Work backwards when creating your design, and express some of what you want to say in the scene changes. If you have more actors than characters there is fun to be had here. Find interesting ways to move from scene to scene.

Staging

Staging the dorms scene
The difficult thing with this scene is to keep clarity. Don't underestimate how important the whole picture is. Alia visualises this with a split stage – on one side boys, on the other side girls, with the corridor centre stage.

Staging the final scene
The stakes need to be high. Explore ways of giving and taking focus in the scene. It can be as simple as sitting back or sitting forward but still playing the truth, only smaller.

When the action they are watching is not physically dynamic, it can be tough for an audience not to 'switch-out'. So it's important to work moment to moment with what these characters want. The interest of the scene is as much with the characters who aren't speaking as it is with those who are.

From a workshop led by Raz Shaw,
with notes by Psyche Stott

Helen Blakeman

Cloud Busting

Based on the novel by Malorie Blackman

Characters

Sam
Mr Mackie
Alicia
Morgan
Claudia
Casey
Jay
Alex
Rebecca
Oliver
Davey
Head Teacher
Sam's Mum
Davey's Mum
Man

Scene One

A hill.

Sam, *a boy, about thirteen years old, lies on his back, staring up at the sky. Deep in thought. He's watching the clouds. He points at them, follows them with his finger. He smiles to himself.*

Bright sunshine.

He sits up and addresses the audience.

Sam It was just a day. Just another ordinary day . . . Not that I thought it would be any other sort of day – why should I? I didn't. I did not think when I woke up that morning that this would be the sort of day when I started to discover . . . When I started to realise . . . I just didn't, you know what I mean?

A pause.

Life-changing days. That is what is so weird about them. They start off the same as all the others. Normal. Head-on-the-pillow normal. Can't-be-bothered-getting-up normal cos the highlight of the next hour is the normal bowl of cornflakes and the normal banana-followed-by-a-bus-to-school normal! Yeah? . . . Well, as it turned out, this particular day wasn't gonna be like that. When I got to school it was just a day. The same as any other . . .

Scene Two

A classroom. The class fills up with pupils. **Sam** *wanders through to find a seat.*

He addresses the audience.

Sam Assembly. Geography first period cos it was Tuesday. Then English with Mr Mackie. Mr Mackie. Licence to backchat.

Mr Mackie Sam?

Sam   Yes, sir?

Mr Mackie   Find a seat and I suggest you sit in it. All of you.

Sam *idles to a seat.* **Morgan** *pushes by, bangs into* **Alicia**.

Alicia   Ow! Morgan.

Morgan   Sorry.

Mr Mackie   Morgan, what did I say?

Alicia   Sir. Morgan's just hit me.

Morgan   I said sorry, sir.

Alicia   Like proper hit me, hit me.

Morgan   You liar, like I would ever hit a woman?

Mr Mackie   Alright, this is really quite enough.

Casey   Oh my God, he just called you a 'woman'!

Alicia   You did what?

Mr Mackie   If we could sort this out later –

Alicia   Under twenty, idiot. I am a girl.

Mr Mackie   Please 8M, let's get along with the lesson in hand. Morgan, there's a place by Rebecca.

Morgan   No, ta.

Mr Mackie   Alicia. Sit.

Alicia   Like, by him?

Mr Mackie   Sit. 8M, listening please.

Alicia *sits.*

Alicia   Women are like, old. You are such a pure monster.

Morgan (*smooches up*)   Can be a monster if you want me to be . . .

Alicia (*recoils*)   Urrgh! Get off of me!

Mr Mackie   Oh please . . .

Alicia's *out of her seat,* **Casey** *pushes* **Alex** *from his chair.* **Alicia** *takes his place.* **Alex** *sits next to* **Morgan**. **Mr Mackie** *hangs his head.*

Sam *addresses the audience.*

Sam   Like I said, any other normal day in our class. The only thing I noticed was outside. Blue sky. No clouds. No clouds at all. Weird. And before I knew it, it was getting weirder . . .

Lighting change. **Mr Mackie** *stands before the class. He commands.*

Mr Mackie   Write a poem. 8M, I want you all to write a poem.

Sam *addresses the audience.*

Sam   Told you.

A pause.

Claudia   Write a what?

Alicia   Like . . . You mean . . .

Sam   A poem, sir?

Alicia   A poem, poem?

Morgan   About what?

Alex   Like, a real poem?

Mr Mackie   You know, one that . . .

Rebecca   Rhymes. Poems rhyme, don't they? I like rhymes.

Oliver   Me too.

Casey   You two shut up.

Mr Mackie   A poem has rhythm. It has meaning.

Alex   Leaves are falling on the ground, autumn leaves are all around . . .

Laughs.

Mr Mackie   A poem about someone. That's what I want you to write. Not just anyone.

Sam   Like who?

Mr Mackie   Someone close to you. Someone special. Someone who means something. To you.

Alex *and* **Morgan** *separate their chairs immediately.*

Alex   Not you, man. Forget it.

Morgan   No way!

Alicia   Got it – 'Sparkle the Dog'. My dog, sir!

Mr Mackie   A person, Alicia.

Claudia   My cat's a Persian. Does that count?

Laughter.

Mr Mackie   Like a friend or a family member. A brother, a sister, or mum or dad. Someone you love. Someone you care about.

Claudia   Sir, if my house burnt down I would only care about the cat. Seriously.

Mr Mackie   A poem. That is your homework.

A pause. The **Clever Kids** *make a note. The other* **Kids** *just stare.* **Sam** *puts down his pen.*

Sam   Sir. I don't want to, sir.

Mr Mackie   I'm sorry?

Sam   Write a poem. No thanks.

The **Kids** *begin to stand and protest.*

Morgan   Me neither, sir.

Mr Mackie   Now please –

Morgan   Poems are boring, sir.

Claudia   And no one reads them.

Mr Mackie   Please class –

Casey   'Cept poets.

Jay   And people who bore you.

Alex   Old people.

Morgan   And teachers who bore you.

Casey   And it's boring.

Mr Mackie   I said –

Alicia   Capital-B boring.

Claudia   First-class boring.

Mr Mackie   I said –

Casey   Second-class boring.

Mr Mackie   I said –

Alicia   Like coach-class boring –

Mr Mackie   Enough! I said – ENOUGH!

Morgan (*mocking*)   Mr Mackie . . . You sure can shout!

Mr Mackie   Yes . . . Yes, I can. And this time . . . I will. And you and all of you, you will listen and you will sit and you will pay attention to EXACTLY WHAT I HAVE TO SAY!

Quietly, the **Kids** *sit down.*

Sam *addresses the audience.*

Sam   And they actually took notice of him. Today, either Mr Mackie had got out the wrong side of bed or he'd eaten three shredded wheat for extra strength or something. On the other hand it might have just been the threat of a school inspection constantly hanging over us which had got to him. But what was already weird, started to get weirder . . .

Mr Mackie   Hands up. Who likes . . . rap music?

The **Kids** *share quizzical looks. Hands go up – including* **Sam**, **Alex**, **Alicia**.

Mr Mackie   Hands up who likes pop music?

Hands goes up – including **Alicia**, **Claudia**, **Casey**, **Rebecca**.

Mr Mackie   Hands up who likes . . . classical music.

Slowly, **Oliver**'s *hand rises.*

Morgan   He would.

Mr Mackie   Good. Because rap music and pop music and punk. And rock music. What do they all have in common?

Morgan   Music, sir.

Mr Mackie   And words.

Alex (*bored*)   And the words are set to music . . .

Mr Mackie   And the words are set to music.

Alex   I said that.

Mr Mackie   Well done, Alex. Well done.

Alex   Well done to me?

Mr Mackie   Yes, you. Songs are words and words are poetry. Set to music. That's all.

The **Kids** *share looks.*

A pause. **Oliver**'s *hand goes up.*

Oliver   What about classical music then, sir?

Mr Mackie   Well . . .

Rebecca   Sir, Oliver wants to know.

Morgan   He would.

Mr Mackie   Classical music – that creates poetry in your mind.

A whoop goes up from the **Kids**.

Jay   Whoo, Oliver!

Casey   Clever boy, Oliver!

Mr Mackie   And sometimes in your heart too.

Oliver   Yes, sir. And in your soul, sir.

Claudia   Not in my soul it don't.

Mr Mackie   But it might. If you just . . . listen . . . Even if no words are spoken –

A brief moment of silence. Classical music starts to play.

There is always poetry. Inside. Trouble is, some people let it out. And some don't. This is your chance.

A substantial pause. The **Kids** *listen, puzzled at first, then quite spellbound.*

Sam *addresses the audience.*

Sam   See what I mean? Something was different. This lot, they haven't been this quiet their whole lifetime. Seriously weird.

The bell rings.

Mr Mackie   Any questions?

The **Kids** *scrape their chairs. End of class.*

Casey   Does it have to rhyme, sir?

Morgan   Can it be a rap?

Alicia   How do we start, sir?

Mr Mackie   You take your love and your pain and you don't hold back.

Sam *addresses the audience.*

Sam   Homework, and they wanted to do it. But what happened next surprised even me.

Jay I could write about my kid sister, sir –

Alex My annoying cousin, but he's like twenty-three.

Morgan My dad. Even though I don't see him, could I write about him, sir?

Mr Mackie What about you, Sam? There must be someone who means something, who's affected you, who is in your head and longs get out. Someone?

A pause.

Sam *is the only child still seated at his desk. He looks up.*

Sam Sir? Can I write about Davey?

Silence.

Mr Mackie Yes, Sam.

He smiles.

You write about Davey.

The class exits.

Sam *stands alone.*

Scene Three

The playground.

Alex, **Morgan** *and* **Jay** *crowd around* **Sam**.

Morgan Dave?

Jay Davey?

Alex David Youngson? What d'you want to write about him for?

Sam We've got to write about someone.

Morgan Mr Mackie said anyone.

Alex Anyone! He didn't mean him.

Jay   So why write about it, man? Why drag up the past?

Sam   Cos Davey was here and now he isn't. Doesn't mean I can't talk about it.

Alex   So talk about it.

They crowd him, they goad him.

Morgan   Tell us, big man.

Jay   Spill it, Sam.

Morgan   Go on, Sam.

Alex   Sam, the big man.

Jay   Sad Sam. He ain't no man.

Sam *walks away. He addresses the audience.*

Sam   The more they went on, the more I could have said . . . But that would have been easy . . . I want to write about Davey cos he's always in my head, I want to write about him because my mum goes on. She says Davey was a good lad and that you don't miss the water till the well runs dry or something like that . . .

Alex   Look at him . . .

Jay   He ain't got a clue.

Alex   Loser.

Morgan   What's up, Sam? Davey got your tongue?

Sam *addresses the audience.*

Sam   And he did, kind of. Thinking about Davey made me silent. Sad and angry, all at once. I wanted to write about Davey because when he was here, I preferred not to give Davey a second thought.

Davey *enters.*

Sam   To me, Davey was just a nuisance who lived down my street. A nuisance who I wished would get out of my neighbourhood and my entire life. Now he's gone, well, he hasn't gone anywhere . . .

Morgan   He looks sad.

Alex   He is sad.

Sam (*to the audience*)   He's in my head and I can't get him out. I miss him. Davey. Dave. David Youngson . . .

He addresses the audience.

Everyone called him Fizzy Feet.

Lighting change.

Davey *dances. A beat dance, his feet flying.*

Scene Four

Assembly Hall.

Davey *sits in a chair.*

Lighting change. The **Class** *are present.*

Sam, **Alex**, **Morgan** *and* **Jay** *sit behind* **Davey**. **Alex** *is playing a Nintendo DS game or whatever.*

Sam *addresses the audience.*

Sam   The first morning Fizzy Feet ever happened. To be honest, it was just another one of them normal, ordinary days . . .

The **Head Teacher** *stands at a lectern.*

Head Teacher   School league tables will be published this Friday and I expect all of your parents will, like myself, be concerned about our position. As a failing school, we fail because you fail. And it is our job to hoist you from failure, to pull you up and set you on the right course for life. However, we can only do this with your help.

Morgan *yawns.*

The **Boys** *taunt* **Davey**, *pull at his collar, his hair.* **Alicia**, **Claudia**, **Casey** *sit to one side.*

Alex   Davey . . . .

Morgan   Dave.

Sam   Oy. David Youngson . . .

Jay   What's up with your hair, Davey? Need a wash?

Sam   He only wears it long to hide all his scruff.

Alex   What's up, Davey? Your neck a bit dirty?

Morgan   Holes in his jumper today. It was holes in his trousers yesterday.

Sam   My mum would never send me to school like that.

Jay   That's cos your mum cares.

The **Boys** *laugh. The* **Girls** *observe.*

Alicia   I think he's cute.

Casey   Shut up, Alicia.

Alicia   Yeah, in one of them lost-dogs sorts of ways. All droopy eyes and matted fur. If you give them a good bath, they'd be alright really.

Casey   Sure they would. Till they flip and bite your fingers off.

Claudia   Face it. He's odd. He deserves what he gets.

Alicia   Yeah. I suppose.

Claudia   He's weird.

Casey   Treat him weird.

Alicia   Yeah. I suppose you're right.

Claudia   And he'd bring your cred straight down to zero.

Casey   Minus zero.

Alicia   I'd still like him if he was a dog, though.

They laugh.

Head Teacher   Litter duty. Recycling bins. One class per week. Paper, plastic, tin cans . . . All recycling receptacles will be clearly labelled and colour-coded. Waste will be deposited only in specified bins.

*The **Head Teacher**'s speech goes under the following:*

Sam   Can we put you in that bin, Davey?

Davey *starts to wriggle.*

Alex   Cos nobody wants you.

Morgan   Rubbish, Davey.

Jay   Do you like food slops and smelly, manky trash?

Morgan   You'll be well at home.

Davey *wriggles more.*

Sam   Just make sure no one recycles him. What'd be the point? Who'd want another Davey Youngson?

Alex   Not me.

Jay   Not me.

Morgan   Not even his mum.

Davey *continues to wriggle, his body, his legs, especially his feet. Slowly, they're starting to dance.*

Sam   What's up, Davey? We making you squirm?

Alex   He can't get away from himself.

Jay   Man! Neither can we!

*The **Boys** laugh.*

Head Teacher   Is that clear? Did you hear me, boys? Is that clear?

*The **Boys** answer, full of boredom. Except **Davey** . . .*

Boys   Yes, sir [or miss].

Head Teacher   And you, Davey? David Youngson!

Davey   Fizzy feet, sir [or miss]! I've got fizzy feet!

Head Teacher   You have what?

Suddenly **Davey***'s on his feet. Jigging and wriggling, he breaks into dance.*

Davey   My feet, sir [or miss]. I can't help it. They're just sort of . . . fizzy.

Head Teacher   They're what? Whatever is the matter with you?

Sam   Davey's lost it. He's gone mad.

Alex   Davey, you on drugs?

Davey   It's my feet, sir [or miss] . . .

Davey *pulls off his shoes, rubs his feet. The* **Girls** *hold their noses, the* **Boys** *shy away.*

Sam   They stink, that's what's up with them.

Claudia   Oh my God!

Casey   Oh my God!

Alicia   No, but like seriously, sir [or miss] . . . Oh. My. God.

Claudia   Weird.

Head Teacher   David Youngson, stop this at once.

Davey   I can't, sir [or miss]. My feet, sir. They're fizzy.

Head Teacher   You mean, you have tingling? Pins and needles tingling?

Davey   Yes, sir [or miss]. That's what I said. They just won't stop – fizzing!

Head Teacher   Well, David Youngson, use the correct
terminology and take them to fizz elsewhere – not in the
middle of a school assembly when I have serious announcements
to make . . . About the school's future, about your future . . .

Davey   They're just fizzy, sir [or miss].

Alicia   Can we look after him, sir [or miss]? We can sit out
of lessons.

Davey, *the* **Head Teacher** *and the* **Girls** *exit. The* **Boys** *fall
about laughing.*

Alex   Oh man! Fizzy feet! I've never seen anything so
funny . . .

Morgan   He will so never live that down.

Jay   Yeah. He sure won't.

Sam *addresses the audience.*

Sam   They were right, of course. From now on, Davey was
rich pickings. Prime bully material. And one person took full
advantage. The one person who I hated most. Not Davey.
The class idiot. The class bully, the sort of person who sees a
weak spot and just never lets it go. I don't miss him. I don't
miss him one bit . . .

Sam *keeps on talking into . . .*

Scene Five

A corridor.

Sam *looks on, watching the action.*

There's a scuffle. The crew – **Alex**, **Jay** *and* **Morgan** *– mess about.
From the scuffle the* **Hoodie Boy** *emerges. He wears a hoodie, pulled
up to obscure or shadow his face. He wears his blazer over the top.*

Davey *walks along. The* **Hoodie Boy** *heads towards him, flanked by* **Alex**, **Jay** *and* **Morgan**. *He deliberately bumps into* **Davey**. *The* **Hoodie Boy**'s *bag deliberately falls to the floor.*

A pause.

Hoodie Boy   Maybe next time you should look where you're going.

Davey   Sorry.

Hoodie Boy   Pick it up.

Davey   I said I was sorry.

Hoodie Boy   And I said – fetch. Fetch it. Go on.

A pause. **Davey** *thinks better of it. He reaches down, picks up the bag.* **Hoodie Boy** *grabs it.*

Hoodie Boy   Thanks, Fizz.

Davey   No worries.

Hoodie Boy   You? You should have plenty of worries.

Hoodie Boy *grabs* **Davey**'s *hair, wrenches back his head.*

Jay   Go easy on him.

Davey   Ow.

Alex   Shut up. He's only mucking about.

Hoodie Boy   Yeah . . . Course I am. And d'you want to know why?

He lets **Davey** *go.*

Hoodie Boy   Cos it's a waste of my time even touching you. Never mind looking at you. Go on, Fizz. On your way.

Davey *doesn't move.*

He stands there. He addresses the audience.

Davey   I didn't though.

Hoodie Boy   I said move . . . Go on.

Davey (*to the audience*)   I didn't move nowhere. I never ran, I never shouted back. I just stood there, cool, like. And I looked at him.

Morgan (*to the audience*)   Telling ya, it was the last thing the bully expected.

Hoodie Boy (*to the audience*)   Davey. He just stood there. He watched and he waited . . .

Davey (*to the audience*)   I thought standing my ground was the right thing to do. But maybe I was wrong. I just never realised –

Hoodie Boy (*to the audience*)   He just never realised the effect that had. Like he thought he could take me on . . .

Morgan (*to the audience*)   Which he couldn't.

Oliver and **Rebecca** *enter, passing by on their way to class. They pause to watch.*

Alex (*to the audience*)   But that was before he did it . . .

Jay (*to the audience*)   The most stupidest thing he could do, man . . .

Rebecca (*to the audience*)   On our way to class, we saw it. We saw what he did.

Oliver (*to the audience*)   Davey smiled.

Davey *smiles to* **Hoodie Boy**.

Rebecca (*to the audience*)   A faint, sad smile. Right across his lips.

Hoodie Boy   What? What are you smiling at?

Davey *smirks.*

Davey   You. I guess.

Sam (*to the audience*)   And that was it. He smiled.

Hoodie Boy (*to the audience*)   A smile. A smile that means it's me who's the waste of space, not him, me who's the loser.

The sort of smile that has to be wiped off his face. Thrown away and washed away!

Morgan   Knocked away –

Hoodie Boy   Smacked right away and destroyed !

He launches into **Davey**. *He grabs him up and hits and hits him.*

Hoodie Boy   And smacked! And smashed!

Morgan   And grabbed . . .

Davey *cowers to the floor.*

Hoodie Boy *kicks at* **Davey**.

Alex   And kicked . . .

Sam   And kicked . . .

Jay   And kicked . . .

Morgan *goes to intervene. The* **Kids** *crowd round,* **Sam** *included.*

In the fracas, a swap takes place. **Sam** *puts up his hood – turning himself into the* **Hoodie Boy**.

Morgan   Stop it, yeah.

Alex   Get off him now.

Jay   Hurry up, Mackie's coming!

Morgan   Get off him!

The **Kids** *run off, exit. Leaving only* **Davey**, **Oliver**, **Rebecca** *and what we think is the* **Hoodie Boy** *onstage.*

Oliver   And that's how it was. Till the bully just couldn't kick any more.

Rebecca   Till Davey's smile was gone.

Slowly, **Davey** *stands up. With dignity, he straightens himself.*

Before **Davey**, **Sam** *takes down his hood – turns back into* **Sam**.

Sam   That's right. It was me. The boy who I hated most, the boy I'm glad is gone and who I don't miss one bit . . . It was me. I was the bully.

Scene Six

Lighting change. A hill.

Sam *stares out.*

Sam   Then one day . . . One of them 'get-up-in-the-morning-and-everything's-alright, I-can-go-into-school-and-bully-Davey-again' sort of days . . . Well, things changed, right before my very eyes . . . And none of it was down to me.

Scene Seven

Sam *in his house.*

He grabs his bag, sets off for school.

Sam   See you, Mum.

Sam's Mum   Bye, Sam. Go and knock for Davey now.

Sam   Davey?

Sam's Mum   Davey Youngson.

Sam   Why? What has he said?

Sam's Mum   He hasn't said nothing. I was just talking to his mum, that's all. He's a lovely kid and by all accounts, he needs some friends.

Sam   But Mum –

Sam's Mum   I told his mum you'd knock.

Sam   Davey's . . . a dork.

Sam's Mum You should be looking out for him then. Even more reason to knock. Go on. I'll watch you.

Sam *sighs. He looks to the audience.*

Sam So I knocked. I had to. Davey . . . Fizzy Feet . . . Lived two doors down.

Davey *exits his house with his school bag. Seeing* **Sam** *he pauses – his worst nightmare.*

His **Mum** *gives him a kiss. Then waves to* **Sam's Mum***.*

Davey's Mum Have a nice day, Davey.

Davey Bye, Mum.

Davey's Mum Thanks, Sam.

Davey *heads off ahead at once.* **Sam** *follows eagerly.*

Sam Alright, Davey. Slow down. Wait for us . . .

Davey's Mum Coffee later?

Sam's Mum You bet. See ya. See ya, boys.

Davey's Mum *and* **Sam's Mum** *exit.*

Sam For the school bully, knocking for Davey – it was like . . .

Davey Sam knocking for me . . . What can I say?

Sam It was the perfect opportunity.

Davey As soon as we got round the corner and out of sight . . .

Sam *grabs him.*

Sam Dance for us, Fizz. Go on.

Davey Get off me.

Sam Don't tell me what to do.

Davey Why not? I can say what I like.

Sam   Or I'll tell your mum you've been pushing me around.

Davey   Tell her what you like . . . She saw my black eye and my bruises.

Sam   Never said it was me though, did you? You're a coward, Davey. A big liar who said you'd fallen over when the bus came to a sudden stop. (*Laughs.*) And she believed you. (*He grabs him closer.*) I can make you do anything I like. Yeah?

Davey   And this time, I'll tell.

Sam   Tell who?

Davey *begins to get breathless . . .*

Davey   Anyone. My mum . . . Mr Mackie . . . Your mum . . .

Sam   You wouldn't do that.

Davey   If that's what it takes . . . You can't keep doing this, OK?

Sam   Says who?

Davey   What have I done, hey?

Sam   You got fizzy feet . . .

Davey   What have I done . . . ?

Sam   You're weird. You don't have to do anything.

Davey   So when will you . . . understand?

Sam   Understand what, Fizz?

Davey*'s growing ever more breathless.*

Davey   You wouldn't do this . . . to your big mates . . . would you?

Sam   Do what, Davey?

Davey   No . . .

Sam   Are you scared of me, Davey?

Davey   Please stop . . .

Sam   So scared you can't even breathe?

Davey   No . . .

Sam   Sounds like it. Can't you breathe, Davey? What's up, can't you breathe?

Davey *pushes at him.*

Davey   I said stop! Stop it now! Stop!

Sam *pauses.*

Sam   Do not touch me. Davey, do not even touch me.

Davey *gasps for air. He gets his breath back, takes in big gulps of air.*

Davey   One good reason. Come on . . .

Sam   Cos you are an idiot.

Davey   Sometimes, yeah. I'll give you that.

Sam   You're just an idiot.

Davey   You've said that already . . .

Sam*'s in his face.*

Sam   A scruffy, dorky idiot with fizzy feet.

Davey   I know . . .

Sam   And I hate you, alright! Why can't you just be normal Davey . . . ? Cos then maybe you wouldn't annoy me so much like you annoy me right now!

He shoves **Davey***. But this time* **Davey** *retaliates. He pushes at* **Sam***.*

Davey   And you think you don't annoy me?

Sam   You what?

Davey   Think you're perfect, is that it? Think you're unbeatable?

Sam   Will you stop?

Davey   Do you, Sam?

Sam   Get off me now . . .

Davey   Cos . . . you're not! You're just nothing!

He gives **Sam** *a forceful shove.*

Sam *stumbles more than he expected.*

Davey   Sam! Watch out!

Sam   Help me . . .

Davey   Sam!

A screech of brakes squealing to a stop. The beep of a horn.

Davey *grabs* **Sam**'s *arm, before he can fall, drags him out of the way.*

They stumble back, both falling to the ground. **Sam** *sits there, in a daze.*

Sam   The car stopped where I would have been lying.

Davey   If I hadn't dragged him out of the way in time . . .

Sam   I would have been dead if it wasn't for . . . If it wasn't for . . .

Davey   I think he was just shocked. Cos he just sat there . . .

Sam   While all these people . . . Everyone asking if I was OK . . .

Davey   If he was hurt . . . That's all they wanted to know.

Sam   And middle of it all, the car sped off. Some bloke reckoned he got the number plate but it's not like I was hurt or anything.

Man   Is the lad OK? You alright, son?

Sam   Davey just looked. Nodding and smiling. His usual smile.

Davey (*to the crowd*)   Yeah. He's fine.

Man   You sure about that?

Davey   My friend . . . Yeah he's fine.

Sam *sits up straight.*

Sam (*to the audience*)   'My friend'? He said 'my friend'? You what? Two minutes earlier I'd been wanting to hammer him and he was having some sort of panic attack and now I was his 'friend'! Things were definitely changing. I felt weird . . .

Davey *helps* **Sam** *to his feet.* **Davey** *dusts* **Sam** *down, picks up his bag, straightens his clothes.*

Davey   You alright, Sam?

Sam   Yeah.

Davey *smiles.*

Davey   Well, who'd have thought it, eh?

Sam   Thought what?

Davey   You. You owe your life to me now. Not the other way round.

Sam   You what?

Davey   I'll have to make sure I take care of you.

Sam   No . . . You don't have to do that.

Davey   Yeah I do. When weird stuff like fate happens . . . Like just now. Well, only me and you know how it felt. It was an accident, yeah, and it was stupid. But from now on, we're interlocked.

Sam   Interlocked with you? Get real.

Davey   I am. No one else in the whole world knows how close you were to . . . not being here any more. Apart from me.

Sam *doesn't reply.* **Davey** *smiles.*

Sam   Alright . . . you can stop smiling now. You can stop smiling . . . I said you can stop!

Davey *smiles on. He shrugs his shoulders. He's happy.*

Sam (*to the audience*)   And that was it! Suddenly I had a 'friend' called Davey. And there wasn't much I could do about it.

Scene Eight

A hill. **Sam** *walks slowly.*

He sits down on the hill and looks out. He puts head in his hands.

A pause.

Davey *joins him.* **Sam** *looks up to see him.*

Sam   What exactly do you want?

Davey   Nothing really. I just thought . . .

Sam   Well don't.

Davey   Just thought you might need some company.

Sam *lies back. Stares up.*

Sam   Doing what? Looking at the sky? I'm alright. Thanks.

Davey *sits beside him. He stares up too.*

Davey   It's not just looking at the sky though, is it? Up there . . . Nothing's the same as down here.

Sam   What are you saying?

Davey   Up there. It's just full of possibilities . . .

Sam   Look, Davey, I know you saved my life and all that, but there's no need to get deep. I came up here to get away from you . . .

Davey   Look at that. A muted rainbow . . .

Sam   You what?

Davey   Dancing . . . Look at it . . . In and out of the
sunlight . . .

Sam   You what?

Davey   A rainbow . . . Only softer . . .

Sam   Oh . . . Yeah. Yeah, I can see it.

Davey   Bet you didn't know that rainbows are really round.
We only see the half of it. But somewhere, beyond the horizon
there's other kids seeing it too. Lying on a hill somewhere . . .
Looking at the other half of the rainbow too.

Sam   How do you know, weirdo?

Davey   I don't.

He lies back. **Sam** *looks to him.*

Sam   Just cos I owe you, right, doesn't mean I'm your
friend.

Davey   Just cos you say you're not my friend doesn't mean
you mean it.

A pause.

Sam *and* **Davey** *sit in silence. They look up into the sky.*

Scene Nine

Corridor.

Alicia, **Claudia** *and* **Casey** *are gathered in the corridor.*

Alicia   Then he looked at me and went, 'You are possibly
the most awesome girl I have ever seen.'

Claudia   And what did you say?

Alicia   'I know.'

Sam *walks in, on his way to a lesson.* **Davey** *follows keenly after him.*

Casey   How cool is that? You seeing him again?

Alicia   Friday.

Claudia   The park?

Casey   Can we come?

Davey   Sam . . . You going to English, Sam?

Sam *doesn't answer.*

Davey   I'll walk with you, then.

Claudia   Lucky you, Sam.

The **Girls** *follow* **Davey***, giggling, imitating the way he walks.*

Davey (*he takes big steps*)   Make sure you don't step on the cracks of the tiles, though. You might fall into another universe.

Sam   Davey, we're not ten any more.

Davey   Fall into it, you're gone. And your life's never the same again. All you have to do is step on one crack – a pavement, a tile . . .

Alicia   What? You really think we're gonna ruin our lives?

Claudia   From treading on lines?

Casey   On the floor?

Davey   In a sort of roundabout way, yeah . . . Make one mistake and that could be it – sucked out of the light and into the dark side. Do not fall into the abyss of life. Stay on the pavement, the corridor of life, the straight and narrow . . .

Davey *exits.*

Sam   Oh man, where does he get this stuff?

Scene Ten

Sam*'s house.* **Sam** *enters.*

Sam's Mum   Hi, Sam . . . Nice day at school?

Sam   Alright.

Davey   Alright apart from Sam stepped on seventy-nine cracks in the corridor floor tiles.

Sam *stops dead.* **Davey** *sits at the table.*

Sam   What is he doing here?

Sam's Mum   Davey's come for tea. Did you forget?

Sam   Who invited him?

Sam's Mum (*simultaneously*)   I did.

Davey (*simultaneously*)   I did.

Sam (*to the audience*)   The weird thing was, even if there was something I could do about Davey being my friend, at this point, I wasn't sure I'd do anything about it. Cos when it was just us . . . Me and Davey, Davey and me . . . life was alright. Life was actually fun . . . Though don't tell anyone, *anyone*, that I said that . . .

Scene Eleven

Sam's *room.* **Sam** *and* **Davey** *are looking out of the window.*

Sam   You know what that is?

Davey   What?

Sam   Behind them trees . . . Back of the science block.

Davey   Science is the answer. Dreams are the key.

Sam   The key to what?

Davey   You don't know what dreams are?

Sam   Yeah, dim-brain. I'm not that thick. They're all your muddled-up, rerun thoughts from the whole day, mixed in a blender and spewed back at night like a previous episode in fast-forward.

Davey   No. Dim-brain.

Sam   What was dim about that? I thought that was poetry.

Davey   Dreams are the way we live two lives. Like me and you. Here. A parallel universe. I'm here but no one else on this earth knows that I am.

Sam   Except my mum. And your mum.

Davey   But no one else. No one else that could alter anything. Like your mates. Question is, would it matter if they did?

Sam   You've got fizzy feet, Davey, course it would matter.

Davey   To you, maybe.

A pause.

I read about a guy once. He dreamed he was this butterfly, right.

Sam   Let me guess, but when he woke up it was just a moth in his bedroom.

Davey   No. When he woke up, he didn't know if he was a man who'd dreamt he was a butterfly. Or a butterfly who was dreaming he was a man. Imagine that . . . This life, what if it's all a dream, a bad dream sometimes and we're just overgrown flying insects?

Sam   Seriously, Davey, how do you think this up?

Davey (*he taps his head*)   My bottomless pit of imagination. There's plenty more where that came from. I hear it, taste it, see it, think it. If I can, so can you.

Sam   You taste your imagination?

Davey   There's more than one way of looking at things, Sam.

Sam   Yeah. My way. Or your way. Your way is strange.

Davey   Strange is good. I quite like strange.

Sam   Never.

Davey   Yeah. Cos do you know what the worst thing in the entire universe would be? To look and walk and talk and spout and think the same way as everybody else.

Sam   Would it?

Davey   While all the time claiming to be an individual. Means you've joined the populist army. And once you've joined you never get yourself back. You've lost your confidence and sold your soul. That's why people like me get such a hard time. I didn't join up and never will. Scares the living daylights out of people . . .

Scene Twelve

The playground.

Alex, **Morgan** *and* **Jay** *kick a ball idly from one to another.*

Alex   That four–one win at the start of the season. He's the best player in the world.

Morgan   The best striker ever?

Jay   Better than anyone. He could take them all on.

Alex   He crosses a ball, sheer perfection.

Sam *and* **Davey** *enter.*

Davey   Think of it this way, earth may well be just a football in the playing field of space.

Sam   Yeah. And we're on it, just waiting to get kicked . . .

Davey   End of the dinosaurs, the cretaceous period, the Ice Age – the earth was well volleyed. One big kick and life was wiped out. . . .

Sam   Now we're just waiting for someone to kick us again . . .

Davey   And when they do . . . When they shoot and score. End of the world . . .

Sam   Perhaps that's why girls don't like football – they're just a load of aliens.

Sam *and* **Davey** *laugh. The* **Crew** *watch.* **Sam** *notices them . . .*

Davey   Maybe they are! I'll pass you that book I was telling you about.

Sam   Oh. Yeah . . . Whatever.

Davey   Promise. I won't lose my thoughts in a void this time.

Sam   I said, whatever.

Davey   Is that all you can say?

Sam   See ya, Davey.

He walks away. **Davey** *watches him. After a moment, he exits.*

Alex *approaches.*

Alex   What was that about?

Sam   What?

Morgan   You and Fizzy Feet . . .

Sam   Me? And him? I can't stand him.

Alex   Why hang out with him then?

Sam   He lives in my street. He follows me, I can't get away.

Alex   I reckon you better start trying, man. Before word gets out.

Jay   Everyone'll think you're his mate.

Sam   No way. Davey is a top-of-the-rubbish-tip idiot. What would I be mates with him for?

Alex *laughs.*

Sam *turns around.* **Davey** *is there. He has a book in his hands.*

A pause.

Davey *goes to* **Sam**, *gives him the book.*

Davey   You didn't say whatever before. You said you were interested.

He looks to the audience.

Sam   So, I had to choose – to be the kind of boy I wanted to be. Or the kind of boy everyone thought I was. Of course, that was an easy decision to make . . .

He looks to **Davey**, *never more certain.*

Sam   Listen, Fizz, I don't know what gave you that idea but . . . it sure wasn't me.

He walks away. The **Crew** *laugh.*

Alex   You crack me up, man.

Morgan   Top-of-the-rubbish-heap idiot . . . You got him spot on, Sam.

Sam   Tell me about it. I cannot get away from him!

Davey *begins to walk away.*

Jay   Truth, mate. At least now he knows it. You are so not his mate.

A pause. **Sam** *watches* **Davey** *exit.*

Scene Thirteen

The playground.

Davey *enters. He has his lunchbag with him. He sits.*

Sam *enters. He stops a distance from* **Davey**.

Sam   Look, I never meant it, alright . . . I never meant any of it. You're not an idiot. You're different, you're funny, you're cool. And you know what? I can talk to you – about mad stuff. You're my friend. And you make me laugh.

Pause. He addresses the audience.

Well, you know, that's what I should have said. But . . . I didn't. (*He calls.*) Dave . . . Davey . . .

He bowls over.

Nice one! I can always rely on Fizz. What you got?

Sam *takes the lunchbag, looks inside.*

Davey   Cheese sandwich. Cheese and onion crisps . . .

Sam   For someone with a big imagination, your food is so boring.

Davey   Never. I just pretend it's other things.

Sam   Yeah? What's this, then? Don't tell me – it's your space food?

*From **Davey**'s lunchbag, **Sam** pulls out an inhaler.*

Davey   Inhaler.

Sam   Durrh. I know what it is . . .

Davey   But you said –

Sam   I know. But how come you've got one? You've got Fizzy Feet but really you're a breath-boy with an inhaler?

Davey   No . . . Never when I dance. Just sometimes. When I . . . panic and that.

Sam   Right. When you panic . . .

Davey   When I panic, I lose my breath. Remember . . . ?

Sam   Alright, don't go on about it.

He tosses the inhaler back in the lunchbag, walks away a little.

Davey   Don't tell no one, right.

He offers out the crisps.

No one. I mean it.

Sam *takes the crisps.*

Sam What's up with you, Davey? Everyone has an inhaler. What's the big deal?

Davey Just . . . please.

Sam Alright. I promise and I cross my heart.

He opens the crisps, eats.

He looks to the audience.

And that was it. Davey had an inhaler. So what? I forgot about it . . . I'd made a promise, yeah, but that just sort of fizzled out as well. Escaped my mind. Clean forgot. Left it. Lost it. Forgot.

Scene Fourteen

The playground. Lighting change.

Sam *looks to the audience.*

Sam Big mistake.

Alex *enters. He paces beside* **Sam**.

Alex How 'asthma'? Bad asthma or what?

Sam I dunno. Just sometimes, he said.

Alex A lot sometimes?

Sam No.

Alex Then how much sometimes? On a scale of one to ten? Come on . . .

Sam I don't know.

Alex So why tell me? If you don't know . . .

Sam I don't. How would I know?

Alex   Some friend you call yourself.

Sam   I am not Davey's friend! How many times do I have to say this . . . ?

Jay *and* **Morgan** *enter.*

Alex   But you know he's got an asthma inhaler.

Sam   I saw it, that's all.

Alex   Then you are his 'buddy'.

Jay   I might have guessed he'd have more than just Fizzy Feet wrong with him.

Morgan   What's right with him?

Jay   Ask Sam. He's his crew.

Sam   No I'm not.

Alex   So keep it that way, yeah.

He offers **Sam** *a drink from his can.* **Sam** *accepts, takes a sip.*

Jay   One of my girl cousins. She's got an inhaler. Runs that bit too far and she gasps like an old man on dirty cigarettes. Imagine Fizzy Feet?!

Alex (*laughs*)   Gasping, yeah?

Jay   Yeah.

Sam   I've never seen him like that.

Alex   Like proper fighting for breath . . .

Morgan   Yeah, I would love to see that.

Sam   What for?

Morgan   Why, you're suddenly his friend again now?

Alex   Yeah, what are you gonna do?

Sam   Nothing. I'm just saying . . .

Morgan   Well, don't. Why would we want to hurt Fizzy? I wouldn't even want to touch him.

Alex   Who would? Not even Alicia, not in a million, I'm telling you.

They laugh.

Jay   You should see her, though. My cousin. Proper fighting for her breath. Funny.

Alex   I like it, Jay. Oh yeah.

Morgan   Yeah. You like it, Sam?

A pause. **Sam** *looks up, to the audience.*

Sam   All down to me. I'd told them about Davey. I'd done it. Big mistake.

Sam *and the* **Crew** *exit.*

Scene Fifteen

The playground.

Davey *enters. He sits alone. He gazes up at the sky.*

He takes out his lunch. He arranges it in a neat line. **Alex, Jay** *and* **Morgan** *enter.*

Alex   Anyone sitting here, Davey?

Alex, Morgan *and* **Jay** *sit beside him.*

Morgan   No one 'cept us. And Davey.

A slight pause.

Davey   Alright?

Alex   Yeah. How's it going, Fizzy?

Davey   Sunshine mainly.

Morgan   Sunshine?

Davey   Yeah. But cloudy as well. A few interesting formations . . .

He looks up to the sky.

A dragon . . . breathing fire. See it?

Alex   You what?

Jay   Yeah, I can see it.

Morgan   Shut up, Jay.

Morgan *and* **Alex** *snigger.*

Alex   Oh yeah. A dragon . . .

Davey   If you look hard enough, everyone can see something.

Morgan   You know what I can see? (*Quiet.*) A pure nuthead.

Alex *takes* **Davey***'s lunchbag away. He looks inside, smiles.*

Alex   Perhaps Davey needs to teach us, that's all. Then we could all do it.

Davey   I don't think so.

Alex   You could always teach us to dance.

Morgan   Yeah. Teach us to dance. Dance your fizzy feet for us, Davey.

Alex   You show us, we'll join in.

Jay   Davey, you don't have to do this.

Alex   Shut up, Jay. You know he wants to.

Morgan   You wanna dance, eh, Davey?

Davey   No.

Alex   Course you do. Fizz up your feet, throw it down, Davey.

Jay   Only if he wants to.

Morgan   Come on, Davey. Up you get. We said dance. Come on. Are you stupid or something?

Alex   Do it, Davey. Come on . . .

Morgan   Dance for us, Davey. Dance . . .

Slowly **Davey** *begins to dance. The* **Boys** *watch him.*

Morgan   That's it.

Alex   Faster now, Davey.

Alex *and* **Morgan** *snigger.*

Morgan   Go on, Davey. Throw it down.

Alex   Tear it up, Davey.

Davey*'s moves get faster.*

Jay   Nice one . . .

Alex   Move them feet, boy. Come on . . .

Morgan   You're so cool. I am loving it, mate.

Davey *begins to slow. He wheezes for his breath.*

Alex   What's up with you?

Davey   No, I can't.

Morgan   Don't stop now, we're just getting to the good bit.

Davey   I need it, alright.

Alex *holds the lunchbag out of his reach.*

Alex   Need what?

Davey   Give it to us . . .

Morgan   Dance more and we'll think about it.

Jay   You can't do that.

Alex   Move it, Davey. Come on.

Davey   I can't . . .

Jay   Give it to him, man.

Davey   Please. I need it. I need it . . .

Alex   Have to catch it first.

Alex *tosses the inhaler to* **Morgan**.

Morgan   Dance and we'll think about it.

Davey   Stop it, I can't breathe . . .

Sam *enters.*

Sam   What are you doing?

Slight pause. The **Boys** *halt.*

Morgan   Back off, Sam. We only want him to dance.

Alex   What are we supposed to do? Stop him doing what he likes?

Alex *and* **Morgan** *run off.*

Morgan   Run.

Sam   Jay, give it to him. He needs it. What have you done?

Jay   It's nothing to do with me.

He runs off.

Davey *collapses. He fights for his breath.*

Sam   Davey! Deep breaths, alright? You can do it. Get help, someone . . . Someone get help . . .

The **Girls** *enter.*

Alicia   What's up with him?

Claudia   What's going on?

Davey   You told them . . .

Sam   Calm down, Davey.

Davey   You told them . . .

Alicia   Told them what?

Davey   My inhaler . . . I told you . . .

Sam   Alright!

Claudia   You have an inhaler?

Casey   I never knew that.

Davey   No one did.

Sam   I didn't mean to, alright!

Davey   I told you not to . . .

Sam   I know what you said, alright. Just keep breathing . . .

Davey   Not Alex, not Morgan . . .

Sam   I never meant to – !

Claudia   You went and told them?

Alicia   What, just so everyone could pick on him more?

Sam   I never meant to tell them, Davey. I never . . .

Alicia   Then what are you? Some sort of idiot? I'll get
Mackie.

The **Girls** *run off.*

Davey   You . . . told him.

Sam   Davey, someone's coming, alright?! Just keep
breathing. We'll find your inhaler. Big, deep breaths . . .

Davey   I can't . . .

Sam   Just keep on breathing, mate . . .

Davey   I can't . . .

Sam   Hurry up, will you! Davey, they'll find it, we'll get it,
alright. Keep on breathing, Davey. . . . Davey. Breathe . . .
Davey!

Lights fade.

Scene Sixteen

School office.

Sam *stands before* **Mr Mackie**. **Alex**, **Morgan** *and* **Jay** *are present too.*

Sam   It wasn't my fault, sir.

Mr Mackie   Really? I thought you were Davey's friend, Sam.

Sam   No, sir.

Mr Mackie   So Davey doesn't go to your house for tea sometimes?

Alex, **Morgan** *and* **Jay** *share a look.*

Sam   No, sir.

Mr Mackie   You don't knock for him and walk to school most days?

Sam   No, sir.

Mr Mackie   Is that the truth, Sam?

Sam   Yes, sir.

Mr Mackie   The whole truth?

Sam   I'm telling you the truth.

Mr Mackie   Are you, Sam? The truth about why Davey's in hospital right now? Why his inhaler was found in the bin when he needed it?

Sam   If I knew anything, I'd tell you.

Mr Mackie   You'd tell the truth for your friend?

Sam   He's not my friend, sir.

A pause. **Sam** *hangs his head in shame. The others look to him. He exits.*

Scene Seventeen

The hospital.

Sam's Mum *comforts* **Davey's Mum** *as they sit in the corridor.* **Sam** *sits nearby.*

Davey's Mum   I swear . . . a place where one boy does that to another? What sort of place is that?

Sam's Mum   A terrible place.

Davey's Mum   If it came to it, I'd move house.

Sam's Mum   You'd have to. I'd do the same.

Davey's Mum   Halfway across the country if it came to it.

Sam's Mum   Well you would. You'd do anything for your kids.

Davey's Mum   I'd even move abroad. If I knew anyone abroad.

Sam's Mum   But you don't.

Davey's Mum   And as for the little so-and-so who did it, what I'd like to do to them . . .

Sam's Mum   I'd join you.

Slight pause.

Davey's Mum   When will there be news?

Sam's Mum   Another tea?

Davey's Mum   Coffee. I've been here all day.

Pause.

Scene Eighteen

The hill.

Sam *looks out, a football under his arm.*

Sam   Remember this, Davey, remember when we used to come up here . . . ? Just me and you.

He lies back. Rests his head on the football, closes his eyes.

Davey *enters. He sits close by.*

Sam   No one else here and no one mattered.

Davey   Two good mates looking up at the clouds. Remember . . .

Sam *opens his eyes. He gazes up at the sky.*

Sam   Now that is definitely a tennis match. See the net across there? That little fluffy one's the ball . . . There's the racquet.

Davey   I can't see it.

Sam   There. The tennis player, arm up, ready to serve . . .

Davey *lies beside him.*

Davey   You haven't spotted the vase of flowers on the table then?

Sam   The what?

Davey   That's the vase, yeah? A few flowers . . .

Sam   That's a bull. With horns.

Davey   You need specs, Sam. That's a vase, flowers, that's the table . . .

Sam   Four legs, it's a bull. Or a cow or something.

Davey   A lot of cows don't have horns.

Sam   Neither does a vase on top of a table!

Davey   Look, I know what I see. Who invented this game?

Sam   You did, you weirdo.

Davey   So I make the rules. Look – that one! Hamburger . . .

Sam   I like it! Caterpillar. You see it?

Davey   Oh yeah . . .

Sam   Roman chariot . . . There. Two horses, a shield . . .

Davey   You're getting good.

Sam   Getting good . . .

He raps.

The grass might be wet, my belt might be . . . rusting, it's gonna be . . . disgusting but now that I am trusting what I see and what I say, we're having fun, in the sun – it is called . . . cloud-busting.

Davey   No way. And you say I'm weird?

Sam   You're my best friend right! You'd have to be!

Davey   What? Did you just say that? Best friend? Did you really just say that?

Sam *smiles.* **Davey** *smiles. He looks up at the sky.*

Sam (*to the audience*)   And he was. My best friend. Not that I ever got a chance to tell him that. I didn't. In the hospital, Davey nearly left us for good . . . For a better place, if you know what I mean. But he pulled through, thank goodness. Not that it made any difference. Davey's mum took him out of our school first chance she could and overnight they moved house . . . (*Slight pause.*) I never saw Davey again. He never came back. No one 'fessed up, no one got punished and that was it. Davey never got the chance to face us. To tell us what he really thought, to tell us all the things we really deserved to hear. I never got the chance to tell him loads of things, like what I really thought of him. What we all really thought of him . . . We couldn't because we never gave Davey the chance just, well, to be Davey . . . Imagine it . . .

The light on **Davey** *fades.*

Scene Nineteen

The playground. A football game.

Alex, **Morgan**, **Jay** *and* **Sam** *kick a ball about.*

Alex   To me.

Morgan   Nice one, Alex.

Jay   Morgan, you're the man. Over here . . .

Davey *runs through the middle. He picks up the ball.*

Morgan   Davey!

Alex   Davey, what you doing?

Davey   Sorry. Did I wake you up? The boys who could never be woken . . .

Sam   Here he goes . . . I feel a poem coming on.

Davey   It is poetic, I suppose. Poetic justice.

Alex   Pass it, Davey.

Morgan   To me, Davey.

Alex   Davey, just give us the ball.

Alex *goes to dive for him but* **Davey** *dodges. He points at the sky.*

Davey   See that. An elephant on two legs.

Jay   Where?

Morgan   Shut up.

Alex   The guy has lost it. Permanent.

Jay   No, I want to see it.

Davey   Too late. It's turned into a vacuum cleaner.

Morgan   What is he on about?

Jay (*pointing to the sky*)   Pancake! Tossed in a pan –

Davey   Nice one. But when it hits it – how will it morph? Like life . . . Stuff happens – and it changes things. Changes people. I made you lot look at the sky. Me. Davey, David Youngson.

He rolls up his sleeves. The **Crew** *share looks.*

Davey   Now I can beat anyone . . .

Sam   Davey. What is up with you?

Davey *shrugs him off. He picks up the football.*

Davey   Sam, why stick to the rules?

Morgan   Cos it's football, you pillock.

Davey *holds the ball high, like basketball. He searches for who to throw it to.*

Davey   No ref. No big, silver trophy. No need. Just – have a bit of fun . . .

He loops the ball around his body. He starts to move.

It's only a ball. The instructions are up to you.

Sam   Davey, are you fizzing?

Morgan   Fizz on, Davey.

Davey (*moving the ball round him*)   You take it up, you let it go.

Alex   You tell us, Fizz.

Davey   You connect, you dive, you score. Or maybe you don't.

He throws the ball to **Jay**.

Davey   Football – two feet, one spherical object and a team of ten other nimble dancers all waiting to dance the best steps of their lives.

Morgan   Football's a dance?

Davey   A dance with a ball. You think about it. It pays to look at things differently sometimes.

He tosses the ball back to them.

Sam   Nice one, Davey.

Davey *walks on, they follow.*

Scene Twenty

The classroom.

Oliver *and* **Rebecca** *enter, sharing earphones as they listen to music.*

Sam (*calls*)   Davey, get us a seat.

Jay   Get me one.

Morgan   All together, yeah?

Alex   Oy. Watch it.

Oliver   Sorry.

Rebecca   Sorry.

Morgan   You will be, yeah.

Davey   Morgan – step out of the atmosphere yeah?

Morgan   What?

Davey   You and them. It's what's called two universes – colliding.

Alex   And they weren't looking where they were going.

Oliver   We said sorry.

Davey   Neither were you. Only they were busy listening. You were just busy not being aware of your own orbit. Apologise.

Alex   Sorry, yeah.

Morgan   Yeah. Sorry and all that.

Morgan *and* **Alex** *take a seat.* **Rebecca** *and* **Oliver** *smile.*

Alex   Davey, you are too much.

Davey   A thousand pound is too much.

Morgan   For what?

Davey   For anything. Except your imagination.

Morgan   What?!

Davey   Imagine. Go on . . .

He takes the earphones from **Oliver** *and* **Rebecca**. *We begin to hear the music they were listening to. Classical music . . .*

The **Class** *begins to settle.*

Davey   Like it?

Jay   Shush.

Slight pause. The **Class** *listen as the* **Girls** *enter.*

Alicia   What's this?

Claudia   What's going on?

Casey   Has someone died or something?

Morgan   Shut up, will you? We're listening.

The **Class** *listen where they sit or stand. The music fades . . .*

Lights fade . . .

Scene Twenty-One

The classroom.

The usual hive of activity before a lesson. **Davey**'s *seat is empty. Only* **Sam** *sits in his seat. Head down, locked down.*

Alicia *walks over to the place where* **Davey** *sat.*

Alicia   Anyone sitting there?

Alex   A girl, Alicia, no way!

Alicia   Why, what is wrong with me?

Morgan *bars her way. Any excuse . . .*

Morgan   Alicia, that is Davey's chair. What if he comes back and some girl, like, just took his place . . . ?

Alicia   Why? You think he's coming back?

Jay   I dunno, ask his mate.

Morgan   Oy, Sam? Has Davey been in touch?

Alex   What's happening, Sam?

Sam   I've told you.

Morgan   You just told us lies, man. Like you told Davey. On the sly you were his mate, in school you weren't. Not that you came clean to us.

Alex   Yeah. What sort of mate is that?

Jay   A bad mate.

Morgan   A sad mate.

Alex   Sad for us.

Jay   Sad for Davey.

Sam *erupts. He addresses the audience.*

Sam   Alright! Yeah. I was – the worst kind of mate you could ever have! But what was I supposed to do, eh? Come right out and say it? 'I'm Davey's friend'! And then what, eh? Then what?

Morgan *and the others look on.*

Morgan   Alright. Calm down.

Sam   No, Morgan, I won't. Because I would have been tormented. Just like Davey. What was I supposed to do? Tell the truth and make my life a living hell as well?

Jay   You were his mate . . .

Morgan   Yeah, you should have stood up for him.

Alex   You should have looked out for him.

Sam   I should? What about you? Every single one of you . . . Well come on. Hands up . . . Hands up whoever asked Davey how he was feeling, if he was alright, cos he looked lonely. Hands up whoever talked to him or saved him a seat? (*No one puts up a hand.*) See. This is not just me.

Jay   We all could have done something.

Sam   Yeah. So hands up . . . Come on. Hands up. Who feels bad about it, eh? Come on . . .

Slowly, around the class, hands go up. **Jay** *is the first. Then* **Oliver**, **Rebecca**, *the* **Girls**. *Then* **Alex**, *then* **Morgan**. *Finally* **Sam** *puts his hand up too.*

Sam   Looks like that's a vote then.

The class stand there, hands still in the air.

Scene Twenty-Two

The classroom.

Mr Mackie *enters.*

Mr Mackie   Homework. Any other homework? Poems anyone?

Pupils *hand in their workbooks.*

Alicia   Sir.

Claudia   Mine, sir.

Mr Mackie   Thank you. Boys? Homework by chance?

Alex   Mr Mackie, sir.

Jay   Sir . . .

Mr Mackie   What? All of you?

Morgan   A poem, sir.

Alex   All of us together, sir.

Jay   It was good.

Mr Mackie   Good . . . ?

Jay   Made me sort of feel better, sir.

Mr Mackie   About?

Alicia   Made all of us feel better.

Casey   About the world. Everything.

Sam *hands in his poem.*

Mr Mackie   Thank you, Sam. Your poem?

Sam   Our poem, sir. About my friend.

Oliver   About our friend, sir. Davey.

Mr Mackie   Davey . . . David Youngson.

Sam   And how he went away.

The **Children** *begin to speak their poems.*

Morgan   Fizzy Feet we called him. Cos he could dance.

Sam   He was persecuted. Pushed around . . .

Alex   Different and strange.

Oliver   Different cos he had a brain.

Rebecca   And he knew how to use it.

Alicia   He was unique . . .

Casey   He was special.

Claudia   He saw different things 'different'.

Morgan   Different. Maybe that was the problem?

Sam   Whose problem? Your problem, my problem, our problem?

Jay   Not his. I never even said sorry.

Morgan   I never even got the chance.

Sam   And if you had the chance, would you? Could you be brave enough? When I fell, I had Davey. Who did Davey have, eh? Not me.

Jay   Or me.

Mr Mackie   I see.

Sam   And now he's gone, he's left a Davey-shaped hole.

Morgan   A little piece of Davey.

Jay   A little piece of sky.

Rebecca   A little piece of different.

Sam   To remember him by.

Lighting change.

Scene Twenty-Three

The hill.

Sam *points up at the sky.*

Sam   Up there . . . A horse . . . Right there . . . Galloping over a fence . . . Its tail, its mane . . . That one's an eagle. A golden eagle . . . Now a wave, breaking over the shore of a perfect summer's day. A day I'll never forget . . . Sunshine. Blue. Not a cloud in the sky . . .

He lies back. He gazes up at the sky.

Lighting change.

Cloud Busting

*Notes on rehearsal and staging, drawn from workshops
with the writer held at the National Theatre, November 2010*

Helen read Malorie Blackman's *Cloud Busting*, which is written
entirely in verse, two years ago and felt that it would be perfect
to adapt for young people to perform. It is a powerful story
about young people's lives that, if performed properly, should
enable both performers and audience to reflect on their own
experiences. The script allows for as many performers as you
want, but moves very smoothly and quickly from scene to
scene, so any production should be swift and light on its feet.

Digging into the Text

PROLOGUE

When you first approach the play, before you start rehearsals,
it is vital to get an understanding of the piece as a whole.
Good stories are held together like pieces of clockwork – they
are structures – so if you can understand what the structure of
your play is before you begin rehearsals it will make directing
it a lot easier.

TIMELINE

Cloud Busting is a 'memory play', which means that the story
happens in the memory of the narrator. Look at the first three
scenes: they are taking place 'now', and then in Scene Four
we go back in time to the assembly when Davey first danced.
It is at this point that the story really begins. The early scenes
are the prologue, but it is only once Davey does 'fizzy feet' in
assembly that the narrative really kicks off. It sounds obvious,
but these jumps in time happen throughout the play – whenever
Sam speaks to the audience he is talking 'now' as his older self,
but the story takes place in the past, and any production needs
to show that change clearly.

THE LATER SCENES

A useful way to get an idea of the structure of the play after the prologue is to break the story down into events. An event is something which happens in the narrative which fundamentally changes everything that comes later. When you string all the events together, you get an idea of the total 'arc' of the story – the simplest way of describing the journey of the audience from the beginning to the end. We identified six events in *Cloud Busting*, and they are:

1   Davey's public shame when he dances in front of the assembly (Scene Four).

2   Sam is forced to meet Davey the Fool (Scene Seven).

3   Davey saves Sam's life – Davey becomes the hero (Scene Seven).

4   Sam betrays Davey – 'Davey is a top-of-the-rubbish-tip idiot' (Scene Twelve).

5   The Crew torture Davey (Scene Fifteen).

6   The Crew and Sam mourn Davey after his departure (Scene Twenty-One).

We have given the events titles because these allow us more clearly to understand the core message of the play. By looking at the arc these events create you can see that the play is about the conflict between Davey the individual and the Crew who want to punish him for being different. Sam is caught in the middle, and the tragedy of the piece is that he feels forced to betray his friend. By breaking the script down like this we know that any production has to show the conflict between the Crew and Davey as boldly as possible.

Character

Once you have broken the piece down into events you can start to look at character, and the role each character plays in the story. A great way to do this is to describe the story from each character's perspective as they experience it. Remember only to use information that is there in the text, not to elaborate around it, and also to pay close attention to the timeline.

For example, Mr Mackie's story could be:

'My name is Mr Mackie and I'm an English teacher in a secondary school. I have a class who are normally pretty naughty, but the other day they responded really well when I asked them to write a poem. I was particularly pleased that Sam wanted to write a poem about Davey. Davey was this quite scruffy kid who did this strange thing in assembly a while ago when he just got up and danced in this really bizarre way. Everyone started laughing and I was worried he'd get bullied. A while later there was that awful incident with his inhaler, and then his mother took him out of school. None of the kids owned up to it, of course, but then when I came in to hear their poems the whole class had responded to Davey's leaving and it was fantastic. I felt they might have realised that they weren't as nice to him as they could have been and were trying to make amends. Hopefully it won't happen again.'

Notice that in the story there's no mention of the dream sequences that Sam has about Davey towards the end of the play, as they could only be part of Sam's story. This exercise is almost more important for the smaller characters than it is for the main ones, since you get important detail which is helpful for actors. If you are all doing it as a company it can be useful to write other characters' stories as well – again, to get a richer understanding of every character's role in telling the story.

Working on the Lines

PUBLIC, PRIVATE, PAST AND PRESENT

We've already established that *Cloud Busting* is a memory play where the storytelling cuts between the past and present – cuts that will need to be made very clear in a successful production. In order to help navigate these changes for the actors, try going through the script line by line, and label whether it is a public or privately spoken line, and whether it happens in the present or the past. Whenever Sam talks to the audience, he is talking privately and in the past tense, but this will often cut suddenly into the public, present tense of (for example) the classroom. The script often moves very quickly between these two different registers, particularly at the moment when Sam beats up Davey in Scene Five, where nearly every character has a private, past-tense aside to the audience. Noting this down for each line will allow you to be much more precise about how to make the jumps between telling the story in the past and telling it in the present. Remember how we established that the story is about the conflict between the individual and a large group – so the private thoughts of the characters are different from how they behave publicly.

RHYTHM, BEATS AND MUSIC

As you read through the script you'll see that it has a very clear rhythm, with parts occasionally rhyming or alliterating. This is not by accident! Helen has written a play where every scene has an almost musical quality, and in order to make a production work you need to be able to unlock this rhythm. A good technique to help you do this is to find a pulse for a scene and make the actors say their lines to this beat. If you look at Scene Seven, you can see that Sam's Mum jumps in at the end of all his sentences, implying that this scene has quite a fast tempo. Try clapping out a quick beat in two while the actors playing Sam and Sam's Mum read the scene. Make sure they don't leave any gaps. You'll see this gives the scene a really exciting urgency. Maybe try changing the tempo when Sam addresses the audience to help you differentiate between public and private moments. After a while you'll find that you won't need to beat a pulse, but the actors will hopefully retain the urgency that the rhythm in the text gives them. Try it for the other scenes – each will have a different tempo. The idea is not to sound as though you are performing the whole text like a song or a rap – you still want to hear the characters – but remember that the rhythm of the text gives a clue to the tempo and urgency with which a text should be performed.

UNLOCKING SCENES

As well as using tempo, there are numerous useful ways of finding the heart and urgency of a scene. Helen doesn't want her play to be 'nice' or whimsical – it is, after all, a story about group of people who bully a boy so badly that he nearly dies, and so while much of it is very beautiful, remember that there is savagery at the heart of the piece. This is particularly true of the classroom scenes, which should have a real undercurrent of aggression. To release this in performance you could try as an exercise staging Scene One as if it were in a prison, an army barracks or a zoo where all the animals are in different cages screaming at each other. Without losing the rhythm and musicality of the dialogue, see if you can unlock how horrible all the kids are to each other. Once you've done that, go back to your classroom staging, but see if you can maintain the essence of the zoo or the prison. You can try different scenarios to unlock different scenes – try Scene Eight, for example, as if Davey is trying to drag Sam somewhere exciting but Sam is holding back.

Stage Language

While we have looked at ways of breaking down the text in order to get to the heart of the story and to the truth of particular scenes, we haven't so far examined any particular staging solutions. Without being too prescriptive, we can see that many of the features of the style and content of the piece suggest some particular approaches to staging. Helen wrote the play to move quickly and be light on its feet; as the piece takes place in many locations and indeed addresses the power of the imagination, it would suggest that a strongly naturalistic staging would be inappropriate – long scene changes with lots of sets would drag down the pace. Particularly as most of the action takes place in Sam's memory, you can afford to be much more fluid and dream-like with your staging. For example, there is no need to bring on lots of actual desks and chairs for the classroom – you'll find more imaginative ways of conveying this.

One thing that should emerge very strongly is the difference between the Crew and Davey. When we workshopped the play we looked at creating a menacing group identity for the Crew built around a particular slouching walk. With everyone walking together in this manner the group had a uniformly intimidating approach. By having Davey alone onstage walking past the group as they followed him with their eyes, we created a really ominous effect that highlighted both Davey's isolation and his independence.

Think as well about Davey's dancing: it would not be appropriate for Davey suddenly to launch, Billy Elliot-like, into a 'beautiful', choreographed, performance of a dance. Take the words 'fizzy feet' as your guide here – Davey does not seem to be in control of his dance at all, and it comes from somewhere very deep. He is expressing something that he can't vocalise, releasing pent-up feelings, in which case it would be quite inappropriate to have him perform a 'pretty' dance. To practise, maybe have everyone in the cast attempt to dance 'fizzy feet', and see what comes out. Remember, the aim is not to be polished but is to express an outpouring of feeling that won't be contained – something quite animal.

Music plays a key role in the play. As discussed, the dialogue has a musical, rhythmic quality, and a musical ear for each of the scenes is vital in getting to the heart of them. The most transformational moment in the play is when Sam imagines Davey making the class listen to classical music in Scene Twenty and it has a magical effect on everybody. In your staging you might want to think about where else you could use music to achieve other effects. You might want something similar for when Sam and Davey are cloud-busting, or something brutal and discordant for the bullying scenes. The script as a whole calls for a very musical ear, and you might want to consider how you could use recorded or live music to complement what is already there in the text.

From a workshop led by Rachel O'Riordan,
with notes by James Yeatman

Noel Clarke

Those Legs

Characters

Carer, *can be played by a male or a female (but is referred to as female throughout the play text).*

Georgia, *tomboy, was a model, fiancée of Aaron, who has been one of her best friends since primary school. Her other best friend is Leon, whom she's known longer. A bright and cheerful girl, she's the one who keeps the group together, although she's currently still dealing with the accident that put her in the chair. All the others live in her house, while saving for their own places.*

Leon, *best friends with Aaron and Georgia. Good guy, loves the ladies, but is actually dependable and loyal when he cares about someone. Works as a graphic designer, so is home a lot.*

Aaron, *Georgia's boyfriend and long-time friend of her and Leon. Good fiancé, doesn't even look at other women, works as a trainee agent so does long hours and goes out loads to premieres, etc.*

Alanis, *yes, like the singer . . . which she hates, so people call her Lana (as shall we). Wannabe actress, works in a café to pass the time. Was Aaron's new flatmate but now lives with them all in the house, average-looking girl. Not as stunning as Georgia should be, but pleasant, if a little competitive and self-obsessed.*

Plumber, *any age, male or female.*

New Carer, *male or female (but referred to as male throughout the play text).*

As suggested, the Carers and the Plumber can be either male or female.

The stage is the upstairs section of a five-bedroom house, and should be able to work in the round or standard. We see the living room, dining area, Georgia's room, a bathroom and Lana's room.

Scene One

House – night.

Lights up on a spacious modern interior of a house, not too much furniture. The TV plays. A person, the **Carer**, *responsible, walks around picking things up. Another woman,* **Georgia**, *sits in a wheelchair near the couch, watching TV. At certain moments the* **Carer** *looks towards her.* **Georgia** *chuckles slightly.*

Georgia You know it's really not gonna help, you looking at me like that. You stop, then start, then stop, then start. It's like watching someone do the robot.

Always smiling, she 'does the robot' while she talks. The **Carer** *pauses, contemplates.*

Carer I would strongly advise against this. You still require a lot of assistance and this isn't something that . . . Well, it does get easier, but I'm assigned to facilitate that.

Georgia's *face changes, deadpan.*

Georgia I've told you I want you to go. I'm not fucking asking you.

The **Carer** *stops packing things and stands staring at* **Georgia**.

Carer I know the change takes time to get used to.

Georgia The change? You're the fifth one I've had in . . .

Carer You've fired three.

Georgia And two left.

Carer Anyway, by change I meant getting used to chairs and us . . . I understand this has been a challenge.

Georgia A challenge . . . A fucking challenge . . . How do you understand? How do you understand what I'm going through? From what? From your degree? Your books? From reading about the stages that I'm supposed to go through, and how it affects my mood? You don't understand anything. You can't empathise . . . at best you sympathise, you pity me . . .

Carer   I don't pity you . . .

Georgia   Then what?

Carer   I realise you're still in a period of mourning.

Georgia *leans over, reaches a book, then throws it at the* **Carer**, *who dodges it deftly.*

Georgia   Straight out of a book . . . Mourning? That the technical term? Is that what you tell your mates when you get your time off? When you take your deep breath as you walk out the door, have your cigarette, relieved you're away from me? When you make your phone calls? When you meet those special friends in the evening and go to dinner? Is that what you say as you recount the story of your day, where you lifted me, carried me, watched me wash, wiped my arse and helped me do other intimate things that I still just can't get my fucking head used to? Is that what you say? 'She's still in a period of mourning'?

Beat.

Carer   I don't talk about work when I'm with frien—

Georgia   How can you not? You spend so much time doing it.

Carer   I try not to talk about –

Georgia   What do you talk about then?

Carer   Well, we just –

Georgia   You're lying.

Carer   You didn't let me finish.

Georgia   Your nose crinkled.

Carer   What?

Georgia   Your nose crinkled.

Carer   My nose?

Georgia   Your nose. And I can tell you're lying . . . Funny what you notice when you can't walk. Your nose crinkles a bit when you lie . . . Oh, and your ears move.

Carer   My ears?

Georgia   Your ears . . . So what do you talk about then?

Carer   Excuse me, I don't see the relevance –

Georgia *shouts, wheels forward, the* **Carer** *shrinks back, almost falling over the coffee table.*

Georgia   Don't lie to me! Is that what you say when you're with your fucking friends? 'She's in a period of mourning'?

Long pause.

Carer   . . . Yes . . .

Georgia *(calm)*   Get out!

The **Carer** *picks up her bags and starts slowly to exit, talking to* **Georgia** *as she leaves.* **Georgia** *watches her go, says nothing.*

Carer   I feel like this might just be about me. I'll tell them your decision and have them send someone else as soon as possible. Can your friends assist you in the meantime? Full-time I mean? I'm aware that your housemates and boyfriend work full-time, but can any of them?

Georgia   Get . . . out . . .

The **Carer** *waits at the door.*

Carer   I hate to say this, Georgia . . . because the truth is, even though you've been horrible to me since the moment I arrived, and you're right, I'll never really understand, because what's happened to you hasn't happened to me. But truth is, I quite like you . . . I think you'll find that you will need help. For a while anyway. And ironically, the first sign of knowing that you'll need it less, is when you accept that you'll need it in the first place . . . If you don't learn that, then . . .

The **Carer** *exits.* **Georgia** *sits for a moment in silence, then wheels herself in front of the TV. She grabs the remote control and turns off the TV.*

Lights down.

Scene Two

House – night.

Lights up: **Georgia** *is in bed in her room, her chair by the side of the bed where she always places it. The living room is quiet. TV off. Voices can be heard getting nearer and coming up the stairs. Three people enter the living room, turn on the TV and make themselves at home.* **Leon** *and* **Aaron** *sit on the couch and* **Alanis**, *otherwise known as* **Lana**, *sits at the dining table, where she opens a shoe box, studying some new shoes.*

Lana   Still think that was one of the best curries I've ever had.

Aaron   I agree, it was.

Leon   I'm not denying that, I didn't say it wasn't good, and I've never had hotter, you know I like it hot.

Lana   I don't get how you can eat that, even mild burns me.

Leon   It's genetics, a palate and pain-threshold thing. Some people can handle it, babe, some people can't.

Lana   Excuse me?!

Aaron   Here we go.

Lana   What do you mean, 'Here we go'? . . . Pain threshold? Can I remind you about childbirth and periods . . .

Leon   Can I remind you about epidurals and hot-water bottles. Plus you haven't had a kid yet so you don't know if you could handle it or not. I could handle it for all we know. Anyway, what I was saying was, yes, it was good but I don't see how any curry can be so good it dominated ninety per cent of our conversation on a thirty-minute journey home.

Aaron and **Lana** *look at each other a moment.*

Aaron/Lana   Because it was that good.

Leon   Whatever, I'm just embarrassed that I've become the person that talks about curry for thirty minutes.

Aaron   It's a sign of the times. We're all so engrossed in our iPods and iPads that conversation is dying. In fact, it's dying so much, it's coming back to life and even a trivial chat about curry now takes up thirty minutes. It's a good thing.

Lana   Wow . . . that was deep.

Leon   That made no sense.

Aaron   I think you'll find that it did.

Leon   Can't we talk about something else? Anything else.

A beat.

Aaron   I might be getting tickets to the Clover Green premiere.

Leon   Jesus!

Aaron   What?

Lana   Oh my God! Can I come?

Leon   Anything but that.

Aaron   You said, 'Let's talk about something else, anything else.' You can't change the goalposts now.

Leon   I designed that poster, my boss cut the trailer and not one of us got an invite. How have you got tickets?

Aaron   When you're an agent like me . . .

Leon/Lana   Trainee agent.

Aaron   More like assistant. Whatever. I move in those circles . . . I'm mates with a girl at Freuds PR, she goes out with one of the actors and said she'll give me her spares. Look, if I get the tickets, do you wanna come?

Leon No!

Aaron No? But you just –

Leon It's the principle.

Lana Can I come? If I could get an audition with Miguel Sanchez-Marks, I would literally piss my pants. Would there be an after party? Oh God, I'm gonna need a dress. Should I bring a showreel in case we meet him?

Aaron What would you show him? The time you asked for a sandwich in *Enders*, or the walk past the camera in *Dr Who*?

The boys laugh.

Lana I've done other stuff. Corporates, ads and things. My agent reckons I'm one audition away.

Aaron From the dole queue.

Leon Everyone's one audition away.

Lana I did that short film.

Aaron And of course there's the other one.

Lana I was young, I needed the money, my hair was a different colour and my nose wasn't done. No one knows it's me, and if we don't talk about it no one ever will.

The boys laugh again. **Lana** *glares at* **Leon**.

Aaron Anyway, the answer is no, too. I'm gonna take Georgia if she's up for it. I only asked him because he was moaning.

He starts to get up.

Lana Oh, see if she wants her food, otherwise I'll eat it. I mean I'm watching my weight but it is a Friday.

Leon I'll ask.

Aaron *slumps back down.* **Leon** *shouts.*

Leon   Georgia! Three things. One. Are you awake? Two. If you are, do you want your food? Curry? And three. Do you wanna go to the film premiere with your fiancé for the film I worked on and never got invited to?

Aaron   Funny.

Aaron *gets up and heads towards the bedroom.* **Georgia** *in bed, chuckles.*

Georgia   Yes, I am awake. I'll eat it tomorrow! And maybe.

Lana   Right, well, I'll go and put this in the fridge then.

Lana *exits stage, as* **Aaron** *enters the bedroom.* **Leon** *spreads out on the couch, flicking channels.*

Scene Three

House, **Georgia***'s bedroom – night.*

Aaron *walks into the bedroom, kisses* **Georgia** *flush on the lips. She sits up.*

Aaron   Hello, babe.

Georgia   Hey. Did you have a nice time?

Aaron   Yep. Do you think the carer girl – what's her name again? – anyway, do you think she'll want food when she gets in? We brought her some too.

Georgia   I fired her.

Aaron   What?

Georgia   I fired her.

Aaron   Jesus, Georgia. It's not gonna get easier with someone new, you know? You need the help.

Georgia   Why don't you help me?

Aaron   I do help you, don't I? We all do . . . I love you, I'll do anything for you but it's not really fair on us, is it? All the time, on Leon and Lana. We've all got full-time jobs. That's why you have a carer. It's not gonna be for ever, babe. Just until . . . If you sold this place.

Georgia   I'm not selling this place, I bought it with my own cash, no rent, no Daddy's help. Me. I'm not selling it. And yeah, you guys do help. I just . . . I'm sorry. I just still can't get used to it. Look at me.

Aaron   There's nothing wrong with you, babe.

Georgia   Do you still think I'm sexy, Aaron?

Aaron   I love you.

Georgia   That's not an answer.

Aaron   Course I do. Come on, you're being silly. Come into the living room?

He leans in and kisses her.

Georgia   I'll get up and come in in a minute.

Aaron   Great. D'you think you'll come to the premiere then? I'd love you to, babe.

Georgia   Maybe.

She watches **Aaron**, *her eyes never leaving him as he takes off his outside coat, strips down to his pants, then puts on a tracksuit. This happens while we go back to . . .*

Scene Four

House – night.

Lana *comes back in, grabs the shoes by the dining table, puts them on and starts walking around in them.* **Leon** *watches her.*

Leon   Where'd you get those?

Lana Jason bought them for me, to say sorry. I love 'em.

Leon How is Shrek? Haven't seen him in ages.

Lana He doesn't look like Shrek. And he doesn't come near here any more because you two – quite immaturely, I might add – were gonna beat him up and he twisted his knee running off.

Leon You're right, he doesn't look like Shrek. He looks like Shrek's dick – that or his asshole, I haven't decided yet. And we were gonna beat him up because you're our friend and he slept with that Vietnamese girl and then tried to use the excuse that as an American he was symbolically healing wounds because he hated what his nation had done there.

Lana *says nothing, still watching the shoes.* **Aaron** *comes in, sits on the couch.*

Leon Is Georgia OK?

Aaron Bit down. She fired the carer.

Leon She fired – shit, what was her name?

Lana Good. I didn't like her. Is Georgia alright? Does she need anything?

In the bedroom. **Georgia** *starts to get up. The process is always the same. She sits up, moves her left hand to her chair, shifts left on to it, before putting her legs in place properly.*

Aaron She said she's fine, she's coming in now. What's going on in here? You got an audition for *Project Runway*?

Leon The goblin king bought her shoes to say sorry for shagging the Vietnamese girl.

Lana He's not a goblin, and he did more than just buy me shoes, thank you.

Aaron Well, it's a start. He's an arsehole, Lana, an ugly one too, you know that. But I guess looking the way he does, he'd have to take any offer he gets.

They chuckle, even **Lana***.*

Lana   Shut up, Aaron. I forgave him, he's an artist, I kind of get what he felt he was . . . doing when he was . . . well, *doing* the Vietnamese girl.

Leon   I'll tell you what he was doing. He was fucking her, like America tried to do to them all those years ago.

Lana   He felt he was making amends, in some weird way.

Pause.

Aaron   Better hope he never goes to the Middle East.

Georgia *enters.*

Georgia   Hey.

They greet her. **Lana** *by walking over and giving her a kiss,* **Leon** *by just giving a wave.*

Lana   Why'd you fire – umm, what was her . . . ?

Georgia   I didn't like her.

Lana   Me neither, I just said that . . .

Georgia   Plus you guys have to let me have some fun . . .

Georgia *and* **Leon** *high-five.*

Leon   How long did she last?

Georgia   Three months, three weeks and a day.

Aaron   Fourth place. She was weak.

Georgia   What you guys watching?

Leon   Nothing that can't be changed for a movie. It is food and movie night. Whose turn is it?

Aaron   The girls.

Georgia/Lana   *Dirty Dancing.*

Leon/Aaron   Fuck sake.

Georgia   Stop moaning, and go and get it. Maybe do a little dance on your way over.

Leon *gets up to find the DVD.* **Georgia** *looks at* **Lana**.

Georgia   Nice shoes, missy . . . Where'd you get 'em?

Aaron   Gruffalo face. She forgave him.

Georgia   What?

Lana   Hello. I'm still here. D'you like 'em, George?

Georgia   They're high . . . I fell on my arse on the catwalk on my fifteenth birthday in a show in Tokyo wearing heels like that. So embarrassing.

Lana   You should try these on. You'd look great in these.

Georgia   Yeah, course I would.

Lana *doesn't even notice* **Georgia**'s *morose reply.* **Leon** *puts the DVD in and sits on the couch.*

Lana   Actually, the only thing I don't like about them, though, is this designer always makes 'em smaller and when I walk about in them, my feet really fucking hurt. D'you know what I mean, George?

Silence.

Georgia *watches* **Lana** *as* **Lana** *takes the shoes off and slumps on the couch between the boys as the film starts.*

Lights down.

Scene Five

House – night.

Lights up: it's late. **Leon** *is not around,* **Lana** *is on the couch watching TV alone.* **Aaron** *and* **Georgia** *are in bed.* **Aaron** *taps* **Georgia**. **Lana** *gradually listens more as things get louder.*

Aaron   Georgia? Are you awake?

Georgia   Yes, babe. What's wrong?

Aaron   I was just. Wondering. Do you think we could . . .
you know, d'you wanna . . . It's just it's been about ten
months since we last . . .

Georgia   Are you counting?

Aaron   No, course not, but, you know. I'm still a man. You
know, you still make me . . . you know.

Georgia   You're a man who gets 'you know' or I make you
'you know'?

Aaron   You do, babe.

Georgia   You barely touch me.

Aaron   What? I always wanna touch you.

Georgia   Not like that. I mean, like you don't hold my
hand like you used to, or stroke my arm when you're tired
any more, or do that thing where you used to put my hair
behind my ear so you could see my face.

Aaron   Don't I? I do.

Georgia   You don't.

Aaron   Babe, this has been tough for me too. One minute
I'm dating the coolest girl in the world, she becomes my
fiancée, she's funny, plays video games, reads comics, gets on
with everyone, used to be a model, and then it's all taken
away from me . . .

Georgia   From you? And now what? You're just with the
girl in the chair?

Aaron   That's not what I meant, babe. You hardly come
out. Two years later and you hardly come out. How can I do
those things you say I don't any more if you never come out?

Georgia   Because when I do, I feel like everyone's watching
me. I feel like everyone pities me, or that I'm an annoyance.
That we can't eat in a certain place, or watch a certain film

because of them having no wheelchair access, I feel like you look at other girls, girls like I used to be who walk around in the summer in semi-see-through summer dresses and G-strings. I feel like you're tense because you're looking around, waiting to see who's gonna be the first idiot to say something about the girl in the chair and you'll have to come to my defence. And mostly . . . mostly I feel like you don't want me there.

Aaron   What a load of shit. I want you everywhere. And I still want you, I want you right now.

Georgia   I don't want to right now.

Aaron *tries to control it, but sighs deeply, frustrated.*

Georgia   Why are you huffing?

Aaron   I don't know. Please . . . Georgia, can we just do something? Anything. I'm a man, I need sex.

Georgia   And I need my fucking legs. Looks like we've both lost.

Aaron   I know it's hard for a woman to get, but we're built differently. A woman could probably go for ever with a man that this happened to as long as the love was there.

Georgia   Is it there?

Aaron   Yes. But with men, the love can be there, but we still need the physical.

Georgia   So without it you'll leave? Is that it? Are men that shallow? Are you?

Aaron   Me, no, men, yes, well sometimes, but I just . . . I could break boards right now.

Lana *can hear the argument in the living room and tries not to listen but can't help it and scootches nearer.*

Georgia   Then go break one.

Aaron *jumps up and out of bed, putting his tracksuit on straight away.*

Georgia   Where are you going?

Aaron   I'm gonna go to one of the bathrooms and sort myself out. Then I'm gonna sleep in the downstairs bedroom.

Georgia   So is that what it's really about? Just a release? You just wanna cum? Well, there's a few other options. Why don't you take your pick with the one you're still actually happy with and we can stop talking about it and go to sleep. (*Mock sexy voice.*) 'I won't put up a fight.' (*Normal, angry.*) I can't.

Aaron   Stop saying shit like that . . . And you know what, I can't stop talking about it, because I'm being honest with you. I'm an adult. I love you, but I need a fucking sexual relationship.

Lana, *still on the couch, scootches even closer to the bedroom door.*

Georgia   We've done it.

Aaron   Not for ten months. And I waited until you were better . . . I waited until you were ready to do that. I never pressured you once after the accident, did I? Not once, and now you wanna mock me and make it about me just wanting a release . . . (*Calm now.*) You know what, partly you're right, anything right now, from 'you', would be good. It's not just a release. It's a release from you, babe, because I love you. I waited until you wanted to . . . But I thought after we did it, we would get back to normal . . . You're one of the lucky ones, you know . . .

Georgia   I'm lucky?

Aaron   In a way.

Georgia   How?

Aaron   You can still feel there.

Georgia   So?

Aaron   I've looked into it online. Do you know how many people lose all feeling?

Georgia   How many?

Aaron   A lot . . .

Georgia   It's not just about that, though. You're supposed to love me. Sex isn't everything.

Aaron   No, it's not, but it is something. And I do love you, but I feel like I've lost you. I feel like I don't always know how to connect with you any more, and I don't know, but I think that might help.

Georgia   I'm paralysed, Aaron, I don't exactly feel very sexy.

Pause.

Do you think about being with other girls?

Aaron   Sometimes . . .

Georgia   Who?

Pause.

Aaron   No one. Everyone. Just more about one thing than them, it's almost become primal. I wouldn't ever do anything though.

Georgia   We can do it if you want. If it'll keep you happy.

Aaron   You have to *want* to as well.

Pause. **Aaron** *opens the door, leaves the room.* **Georgia** *starts crying, leans back and turns off the light.* **Lana** *scootches back to her original position on the couch.* **Aaron** *doesn't notice.*

Scene Six

House – night.

Lana   Hey.

Aaron   Hey . . . what you doing up?

Lana   I was waiting for Jason to call. He didn't, so I just sat up watching films. I watched *Hurt Locker* and was about to put in *Avatar*.

Aaron   Fucking hell. Not planning on sleeping, then? I heard that's why James Cameron left Bigelow.

Lana   Why?

Aaron   She didn't like it in the hurt locker.

A beat. **Lana** *doesn't laugh.*

Aaron   Bad joke. Wrong time. Ignore it . . . Go to sleep, Lana.

Lana   I don't wanna miss the call if he does call.

Aaron   He's a dick, Lana, you're better off without him . . . Did you hear all that just then? In there?

Lana   All what? What? Well, vaguely. I wasn't listening really.

Aaron   Sorry.

Lana   No problem.

Aaron   Get some sleep, babe . . . Night.

Aaron *walks towards the living room door.*

Lana   Night. Oh and Aaron . . . if you do go to the downstairs bathroom. Can you please clean up properly? I slipped last time.

Aaron *nods and exits.* **Lana** *watches the TV.*

Lights down.

Scene Seven

House – day.

Lights up. It's a bright morning. **Leon** *is walking back and forth, in and out of the living room, as if he keeps forgetting things. He brings in the laptop, then charger, then paperwork, then coffee.* **Georgia**, *in the same clothes, looking slightly bedraggled, yawns, and goes through her same routine to get up: sit up, hand on chair, scootch left. She gets in*

*her chair and wheels into the living room near the couch and flicks the
TV on.*

Leon   It's alive . . .

Georgia   Morning. What you doing up here, haven't you
got cool things to design?

Leon   Took the day at home, there's this amazing technology
called a laptop, heard of it? Thought I'd do my work up here,
because Lana's out and the light's better up here. That and
Jessica Alba's on the lunchtime show. How are you? Haven't
seen you for a couple of days, was gonna give it until the end
of today then send in a search party.

Georgia   I'm fine. I just haven't felt like hanging out or
anything.

Leon   D'you need anything?

Georgia   Cup of tea would be good if that kettle is still hot.

Leon *comes over to the couch and sits next to* **Georgia***.*

Leon   No. Do *you* need anything? I can't imagine how tough
it must be and I know it gets you down, but recently you seem
different. I'm worried about you. Both of you. Not as simple
as it was in school, eh? So anything you need. Absolutely
anything you want, I'm here for you. We all are.

Georgia   Yeah.

Leon   We all love you. Especially Aaron. But I don't think
he likes the bedroom downstairs. It's cold, and there's
monsters down there.

Leon *leans forward and moves* **Georgia***'s hair behind her ear so he
can see her face.*

Georgia   I know . . . Called my dad yesterday, thought
I could go down there for a bit. He said it was just too much
with the chair and stuff and they may visit next month.

A beat.

Leon   That'll fly by . . . In the meantime . . . you want, I get.

Georgia   That tea would be good.

They smile at each other. The doorbell rings.

Leon   OK . . . That'll be the plumber, so I'll get that and make you a fresh tea. Be up in a sec.

Leon *exits. We hear him talking to someone downstairs. Then footsteps start coming up the stairs and the* **Plumber** *enters. He spots* **Georgia***, nods. Then starts looking around the room.*

Georgia   Can I help you at all?

Plumber   I'm . . . just . . . looking . . . for . . . your . . . bathroom.

Georgia   Excuse me?

Plumber   I'm . . . just . . . looking . . . for . . .

Georgia   I heard you . . . Why are you talking to me like that?

Plumber   Like . . . what?

Georgia   S-l-o-w-l-y and . . . loudly!

Plumber   Sorry, love I, um . . .

Georgia   It's back there.

The **Plumber** *goes back and into the bathroom and immediately starts fixing whatever he's been told to fix.* **Leon** *comes up, the doorbell goes again.* **Leon** *leaves again. More voices. More footsteps. A man walks in, looks at* **Georgia** *and makes a bee-line straight towards her.*

New Carer   Hi . . . Georgia Stark? I'm here for the interview to be your new carer. A Mr Aaron Jones called two days ago . . . and then a Lana Jefferies, yesterday . . . and than a Leon Welsh this morning.

Georgia   You should leave. I don't want a carer.

New Carer   OK, so why did they all call me?

Georgia   Because they're busybodies and they think they're helping me, but actually they're not. I don't need anyone else to carry me anywhere, I don't need anyone else I don't know, having to do things for me that I would do in private.

New Carer   Well, it's not that we want to. It's our job. So from what I've read from the report from the last carer . . . um, I forget her name, you still can't do a lot of things without assistance.

Georgia   I was out on my own modelling from the age of thirteen. I'll learn.

New Carer   Right. You also haven't attended physio in two months. You have to go to physio.

Georgia   Don't tell me what I have to do.

The **New Carer** *takes a deep breath, leans forward and touches her hand.*

New Carer   Look, Georgia . . .

Georgia   Don't act like you know me, and don't you ever touch me.

New Carer   Right, well, I guess we are done here, because I'm not prepared to have this.

Georgia   Have what? Have the girl in the wheelchair tell you to fuck off?

New Carer   Do you have respect for anyone?

Georgia   Not you.

New Carer   Do you ever think for a second about what people like me sacrifice in our lives to look after people like you, or why we do it?

Georgia   Because if you don't Daddy will cut off your trust fund money?

The **New Carer** *snaps and grabs* **Georgia** *by the collar.*

New Carer   Fuck you . . . fuck you. You have no idea what my life is like, and why I do this . . .

Leon, *who's heard the commotion, rushes into the room. He grabs the* **Carer** *and throws him down on to the ground, straddles him and goes to punch.*

Leon   What the hell do you think you're doing?

New Carer   I'm sorry, I'm sorry, I'm sorry . . . Please just let me go. Please, please . . .

Leon *gets up and steps back so the* **New Carer** *can stand, grab his things and leave. He pauses at the door.*

New Carer   I don't suppose there's any chance you could not mention this. It's just I've trained for so −

Leon   I'm gonna mention this to everyone I can. I'm gonna report you to the fucking astronauts on Mir if it means you don't get to work again.

New Carer   Please.

Leon   Get out!

He leaves. **Leon** *crouches down to* **Georgia**, *puts her hair behind her ear so he can talk to her, she stares at him.*

Georgia   Don't tell Aaron about this.

Leon   George.

Georgia   Promise me.

Leon   OK.

Silence.

Georgia   God, I was so rude. What is wrong with me? And I do need to go to physio, I haven't been in so long.

Leon   Why not? I thought you were . . . Do you want me to book an appointment for you?

Georgia *nods. The* **Plumber** *comes out of the bathroom.* **Georgia** *sighs.*

Georgia   I need a shot of rum or something.

Plumber   Let her drink, do ya? That safe?

Georgia   Excuse me?

Leon   What did you just say? 'Do we let her drink?' What the fuck do you mean, 'let her'?

Plumber   I didn't mean nothing by it. Sorry, mate.

Georgia   You can talk to me you know, being in the chair doesn't affect my ability to hear, or communicate. Look. You . . . are . . . a . . . twit.

Plumber   I'm really sorry. I just meant cos of like drink driving, with the . . . chair . . . and . . . Hundred and twenty quid, mate.

Leon *fishes out the money and gives it to the* **Plumber**, *who does his invoice and leaves quickly.* **Leon** *crouches back down.*

Leon   What a day. I'll tell you what, forget work. Let's take you to physio, then go out and get lunch, maybe watch an afternoon film or something.

Georgia   Isn't the work you have to do important?

Leon   Yes . . . yes, it is. But being behind one day isn't gonna kill me, and I can catch up later.

Georgia   What if I can't get an appointment?

Leon   We'll go get lunch and a movie anyway. As long as you don't get the mixed popcorn. That really fucks with my head, either get sweet or salt, mixed is just senseless, absolutely senseless.

Georgia   What if there's no chair access?

Leon   Then we'll find a place that has it.

Georgia   But . . .

Leon   Georgia. Stop making excuses. I'm taking you out.

A beat.

Georgia   I need a shower.

Silence. The two friends look around awkwardly.

I guess it's not gonna get much more awkward than this. So I'll just say it. Will you help me?

Leon *nods, and pushes the chair into the bathroom. They both stand in silence a moment.*

Leon   OK so . . . what do I do?

Lights down.

Scene Eight

House – evening.

Lights up. **Lana** *in casuals, sits on the couch watching TV in the living room. She's been crying and is still on the phone.*

Lana   So when am I gonna see you, then? But I thought you were . . . OK, and can I come, then? Oh . . . Who's that? The person that just told you to hang up? Who's Caitlyn? Have I? I don't remember meeting her. Well, why are you with her? Oh, OK, but when . . .

He's hung up. **Lana** *sits for a moment then breaks down crying. We stay with her. She then gets up, goes to the fridge, grabs a tray, piles it with food and goes back to the couch. Starts to eat. We watch her eat until* **Aaron** *walks in. He throws off his jacket and stands in front of the TV and smiles.*

Aaron   Hey. Look what I've got. Premiere tickets. Georgia!

He walks towards the bedroom, opens the door, and peeps in. No one is there. He comes back out.

Aaron   Where's Georgia?

Lana   She's with Leon.

Aaron   Oh . . . Did the new carer come?

Lana   Dunno. Bathroom's fixed.

Aaron   Cool. Did they say where . . .

Lana (*still sniffing*)   There's a note on the table.

Aaron *double-takes at* **Lana** *then walks to the table and reads the note. He checks his watch.*

Aaron   They need to hurry it up, I wanna take her to this premiere. What's wrong with you? You've been crying? Is it Cerberus again?

Lana   I think he's seeing another girl. I know he is. People tell me all the time I should leave him. I always try to think the best about people. I guess I'm just naive.

Aaron   I'm not being funny, Lana, but how many chances can you give him? It should have ended the first week when you found that tiny thong in his living room and he said it was his mum's and she left it when she came to visit. I mean, fuck me, not even Jordan, or whatever she calls herself these days, wears pants that small, let alone someone's mum. And if his mum does, I wanna meet her.

Lana *stuffs more ice cream in her mouth.*

Lana   Want some ice cream?

Aaron   Flavour?

Lana   *Dulce leche.*

Aaron   Yes. Yes, I do.

He grabs a spoon from the table, wipes it and goes to sit down with **Lana**.

Aaron   What's on TV?

Lana   Nothing? What did you do today?

Aaron   Paperwork, all day. Had a nice lunch at this little sandwich bar off Dean Street. You?

Lana   Another boring shift in the café. Was hoping to get an audition for this Channel 4 thing, but I heard they offered it to that girl from *Dr Who*.

Aaron   Who?

Lana   Yeah.

Aaron   No . . . Who? Billie Piper?

Lana   No, the other one.

Aaron   Freema Agyeman?

Lana   No. The ginger one.

Aaron   Catherine Tate?

Lana   The latest one.

Aaron   Matt Smith?

Lana   Not the doctor, the girl, the assistant . . . The stripper. Karen Gillan, I think her name is.

Aaron   There's a stripper in *Dr Who*? I gotta start watching.

Lana   No! Not really. She's not a stripper, her character was a kissogram.

Aaron   Which equals stripper.

Lana   Exactly . . . Anyway, it's not real and she got the part I wanted an audition for.

Aaron   Yeah . . . she's hot.

Lana   Aaron!

Aaron   Sorry, Lana, I wish you'd got it.

Lana   Do you think you can get one of the agents at your work to take me on?

Aaron   Dunno, Lan – I've only been there a few months . . .

The door slams, and footsteps start up the stairs. **Leon** *comes in, carrying* **Georgia**.

Leon   Hey, guys.

Georgia   Hello.

Lana   Hiya.

Aaron   Hello, babe.

Leon *transfers* **Georgia** *to* **Aaron**. *They kiss, then he places her on the couch.*

Aaron   You guys have a good day?

Leon   Yeah. I think we need a chair lift.

Georgia   You saying I'm heavy?

Leon   Um . . . let me go get the chair.

Georgia   You cheeky bastard.

Leon *leaves.*

Aaron   So what did you guys do?

Georgia   Leon took me to physio, then we went and had lunch at that new sushi place . . . then the cinema to watch . . . Lana, what's wrong with you? Have you been crying?

Aaron   Mothman.

Georgia   Again . . .

Aaron   I can't believe you went out, did all that, why didn't you wait till Saturday we could have all gone?

Georgia   It wasn't planned. It just kind of . . .

Leon *enters carrying the chair.*

Leon   This chair is heavy. Think I'm gonna need the chair lift. This place isn't very practical for you, George.

He places the chair in a position where **Georgia** *can get in it. She does.*

Georgia   Yes, we know this. But it's mine.

Leon   Yeah but . . . Lana, what's wrong with you? Have you been –

Georgia/Aaron   *Golem!*

Leon   Again.

Aaron   So listen, babe, I've got those tickets to the premiere. You wanna get ready so we can go. We need to get there by six thirty.

Georgia   I'm not sure, Aaron.

Aaron   Why not? You just went out all day?

Georgia   Yeah, but that was just to lunch and cinema . . . with a friend.

Aaron   For God's sake . . . And I wanna take you to a premiere. Am I not your friend? I'm your fucking fiancé.

Silence.

Leon   We're gonna leave you guys alone for a bit. Come on, Lana.

They leave into **Lana***'s room and sit down on the bed, switching on the TV in there.*

Georgia   Do you have to talk to me like that in front of everyone?

Aaron   I just can't deal with this any more. I wish I could just have my Georgia back. The girl I grew up with, fell in love with.

Georgia   I'm here, but you're not happy. You don't actually want me. You probably never knew that yourself. You want the mould I was made from. The aesthetics. People talk about me not handling being in this chair. You can't handle it.

Aaron   Right now, you're right, I'm fed up with waiting for you to decide when you're ready, all the while forgetting about everyone else around you. This is not just about you. You know what I'm gonna do? I'm gonna go out tonight, I'm gonna get drunk, chat to people, have fun, laugh, eat popcorn, not mixed, flirt, and see where the night takes me.

Georgia *starts to cry.* **Aaron** *shouts, frustrated, at the top of his voice and walks out, leaving* **Georgia** *there.*

Lights down.

Scene Nine

House, **Lana***'s room – evening.*

Lights up: **Georgia** *is now in her room, crying.* **Lana** *and* **Leon** *sit on her bed watching TV. They glance at each other as they hear the downstairs door slam and a car start.*

Lana   That was a big row. Do you think they'll be OK?

Leon   I don't know. I've never seen them like this.

Lana   I've been thinking about moving out. I like them and everything and I haven't known them as long as you, obviously, but I feel like I do too much, you know, for Georgia. I mean I don't mind but . . . well, I guess I do a bit. I reckon a fifth of my time is taken up helping her when I could be going to acting classes or . . . Oh God, that's so mean. That's mean, isn't it? She gives me cheap rent, she's been so kind and I . . . I just feel like I'm walking on eggshells recently. Do you know what I mean?

Leon   It's hard for me to really say too much, cos I've known them so long, and I'd do anything for Georgia, for both of them. You didn't know her long before this, she was the coolest girl in the world. Everyone wanted her, everyone liked her, girls wanted to be her and guys wanted to be with her.

Lana   You as well?

Leon   Nah, she was with Aaron . . . She's always just been my best friend, but to answer your question. Yes, I know what you mean . . . (*A beat.*) I should go, I'm gonna check on George and then catch up on some work I didn't do today.

He stands. **Lana** *quickly stands in front of him holding his shoulders.*

Lana   Oh God, please don't tell her what I just said. I didn't mean it in a bad way. I feel like such a bitch . . .

Leon   It's fine, I'm not gonna say anything. It's tiring, I get that too. Especially when you're around, you feel compelled to help and consequently get less done. Don't worry.

Lana   Thanks so much.

He grips her shoulders as well.

Leon   You can let go of my shoulders now.

Lana *looks at him then leans in and kisses him flush on the mouth.* **Leon** *backs off.*

Leon   Whoa!

Lana   Sorry, I just . . . What with . . . it's just you're so nice . . . to me. The kind of guy I should be with and . . . Oh God, I'm sorry.

Leon   Stop saying sorry, it's fine. We're mates, OK?

Lana   OK . . . I'm so embarrassed.

Leon   Don't be.

He gives **Lana** *a cuddle and then exits, heading to* **Georgia**'s *room.* **Lana** *stands frozen, berates herself quietly then slumps down on her bed.* **Leon** *knocks on* **Georgia**'s *door.*

Georgia   Come in.

He enters. Footsteps up the stairs. **Aaron** *comes up and knocks on* **Lana**'s *door and enters when she answers.*

Lana   Yeah. I said I'm sorry.

Aaron   What?

Lana   Aaron.

Aaron   Listen. Lana . . . do you wanna come to the premiere? I feel like if I go on my own I might do something I regret, but with a mate there, who knows me and Georgia, I'll be . . .

You know, if I get drunk, which is what I feel like doing . . .
Just in case, and I wouldn't wanna . . . I love her.

Lana   I know. You sure . . . ? Seriously?

Aaron   Yeah. Leon said he won't go on principle . . . And
I know how much you wanted to. So if you can get ready in
five mins, then yeah, seriously.

Lana   OK . . . oh my God, I'm so excited.

Aaron   I'll wait in the car.

Lana   Cool.

Aaron *leaves and goes downstairs.* **Lana** *does a celebratory dance.*

Lana   Yes!

Lights down.

Scene Ten

House – evening.

Lights up. **Leon** *moves* **Georgia***'s chair to the end of the bed. He
comes back round and sits next to her on the bed. She sits up.*

Leon   Hey.

Georgia   Hey.

Leon   You alright?

Georgia (*sudden shock*)   Oh my God! I can't move my legs.

Leon   Seriously . . . You know what I mean.

Georgia   I'll be fine.

Leon   It'll get better, you know . . . I promise.

Georgia   When?

Nothing.

Part of me understands what he means. I'm not me. You know that, he knows that, and the worst thing is, I know it. I don't know where I am . . . I haven't been me since the accident . . . I never realised how much of my personality was in my legs. Never thought so much of me would walk away with . . . my walk . . . I never thought about it at all. You never do. I never thought about giving money to any sort of charity because I was never in the situation. That's how it is, though – you walk past those people and see them as an annoyance . . . But now I just want everyone to put money in the bucket so they can cure me . . . Just me . . . I don't give a fuck about anyone else . . . I just wanna walk again . . . to the shop to get milk, for a bus, to get the remote. Anywhere. I just want my legs back.

Leon *hugs her, then* **Georgia** *lies back down.*

Leon   Get some sleep, babe. Apologise to Aaron in the morning. Get everything back on track?

Georgia   Yeah.

Leon   Good. I'm gonna do some work downstairs, you need anything . . . Anything, you just shout me.

He gets up, leaves the room and exits. **Georgia** *waits for a moment, thinking, then turns out the light.*

Lights down.

Scene Eleven

House – night.

Lights up. We let the place settle a moment, then footsteps up the stairs. **Aaron** *and* **Lana** *walk in, drunk.*

Lana   Shhhh. Don't make noise. Everyone's sleeping.

Aaron   How are they sleeping already?

Lana   It's four in the morning.

Aaron   Really? Then you shush.

Lana   You shush.

Aaron   I am shushing. That film was so good.

Lana   I had such a good time, I couldn't believe when Shia actually looked at me.

Aaron   Don't know if he was looking at you or the guy choking behind you . . .

Lana   It was me.

Aaron   The guy was getting the Heimlich by Shia's girlfriend, he . . .

Lana (*shouts*)   Just let me have it please!

Aaron   Shushh.

Lana   Shushh.

They start laughing. That wakes up **Georgia***. She sits up in her bed and stretches, then starts rubbing her tummy. She hasn't heard them yet, and keeps rubbing her tummy while they talk. They keep talking, slumping on the couch.* **Aaron** *takes off his jacket.*

Aaron   OK. You can have it . . . I thought Penelope Cruz was giving me the eye.

Lana   Now that I won't give you . . .

Aaron   You're right. I can dream.

Aaron *stands.*

Aaron   Anyway, I'm gonna go to bed.

Lana   Up here or downstairs?

Aaron   Don't know yet.

Lana   Listen.

She stands. Throws her arms around him, kisses him drunkenly on the lips.

A moment between them as she pulls away, knowing that shouldn't have happened. She pats his chest.

Thank you, so much, for taking me tonight . . . I'm gonna go to my room now.

She turns to walk away, but **Aaron** *is still holding her hand. She turns back, they stand at arm's length. Staring at each other.* **Aaron** *pulls* **Lana** *back gently.*

Lana   Don't, Aaron . . .

He kisses her.

Aaron, we can't . . .

He kisses her again. It lingers. It starts off slowly then becomes more frantic, as they fall on the couch pulling at each other's clothes. Breathing heavily, they roll off the couch on to the floor. This noise makes **Georgia**, *who is still sitting up, turn on her nightlight.*

The lights go down on **Aaron** *and* **Lana**, *and we stay on* **Georgia** *as her lights rise slightly as she listens. We hear a few sounds, muffled noises through the door.* **Georgia** *can hear this and listens intently, she covers her mouth in shock, then vomits. She goes to get into her chair and leans to the left for her regular routine of getting up, but falls out of the bed, clunk, on to the floor: the chair's not there. It's still at the end of the bed where* **Leon** *left it. The lights come up on* **Aaron** *and* **Lana**. *They stand, breathe deeply, fix themselves.*

Lana   Did you hear something?

Aaron   Where?

Lana   I thought I heard a bang.

Aaron   Nope.

He paces, already regretting what he's done. **Lana** *stands, the two face each other.*

Aaron   I'm so sorry.

Lana   Don't be stupid . . . We both did it. I feel horrible, though. I'm a girl who gets cheated on, I should know better.

Aaron   How the fuck do you think I feel?

Lana   Well . . . I know. I didn't make you do it.

Aaron   I know . . . I know . . . I'm sorry . . . Fuck!

Lana   Shhhh. I'll get the morning-after pill tomorrow.

Aaron   Yeah . . .

He sits on the couch and puts his head in his hands.

Lana   Oh God, why did that just happen? Are you gonna tell her? You're gonna tell her, aren't you? Georgia?

Nothing.

Aaron?

Aaron   I don't know . . . No . . . I'm not planning to, no. Why? You're not, are you?

Lana *shakes her head. Silence.*

Lana   Do you . . . Do you have feelings for me? Or was it just a, you know . . . I'm cool either way. I'm splitting with Jason anyway . . . so it'd just be good to know . . . where we, where I, stand . . . you know, with you.

Aaron   We don't stand anywhere, babe. I'm with Georgia.

Lana   Of course. I was . . . I know I seem needy but I'm not, just if you did like me, we'd probably have to move out, which I'm thinking about doing anyway . . . and . . . well, whatever, either way I'm good with whatever.

Nothing.

So what do we do now?

Nothing.

I'm gonna go to bed then . . .

She waits a moment, then exits off to her dark room, takes off her dress and gets into bed. **Aaron** *stays still. Eventually he stands. Walks to* **Georgia**'s *bedroom. He puts his hand on the door, is about to open it, then exits towards the front door. We hear a car start and drive away.*

Lights down.

Scene Twelve

House – morning.

Lights up. **Georgia** *is laid out on the floor in the same place she was last night, clambers up, trying to pull herself up on to the bed, but can't. She's been crying, we watch her try for a bit, then rest. In the living room* **Lana**, *in her usual trackie bottoms, hair pulled tight back, no make-up, eating, is sitting on the couch watching TV.* **Leon** *walks into the living room, dumps some work on the table and starts having a drink.*

Leon   Morning.

Lana   Morning.

Leon   Pwoor! What's that smell?

Lana   What smell?

Leon   You can't smell that?

Lana   Nope.

Leon   Like shit . . . or puke, or puke and shit? Is the toilet blocked up again? . . . I knew that plumber was useless.

Lana   It's not blocked up.

Leon   How was last night?

Lana   What?

Leon   The premiere?

Lana   Oh yeah. Good.

Leon   Was the film great? Tell me it wasn't great . . . It was great, wasn't it?

Lana   Yeah, it was really good. It was . . . great.

Leon   Fuck, I knew it . . . Where's Aaron? Did he like it?

Lana   Dunno.

Leon   What's wrong with you?

Lana   Nothing . . . He went out early, didn't say anything, just left.

Leon   Where's Georgia?

Lana   Dunno. She hasn't come out of her room.

Leon   What?

He walks over to **Georgia**'s *room, then reels back.*

Leon   Fucking hell. The smell's coming from here. Georgia!

Lana *jumps up off the couch, and immediately starts panicking.*

Lana   Oh my God, she's dead, she heard and she killed herself and she's in there and . . .

Leon   What? Heard what?

Lana   Oh my God, check if she's OK.

Leon *bursts into the room to find* **Georgia** *on the floor. He rushes over to her.* **Lana** *stands apprehensive in the living room.*

Leon   Georgia . . . Georgia.

Georgia   Leon.

Leon   Are you OK?

Georgia   I fell out of bed.

Leon   Do you need an ambulance?

Georgia   No . . . no, I'm fine.

Leon   Why didn't you call out for one of us.

Georgia   I didn't want to.

Leon   Why? Cos you'd rather lie on the floor . . . ?

Georgia   Because I've fucking shit myself, OK, and I threw up.

Pause.

Leon   Oh, George . . . We'll sort it. Lana, get in here.

Lana *comes in.* **Georgia** *sees her.*

Lana   Is she OK?

Georgia *flips out. Clawing and reaching for* **Lana**.

Georgia   Fuck off. You fucking whore . . . You fucking bitch, I'm gonna fucking kill you. You fucking whore.

Lana   Oh my God! I'm sorry . . . I never meant . . .

Georgia   I don't wanna hear it. I heard enough last night, you fucking slag. Get out . . . Get out, get out, you whore, how could you do that . . . ? Why did you do that . . ?

Leon   What's going on?

Georgia   She fucked him . . . She fucked him . . . Why did she fuck him? Why can't he love me? I hate you.

Lana *leaves, rushes into her room and starts packing stuff.*

Georgia   I hate her . . . I hate him . . . Why did they do that . . . ?

Leon *rushes to* **Georgia**'s *chair, brings it around and puts her in it. She sits there, crying.* **Leon** *then rushes to* **Lana**'s *room, pushing the door open.*

Leon   What did you do?

Lana *has finished packing. She walks passed him, he grabs her.*

Lana   I didn't mean to, but I can't take it back so I'm going. If you want me to say I wish I hadn't, fine, I wish I hadn't, and I really mean that, but it's done and now I have to go. I'm sorry . . . I'll call and arrange to have my stuff picked up.

Leon   Where are you going?

Lana   I dunno.

Leon   Don't go to Jason's.

A beat.

Lana   You know . . . I actually won't . . . Thanks. Caring until the end. You do anything for your friends, don't you?

Leon   That's what friends are supposed to be for.

Lana   Wish I had more friends like you. Though I don't suppose we can be friends any more, can we?

Pause.

Leon   No. Probably not.

Silence.

Lana *hangs her head. She regrets it more than ever now. It wasn't worth losing all of this.*

Lana   Tell Georgia I *really* am sorry.

Leon *nods. And* **Lana** *is gone.* **Leon** *goes back to* **Georgia**. *Stands for a moment looking at her. She looks up at him, a mess.* **Leon** *sighs.*

Leon   Come on. Let's give you a bath.

Lights down.

Scene Thirteen

House – morning.

Lights up. **Georgia** *lies on top on her bed wrapped in a towel, and with a towel round her hair as well.* **Leon** *sits on the couch in the living room on the phone.*

Leon   I'm just saying . . . No, I really don't think you should. Just leave it a few days . . . Of course she's upset, you fucked our housemate. You couldn't have done a random? It had to be Lana? Lana? Everything is messed up. You shouldn't have fucked anyone . . . Yes, I know I'm not an angel and yes,

I know the man code, but it's fucking Georgia, man . . . When you started going out with her, man code went out the window. She's . . . she was our best friend, and friends always come first, you know how I feel about that . . . Alright. I'll call you and let you know when's good. Alright, you call me . . . Yes, I'll talk to her, but I don't know what I can do . . . OK . . . Alright, mate. Bye.

He goes back and sits with **Georgia** *in her bedroom.*

Leon   So Lana's brother is gonna come and pick up all her stuff on Saturday. And Aaron is gonna stay away for a few days unless you wanna see him or speak to him beforehand. You OK? D'you wanna get dressed?

Georgia   Stay with me.

Leon   OK.

Georgia   I love you, ya know.

Leon   I love you too.

Georgia   I don't know what I'd do without you.

Leon   Same here.

Georgia   Best friends since we were kids . . . Do you think I'm pretty?

Leon   Course you are. If you're thinking that's why he . . . He was just a twat.

Georgia   No. Do *you* think I'm pretty?

Leon   Yeah. As much as a friend can.

Georgia   Do you think I'm sexy?

Leon   What?

Georgia   Just . . . people don't look at me in that way any more. I'm just wondering if I still am?

Leon   Yeah. Course you are. Aaron thinks you are.

Georgia   No, he doesn't . . . He doesn't.

Long silence.

Leon *sits, made a bit uncomfortable by the questions.* **Georgia** *unwraps the towel from her body and lies there in her underwear.*

Georgia   Make love to me?

Leon *stands.* **Georgia** *leans up on her elbows.*

Leon   What? No . . . What?

Georgia   I want you to make love to me.

Leon   No . . . that's what Aaron's for.

Georgia   He just wants a release. I want to be wanted. Haven't you ever wanted me? Don't you want me when you see me lying here? Like a guy wants a girl? Isn't there . . . that primal instinct in you? Something that just makes you want to take me . . . Because that's what I used to get. I could walk into any room and men wanted me, I could feel their eyes, burning into me, their thoughts stripping me, and I didn't want or need any of their chauvinistic, sexist objectification. You know why? Because I felt good about myself. I felt like it was my choice. But I never knew how much I needed it until it wasn't there. We all need it a bit on some level, and now I'm here, paralysed, begging you to have me because I need to know that people, someone, still feels that . . . I need to feel something, because where I was is just a chair. People open doors for the chair, talk to the chair, smile at the chair – and me . . . I'm just . . . invisible.

Leon   I can't do it.

Georgia   Tell me the truth. You must have wanted me at some point? I saw you staring at me when you gave me a bath, trying to look away. Have you ever wanted me like that?

Pause.

Leon   . . . It was a long time ago and I would have never, never have acted on it, betrayed myself, you, or Aaron because you're friends and . . .

Georgia   And anything for friends right? Right? Whatever they need?

Pause.

Georgia   Well I need this . . .

Leon   I can't do that. It's not right . . .

Georgia   Why? Because of Aaron? There is no Aaron any more. He shagged our housemate and ruined everything . . .

Leon   I'm not getting back at him . . . He's our mate . . . Maybe if . . .

Georgia   It's not about revenge. He doesn't want me . . . Not like you did, not like you do, like you've thought about, what it'd be like with me. I can still feel, Leon . . .

Leon   What are you saying? I can't do this . . . You're . . .

Georgia   What? Paralysed?

Leon   No!

Georgia   That's all I am, right? Even you can't see past that to me any more? I wanna be more than that. I'm still me. I still want to be me . . . Yes, I'm intelligent, yes, I had a career, two careers, yes I could pick and choose men back when I was working and yes, I still have or could have all of that, except one. And that's what I want . . . I still want to be wanted, I did then and I do now.

Leon   You'll find someone who . . .

Georgia   I want you.

Leon   Stop. We're just friends . . . I . . .

Georgia   Please. For me . . . if you really love me, if you really see me as the friend you say you do, then do this for me. But not as a mercy fuck and not because I'm here baring everything I have left to you but because you want me. Because you secretly always have, because you still do. You can imagine my legs wrapped around you if you want. I just need to know that someone still desires me . . . wants to make love to me . . .

Leon *leans forward and kisses her, she kisses back. He leans her back gently on the bed.*

Lights down.

Scene Fourteen

House – afternoon.

Lights up. **Leon** *sits on the side of the bed, putting his clothes on.* **Georgia** *is now under the sheets. He stands.* **Georgia** *grips his arm.*

Georgia   You don't hate me, do you?

Leon   Course not . . . I could never hate you. It was great, little weird at first, but great.

Georgia   And we're still friends, right?

Leon   Course we are. Nothing could ever change that. I'll be back in a bit, call if you need me.

Leon *walks out of the bedroom and closes the door.* **Georgia** *settles for a nap.* **Leon** *walks to the couch and sits down. He stares into space, stoic. His face changes, sombre, and he holds his head in his hands.*

Nothing will ever be the same, and he knows it. We hold on him and then . . .

Lights down.

Scene Fifteen

Bar – day.

Lights up. The background noise hum of people talking. The stage has been cleared, the furniture moved around, one couch is joined by another.

A table in the middle. **Aaron** *and* **Lana***, both looking different, younger, fresh, sit around on opposite sides, waiting with coffees.*

Lana   What do you think she'll say?

Aaron   She'll be fine. Georgia's cool. There's not another girl like her. She was fine when you became my flatmate. Admittedly that was only two weeks ago, but no one knew she'd get this house, but three big contracts and that was it. We'll all get cheap rent, helping with the rest of the mortgage and it'll be a laugh. She's already said yes, it's just about meeting you properly.

Lana   I mean, I won't be there a lot, because I'll be auditioning and filming and stuff, but a place to hang my hat when I'm in London would be great.

Leon *walks in. Greets* **Aaron***.*

Leon   Hey

Aaron   Hey, man. This is Alanis. The girl that had just moved in. This is Leon.

Lana   Lana. Heard so much about you, nice to meet you finally.

Leon   Leon. Nice to meet you. Where's George?

Aaron   Two minutes.

Leon *sits.*

Leon   So what do you do? And is it Alanis like the singer?

Lana   Yeah, but I hate it. That's why I use Lana . . . I'm an actress.

Leon   Oh, sweet. Have I seen you on TV?

Lana   Bits maybe, nothing major.

Aaron *stands.* **Georgia** *has walked in. Tall, beautiful, stunning, hair down, very natural make-up, looking every bit as amazing as we imagined she would and better, smiling from ear to ear. The sound dims* *as many men and indeed women watch her as she walks over to our guys. She hugs and kisses* **Aaron**, *then hugs* **Leon**.

Georgia   Hey . . . sorry I'm late, guys, traffic was killer. (*To* **Lana**.) Hiya, I'm Georgia. So nice to meet you.

Lana   Lana. Nice to meet you too.

Georgia   Aaron said you were pretty.

Lana   Me pretty? You're amazing.

Georgia   Thank you.

Lana   And possibly the only girlfriend I know that wouldn't be straight round if their boyfriend got a female flatmate.

Georgia   I trust him . . . Plus no one else will have him, wish they would. Might give me the night off.

They laugh. **Georgia** *sits next to* **Aaron**. *We see from their body language that they are so in love.*

Georgia   Listen, I'm so sorry I messed up all your plans, I know you've just moved down, but the house thing was quite short notice, so you're more than welcome to come and join us if you want. It's five bedrooms so it's fine for you to stay.

Lana   How much would I . . .

Georgia   Don't worry about that now, we'll sort something out. Do you guys want another coffee?

Leon   I'll get 'em . . .

Aaron   Grande latte.

Lana   Skinny mocha latte.

Georgia   Just regular tea. Thanks.

Leon *walks off.*

Lana   I love your shoes. Where did you get 'em?

Georgia   I did a show in New York and the designer gave 'em to me. I can get you some if you want.

Lana   Oh my God . . . That'd be great. What's it like? Modelling?

Georgia   I don't love it, it's OK. Parents hate it, cos I did so well at school. Dad wanted me to be a barrister, I think. Half did it to get away from them . . . I read books most of the time, and stay away from the bitchy ones, but it's fun.

Lana   Aaron. You were right. She is awesome. I need to pee, excuse me.

She gets up and leaves. **Georgia** *and* **Aaron** *are alone.*

Georgia   She seems alright.

Aaron   Yeah, she's cool, bit excitable.

Georgia   But nice . . . and I'm awesome, am I?

Aaron   You know you are, the coolest fucking girl in the whole world.

Georgia   Is that my official title? Cos I may get it tattooed.

Aaron   Yep.

Georgia   Is that all I am, baby? Cool?

Aaron   Nope . . . you are the sexiest, most beautiful, funniest, kindest girl ever known to humankind, and I love you.

Georgia   I love you too. What do you love about me?

Aaron *whispers in her ear. She smiles flirtatiously, kisses him on the lips.*

Georgia   Naughty . . . Yeah . . . and what else?

Aaron *whispers in her ear again. She smiles and play-hits him.*

Georgia   Behave!

Aaron   Oh, did you get my text about Leon's surprise party?

Georgia *looks for her phone.*

Georgia   Sugar! Where's my phone? I must have left it in the car . . .

Aaron   Leave it.

Georgia   I need it, babe, I'll be back in a sec . . . So anyway, you were saying . . . ?

Aaron   Saying what? About the party . . . ?

Georgia   No, before that, you were still telling me what you love about me . . .

She stands, starts to walk towards the door, getting further away as **Aaron** *talks. His voice getting steadily louder.*

Aaron   Oh yeah . . . I love your eyes . . . nose . . . mouth . . . lips . . . hips . . . laugh . . . belly, bum . . . (*Shouts.*) Oh, and those legs. How could I ever forget those legs?

Georgia *smiles and steps out of the bar.* **Leon** (*with drinks*) *and* **Lana** *approach* **Aaron** *as we hear the sound of screeching tyres from outside and a hard thud. The other three look up concerned.*

Black.

Those Legs

Notes on rehearsal and staging, drawn from workshops with the writer held at the National Theatre, November 2010

Noel spoke to two young women who had become paralysed and they both described the way in which people's interaction is affected by seeing a person in a wheelchair. Their experience was that people speak to the chair, people open the door for the chair – they see the chair, not the person.

This prompted a process of self-analysis in Noel. He wanted to explore his own prejudices and behaviour honestly. Although he believes in equality, and was raised to treat everybody the same, he started thinking perhaps there are instances where he doesn't live up to this ideal. This line of thought was the genesis of the play.

Ways to Begin Work on the Play

THE PREVIOUS CIRCUMSTANCES

It has been two years since the accident. As the First Carer states, Georgia will go through 'stages of mourning'. As a group, plot a timeline for the last two years.

- When did she come out of hospital?

- How often did Aaron visit?

- When did Lana move in?

- When did Georgia go/stop going to physio? And so on.

THE IMMEDIATE CIRCUMSTANCES

The play opens mid-conversation between Georgia and her Carer. It is important to establish exactly what has just been said before, and at what emotional temperature.

To make the conversation in the opening scene valid, we need to know what they've been saying for the last three months.

They have to have an existing relationship so that it is real and doesn't sound like exposition.

A useful exercise would be to improvise Georgia and the Carer spending time together in the flat: over lunch, the Carer doing Georgia's ironing, etc.

- How formal or informal is the Carer with Georgia?
- How aggressive or friendly is Georgia with the Carer?

Perhaps improvise a good moment where they get on well together.

Character

Ask each character to read the character descriptions aloud and discuss them.

Explore the characters by posing questions and discussing the answers in detail. Allow the actors space to discover answers for themselves.

GEORGIA

Does Georgia want a carer?

A carer is a constant reminder of her disability, but without one she'd be alone a lot.

Why doesn't Georgia refurbish her house to make her life easier, for example by getting a stair-lift?

Does she want others to look after her? Does she crave that interaction?

What is her concept of 'normality'?

She had only just bought the house when the accident happened. How long had she lived here previously, when she was able to walk round the house?

Why won't Georgia sell the house? Is it perhaps a statement of her independence and achievements?

How long have Georgia and Aaron been engaged?

When did they plan to marry?

How is this affected by her being in the chair?

What has happened between Georgia and her parents since the accident?

Does Georgia feel any jealousy towards Lana before Lana sleeps with Aaron?

Has Georgia wanted to have sex with Aaron in the last ten months?

What causes her to reject him?

What does sex mean for Georgia?

Does Georgia enjoy her interaction with her second Carer? No one has been rude to her for two years!

Why won't she go to the premiere?

Why does Georgia want to sleep with Leon so much?

AARON

How much does the chair affect Aaron?

Has he accepted the change?

How much have they discussed the accident before what we see in the play?

Why is it coming up now?

Does Aaron want to talk about it?

Aaron and Georgia haven't had sex for ten months. Why does Aaron feel he needs to ask permission from Georgia to have sex?

Is he frightened that he is losing her?

Has he tried to have sex with her before during those ten months?

What physical contact do they have in bed? Do they cuddle?

What does sex mean for Aaron?

Why does the premiere matter so much to Aaron?

What was a typical Saturday night for Aaron three years ago?

What did Aaron and Georgia do on their first date?

LANA

When did the relationship between Lana and Georgia emerge? (Lana had just moved into Georgia's house when the accident happened.)

Did Lana visit Georgia in hospital?

How does Lana feel about Georgia?

Why does Lana sleep with Aaron?

Why can't Lana be alone?

LEON

Has he always loved Georgia? (Perhaps her seduction of him is more interesting if he hasn't.)

Who is Leon most loyal to?

How does Leon cope with confrontation?

Why does Leon sleep with Georgia?

Does he want to? Is it for her or for him?

Does he enjoy it?

Can Leon lie?

CARER ONE

Does she/he enjoy her/his job?

Although she/he uses 'carer-speak', directors needn't necessarily portray this Carer as a baddie. It is in the power of the interpretation to make her/him warm or cool.

CARER TWO

What are the motives for the Second Carer's behaviour?

What has happened in his past to lead to this?

What has happened today to lead to this?

There could be a moment for an ad-lib with Leon as Carer Two comes into the space to indicate his mood. For example, 'I've had a nightmare with the traffic . . . '

PLUMBER

How educated is the Plumber?

How old is the Plumber?

What is his/her experience of disabled people?

Playing a Scene

Within these scenes large topics are being raised. Ask your actors how many times they think they have said certain things before. For example, on page 172, Georgia says to Aaron, 'Look at me.' Does she say that to him a lot? Or is this the first time she is daring to say it? This will colour the actor's thought process and how they deliver the line.

Examine the subtext of key lines. On page 171, Georgia says to Aaron, 'Why don't you help me?' This is an interesting line as it seems to mean more than what she actually says. It could mean, 'Why don't you love me?' or 'You seem to resent helping me,' or 'I feel like I'm losing you.' Discuss the meanings of key lines; try to be specific and pin the subtext down.

The reactions of the actors should be innocent and natural. Nothing should feel premeditated or pointed.

Be specific in the execution of any stage direction. For example, on page 194. '*Georgia waits for a moment thinking, then turns out the light.*' What is she thinking about?

It is important to find the moments of lightness within this dark play and within Georgia. When is Georgia joking, happy, relaxed?

Work out the endings of any broken lines. For example,

Georgia   . . . And yeah you guys do help. I just . . . I'm sorry. (page 172)

What is Georgia going on to say after 'I just…?' If the actor knows specifically what they're going to say it will inform their thought process and delivery.

The Play in Performance

Noel hopes that he has written an uncompromising play which presents Georgia's challenge in a way which is clear, sympathetic and full of truth. He hopes that seeing his play in performance will provoke questions in the audience: each character should inspire a debate. We are all one second – one accident – away from disability and like to believe that we live in such a liberal society that these things become almost irrelevant, but how would we actually cope? The lack of hope in the play is in balance with its energy and the sparkling dialogue of the household. If your production is staged in an open way, it will leave room for the audience to engage with these complex issues from many points of view and hopefully inspire real debate and a charged evening of theatre.

From a workshop led by Richard Wilson,
with notes by Abbey Wright

Molly Davies

Shooting Truth

Characters

From the present day:
Alice
Liam
Sid
Leanne
Jake
Sadie
Luke

From the seventeeth century:
Freya
Billy
John
Len
Sal
Lou
Marley
Gran

Scene One

The present. A classroom. All is quiet. **Alice** *sits alone at a desk, staring into space. Her peace is disturbed by a hubbub outside, which sounds as if it's making its way towards the classroom. She quickly grabs some exercise books and keeps her head down.*

Liam, **Leanne** *and* **Jake** *enter, closely followed by* **Sid**, **Luke** *and* **Sadie**. *They don't notice* **Alice**.

Liam   Anyway, glad you all could make it.

Luke   How long this gonna take, mate?

Sid   Yeah, I've got a game in a minute.

Luke   Against Reckinhull Village?

Sadie   Reckon I need to get at least sixty per cent or it ent worth me doing.

Leanne   So. Me, Jake and Liam had this idea for the project. Basically, I'm gonna be the female lead and –

Liam   Leanne, leave it to the director, yeah? (*Sees* **Alice**.) Oh, Alice, we booked this room for a meeting, sorry.

Alice   I think I booked it actually, for Homework Club.

Leanne   Oh *you're* Homework Club.

Alice   Maybe you booked 2*L*, instead?

Jake   Let's just get on, we don't have time to be traipsing round for another room. There's enough space.

Leanne   Unless *all the others* in Homework show up.

Liam   So. As I was saying: welcome. I've asked you here today because I believe each of you have a unique set of skills.

Leanne   What skills did we say Luke has?

Luke   I got the best camera, baby. No me, no film.

Liam   Anyway, welcome –

Jake   And congratulations.

Liam   Yes, welcome and congratulations. You've made it into the most exciting event of the summer: Liam Rayner's 'Untitled Film Project, 2011'.

Leanne   Excuse me?

Liam   Until, you know, we get a proper title.

Luke   Ent gonna be like Liam Rayner's 'Unsigned Band Project, 2010', is it?

They all laugh.

Leanne   Don't be stupid, this'll be *good*.

Sadie   What grade was it you got for that again, Liam?

Sid   I ent gonna be no laughing stock.

Liam   Listen, no one'll be laughing, trust me. Crying, maybe. Quaking in their boots, definitely.

Luke   We ent just gonna be bossed around all day?

Leanne   No, this is a real group effort. We got the (*gestures to* **Liam**) director, the (*gestures to* **Jake**) producer-stroke-art-director-thing, the (*gestures to herself*) talent, the (*gestures to others*) . . . cast and crew.

Sadie   Are we even allowed to work as a group, though?

Leanne   Yeah, the twins are doing that Post Office made out of Pot Noodle thing.

Sadie   What?

Luke   It's about the Post Office in town going to pot and all that.

Sadie   Yeah, but they're twins, ent they, it don't count as a group.

Luke   Could be a laugh.

Sadie   Ent heard of anyone else making a film, which means it's easier to get a good mark, I suppose.

Liam   Listen, I don't want you to see this as just another school project. We're gonna show people somethin' they've never seen before. I'm thinking Polanski, I'm thinking Lars von Trier and the Dogme 95 collective – (*Silence, blank faces.*) I'm thinking, something along the lines of *Saw VI*?

Sadie   I'm thinking Miss Rusk's never gonna pass us for making a film.

Liam   Right. What was the brief?

Sadie   I dunno. 'Respond to your local area' or something.

Liam   Exactly.

Leanne (*sarcastic*)   What do that even mean, 'respond'? Like our local area ask us a question. Stupid, ennit.

Sadie   It's like, say something about it or be affected by it or whatever.

Leanne   My boots have been affected by cow pat, she can mark them.

Liam   Well, we're gonna show our local area in a way it's never been seen before. We're gonna show the horror in it. Yeah, we'll make the sickest film known to man. Seriously, right, not to sound like a tosser, but this is gonna change our lives. Believe me. This film is gonna turn the world upside down.

Sadie   Hang on, wait, it was' artistically'. Respond *artistically* to your local area.

Jake   Well, if this ent art, I dunno what is. (*To **Liam**.*) Do yer mind?

Liam   Go ahead.

Jake   It's gonna be a huge creative challenge, inventing this atmosphere of, like, sheer terror, using smoke machines and fake blood and wigs and that. Just picture the blood, the entrails, the bits of mashed-up hair in the mud – this is all just off the top of my head. It's really technical. All the small details you probably don't even think about. All the ways our local area get mixed up in the horror.

Sid   So what actually happen?

Liam   What?

Sid   The story?

Liam   Well, there's you – actually, the character's name is Bronx. And Bronx is strong, he's decent, he's, supposed to be, you know, smouldering and that. Anyway. He gets his leg cut off by the murdering village psycho –

Jake   I'm working on a realistic leg substitute.

Liam   Hang on – get this, right – *then* he has to eat his own leg.

Pause.

Jake   Can you imagine?

Sid   What's the plot?

Liam   Uh. You're trapped. You're tortured. Your leg get cut off, you have to eat it.

Luke   That's not a plot, mate.

Liam   I mean, there's a lot leading *up* to the leg incident. A lot of torture and just mental sort of messed-upness and then –

Leanne   Thought the main part was female?

Jake   Uh, yeah: *Murdering Village Psycho*.

Sid   What about the story? What's it actually *about*?

Jake   Just told yer, a bloke eating his own leg.

Liam   No Jake, what it's *about* is how a man's immediate surroundings make him –

Sid I dunno if I wanna do it. Can't it be something like, there's a bloke and . . . he seem normal, but you can tell right, you can just tell he's got a *past*. He's fighting some kind of demon.

Liam Now, demons I like.

Sid I mean, you know, demons within himself. And his journey is –

Jake Oh, we can't have more locations than one. Let's just say, whatever we end up doing, there will be no journeying around.

Sid *Emotional* journey.

Leanne Oooh. I get it. He's stuck in a state of of of, you know, when yer stuck in a rut?

Alice Inertia?

Luke In what?

Alice Well . . . this character, maybe he wanna *change*. Connect with people. Have them see him the way he see himself, but he can't 'cause he's inert.

Jake Huh?

Alice Maybe he's really funny and interesting but no one even know it. Remember doing it in Chemistry? It mean something ent reactive with other elements and can't form any compounds.

Sadie Yer mean he can't make friends?

Alice (*shrugs*) Inertia.

Leanne Yeah, that. And he's looking for something to get him out, to make him *feel* again, right?

Sid Right.

Leanne And then, when he's at his lowest point, he find her – me – and he completely fall for me. Her.

Sid   What?

Luke   This sound like a total girl's film.

Liam   We're not doing a rom com. There has to be some sort of supernatural element or –

Sid   Gotta have a plot, though, or it'll be rubbish.

Jake   Well, I ent heard a better one than Bronx and his leg yet.

Sadie   It's ridiculous, there's no story.

Jake   More of a story than that Jennifer Aniston rubbish –

Sadie   Did I say I wanted to do a romantic comedy?

Liam   Can you provide us with a better plot?

Sadie   Did I?

Alice   I've got a story you could use.

Liam   No thanks.

Alice   And the perfect location.

Sadie   Where 'bouts?

Alice   In between Swumfuld and Halebrough. It's an abandoned village. Used to be called Auldem.

Leanne   Sound thrilling.

Alice   Well, it could be. And no offence, but I don't really see how your idea responds to our surrounding area, actually.

Liam   Alice, we're not looking for some *Pride and Prejudice* thing.

Alice   I'm writing a poem for the project –

Leanne (*sarcastic*)   Rock'n'roll.

Alice   It's about this girl, I did some research and –

Luke/Liam/Jake   Shuttup. / Come on. / Alice –

Leanne   Hang on. There was this *girl* . . .

Alice   Freya, the youngest-ever witch. She was fourteen. It would need to be set in like the 1640s –

Jake   No way.

Leanne   What was she like, Freya?

Alice   Well. Everyone thought her family was weird. Her parents died when she was two – her dad of some random illness and then her mum died of like a broken heart. There was all this gossip about them. People thought maybe her mum had been a witch.

Liam   Bit more like it!

Alice   Her gran was also a witch – at least everyone thought so, 'cause of her of being so close with her cat.

Sid   What?

Alice   They thought it was her . . . familiar. A spirit that's like a sort of evil helper or something – all witches had them. So, because at that time witches were killed, Freya's gran murdered her cat to prove that the bond was not as strong as everyone reckon –

Sadie (*sarcastic*)   Nice.

Jake (*to* **Liam**)   Do-able.

Alice   But I think actually the real story start after all of this. It would make a good film, what happen to Freya. How she suffered years and years of teasing about her family and how she was always on her own –

Leanne   'Cause no one like her?

Alice   Yeah, or maybe because she preferred being by herself. But this group of kids picked on her. They'd been doing it for years –

Luke/John   Freya. Oh Frey-uh.

Alice   For ever, it seem like to Freya. And one day, she snap –

Luke/John   Where are ya, Freya? We know yer 'bout here somewhere.

Leanne   Right, I'm being Freya.

Len   Come on, ya little witch runt.

Alice   – and when she did, it was horrible, what they did to her. It's right up your street. It's true. And it's local. And it's real.

Sid   Sound perfect.

Beat.

Liam   Let's do it.

Scene Two

The seventeenth century. **Len**, **Sal**, **John**, **Marley** *and* **Billy** *in the woods.*

Freya *reveals herself.*

Len   There y'are.

Billy   Hello, Freya.

John   Here she is, come to play.

Freya   I got somethin'. For you, Sal. (*Hands it to* **Sal**.) I got a purse.

Sal   Look at that.

Billy   'S pretty.

Sal   Who ask you? Silk is it, Freya? Musta been expensive (*Pause.*) Where d'yer get 'at?

Silence.

Len   Cat got yer tongue?

John   Can't have – 'at's dead.

They laugh.

Lou   Got anythin' else?

Freya   Some liquorice.

John   Give it.

He hungrily divides it out between them.

Len   Where did yer get the purse, Freya?

Marley   Are yer rich now?

Len   Maybe her gran did some trickery. Did she magic yer some riches?

Sal   Did she, Freya? Is that what happen'?

Freya   No.

Sal   So how d'yer get 'at?

Freya   Thieved 'at.

Sal   What a surprise!

Freya   'Cause I thought you'd look pretty in 'at.

Sal   An' yer right, ent yer? I do look pretty.

Beat.

Freya   Yes.

Sal   Well, thank yer very much, Freya. But I dun want these little gifts no more. See, I think I'm growing out of them. Hairpins and ribbon and buttons and –

Billy   A ladybird in a box.

John   That was a rubbish one, you idiot.

Sal   *I'm* speaking – and aprons, and a pipe, well, they're all very nice and I am grateful . . .

Pause.

Freya   Yer welcome, Sal.

Sal   But now I think I need some shoes. Embroidered ones, like Mrs Pilmer have.

Billy   Sal! She'll never get 'em.

Sal   Don't be stupid, Billy. She will, if she want to be my friend.

Billy   Yer should choose somethin' easier.

Sal   Should I? Where's the fun in that?

Len   Course she can get 'em – right, Freya?

Freya   I, I don't know where.

Len   Sal just told yer, Mrs Pilmer wears them. What more d'yer need to know?

Freya   I can't take them right off her feet.

Len   Yer can if we say yer should.

Freya   But what about when everyone see yer wearing 'em? They'll know 'at was you.

John   Ent your place to ask questions, Freya Quicke.

Sal   And don't try and be clever. If I want somethin' done, you do 'at. Otherwise, what are yer good for? (*Throws the purse at* **Freya**.) So take this and magic me up some shoes for next time we meet.

Lou   Bye then, little witch.

Freya   Wait! I can't do it, I can't, Sal. I mean, buttons and hairpins and that, they're easy. No one notice. But *shoes*? How can I? She'll be wearing them, I can't just –

John   Knock 'er over and pinch 'em?

Freya   What if her husband see? I shouldn't creep into their house, or . . . Maybe I could follow her in the woods and . . . But what if she hurt herself? What if she die and 'at's all my fault? I can't do 'at.

Len   Did yer just say yer *can't*?

Len, **John**, **Lou** *and* **Marley** *begin to round on* **Freya**.

Lou   Even after Sal tell yer to?

Freya   Don't make me do 'at.

Marley   Not very polite is 'at?

Freya   *Please.*

Len   Are yer offended, Sal?

Sal   I think I am, yes.

John   That's it then.

John *grabs* **Freya** *by her hair and pulls her to the ground.* **Lou** *and* **Marley** *pin her arms behind her back.*

Freya   *Sal!*

Sal   There's nothing I can do, Freya. You should've said you'd get the shoes.

She turns away as **John** *and* **Len** *advance on* **Freya**.

Freya   Curses on yer then! Curse the lot of yer!

Len   Proper little witch, en' yer?

Freya   What if I am? What if I am a witch?

Pause. **Len** *and* **John** *stop.*

Freya   See. For three year now, I've been learning off my gran. But. She say I mustn't do trickery till I'm ready. Till I've learnt as much as the devil himself. And I'm nearly there, I am. So yer better beware.

She breaks free from **Lou** *and* **Marley**.

Sal   Don't tell lies, Freya.

Freya   I've been doin' small bits for ages, and yer ha'n't even noticed. Yer know when Jimmy Partridge faint in church? That was me. How we have two years bad harvest?

I did 'at. When Meg Rowe lost her little baby? My trickery caused 'at.

John   What's she / sayin'?

Freya   My gran, she killed our cat. But. He come back, as my familiar. And. And, I did tell him to eat Meg Rowe's baby. (*Beat.*) 'At's all true.

Len   So, you're saying you're possessed by the devil?

Freya   I am.

John (*walking towards* **Freya**)   Where's yer devil's mark, then?

Sal   No, John. Careful!

Len   John! Freya Quicke, are yer – in all honesty – a witch that do practise the devil's work?

Freya   Yes, I am, so yer better look out. (*Beat.*) And I en' gonna be thievin' nothin' for you no more.

Pause.

Len   Lies.

Sal   Come on, Len.

Len   Prove it, then. Call your familiar. Bring sickness upon us.

Sal   Stop!

Len   She can't do it, don't yer see?

Sal   But her family –

Len   Show us then, Freya.

Silence.

John   Come on, Freya, we're waitin'.

Silence.

Len   So you'll have Sal's shoes next time we see yer. (*To* **Sal**.) No witches here. Just lies.

Lou   Len, she'll come after yer.

Sal   If this is true, Freya Quicke, they'll drown yer for witchcraft.

Len   An' if it en', we'll kill yer for lyin'.

They exit.

Freya (*to herself*)   I am. I am a witch.

Scene Three

The present. In the woods of the abandoned village.

Sadie *is trying out make-up on* **Alice** *and* **Luke**. **Luke** *already has a scar across his cheek. Silent concentration as she works on* **Alice**.

Sadie (*as she paints a cut on* **Alice***'s arm*)   Gross. Gross. (*To* **Luke**.) Ennit?

Luke   Sick.

Sid *enters.*

Sadie   Hey, Sid, don't Alice look gross?

Sid   Uh. Yeah.

Luke   Can yer get this stuff off me now?

Sadie   Come.

Sadie *and* **Luke** *exit.*

Sid   A'right Alice.

Alice   A'right.

Sid   What's goin' on?

Alice   Just waitin' for everyone. Liam's gone to find Jake.

Sid   Right.

Alice   Something about props.

Sid   Oh.

Alice   Learnt yer lines then?

Sid   Sort of. You sent the script through pretty quick.

Alice   Done all the research, ha'n't I? Anyway, it seem a screenplay's easier to write than a poem.

Sid   Oh, guess who did some research of their own?

Alice   Um. You?

Sid   Looked up some facts about Auldem.

Alice   You mean, what used to be Auldem.

Sid   Well, whatever, *this* place. I'll show yer, I googled.

Takes out his phone.

Sid/Alice   No reception.

Leanne *enters.*

Leanne   Hey, kids.

She is dressed as a 'sexy witch' – Christina Aguilera meets Dita Von Teese.

Alice   A'right.

Leanne   Thought I'd come in costume, save getting ready in the cold.

Sid   It's set in the seventeenth century.

Leanne   And?

Sid   I don't think they had stilettos in those days.

Leanne   Well, it's never gonna be a hundred per cent accurate, is it? (*Looking around.*) This is proper no-man's-land. Can't barely see Swumfuld.

Sid   It's where my brother learn to drive.

Leanne   In the woods?

Sid   Fields – between Marley Farm and here.

Alice   Yer know, Leanne, it probably all happen to Freya really close to here because –

Leanne   I didn't know, Alice, but wow, thanks for that thrilling information.

Liam *enters*.

Liam (*seeing* **Leanne**)   Woah!

Leanne   You like?

Liam   I *like*, I'm just not sure it's –

Sid   You gotta tell her.

Liam   It's just, I was thinking something a bit Kristen Stewart or Ellen Page or . . . something *dark*, you know.

Leanne   Uh, hello: black nail varnish, wig, fishnets.

Alice   It's 1645.

Leanne   What's your problem?

Liam   Well, let's just see how it look on camera yeah?

Jake *enters with* **Sadie** *and* **Luke**, *carrying a 'leg', and some other props*.

Liam   Ah, here's our prop man.

Jake   Thought maybe we could still find a use for this, if yer think? (*Seeing* **Leanne**.) Jesus.

Leanne   Not you an' all.

Liam   Forget it, you look hot. Come on, let's go. We'll have . . . Yeah, Leanne, we'll see you run on and hide behind this tree. Your tormentors – that's you guys – are on her tail. Jake will cue you. Everyone ready? So this is scene one, chase sequence, establishing shot.

They all get into starting positions, **Liam** *'films'*.

And. *Action.*

Leanne *walks on. Pouts. Hides behind tree.*

Liam   OK. *Cut.* Leanne. Um. I'm thinking. You're being chased by people who really wanna hurt you and. I'm just not sure it's reading as *fear* you're feeling.

Leanne   I think I need more powder.

Sadie *does her make-up.*

Liam   I know, let's up the stakes a bit and say you fear for your life.

Alice   You're petrified, you're exhausted.

Liam   It's alright, Alice, I'll do the talking to the actors. Leanne: You've been running for so long you're out of breath. Yeah?

Leanne   Whatever you say, Mr Director.

Liam   OK. So. We'll go again guys. *Action.*

Leanne *does it as before, but this time with a lot of panting.*

Liam   OK, sorry, Leanne. I'm not sure about the. Panting.

Leanne   You said breathless.

Sid   Out of breath, he said. How many times are we gonna do this?

Liam   Until it's right.

Leanne   Wait till we get to your bit. It's not as easy as it look.

Liam   Right. Let's go again, please.

Leanne *does it exactly as before, but* **Liam** *lets her continue as she is clearly unable to follow his direction.*

Sid   Freya! Whither art thou?

Luke   Freya! We know that thee is there!

Sadie   Freya! We will torture thee in the most terrible and frightful manner!

Liam   And *cut*! Well done. Great. Now. Let's do the close-up on Freya's face when she's hiding up the tree.

Leanne   You want me to climb a tree?

Liam   No, we'll just do the close-up here. So, you've been bullied for years. You've had enough. You're no longer scared – you're angry. Ready? And, *action*.

Leanne   Ahhh. (*Pout.*) Ahhh.

Sid   She's not supposed to be a sexy witch.

Leanne   Am I asking you to find me sexy, Sid?

Sid   Pretty much. (*To* **Liam**.) People are gonna laugh at us.

Liam   OK, we'll go again. And . . . *action*.

Alice   Think *angry*, Leanne.

Liam/Jake   Alice!

Liam   Right. Quiet. Everyone shut up apart from me. And, action.

Leanne *does it as before.*

Liam   OK, cut.

Luke   That's brilliant!

Leanne   Yeah?

Luke   Hilarious.

Sid   Not supposed to be funny though, is it?

Liam   No. It's not.

Luke   Come on, it's like a seventeenth-century porno.

Liam   Right. Again.

Leanne   I'm tired.

Sid   This is what it's like being an actor. If you're not serious about it –

Leanne   I *am*. God you're boring. Let's do it then.

Liam   Action!

Leanne *does it as before.*

Liam   And *cut*!

Leanne   Well?

Beat.

Liam   Better.

Sid   Worse.

Jake   She's not good enough. This is supposed to be art and it look like a joke.

Liam   OK. One more time. Really go for it, Leanne. Remember, this is a scream of anguish and frustration, built up after years of torment.

Leanne   But –

Sadie   Just listen, Leanne.

Alice   Yeah, listen, then you'll understand the character better.

Leanne   Shut *up*, Alice. No one even ask your opinion. Yer only here 'cause you wrote the script.

Liam   Right. Leanne. Think of a time you've felt frustrated, like people don't understand who you really are, your voice ent being heard, no one get you. And all you wanna do is –

Sid   Is it really that hard?

Luke   It look easy.

An argument breaks out between everyone on set. They are all shouting over one another. Out of frustration.

Alice   AAAAHHHHHH!

Beat.

Sorry. This is doing my head in.

Sid   Wow.

Liam   Yeah. Like that.

Leanne   That's gonna kill. Maybe she can be my scream double?

Jake   That might be a bit difficult, technically speaking.

Sid   Why don't Alice just play Freya?

Leanne   You can't sack me, I'm on the production team.

Jake   But you were never exactly given the part, you just took it.

Luke   It's gonna take for ever this way, and I've got better things to be doing with my holidays. No offence.

Sadie   Shall we just see how Alice go?

Leanne   But I thought she was playing the cat?

Alice   The cat's dead.

Beat.

Leanne   Oh yeah.

Liam   Alice, you OK for lines?

Sid   She did write it.

Alice   I dunno, I might not be any good.

Leanne   Thank you!

Liam   You wrote it, surely you can do it.

Sid   Remember that poem, the one Miss made you read out in assembly and you used different voices –

Sadie   Yeah, the roast dinner one, you did the voice of the chicken and the carrots and that?

Sid   That was acting, weren't it, doing all them voices?

Alice   Suppose. What if I'm rubbish?

Luke   You're not gonna be any worse than Leanne, are yer?

Leanne   What?

Sadie   We *need* you, Alice.

Leanne   You lot are ridiculous. Takin' it from me and giving it to . . . *that*. Losers.

Luke   Broken. Hearted.

Leanne (*as she exits*)   Urgh. I hate you.

Sadie   Leanne –

Liam   We'll find another part to showcase your talent.

Sadie   Leanne!

Sid   Leave her.

Sadie   She's going the wrong way.

Jake   We need to get on. There's a lot to do before it get dark.

Liam   Absolutely. Right, so we'll rehearse it as before then, but with Alice. And *action*.

Scene Four

The seventeenth century. Gran's kitchen.

Freya *and* **Gran** *are sewing.*

Gran   Need to work a bit faster there. Practise that stitch.

Freya   Sorry. I was distracted.

Silence.

I had something on my mind.

Silence.

I was thinkin' about that Evie Tucker over in Slophum. They just tried her fer witchcraft, dun ya know? They swum 'er.

Gran *pricks her finger on needle.*

Gran   Ouch.

Freya   Are yer a'right, Gran?

Gran   Poor soul.

Freya   You'd think, wouldn't yer, that if you was a witch and people were after yer, that ye'd put a spell on 'em. Or get yer familiar to see to 'em. Dun yer reckon?

Gran   Maybe.

Freya   That's what I'd do. Magic them away for ever. I bet there's a spell that could do that, en' there? One that dun hurt no one, just makes 'em go away. Gran?

Gran   I suppose there probably is.

Freya   How d'yer reckon 'at would go? Would yer need flowers an' herbs an' that as well as chanting, or –

Gran   I dun know, they'd probably just use things they'd find about their house.

Freya   Like what sort o' things?

Gran   Why you asking me, child? I en' no witch.

Freya   Course, I know yer not. I was just wonderin', *if* yer were, how you'd make a spell fer –

Gran   I know yer, Freya Quicke, and dun you forget 'at. Why are yer asking about witchery?

Freya   No reason.

Gran   Tell me. Truthfully, Freya.

Freya   I dun really know.

Gran   Yer know I'll help yer how I can, but dun be tellin' me no lies.

Freya   Remember Lizbeth? Lizbeth Grout, she knew Ma?

Gran   I remember.

Freya   She got a daughter, Sal Grout. Always with them two boys.

Gran   Oh yes, Joan Gooderham's?

Freya   They pick on me, Len and John Gooderham and Sal Grout. Every day, Gran.

Gran   Yer never said.

Freya   I never wan'ed to worry ya.

Gran   Just avoid them, gal. They'll give up.

Freya   I've tried. 'At's not that simple. They follow me. They look for me.

Gran   They din lay their hands on yer?

Freya   No.

Gran   I'd have a word with their ma if they did.

Freya   No, Gran. Best yer don't. Dun wanna get y'self in trouble.

Pause.

And. Because them kids were grieving me every day (*beat*) I told 'em I'm a witch.'Cause yer dun understand, Gran, what at's like.

Gran   I dun understand what 'at's like? When I were accused of witchcraft and threatened with swimming and had things thrown at me? How dare yer, child. I didn't sacrifice my moggy for you to go round sayin' things like that.

Freya   Sorry, it just –

Gran   Ye'll have to tell them 'cause's not true.

Freya   I can't, they'll kill me.

Gran   They'll kill you if yer keep saying it. What would yer mother think?

Freya   You know better than me. They say she was a witch, dun they?

Gran   Leave these things in the past, Freya.

Freya   Come on, surely I'm old enough for the truth. What if it pass in the family?

Gran   Dun' be silly. 'At en' right goin' into 'at all.

Freya   But they'll leave me be, if they think my mum and my gran are –

Gran   No! It break my heart that I ha'n't manage to teach you the value of life yet. 'Cause we'll lose ours, if yer keep on with this. Your ma was a good woman, that's all yer need to know. No gossip can change that. You're riskin' our lives with this silly talk. There's been too much death in this family. I en' gonna let yer cause more. I couldn't stop yer mother from ruining her life, but I can stop you.

Freya   I'm sorry, Gran –

Gran   Oh, fetch my nightshade, would yer, child? This talk make my head ache and 'at'll help me sleep. What am I gonna do with you?

Freya *passes* **Gran** *a phial of nightshade.* *Gran dilutes a few drops in a glass of water and drinks.*

Freya   Yer don't have to do nothin'.

Gran   Yer gon' tell 'em it's not true?

Beat.

Freya   Yes.

Gran   Good girl. Yer dun want to make waste of this life. Bad things you can handle, child. Words are just words.

There's a lot worse. Yer dun need to be messin' with rhymes
and pentangles and candles.

Freya   You're right. I din mean to upset yer. I'll tell 'em. I'll
tell 'em now.

Gran   That's right, be brave, girl.

Gran *kisses* **Freya** *and leaves.* **Freya** *picks up a candle and the
phial of nightshade and puts them in her pocket.*

Scene Five

The present. Abandoned village.

Luke *in apron and bad wig.* **Alice** *is in a modest 'Freya' costume.*
Jake *and* **Sadie** *are standing by with props and make-up.* **Liam**
films while **Sid** *watches.*

Liam   OK. Are we ready? Let's go for a take this time.

Sadie   What about Leanne? She'd be much better than
him.

Jake   We can't wait all day.

Sid   Didn't exactly sound like she was planning on coming
back.

Sadie   But she'd have to come back. She went in the total
wrong direction. What if she's –

Sid   She'll just be sulking, plotting her revenge.

Jake   We've gotta start this scene without her.

Liam   Yeah, we have. Luke? Ready?

Luke   Can't wait.

Liam   Right then. Action.

Throughout filming, **Alice** *keeps looking down, embarrassed.*

Alice   Grandma?

Luke   'S up my dear?

Alice   Children have been –

Luke   By heavens! Darling, what happen to your face. Prithee?

Alice   The children, Gran, they threw twigs and stones at me.

Luke (*turns suddenly*)   Goodness me!

Liam   Luke! Yeah, *cut*. You did it again.

Luke   But she would turn, wouldn't she? She gotta react.

Liam   But every time you turn, we see your face!

Luke   I'm just being true to the character.

Liam   OK. Take 3. Please just *try*. Alice, don't look down so much, yeah? And action.

Alice   Grandma?

Luke   'S up my dear?

Alice   Children have been –

Luke   By heavens! Darling, what happen to your face. Prithee?

Alice   The children, Gran, they threw twigs and stones at me.

Luke (*turns suddenly*)   Goodness me!

All   *Luke!*

Alice   Luke, it don't actually say ''S up' in the script.

Luke   So?

Liam   Right. Again! Action.

Luke   'S up my dear?

Leanne (*off*)   Urrggh.

Sid   Hang on.

He pulls **Leanne** *out from behind a bush.*

Leanne   My bloody heel's broken. Get off.

Sid   Listening in, were yer?

Leanne   No. How's it going?

Liam   Yeah. Great.

Leanne   Looks it. Loving your work, Luke.

Luke   Glad someone appreciate it.

Sid   Let's have Leanne play her, then we don't have to worry about it.

Leanne   I'm not playing some nan.

Jake   Sadie, can't yer do something else with him? Make him look more like an eighty-year-old woman?

Sadie   I'm not a miracle worker.

Liam   Right. Fine. We'll come back to it. OK, let's go to Freya's big speech. Ready, Alice? Both of you, at the table. Gran, maybe you have your arm around Freya?

Luke   Right.

Liam   And *action.*

Alice   But you don't get my pain, Grandma. They set out to –

Sadie   Cut! Wait wait wait, she needs blusher.

Liam   You can't just shout 'cut' like that. It's my job.

Sadie   It's important, this is a close-up. (*To* **Alice**.) You're so peaky-looking, aren't yer?

Alice   Sorry.

Sadie   OK. All done.

Liam   Right. *Action!*

Alice (*keeps sneaking looks to 'camera' throughout this speech*)   But you don't get my pain, Grandma. They set out to terrify me out of my wits. Is it not enough that my dear mother and father are no longer with us? Is it not enough that my darling grandma is accused of witchcraft? That we had to lose our sweet Dusty? (*She starts to cry.*) Must I also have to bear this tormentious bullying? Must I? Who is it that hate me thus?

Liam   And *cut*! That was . . . better, Alice.

Alice   Really? I felt a bit –

Sid   It's a definite improvement.

Alice   I dunno. Maybe it's a bad idea. (*To* **Leanne**.) You should do it.

Leanne   No. No, you do it. You understand the character better.

Sadie   Changed yer tune, ha'n't yer?

Leanne   Well, it make sense, don't it, that she play the loner.

Liam   OK, fine. Let's break, guys.

Leanne (*to* **Liam**)   Can I have a word? Privately. Had an idea.

Scene Six

The seventeenth century. Woods.

Freya *lays out some things she took from her gran's kitchen. She starts to draw a circle with the chalk.*

Freya
    I draw this circle . . .
    I draw this circle around me for protection.
    I call upon nature and the sphere
    To give me witchcraft . . .

No.

> I draw this circle around me for protection
> I call on the devil, the devil himself,
> Give me witchcraft an' the skills of magic,
> Make me mighty, build me strong.

Freya *tries to draw a pentangle. It goes wrong, she crosses it out and tries again.*

> Bring me the power
> To . . . something . . . hour

Or –

> Cower! Make them cower

Yes.

> Bring me the power
> To make them –

Sound of a twig snapping.

Freya   Who's there? Come out.

Billy *enters.*

Freya   Billy. Where are the others?

Billy   Dun know. Promise!

Freya   Go away, I'm busy.

Billy   Just wan'ed to talk to yer. I wan'ed to say, I dun agree with how they act. Sal an' that.

Freya   Din hear you sayin' nothin' at the time.

Billy   I wan'ed to.

Freya   Then why din yer? Scared? Scared of Sal, are yer? Scared of a girl?

Billy   Look. I'm try'n'a tell yer, I like yer, 'at's good how yer stand up to 'em.

Freya   Yer don't wan'a like me. I'm bad. I was doin' witchery, just now.

Billy   Wha – No yer weren't –

Freya   I'm a *witch*, Billy Battrick.

Billy   Yer not, Freya. I –

Freya   You dun even know how it work. Yer dun / know nothin'.

Billy   I know –

Freya   You're too small to understand. You're an idiot / just like they say.

Billy   I know because I saw. I saw yer couldn't even draw a pentangle properly an' yer couldn't do a rhyme an' –

Freya   Leave me alone, Billy. Go away.

Billy   Alright, I will, I'll go an' tell them all Freya Quicke's a liar. I'll say, I saw it myself, she can't do no witchcraft. An' yer know what they'll do, dun yer?

Freya   Don't –

Billy   They'll kill yer, won't they? That's what they said.

Freya   Billy –

Billy   So I'll leave yer alone an' I'll go an' tell Sal an' Len. Yer done for an' yer know 'at. I'm tellin' 'em.

He goes to leave.

Freya   Or. *Billy wait!* Or, yer could stay. Join me. (*Beat.*) I see how they look at yer, Billy Battrick. Down their noses. Just playin' with yer 'cause yer live across the way, but callin' yer names all the while. Silly Billy. Billy No-Brain. If I weren't here, you'd be the one they'd go for. They dun like us, Billy. But we could take our revenge. You could be my apprentice.

Billy   I dunno what that –

Freya   Helper. You could assist me in a trick. Then they'd leave us be. I might only be learning, but I'm a *natural* witch. 'At's in my blood, 'cause my mum was one, and my nan is too, only she don't practise no more.

Billy   I dunno.

Freya   It'll be great, we'll trick 'em and they'll be scared of us for ever.

Billy   Really?

Freya   They'll never dare be horrible then.

Billy   They'll never be mean?

Freya   No.

Billy   So, they won't pick on us no more?

Freya   No, Billy, never! We'll show 'em what's what. We'll do a magic on them they'll never forget.

Scene Seven

The present. The abandoned village. **Liam**, **Leanne** *and* **Jake** *are having a meeting.*

Jake   I dunno if we've got time for this.

Liam   All film-makers have production meetings, Jake. And Leanne got a point to make. (*To* **Leanne**.) Go on.

Leanne   Look, I know I've been a stupid, terrible –

Jake   Yeah, yer have – can we get on now?

Leanne   But I'm back on board, and I've realised we have a serious problem.

Jake (*reluctantly*)   What?

Leanne   Maybe you haven't noticed – and I'm not saying this 'cause I want the part, 'cause I totally don't – but Alice seem really conscious of the camera.

Jake   She's shy, ent she? Surprised she's doing it at all.

Liam   Thing is, when we watched it back, you can see she keep on looking right down the lens.

Leanne   Let's show him on the monitor.

Liam   Take too long to set up. Look, mate, it's bad.

Jake   Man, we ha'n't got time to get a new actress.

Liam   I reckon the best we can do is just make it all less intimidating for Alice.

Leanne   Hide the camera and tell her it's a rehearsal, but actually we're filming. Or something.

Liam   Actually. (*They laugh – he sounds like* **Alice**.) Actually, I was thinking – you've seen *Alien*, right?

Jake   Of course.

Liam   You know when the alien first come out of Kane's stomach?

Jake   It's committed to memory.

Liam   Well, none of the other actors knew it was gonna happen.

Jake   No way.

Liam   That's why yer get such a pure, realistic reaction. It was a total surprise.

Jake   Awesome. I know what yer saying –

Liam   Alice think she's filming one thing –

Leanne   But we know she's filming another.

Liam   The truth.

Jake   Not exactly got the budget of *Alien* though, have we?

Leanne   That just make it more challenging.

Liam   We do have that fake blood.

Jake   And all them props I made for the Bronx leg film. Just gotta get creative with them.

Liam   Right, so, we're up to Freya running away, having just done her first bit of witchcraft. She's in the forest and . . . I know, we'll tell Alice it's a rehearsal, but once she start running we'll scarper, so she really do feel alone in the woods. She'll feel abandoned and scared, just like Freya did, and then maybe –

Leanne   Something come and attack her? Or, you know, anything that improve the quality of the acting.

Jake   Wait, I've got the perfect thing.

He exits.

Leanne   This should be interesting.

They laugh.

Liam   Yeah, this film has definitely just got better. Imagine the look on everyone's faces when they see it. They won't be laughing this time. Thanks, Leanne.

Leanne   No problem, I think producing actually suits me better than acting – and I don't wanna be part of something rubbish, do I?

Liam   You won't be. It'll be brilliant, I can feel it.

Scene Eight

The seventeenth century. The woods.

Freya *holds up a phial.*

Freya   So here it is.

Billy   'At look murky.

Freya   Should be delicious, 'at's got some excellent ingredients. Started with Gran's medicine, then added a few sprinklings of black nightshade berries – that's the bits floatin'.

Billy   Right.

Freya   Then some hemlock, from around the marshes, mixed together with cider and – the reason 'at's gonna taste so nice – a dash of milk and sweet wine.

Billy   Sweet wine! Where'd yer get 'at?

Freya   Ask me no questions, Billy Battrick.

Billy   Are yer sure 'at'll make me sleep?

Freya   Definitely, nightshade droplets put my gran to sleep every night since her moggy died. I promise yer, yer'll have a deep, deathlike sleep, till I wake yer with the salts.

Billy   'Cause if 'at don't, I might sneeze or blink or –

Freya   Have faith. I, Billy Battrick, I am from a family of witches.

Billy   I feel a bit nervous.

Freya   Hush an' take 'at.

Billy *sips from the phial.*

Freya   Nice?

Billy   I can taste that sweet wine.

He swigs it all down.

Freya   Wait, I got'a say my spell . . .

Billy Batterick:
May this bittersweet and woody potion
Run through yer veins and
Relieve yer of yer warmth, yer pulse, yer breath
And put yer into such a sleep that
All might think yer dead.

Billy   Right, what shall I do n——

Freya   Hang on!

May yer become awake only when I produce
Special salts under yer nose.

Billy   Where'd yer –

Freya   Doctor Webb.

Children's voices, offstage.

Freya   That's them, they won't be laughin' so hard once
they know the power of Freya Quicke.

Billy   I feel a bit . . . I need to sit down.

Freya   Yer should lie down, I'll put blueberry stain on yer
lips so yer look even more deathly.

She rubs blueberries on his lips.

Billy   Freya –

Freya   And the blood, the fox blood, I nearly forgot.

Billy   Freya, I –

Freya   I'm just gonna smear it, alright?

*She smears blood on **Billy**'s arms and legs.*

Billy   I can't –

Lou *(off)*   Said the clearing, din she?

Len *(off)*   John, make sure yer stick by me.

Freya *freezes.*

Billy   Freya?

Freya   What, Billy? They're comin'.

Billy   I can't move my legs. I can't feel –

Freya   Hush. Soon yer'll be sleepy. It take my gran a few
minutes every night. I'll cover yer up a bit to stall 'em from
finding yer.

She kicks some leaves over him.

Billy?

Beat. No answer.

I'll see yer when yer wake, Billy Battrick.

She takes out some knitting and tries to appear nonchalant.

Len, **Sal**, **John**, **Lou** *and* **Marley** *enter.*

Lou   A'right, Freya Quicke.

Freya   Oh, so yer came.

Lou   Course.

Len   Where is 'at then?

Freya   What?

Len   The corpse.

John   Yer told us there'd be someone dead, now if yer lied –

Sal   'At ent here, let's just go.

Marley   You're scared.

Sal   I'm bored 's all.

Freya   The corpse is here, but yer needn't be scared, Sal, 'cause yer know 'at.

Sal   'At's not Mrs Pilmer?

Lou *screams – she has uncovered* **Billy**.

Lou   Billy. Billy Billy Battrick covered in blood!

Freya   Ah yes, that'll be the blood from where my familiar ripped at his flesh.

John   Let's see.

Len   Billy?

Len *picks up* **Billy**'s *arm and drops it. He listens to see if* **Billy** *is breathing. Nothing.*

John   Shall I pinch his toes?

Len   No. He's dead.

Lou   Freya, yer killed Billy Battrick.

Freya   Well, my familiar did, actually. My moggy. Told yer I'm a witch, din I?

Sal   But that en' witchery, that's plain murderin'.

Freya   The real witchery's in bringing him back to life.

Marley   What?

Freya   That's right. I will fill him with life an' power. An' none of yer had better be mean to him again, for if y' are, some dark spirit will settle upon yer.

Lou   We won't, just bring him back.

Freya   Alright then, I will. Stand back.

Sal   Please, let's go.

Len   Never, I wanna witness this.

Freya
    Behold, behold the power that is Freya
    Beware, beware the power that is Freya
    No one shall make her steal embroidered shoes no more
    And no one will dare call her 'little runt' again.

She takes salts.

I shall now return life to the body of Billy Battrick.

She hold the salts under his nose. He doesn't respond.

    Billy, I will bring colour to yer cheeks –

Tries salts again – still nothing.

(*Whispers.*) Come on, Billy, yer get up now. Billy?

She stops for a moment – looks at the others.

Yes.

She grabs **Billy** *under his arms and hauls him up.*

Freya
  I will breathe air into yer lungs an'

She struggles to hold him. He is completely lifeless.

  Billy! I will make the blood run in yer veins.

Billy! Wake up!

  Yes . . . Behold, the power that is Freya.
  Beware, the power that is Freya.

Freya *can hold* **Billy** *no more. They slip down to the floor.*

Freya   *Billy! No!* It's not working.

Len   Step back from him, Freya.

Freya *(crying)*   'At's not working.

Lou   Stay away from him, yer murderin' witch.

Freya   'At ent my fault –

Len   Come on, we'll get our fathers and show 'em what happen.

Freya   No, yer dun understand. 'At's a trick is all, gone wrong. Yer have to believe me. Sal?

Sal   Keep away, I hate yer.

Marley   Yer dead, Freya Quicke.

Freya *starts to run.*

John   Go on, run, run for yer life.

Scene Nine

The present. The abandoned village.

Alice, *as Freya, alone on stage, running through the woods.*

Luke *(off)*   Run for yer life, go on, run.

Sid (*off*)   We'll hunt yer down.

Luke (*off*)   We'll kill yer when we find yer, Freya.

Alice *stops. She acts 'scared'.*

Alice   Not if I see thee first, you will not. For I will hide wherein thee shall never find me. (*Pause.*) Is it my line? (*Silence.*) Hello? Liam? Jake? Are you messing around? Say something! Please, I don't know the way back by myself. Come back. Sid? It's too dark I can't −

A bright light suddenly dazzles her.

Who's . . . Who is it?

Something comes flying through the air towards her − it is the false leg Jake made, with 'blood' on it.

Aaaaahhhhhhhhh!

Sid   Enough!

*The spotlight is switched off and **Sid** enters, closely followed by the others.*

Alice   What was that, what was, Sid, what −

Sid   It's just that stupid leg, see.

Alice   Where did you go?

Jake   We were using this special acting technique, it's completely harmless. And it look totally amazing.

Alice   Oh.

Liam (*sarcastic*)   Thanks, Jake. Alice, the idea is, because the actor doesn't know what's coming, their response is completely truthful.

Alice   Oh. I think I −

Sadie   Are you OK?

Alice   I'm gonna be sick.

Sadie   Quick, come with me.

Sadie *and* **Alice** *exit.*

Leanne   Oh. My. God.

Jake   Did yer see her face?

Luke   Priceless!

Liam   This is something else. Seriously. This is. This could win awards. It's something else.

Sid   *You* lot are something else. She was terrified.

Leanne   That's the point.

Luke   Well, she know now anyway, don't she?

Leanne   Yeah, Jake, you knob, why d'yer have to tell her? Can't use that idea no more.

Liam   Ent necessarily over. I mean, Alice now know that we might surprise her, but she don't know *how*.

Luke   Right, she don't know *exactly* what could happen –

Liam   So maybe we turn it up a notch. We'll have to, won't we, now she know something's coming. We gotta make sure it's that little bit *more* than she's expecting. And it gotta last for longer this time, we only got a few seconds before.

Jake   I saw a dead cat by the side of the road near the hall, I reckon we could use that in some way. And what about that pit thing, in the middle by the clearing?

Liam   Yeah, we should totally collect some road kill, make it more *real*.

Sid   You gotta be joking me, a dead cat? No way. There's no way I'm being part of this.

Sadie *and* **Alice** *enter.*

Liam   Alice. How you feeling?

Alice   Better. Thanks.

Sadie   She threw up.

Liam   Well. I have a proposition for yer –

Jake   It's really exciting –

Liam *gives him a 'look'.*

Liam   The proposition is this: we continue using the same technique we did in the last shot. It enables you to give us some of the best acting I've ever seen –

Alice   Really?

Sid   Yer don't have to do this, Alice.

Liam   Of course you don't. We've got two options. One is to carry on as we started: making what I believe is quite a good teen horror film. Maybe worth a '12' certificate. At best I think the rest of the year are gonna find it amusing.

Leanne   The second option?

Liam   Is to work with what we've just hit upon with this technique, which take it to a whole other level. And truly connect us to our local environment and all that.

Leanne   What d'yer reckon, Alice?

Alice   Is it definitely better like this?

Liam   Totally. Maybe you're just one of those actresses that need to immerse themselves.

Sid   Are you serious? You were just chucking up.

Alice   Yeah, but that's 'cause I didn't know, ennit. I didn't know it was you lot an' that yer could see I was OK.

Liam   Look, the story of Freya is such a powerful one that, personally, I think we can only do it justice using this approach.

Sid   This is the most stupid idea I've ever heard.

Leanne   Go then, you won't exactly leave a gaping hole, will yer?

Sid   You know what, yer right.

Luke   Come on, mate, this is just getting interesting.

Alice   You gotta stay, we need you.

Sid   Why?

Alice   You're the best actor.

Sid   I've barely got a part. You don't have to do it, Alice. It's stupid. Liam's on some power trip, we could join the twins or something.

Leanne   Do it take four people to make a *Pot Noodle*?

Liam   This is Alice's choice, Sid.

Alice   I'm gonna stay. It's important, ennit. An' artistic. And I reckon I can be good.

Liam   We've really gotta get on, so . . .

Sid   Well. See yer then. Good luck.

He leaves.

Leanne (*to* **Alice**)   Don't worry, he's probably just intimidated 'cause yer acting's so good.

Alice   D'yer think?

Liam   OK, Luke, you're playing Sid's part now, so start looking over the script. Sadie, why don't you make Alice look a bit less like she's just thrown up. Jake and Leanne, I need you to help me set up for the next scene.

Leanne   Yes, sir.

Liam   Let's go.

Scene Ten

The seventeenth century. The woods. **Len, John, Sal** *and* **Lou** *are waiting for* **Marley**.

Sal   So my mum just wail 'poor foolish boy'. She say, 'He always were a bit simple.'

Sal, Lou *and* **John** *laugh.*

Sal   But 'at's true en 'at.

Lou   Mine say the same. 'Silly Billy.'

John   Well, our dad just reckon we're lyin'. He say –

Len   John, watch yer mouth. None of this matter. We saw what happen, we gotta work out a plan.

Marley *enters.*

Len   Well?

Marley   I told 'im. I say, 'Da, we did see Freya Quicke perform magic on Billy Battrick.'

Len   And?

Marley   An' he say, ''At's foolish tales. Billy probably die through fault of his own,' my Da say. There ent no bite marks from a cat on 'im. Also he reckon he never hear of a child witch, so he en' gonna lead a hunt over what we saw.

Len   That en' fair.

Marley   'If 'at's true Freya killed Billy, she will be found an' punished,' he say. But he ask if we saw 'at with our own eyes.

Len   An' what did you say?

Marley   Well, we din', did we? We din'.

John   We gotta do somethin'. If we don't get her, she'll get us, won't she?

Marley   Well, she'll get Sal.

Sal   What?

Lou   'At's right, Sal. You'll be next. 'At was you she wan'ed to be friends with, and you were meanest.

Sal   No.

Marley   'At's true.

Sal   Oh Len, we gotta stop 'er.

John   Dun' worry, Sal. We'll find that witch an' drive a stake through 'er evil heart. We'll kill 'er so badly that –

Len   No, John, we won't, 'cause then they'd drive a stake through our hearts as that'd make us nothin' but murderers.

Sal   Len, *please*!

Len   No, we gotta do this right. We gotta show 'em that Freya really is a witch, ha'n't we. Marley, yer ever see a trial?

Marley   Lots.

Lou   A proper trial, like the men do?

Marley   Course, with my dad. I've seen 'em swum, I've seen 'em pricked, I've even spotted a devil's mark myself.

Len   Now what I reckon is, in order to prevent the witch Freya Quicke doin' further damage –

Sal   Oh, no –

Len   What we'll do is bring 'er to trial. Ourselves. I'll lead the hunt, Marley can lead the trial and if she's found guilty –

John   She will be, she will be –

Len   – we'll take her to Marley's dad ourselves.

Marley   We'll be heroes. There's a witch in our midst – 'at's obvious 'cause we've all been goin' hungry – an' *we're* gonna catch 'er.

John   An' just in time, afore she kill Sal.

Sal   She's probably hexin' me right now 'cause yer takin' so long.

Len   We're gonna do this the sensible way, Sal, I ent gonna be rushed. We'll start in the woods. 'At's where she spend all 'er time, an' she en' gonna go back to 'er gran's as she know we're coming for 'er. We're gonna need lanterns to see our way –

Lou   I can get them.

Len   Right. Marley, you'll need to borrow some of yer dad's equipment won't yer –

Sal   I'll pack some bread and water –

Len   Do everyone know what they're doin'?

All   Yes, Len.

Len   Back here, soon as yer can.

John   Can I check fer the devil's mark?

Marley   Might do, it depend.

Len   If yer good yer can have a go.

Scene Eleven

The present. It is now dark.

Jake, **Leanne**, **Sadie** *and* **Liam** *are watching a monitor.*

Leanne   So how do it work? Why can't we see her yet?

Liam   Because this picture here, using the rubbish Drama Department camera, shows the hole Jake found.

Leanne   Don't look like much.

Liam   Covered it with leaves, didn't we? And when Alice break through 'em, we should get a nice picture of her in the hole. Camera's hanging from a tree by a rope, so 'at's pointing straight down –

Leanne   Which is why it's wobbling.

Liam   Exactly. And this picture Luke's filming with his camera. He's our man in the field, as it were.

Leanne   Right.

Liam   When Alice get to the arrows you put down she gotta start running, and that's when Luke'll get nearer to her, so we'll see her on the screen. Then –

Jake   Wham! She fall in the pit!

Liam   And so we switch to the Drama camera, and hopefully get a good shot, 'cause it's zoomed right in.

Jake   Sweet.

Sadie   How deep is it, the pit?

Jake   I dunno, couldn't see the bottom clearly. It's fine. Camera should still pick her up, 'cause of the zoom.

Sadie   It's not fine, Jake. If yer want people to get involved with something yer need to tell them what's happening.

Jake   Alice *know*, Sadie. Well, she know to expect the unexpected.

Sadie   But *I* didn't. I didn't know about some pit that could be full of rats or something. *As if* we won't get in trouble for this.

Leanne   Shut up, we'd get detention at the worst –

Liam   Right, we're nearly there, he's on her.

Leanne   Let's see.

Sadie   You do realise there is now evidence on *two* cameras of something we shouldn't be doing.

Liam   The best thing about this is that we could get like half an hour's good footage, rather than the couple of seconds we got last time.

Leanne   Half an hour of what, though? Someone down a hole? Ent exactly terrifying.

Liam   Yeah, but think about it. Close-up on her face. First, there's the shock, imagine: wide-eyed confusion. Then there will be tears, 'How can this have happen?' Then, there will be the terrible, terrible realisation: she is alone – trapped down a hole in a wood, in the middle of nowhere and anything could happ—

Sadie   Exactly. Is anyone listening to me?

Jake   Look, she just nearly trip!

Leanne   My first arrow!

Liam   And – she's running!

Freya *enters, running.*

Sadie   Liam, I'm going.

Liam (*still watching monitor*)   If yer sure.

Freya *looks behind her, as if hearing something.*

Sadie   Well, no one listen to my opinion and –

Jake   We're getting close.

Sadie *exits.* **Freya** *looks behind again.*

Leanne   I can't look, it's gotta be soon.

Freya *keeps running, more desperate now, she knows she is beat.*

Jake   Any minute now, any –

Liam   Omigod omigod omigod . . . .

Liam, Leanne and **Jake** *react simultaneously as* **Alice** *falls into the hole,* **Len** *and* **Marley** *enter and grab* **Freya**.

Liam   Yessssss!

Leanne   Oh God!

Jake   Whoa.

Len   Got yer.

Liam   We need to see her *in* there –Luke gotta shine the light in.

Lou, Sal *and* **John** *enter.*

Liam, Leanne *and* **Jake** *react simultaneously as they see* **Alice** *in the hole.*

Leanne   Aaaaaahhh!

Jake   Oh. God.

Liam   That's more like 'at.

Marley   Lou, bare her arms.

Lou *pulls back* **Freya***'s clothing.*

Lou   I see no mark of the devil.

Sal *and* **Lou** *go about checking* **Freya***'s hands, her face.* **Freya** *puts up as much resistance as she is able.*

Leanne   It do look very deep.

Jake   Probably six foot or somethin' I reckon.

Liam   Imagine Mr Bailey. The height of him, that's what she fell down. Beautiful.

Leanne   Mr Bailey's pretty tall –

Jake   What's all that stuff underneath her?

Liam   Wait! Where'd Luke go? He's supposed to stay with her, we need both angles.

Jake   This is good enough ennit? Look at her face!

Liam   No – we need options. Different views to pick from.

Sal   There ent no devil's mark.

Freya   Sal, yer gotta believe me –

John   I see one.

Marley   That's a freckle.

Freya   Get off, get off me –

Sal *and* **Lou** *check* **Freya***'s other leg.*

Leanne   Is she saying something? Can yer lip-read?

Liam   Man, we should've sorted the sound.

Jake   It's like she's looking right at us, it's –

Liam   Amazing.

Leanne   Weird, more like.

Luke *enters, out of breath.*

Jake   It look great, Luke.

Liam   What're yer doing back here? You were meant to –

Luke (*still out of breath*)   Quick. It's – Call an ambulance. She screamed and –

Marley   Freya Quicke, now yer must reveal to us yer familiar.

Freya   I ent got no familiar.

Marley   We all know yer familiar killed Billy Batterick.

Lou   But there ent no devil's mark, so how do 'at feed off her?

Marley   What?

Lou   How do her familiar suck her blood if –

Len   Keep out o' this, Lou.

Freya   I lied about a familiar, I lied!

Liam   Hang on, she's supposed to be down there, remember? She agreed to this. She's *acting*.

Luke   No! She fell on all this stuff, this rubble or something –

Liam   Leanne, see if the camera's picking that up.

Leanne   Liam!

Luke   Like bricks and glass and that –

Leanne   Oh my –

Liam   Well it can't be that bad, six foot ent –

Luke   Six foot? There's no way that's six foot, it's way deeper.

Leanne (*to* **Jake**)   But you said –

Jake   I dunno, do I, it was an estimate. I dunno *exactly* how deep –

Leanne   Yer know if it's *too* deep.

Jake   And I couldn't see the bottom, ent my fault –

Luke   We gotta go and call –

Sal   What now?

Marley   Now, Freya Quicke must admit that she met, and is in a pact with, the devil.

Freya   I am not. I have not met the devil.

Marley   You are in no agreement with him?

Freya   No, I promise.

Len   She's a liar though, she said so herself.

Marley   Repeat after me, Freya Quicke: Jesus –

Freya   Jesus.

Marley   God –

Freya   God.

Marley   Good –

Freya   Good.

John   What happen next?

Marley   Well . . . I have acquired all the information I need, so I shall now announce my findings. Freya Quicke, we did witness thee perform on Billy Batterick what look like witchcraft, though we found on ye no mark of the devil. The accused neither flinches at the words Jesus, Good or God. Nor can she produce her familiar. Therefore, I can only proclaim her innocent. Freya Quicke is not a witch!

Liam   Hang on! There ent no reception till Swumfuld.

Luke   Well, I'll run up there, then.

Liam   Look . . . We got an opportunity here.

John   What about swimmin'?

Lou   But she passed all the tests, she ent a witch.

Sal   She ha'n't passed all the tests, Lou, 'cause we ha'n't swum her.

Freya   Marley, no!

Marley   We can't. 'At need to be in a mere or a river.

John   There's the well?

Liam   Come on, Jake. Let's just get five, ten more minutes of this, then we can get help.

Leanne   She's stopped moving. She's stopped.

Jake   OK. Me and Luke'll go Swumfuld. You two wait with Alice.

Liam   I thought you understood what we were doing here? *Alice*, get it. We won't just be the talk of the school. What we could do here, it could *influence* people further afield. This is *art*. Yer seen *Antichrist*?

Luke   Let's go.

Liam *grabs* **Luke***'s camera and stands in his way.*

Liam   Look, if Alice is suffering, or pretending to suffer, *this much*, then the least we can do is film it. She'd be gutted if we didn't. She's doing a great job. Look at her.

Pause. They all look at the monitor.

Len   What's the matter? Dun yer know how to do 'at?

Marley   I know how.

Sal   Yer got'a do 'at, Marley, so we know fer sure.

Freya   Marley, no. I swear yer'll regret 'at if yer do.

Len   Marley?

Pause.

Marley   John, get the rope.

Sal *and* **John** *tie* **Freya***'s wrists and ankles.*

Jake *jumps on* **Liam**.

Jake   The rope, Leanne – in the prop box . Run, Luke – I'll follow yer.

Luke *exits.* **Leanne** *and* **Jake** *begin tying* **Liam***'s wrists and ankles together.*

Liam   This is ridiculous. You're over-reacting completely, it's only like citizen journalism or something, that's all. Or, or, actually it's not out of reach for us to make a lot of money from this. People love all that low-budget stuff. Think *Paranormal Activity. Blair Witch.* Only better, 'cause we're shooting the *truth.*

Freya   No! Yer'll be sorry, yer will. I'll haunt yer all and this very place.

Marley   Water rejects servants of the devil, Freya Quicke.

Freya   I will not rest!

Freya *is thrown into the well.*

Leanne   Wait! Look – on the monitor.

Leanne, **Jake** *and* **Liam** *look at the monitor. Stop struggling. Stare.*

Len, **Marley**, **John**, **Lou** *and* **Sal** *crowd around the well. They squint out / down into it.*

Leanne   D'yer see – movin' across Alice?

Liam   What *is* that?

Jake   Her face . . . It don't even look like Alice any more.

Blackout.

Scene Twelve

Some time. The well. **Leanne**, **Lou**, **Marley**, **Sal**, **John** *and* **Len** *are standing around it.* **Alice** *and* **Freya** *are at the bottom.*

Leanne   Alice?

Can yer hear me?

It's gonna be . . . OK.

The boys have gone for help.

Well, Liam hasn't, he's, he's . . .

Len   Are yer sure this is how yer do it?

Marley   Course.

Lou   But she sunk. That en' right.

Marley   Witches float.

John   How long d'we have to wait?

Sal   We need to make sure.

Leanne   I wonder if, do it feel

Nice, in a way?

You know sometimes how pain do? Drowning do, they say

Feel nice. Wonder if Freya felt

That.

Len   But she kill Billy. She ruin the crops.

Marley   Ask my dad, a witch float.

Sal   Maybe she's a really clever one?

Marley   'At's been long enough. I'll get Dad to fetch 'er body out.

John   So, she ent a witch? She's just a girl?

Leanne   I know yer must hate me, but please just

– Even if it's only 'get lost' –

Please say *something*.

Alice?

Sound of sirens, getting louder, closer.

They're here!

Leanne *runs off towards the ambulance.* **John**, **Marley**, **Sal** *and* **Len** *leave to get Marley's dad.*

Freya *and* **Alice** *are left alone onstage, in the well. We are now in a dreamlike state.*

Freya   Alice?

Alice   Freya.

The final moment of the play is without words. Movement, projections, song or sound should be used to communicate an uplifting exchange between **Freya** *and* **Alice**. *It should be a moment of contact and healing. If the girls were to speak, they might say 'I understand' or 'You're not alone'.*

Molly Davies is from Norfolk and her play was developed in collaboration with a group of young actors at The Garage Theatre, Norwich.

The writer has provided some character background notes that will help during character generation exercises and in rehearsal. The characters in both of the time periods are of a similar age.

The Present Day

The Setting

Though a production need not be based in East Anglia, the play is defiantly not inner-city and the rural setting is critical to the play. There is a sense of the 'smallness' of life, of Saturday jobs and babysitting – things to keep the characters ticking over. There is little mention of wealth or travel.

The Characters

The characters are all in the same year at school, possibly the same class, but they are not a tight group, and there is mistrust.

They are not out for an adventure together. They are together because they want to make a film, and their ambitions for the film have brought them together, not their enjoyment of one another's company. It is a holiday project proposed by their school. They all have personal motivation for their involvement. For example, Sadie, with her ambitions in the make-up world, is enticed by the glamour and the potential for forwarding her career, while Liam wants to prove himself after the intimated disaster of his previous project, 'Liam Rayner's Unsigned Band Project 2010'. There is not a pre-existing status structure to which the characters all adhere but a desire to be older, freer, maybe to define some sense of self and spread wings. The power stutters and slides within the group.

It would be interesting to make decisions on the style of film they are making. There are references to (amongst others) Polanski, Dogme 95 and *Antichrist*, so are these the kind of films the boys watch and want to emulate or do they want to develop a style of their own?

ALICE

Lives with her mum (a librarian), her stepdad (a carpenter) and her three-year-old twin sisters Lexi and Holly. Her dad, a teacher, lives two villages away. Alice loves going to the cinema with her dad. She is a prolific writer, and often on their drives there they plan stories she will write. She writes a film review after every cinema trip.

At primary school, Alice had a best friend, Becky, but they fell out in Year Five and Becky turned everyone against Alice – which means Alice now finds it hard to make and trust friends.

At home, Alice writes character assassinations of her schoolmates, reads them out to her mum and stepdad (who find them very funny), then files them in a box.

Alice can't wait to go to university, where she's told by her mum she'll meet people like herself.

Alice frequently chooses to be alone. She may have a sense of superiority that contradicts her shyness, a way of being condescending that contradicts her insecurity, and though she may be running scared she can still assert herself. Alice is not bullied but avoided. A loner, she doesn't need other people.

LIAM

Lives with his parents, who both work for the *East Anglian Daily Press*.

At primary school, Liam got in lots of trouble for screaming non-stop when he didn't get his own way, but he stopped doing it by the time he was in Year Five.

Ambitious and out to impress, Liam finds it difficult to take orders. He is competitive, which prevents him from having friends at school – although Jake follows him around.

He is passionate – and is sometimes ridiculed for it.

He was teased for the Unsigned Band Project last year, and is now out to make a point.

Liam feels that at school he does get the respect he deserves. He loves to correct his teachers.

SID

Has an elder brother (at Otley College studying agricultural engineering) whom he looks up to.

He lives with his brother and parents on a small farm.

When he was eleven, Saxon treasure was discovered on the farm by his father, and the family hasn't had to worry about money ever since.

He is popular at school, where he is a 'good all-rounder'.

Luke is the only person in this group that Sid would usually spend time with. The friendship between Sid and Luke is the closest in the group.

He works in a corner shop at the weekends.

He would like to be an actor or a footballer.

Sid is nice to Alice. Sid is nice to everyone. He has no agenda, and is impressed by people who are what they are.

LEANNE

The second of four daughters, she lives with her dad, who is a plumber, and her mum, who looks after her sisters.

She has lots of friends at school as she's usually fun to be around, despite being bossy.

Leanne has had boyfriends ever since Year Three of primary school. At primary, she got 'married' six times.

Leanne currently has a bit of a crush on Sid.

She does quite well academically at school, and thinks she'll probably go to a local-ish university like her sister, so she can still live at home.

Leanne wouldn't usually spend any time with Liam, but he sold her the idea by telling her she'd be the star of this film as he thought her popularity would increase its success.

There may be a 'thing' going on between Leanne and Sid: she's the 'it girl' he's the all-rounder.

JAKE

Jake lives with his mum, who works as a researcher at the university, and his elder sister, who's doing A-levels.

He has two imaginary friends, Sallah and Badandah, who have been with him since he was four. They only visit him occasionally now.

Jake enjoys maths, physics, chemistry and art at school but switches off during other lessons.

He has always been a bit OCD, but it only really comes back now if he's tired or stressed out. Other children tend to find Jake a bit intense.

He shares a love of film with Liam, whom he has begun to feel quite attached to. Jake and Liam share a 'prowling fascination' with one another.

SADIE

Lives with her parents, who run a bakery chain. She doesn't have any siblings. She works as a babysitter and in her parents' bakery on Saturdays.

It's important to her to do well academically. She wants to do a foundation course at Norwich School of Art, after GCSEs. She always has one eye on the future.

Sadie has been buying *Vogue* since she was twelve. She would like to be a make-up artist or costume designer.

Sadie and Leanne have a complex relationship. Both are bright, Sadie perhaps having the lioness's share of the nous.

Leanne wants it all *now* but Sadie perhaps will wait to be 'herself'.

The second of three children. His parents run a very successful building firm, which his elder brother also works for. Luke hopes to do the same one day.

Every year Luke, his younger brother and his mum go on holiday for a month.

Luke can't wait until he can leave school. He also can't wait until he turns seventeen as he's already picked out the car he wants, and is three-quarters of the way into talking his mum into buying it.

The Seventeenth Century

These are brutal times: bad harvests, violence, deprivation, death. For many of the group their future will be to follow in their parents' footsteps and do as they have done.

FREYA

Freya's parents died when she was two, and she's been brought up by her gran ever since. Freya's father died as the result of a fever, and her mother of a broken heart.

Although Gran loves Freya, she never made any effort to educate her or tell her how to present herself. Which is why, even though all the children are poor, Freya looks the scrappiest. They sell all the best clothes they make, and Freya is left with the rejects.

Freya has always entertained herself. She is imaginative. The only person she would really like to be friends with is Sal, as she respects her fierceness and the way she bosses the boys around.

Freya has been stealing things for Sal for the last few years, and she's been picked on by the local children for as long as she can remember.

GRAN

Name: Joanie Copperwhart. She makes clothing at home which she sells to make money.

Her father was a farm hand, and she grew up surrounded by farm animals. On the rare occasions Joanie has been able to afford meat, she's chosen not to buy it as she has such an affinity with animals.

When she was fourteen, she saw a man from the village kick a whimpering dog in the stomach. Joanie felt a wave of cold, white hatred flush through her and wished he would feel the same kind of pain. The next day she heard the man had suffered a terrible stomach ache in the night and that by morning he was dead. His wife said he whimpered the whole night through. Joanie never told anyone about her wish.

Two years ago, Gran was suspected of being a witch after she was overheard talking to her cat, Moggy. Knowing what was at stake, she killed her cat to prove they had no special bond.

She suffers great guilt about killing Moggy, which means she has problems sleeping at night, and during the day she hears meows and sees Moggy in dark corners.

LEN

Len suffers frequent beatings at the hands of his father, who is an agricultural labourer and a violent bully. He doesn't have a mother, who died giving birth to his younger brother John, of whom Len is very protective.

As his dad hardly pays them any attention, Len attends to household chores like cooking and cleaning. His dad ridicules him for this, although he eats the food Len prepares.

Every time Len receives a beating from his father, he takes it out on Freya, or one of his group.

Len is the leader of a small group of local children. They hang around together when they aren't working, which due to the poor harvest is increasingly often.

Len hates to see weakness or fear in others; in fact it scares him. He is the boss in the group. The first impression may be that Sal is the leader but there is a power tag-team between the two of them that Len ultimately wins.

JOHN

Len's younger brother. He has never learned to think before he speaks or acts, as Len has always been there to clear up any mess he gets himself into.

He is scared of his father, especially as his behaviour has been worse recently.

He is the most bloodthirsty of the group and spends his spare time killing insects.

SAL

All of Sal's siblings died at birth, and as the only surviving child she has always been spoilt. Her mum is a washerwoman and her dad an agricultural labourer.

After Len, Sal has the most power in the group as she's forceful and direct and used to getting her own way.

Her dad is good friends with John and Len's father, and she has been bossing the boys around since she was able to speak.

She doesn't like Freya because she thinks it's weird that she spends so much time on her own. Occasionally she pretends to like her as a joke, then laughs when Freya falls for it.

She has always imagined that she'll one day marry Len.

LOU

Lou isn't stupid, just a bit of a sheep – she follows the others and doesn't question their behaviour.

She has one brother, who works helping their dad farm the small piece of land he owns.

Lou's family have a bit more money than the other children's, which gives her confidence.

She is the least afraid of Len, as he's not as big as her brother, which gives her strength.

MARLEY

The eldest of four children, Marley is Len's best friend (although he fears him a bit) and is financially the best off of the group.

His dad worked with Matthew Hopkins (the Witchfinder General), and has identified and brought to trial several witches (so the family have a bit more money than the others). Marley has been allowed to accompany his dad at these trials.

Marley has always wanted to impress his dad. He is possibly the only one that has been privileged enough to have some kind of education.

Marley could be cast as a girl, and if doubling is needed Lou and Marley could be merged into a single character.

BILLY

Billy has five brothers, all younger than him. His dad works in a brewery.

Billy is slower than other children in every way. His mother blames a fever he had when he was a baby.

Billy hangs around with the other children because he's afraid not to. He's most scared of Sal, and would rather spend time with Freya as she's quieter.

Feeding the Back-story

For both groups of characters, it may be interesting to formulate a Top Trumps-style system for character development: who has the most money, the highest status, greatest ambition etc.

Create Facebook pages for the contemporary characters and Ye Olde Facebooke pages for the seventeenth century characters: what might kids have on their walls? Status updates? What parties have they been to – or wish they could go to, or wish existed? Include a profile picture that may indicate how they want the world to see them (or maybe how they already regard themselves).

The director suggested watching *The Crucible* and *The Village* as interesting reference points for the seventeenth-century scenes.

Research regional folk tales, witch stories and about local superstitions.

Look at the folk art of the period: paintings, woodcut prints and carvings. Can these shed light on how you could represent seventeenth-century life: the way people dressed, walked, sat, ate, travelled?

What about the Norfolk Accent?

The dialect of the seventeenth century characters is a language of the past. Though the director may choose not to simulate a Norfolk accent it is important that the accent selected has some 'history' – your own local, rural equivalent. It is important that the language of the past has a forward momentum, and not the modern tendency of allowing the energy to 'drop off' at the end of the line.

If learning a new dialect for the seventeenth-century world is not feasible for your cast, then maybe choose a dozen interesting sounds from a rural accent and incorporate these into the actors' dialogue, creating your own distinct patois.

A Diagnostic Character Study Exercise

Get the actors in character to stand between two designated separate points, one representing 'Yes, lots, great!' the other representing 'No, not at all, terrible.'

Ask the actors some of the following and similar questions and then to move towards the 'yes' point or the 'no' point, or place themselves somewhere in between:

- How well do you sleep at night?
- How much do you enjoy the company of the opposite sex?
- Do you like animals?
- Do you enjoy your own company?
- Can you tolerate the sight of blood?
- Do you believe in witches?
- Usually, how hungry are you?
- Do you have a healthy diet?
- Do you have a healthy relationship with your mum/dad?
- If you found £50 (or the seventeenth-century equivalent) on the street, what would you do with it?

Try to avoid extremes of behaviour when developing characters. Try to avoid big, abstract questions during this exercise, such as 'how evil are you?' or 'how frightened are you?'

The 'Dangerous Characters'

The director suggested that in each time period there was one character that particularly needed to be dealt with carefully and sensitively:

Leanne (present day): to play her as the mean girl, the bitchy it-girl, could result in all the characters being interpreted as stereotypes. Leanne is not a TV-show parody, and these are not stock characters.

Billy (seventeenth century): he doesn't want to be in this situation at all. He's caught between exile and bullying. He is a sickly, poorly boy, and it is not unsurprising that the vulnerable Billy and Freya maybe find solace in one another. The death of Billy is a huge trigger and has considerable resonance in the play, so the audience need to have an opinion, to be drawn to, to care about Billy. (NB: he is definitely dead after the poisoning, not in a coma which he'll recover from after the play.)

Production Notes

Be careful when moving from a significant moment into a new scene, with particular reference to the shift from Scene Eight to Nine. Could the beginning of a bright new scene undermine the resonance of the dramatic events of the previous scene? How could this transition be sensitively handled – through lighting, volume, pace? Rhythm and cue-pick-up games could change the tempo of the following scene.

Start early on special effects – you need to find a solution! Work out how you are going to achieve these. If you're using a student technician, there could be a workshop making the different kinds of fake blood to explore their different viscosities and colours.

The end is a big visual opportunity – think about how you are going to tackle it.

COSTUMES   There is an exciting visual opportunity with the seventeenth-century costumes. Look online for ways of making – don't just raid the costume cupboard.

VIDEO   The piece has obvious video potential. There are three options:

> No video at all – do all the videoing and watching theatrically, through acting and reacting.
>
> Pre-record some video to be watched.
>
> Use a live relay.

Molly did not think video was essential and could be distracting. The emphasis should be on the reaction to it. The play was not written thinking the audience were going to see video. The director added that there is a chance that the use of technology could impinge on the pace of the play.

The chase sequence poses a big challenge. Consider early on the level of abstraction necessary to achieve this, and practically how you think you can make it work.

Music is important, and could help blend the two worlds moving from the seventeenth century to now. If working with a composer, get moving now and try things out.

For Scene Eleven, many different options are possible – it could be good for the audience to see reactions, or to see the video. It's up to you.

A warning against literalism – with a piece of this length and with many different locations, the director would be wary of using blackouts.

There is enjoyment and thematic resonance in seeing the transition between the time periods. As with staging, it would be useful to think about the level of abstraction necessary. Think about exits and entrances from surprising places – find the exciting place where the other world can appear.

PRODUCTION EXERCISES   Split into four groups. Each think about the play with specific focus and discuss for ten minutes.

- How would you direct the play if you only had lights?

- How would you design it if you only had sound?

- How would you direct the play if you only had movement?

- How would you direct the play if you had a big empty warehouse and the only thing you could change is the relationship between the actors and the audience? Come up with one idea that works through the whole play or a solution to one specific moment.

LIGHTING IDEAS

The light could pass over the stage through the course of the play – like the sun.

Move from front-lit to back-lit.

For the spell – have candles round her and a cool pool of light that shrinks in focus to her face.

One bright light on a tripod could move around and change the shape of each individual scene – like the lamps you have on a film location.

SOUND IDEAS

The transition from one world to another could be done using music that is electronic for the present day and becomes acoustic when moving into the seventeenth century.

The use of sound could distort reality – voices in the head while running, heartbeats, breathing, etc.

Artificial sounds in contrast to natural sounds – for example, a phone becomes a bird cheeping.

Using the sounds of humming and song.

MOVEMENT IDEAS

Experiment with the proximity of the different worlds: for example, they could be separate at the beginning, but move closer together as the play progresses.

In transitions, play with the idea of watching – the past watching the present, growing in intensity as the play progresses; the return of looks between similar characters.

The touching or passing of a prop to switch between time periods, for example an apple or handkerchief; a sneeze that characters share across time.

EMPTY WAREHOUSE IDEAS

Different periods start at different ends of the space, gradually moving together by the end of the play.

Performing in the round is an option, with pockets of space demarcated by the design, so that the play can happen in amongst the audience.

The director suggested that in-the-round staging might serve this play very well, and that scenes starting as others are finishing could be useful in giving the piece momentum.

Two stories start at the same end of the space but on different platforms, and the audience move through the space and through levels as the play progresses, moving eventually to the same place. The non-literal nature of platforms could be very useful to a play such as this.

All ideas seem to lead towards the idea of blending, merging, casting a spell, breaking a spell. This exercise should not be taken literally but the elegant simplicity of some of the ideas it gives could be worth holding on to.

BILLY'S DEATH

Billy's death provides the opportunity to 'kill' Billy twice: the mock death orchestrated and styled by Freya and acted by Billy will need to be repeated for his actual demise.

What could be the difference between the manifestation of death that Freya decides for Billy and the real suffering that he experiences? What are the effects of ingesting deadly nightshade? Frothing at the mouth, fitting, biting his tongue? There needs to be a distinction between the false death and his genuine suffering, almost as blatant as the shift from the real Gran in Scene Four and 'Luke in an apron and bad wig' at the beginning of Scene Five.

IDEAS FOR THE PIT AND THE WELL

A number of suggestions were made for how the pit and/or well might be presented on stage. Representing it with light, a gauze box, a lower space, an elevated space or video effects were among the ideas, as was the fact that the action *in* the hole and the action *above* the hole may be taking place in separate parts of the playing space: having an actual hole was not the most interesting solution. The fact that Freya is submerged in water and Alice is on stones and broken glass offered interesting design possibilities. We decided on the abstract!

SIGNIFICANT MOMENTS AND KEY EVENTS

A group exercise to locate the key moments, to decide on the climactic or pivotal point in each scene.

Suggestions for Scene One:

Alice   I've got a story you could use.

Or

Liam   Let's do it. (*The last line of the scene.*)

Suggestion for Scene Two:

Freya   What if I am? What if I am a witch?

Suggestions for Scene Three:

Alice   AAAAAHHHHHHHHHH!

Or

Sid   Why don't Alice just play Freya?

Or

Sadie   We *need* you, Alice.

The director suggested that these key moments may be sudden (a shock, a 'masked gun-man in the room') or sustained moments, the beginning of a 'slow burn'.

SCENE ELEVEN

The director asked a group of actors to work on the first two pages of Scene Eleven and develop this, first playing the characters as strongly and clearly as possible and next 'playing the scene', presenting what the characters want, not who they are, and allowing the action, not the attitude, to drive the scene. The result was two quite different interpretations of the same scene: the work driven by character was seen by the audience as being bolder, clearer, brighter; the scene with the concentration on actions and objectives as much more focused, subtle and intimate (though not necessarily more successful).

The participants set about working on other short excerpts from Scene Eleven (where the two worlds appear together) to investigate some of the staging techniques that could be considered. One version ran the action from the modern-day and the seventeenth-century worlds in the same space and at the same time, with clear shifts of focus and the use of freezes and slow motion. Another group developed the section almost as two films running simultaneously in separate parts of the performance space with no 'relationship' between the two. The action in both worlds was continuous and activities needed to be found to justify the 'gaps' as the text moved to the other world. Though this was high-energy, it did raise the issue of the audience not knowing where to look, with almost too much going on at once. The use of lighting was considered as a means of switching focus from one time period to the next, with particular reference to the use of blackouts. This raised the question of what happens when the lights go out. Does the action in that sector stop? Would it hinder the actors having to stop and start? Would the scene lose its momentum?

SCENE TWELVE

The writer said that she imagined the conclusion offering many possibilities. The audience should be left thrilled to speculate about what happened to the two girls. To achieve this, the ending should be strong and assured, but remain ambiguous. It is intentionally free for interpretation, but take care not to leave your audience feeling uncertain as this may lead to disappointment.

The uplifting and crucial moment is the connection between the two girls who share an empathy, a loneliness that the other understands. There are, have been, and will be more Alices and Freyas.

PERSONALISING THE TEXT

Changing names and the trimming of lines to fit specific dialects would not be a problem, but the incorporation of new writing and additional material is not allowed.

Songs etc. would be fine, but do be aware that this could have a negative impact upon running time, so consider the use of music carefully, as it's crucial that we flit between past and present as swiftly as possible.

From a workshop led by Lyndsey Turner,
with notes by Jonathan Humphreys and Phil Sheppard

James Graham

Bassett

Characters

Leo, *boy*
Kelly, *girl*
Spencer, *boy*
Rachel, *girl*
Amid, *boy*
Joanne, *girl*
Russell, *boy*
Shanti, *girl*
Jonathan, *boy*
Aimee, *girl*
Dean, *boy*
Lucy, *girl*
Graeme, *boy*
Zoe, *girl*

Notes on the Text

A slash mark (/) indicates that the character who speaks next should begin their line, overlapping with the preceding one.

An ellipsis (. . .) indicates hesitation.

A dash (–) indicates a change in thought or broken speech.

(Text in brackets) indicates a line spoken almost privately, to oneself, but still aloud (just).

A Classroom in Wootton Bassett School.

A map of the world on the wall, a whiteboard, a window, some tables, some chairs.

We open in darkness.

A school bell rings for lunch.

Lights up just as the classroom door is slamming shut.

A class of Year 11 pupils is dotted around the room, all standing, staring at the closed door – except for one boy, **Spencer***, who is against a wall, facing it.*

The sound of keys rattling as the door is locked from outside.

Leo *is standing closest to the door, staring at it. A short pause . . .*

Leo   She hasn't.

Rachel   She has.

Leo   She hasn't, she wouldn't dare.

Russell   She has though, you know.

Leo   She's still on the other side of the door, she's just joking – Miss, we know you're still there!!

Kelly/Rachel/Dean/Shanti   Leo!

Spencer   Don't!

Rachel   She'll keep us after school if you carry on.

Zoe   She can't do that.

Kelly   She will.

Zoe   She wouldn't!

Kelly/Spencer/Graeme/Dean/Amid/Jonathan
SHE WILL!

Joanne   Shush! Listen.

They all stop and listen. The sound of a plane flying over.

Jonathan   It's coming in to Lyneham.

Leo   We're gonna miss it!

He goes to the door and tries the handle. It's locked. He tugs at it hard, banging and kicking the door.

AAARRRGGHHH!! You bitch!

Russell   Leo! Leo, calm down mate, yeah.

Zoe   This must be against the law or something.

Joanne   It's against thingy, isn't it? Human Rights – what's that thing?

Aimee   What thing?

Joanne   Convention thing.

Jonathan   Geneva Convention?

Joanne   Is that the one I mean?

Jonathan   I don't know, what do you mean?

Leo (*paces around*)   God's sake.

Zoe   Yeah, Joanne's right, it's against the Geneva Convention, locking us in at lunchtime. We could get her put on trial and banged or something.

Jonathan   I don't think / she's –

Kelly   Well, she clearly can do it because she has, so.

Jonathan   I don't think she's breaking the Geneva Convention, but I think it probably is against Health and Safety, though.

Kelly   What?

Zoe   See.

Jonathan   Fire safety.

Leo *sits. Head in his hands.*

Shanti   I can't believe that just happened. She just completely flipped.

Rachel   She completely lost it – went mental.

Russell (*going to* **Leo**)   Mate, you all right?

Kelly   I'm not surprised she went nuts, all you lot teasing her.

Zoe   Who?

Kelly   Everyone.

Jonathan   I wasn't –

Graeme   I wasn't –

Zoe   Oh what, because *you* handed *your* project in, did you, Kelly?

Kelly   There's a difference / between not handing a –

Zoe   Did you? Did you hand your project in? No.

Kelly   Zoe, there's a difference between not handing something in and taking the piss out of the teacher for an hour / so that she goes all –

Zoe   Who took the piss, Kelly?

Kelly   Like you all coughing when she was talking all the time.

Russell   That was funny.

Aimee   I actually do have a cough, though.

Kelly   Well, that's interesting because you're not coughing now.

Aimee   It comes and goes.

Zoe   Why you so bothered, anyway? It isn't even a proper class and she isn't even a proper teacher.

Aimee *coughs*.

Kelly   I'm bothered because thanks to you lot I'm missing the repat. Everyone else, all those people and tourists and journalists and whoever all out there lining the street and I'm locked in here? I think that's a bit not right, I do. Is all I'm saying.

Amid (*looking out the window*)   Look. At the bottom of the drive.

*A few of the other pupils scramble and join **Amid** at the window.*

Spencer   What? What is it?

Amid   They've already started stopping the traffic.

Spencer   Who?

Shanti   Police.

Joanne   Already? That's early.

Jonathan   It's because it's busier today. Because of Charlie.

Leo *holds his head, and groans.*

Russell   Oy, fella, what is it?

Rachel   What's up with Leo?

Zoe   Leo?

Russell   Nothing, just leave him for a bit, all right?

Leo   I just wanted to be there.

For when he came home.

That's all.

Kelly   What, and you think I didn't? We're all missing it.

Zoe   Kelly. Just –

Leo   Uh, sorry, Kelly, but at what point did this become about you, eh?

Kelly   This isn't about me, you're making it / about you.

Leo (*standing*)   Pretending like you even knew him when you didn't.

Rachel/Aimee   Leo.

Leo   It's wrong.

Kelly   You're wrong.

Leo (*imitating, mockingly*)   'Urgh, you're wrong.'

Kelly   Pff. Is that meant / to be me?

Leo   'Pff, is that meant to be me?'

Russell   Oy, oy, oy, can we just chill out and calm down, yeah?

Leo   And you can shut up, Rachel, Aimee; why does everyone listen to her, why does everyone believe her lies, you didn't know him, / I knew him.

Dean   No one really knew him, he was like five years above us.

Kelly   I knew him pretty intimately actually, mate, / if you know what I mean.

Leo   Oh what, and it's nothing to do with there being more people out there today, then?

Kelly   What do you mean, what kind of people?

Leo   You know what kind of people.

Kelly   What kind of people?

Leo   Cameras. Photographs, kind of people.

Rachel   Leo.

Kelly   No, I don't get what he's saying. What are you saying, / I don't get it.

Leo   I'm saying, I'm just saying, I think it's interesting the way you look today, that's all.

Rachel   Leo.

Kelly   And what's the way I look today?

Leo   I dunno, just a little different. In the face.

Rachel   Leo!

Leo   Stop saying 'Leo', Rachel. 'Leo, / Leo, Leo' . . .

Kelly   In the face? What? This is just my face, what are you talking about?

Leo   It isn't just me, Spencer said he thought you had more make-up on today, didn't you, Spence?

Kelly   What?

Spencer (*still facing the wall*)   What?

Leo   You did.

Kelly   Spencer?!

Spencer   No, I said you looked . . . you know. No. I meant . . . nice. Today.

Leo   Erm, well, no, you didn't, but . . .

Rachel   I think you look nice, Kelly.

Kelly   And Spencer, what the hell would you know about what I look like, you've been facing the wall all bloody morning, nearly.

Russell   Spencer, you muppet, why are you still doing that?

Spencer   Miss Kirmani told me to.

Rachel   She's not here, idiot, she stormed out –

Spencer (*shouting and stamping*)   SHE TOLD ME TO FACE THE WALL AND THAT'S WHAT I'M DOING! (*Brief pause. Calmer.*) I'm sick of being in trouble all the time. I'm sick of other people getting me in trouble all the time. I'm sick of getting detention every other lunchtime and after school 'cause of mucking about or other people mucking about and making me laugh or making me join in or making me do things that get me in trouble, I'm just sick of it. OK? She told me to face the wall until she said otherwise and she hasn't said otherwise yet, so I'm facing the wall! OK?

Russell   Man, that is fucked up, Spence.

Spencer   I DON'T CARE IF IT'S FUCKED UP! I don't care. This is what I'm doing. I don't want to fail any more.

A slight sense of calm descends. Momentarily.

Dean   Erm. I don't want to worry everyone, but I really need a piss.

Russell, **Kelly** *and* **Rachel** *laugh.*

Kelly   Dean's gonna wet himself.

Dean   It's not funny!

Russell   Mate, you'll be fine, hold it.

Dean   That's what my hand was up for, to go to the toilet, and then it all kicked off, thanks to you lot.

Kelly   Leo, I want to know what you meant about looking different today.

Jonathan   Oh God, can't we just drop it?

Kelly   I look exactly the same as I always do and that's that.

Zoe   Aren't you a bit colder today, though?

Kelly   What? Why?

Zoe   In that skirt.

Kelly   No. What do you mean?

Zoe   Not exactly boiling today, is it?

Kelly   You're wearing one, Zoe – you're wearing a skirt.

Zoe   Yeah, but you're only *just* about wearing one.

Russell   Haha! (*Snaps his fingers.*) Yes, Zoe. One-nil.

Kelly   Zoe, I think I'd rather you just came out with what you think that . . . (*Stumbling over her words.*) And say what the thing what − is that / you're thinking −

Leo   What? What? What's that, Kelly? Got your false teeth in today, as well?

Kelly   Piss off! It's you lot, all looking at me and judging me, making me all . . .

Leo   Making you what? Guilty?

Joanne   Leo.

Kelly   Back off, Leo, I mean it.

Leo   Oh why, what, you gonna come round mine with your big brother? Because I'll tell you something, he isn't as tough as everyone thinks he is.

Kelly   I don't go down Eveleigh Road, Leo, because I don't want to get stabbed.

Zoe (*at the window*)   God, there is literally no one about, we're like the only ones here.

Leo   Oy, Zo, does that window open?

Zoe (*tries it*)   No.

Jonathan   It needs a key.

Zoe   Where's the key?

Jonathan   Dunno. I suppose Miss Kirmani will have it.

Leo   Right.

He empties his rucksack on to a table − some books, crisps, a rounders bat, paint spray cans and other crap falls out. He takes hold of the bat.

Leo   I'm smashing the window in.

Dean   Leo, no!

Leo   Then I can drop down from here.

Russell   Yeah, go on, Leo. (*Laughs.*)

Rachel   You idiot, it's too high.

Leo   No, it's the second floor, not too high.

Kelly   Oh, just let him, Rachel, do us all a favour.

Russell (*looking out*)   Actually, mate, that does look quite high.

Shanti   Why have you got a baseball bat in your bag?

Russell   It's rounders, we're gonna have a game, Noremarsh Park, after school.

Dean   Are you?

Russell   Yeah, come, Dean, if you haven't pissed yourself by then.

Dean   Awh, don't, I'd almost forgotten.

Russell   Well you can't be that desperate, then, can you?!

Leo   I'm doing it.

Spencer   Don't, Leo, we'll get in trouble.

Leo   Spencer, it's all right, if anyone asks, you don't even have to lie, just tell them you didn't see anything.

Jonathan   Leo, you'll get suspended.

Aimee   If not expelled.

Spencer   The rest of us will get in trouble, we'll all be expelled.

Leo   I'll say if was for Health and Safety, right. Jonathan?

He raises his bat . . .

Graeme/Dean/Kelly/Amid/Shanti   Don't!!

Leo *holds the bat in the air. He thinks. He lowers the bat, and drops it on to the desk, smiling at the others, wandering around.*

Zoe   Still can't believe Miss Kirmani's done this.

Leo   She's not allowed. She can't stop us from going to a repat, when she's not even from here!

Shanti   She lives here, Leo.

Leo   I meant from Bassett, Shanti, she's not from Wootton Bassett.

Rachel   I'm not from Wootton Bassett, I'm from Swindon, so / what? Does that mean –

Leo   It's the same thing, you know what I mean, you go to this school, don't you, this is our town, it's our thing that we do, this is for us –

Jonathan   Well, it's for the families.

Leo   You know what I mean! What's this, pick on Leo day?

Russell   Mate –

Joanne   It's been completely ruined now, anyway. I don't think we should do any more. I don't like it.

Zoe   Oh God, you're not one of them, are you, Joanne?

Aimee   I know what she means, though.

Leo   Shut up, both of you. 'Completely ruined'.

Joanne   Don't tell me to shut up, Leo. / I mean it.

Aimee   It's just turned into a media circus. Loads of people just turn up to see what's happening and they shouldn't.

Leo   You don't know what you're talking about, Aimee, you're just chatting shit.

Aimee   Oy, it's my opinion, it's not chatting shit, it's / just my opinion.

Leo   It's about being respectful, it's about paying your respects.

Aimee   I pay my respects, whenever I've seen one, I just don't want to go to them all the time, I don't think it's for me.

Zoe   It's not about 'wanting to', it's about 'should do'. I always go to them. If we're off.

Dean   So do I.

Aimee   Fine. Good for you. I just don't like to see all the men crying. The dads. It makes me upset. And I'm pretty sure they don't all want me standing there gawping at them either.

Graeme (*quietly, speaking for the first time*)   This mor— This morning. On the way here. There, erm . . . there was this . . . a, a photographer man.

Kelly   Pap. Paparazzi. That's what they are.

Graeme   He –

Rachel   Paps are for celebs, Kelly.

Kelly   Yeah, it is a celeb.

Leo   Not celebs. Soldiers. Better than celebs. Celebs are scum, celebs are dogshit.

Kelly   I meant like our town, like our town is a celebrity now. That's all I meant.

Leo   I need to get out of here. You – none of you know what you're . . .

Graeme   I was walking to school and the vans with the satellite dishes had started turning up and I was walking down the High Street and he came up to me and asked me to give him a leg up on to the branch of the tree so that he could scramble up on to the roof of the what'sit – the thing. The shelter thing. So he could get a better view. But I didn't.

Rachel (*sarcastically*)   Wow, good story, Graeme.

Russell   Oy, leave him alone. Well done, Graeme.

Amid   Well done, Graeme.

Russell   Don't help the bastards, let them break their necks. Ha ha.

Leo   Why are they all here today, he was just a normal soldier, wouldn't have wanted all this attention, just to be treated like everyone else, all he would have wanted.

Joanne   He *wasn't* like everyone else, he was amazing.

Shanti   Oh my God, do you remember him as Danny Zuko?

Joanne/Rachel/Aimee/Shanti (*swooning*)   Awwwwwh.

Joanne   My God.

Rachel   So fit.

Aimee   We were only Year 7, what was he? 11?

Leo   Ten.

Aimee   What?

Leo   Ten. Deafo. He was Year 10 when we were Year 7.

Rachel   I always thought he was older, looked older.

Leo   He was Year 10 when we were Year 7! Listen, I played football with him, we were mates.

Kelly   'We were mates', yeah right, now who's chatting shit.

Leo   We. Were. Mates. Fuck. You. Kelly. You. Silly . . .

Pause.

Kelly   What?

Leo   Fill it in yourself.

Kelly   Silly what?

Leo   Fill in the blank yourself, you know what you are, I can't be arsed.

Russell   I'm not being funny or anything, but he always a little bit pissed me off –

Zoe/Rachel/Leo   Russell!

Russell   God rest his soul, nothing personal, and thank you for going off to fight for my country, but what I actually meant was, like, a backhand compliment – I mean, Mr Southwall basically rated him as God.

Leo   It's true, he did, / he was . . . like . . .

Russell   And no matter how well you did or what you achieved, Charlie had done it about three years before and better. All them trophies in the cabinet, they're mostly him –

Aimee   Not the hockey, that's mine –

Rachel   Ours.

Aimee   Ours.

Kelly   I'm gonna miss him.

Rachel   Awh. (*Hugging her.*) It's all right, Kelly. Just got to be strong.

Leo   Oy, shut up! Seriously, Kelly.

Kelly   Do one, Leo!

Leo   You didn't know him, he never went out with you, it's all bollocks.

Kelly   He did.

Leo   It's bullshit. I know it is, we were mates, he'd have told me.

Rachel   He might not have done.

Russell   Actually, yeah, if I shagged you, Kelly, I'd probably wanna keep it a secret.

Kelly   Fuck you, Russell –

Russell   Joke!

Kelly   This is nothing to do with you.

Russell   Was a joke, wasn't it, laugh, 'ha ha ha'.

Rachel   Leo, if Kelly says she went out with him, then she went out with him, why would she lie?

Kelly   Why would I lie?

Leo   Right. (*Picks up his bat again.*) I'm going out the window.

Spencer/Rachel/Aimee   Don't!

Leo *moves away, pacing, swinging his bat, towards the desk.*

Leo   Must be another key. (*Pulls at a locked drawer.*) Man, everything's locked in this school, don't they trust people? (*Tugs harder.*)

Rachel (*sarcastic*)   Oh yeah, that's a great idea, Leo, go through her drawer, that won't get us in trouble at all.

Jonathan   I'm really against this, Leo. It's her private belongings.

Leo   Not private – school. And anyway, she's only a supply teacher, supply teachers don't have any privacy.

Russell   Come on, I'll help.

Leo *smashes the drawer a few times with the bat, and with force he and* **Russell** *manage to yank it open.*

Dean   Leo! She'll know!

Leo   All right, Dean, don't piss yourself.

Dean   I'm trying!

Leo *and* **Russell** *root around the drawer.* **Leo** *pulls out a set of small keys.*

Leo   Is these them?

Jonathan   Dunno, could be.

Leo *goes to the window and tries while* **Russell** *roots around the drawer more.*

Spencer   He's not really going to go out the window, is he?

Kelly   No, don't worry, he's just showing off, as always.

Russell   Awh man, look at this. Miss Kirmani's notes. (*Laughs.*) They're all from Wikipedia!

Joanne   What?

Russell   She's just printed a load of stuff off of Wikipedia. Jesus Christ, I could do that, maybe I'll be a teacher. What do they get, like a hundred grand a year?

Jonathan   Supply teachers do.

Russell   Urgh, it's just history and war and things.

Dean (*hands between his legs*)   Oh God, seriously, if she's not coming back in the next ten minutes then we're gonna have to think of something.

Russell (*holding up an empty bottle of Cola*)   Dean, why don't you just go in this?

Dean   I'm not pissing into a bottle.

Russell   Fine, piss into your pants instead then.

Zoe (*with* **Leo** *at the window*)   Have you tried that one?

Leo (*fiddling with the keys*)   Hold on, hold on.

Dean   Shit, all right then, give me the bottle.

Rachel   Urgh, don't, Dean, that's gross.

Dean   No one watch.

Kelly   Dean, trust me, no one's gonna wanna watch, OK?

Dean (*reaching to take the bottle from* **Russell**)   Here.

Russell   Fiver.

Dean   What?

Russell   Five pounds please.

Dean   What?

Russell   Supply–demand, mate.

Dean   You're a bastard, Russell.

Russell   I can see it on Facebook now. 'Dean peed his pants today in Citizenship class.' Stuff of legends, mate. That shit never goes away.

Dean   I'll hold it.

Russell   You sure?

Dean   No.

Russell   Have a think then, come back in a bit.

Dean   All right.

Russell   But it'll have gone up to a tenner by then.

Dean   What?!

Russell   Inflation mate, recession's a bitch.

Leo   Done it!

He opens the window.

Shanti   Ah, some fresh air at last.

Zoe   Well done.

Leo   Right.

Leo *swings his leg over and sits on the ledge. Some others run over to stop him.*

Jonathan/Russell/Graeme/Joanne/Shanti/Amid   No!

Leo   What?

Amid   It's too high.

Russell   Leo, don't, mate.

Leo   Honestly, I know how to land, land and roll, I've seen it, like on *Call of Duty*. Then I can go find that bitch, get the key off her, come back, and let you out. Simple as.

Russell   We need you for the game on Saturday, if you twist your ankle or break a leg –

Zoe   He's right, Leo, I don't think you should.

Pause, as **Leo** *sits on the ledge, looking down.*

He climbs off the ledge and back into the room. A sense of relief.

He takes hold of his bat and paces again, swinging it.

Leo When she comes back, I'm telling you . . . (*Swinging the bat.*) Making me miss it.

Jonathan Do you . . . do you have *Call of Duty* on Xbox or PS3?

Leo PS3.

Jonathan Me too.

Leo Yeah? Have you completed any of the Special Ops on *Call of Duty – Modern Warfare 2*.

Jonathan I just did the Delta Special Op, completed it on Veteran level.

Leo No fucking way.

Rachel Urgh, boys and their stupid games.

Leo 'S not games, it's good practice.

Rachel For what?

Leo For war. In case we ever have to go.

He pulls an imaginary weapon and points it at **Rachel**'*s head, firing it several times.*

Russell Incoming!

Leo Get down!

Russell *mimes tossing a grenade.* **Leo** *rolls on to and off a table, making firing noises as he goes, followed by the noise of a fake explosion.*

Dean My brother showed me *Call of Duty – Black Ops* on his PC. It's a–ma–zing.

Russell I prefer *Halo 3*.

He imitates the character in the game, ducking and firing a weapon.

Leo   Favourite weapon?

Russell   Easy, plasma gun, no question. No, no, no, wait, shotgun! Shotgun. Simple, clean.

Leo   No, man, what about the Magnum, semiautomatic, that shit rips through flesh.

Russell   Oh yeah, yeah, and when you get a headshot it just completely explodes. (*Mimes his head exploding.*)

Graeme   . . . laptop.

Dean   What? Squeak up, Graeme.

Graeme   I've got my laptop.

Dean   Lucky you, so what?

Graeme   The projector. Like what Mr McPherson does in Drama, to watch films. I could connect it to the DV projector and go online. We could maybe watch it online. The repatriation. Project it on to the whiteboard.

Leo   Yeah? Could you?

Russell   Can you do that?

Graeme   Maybe, yeah.

Rachel   Like a cinema.

Leo   Awh man, go on then.

Jonathan   I'll help.

Russell   Finally, clever people are becoming useful at last.

Graeme *starts opening up his laptop as he and* **Jonathan** *begin working on the projector.*

Joanne   It might not be live, will it? The repat.

Jonathan   I bet it is on the BBC News Channel. Rolling twenty-four-hour news, they're always struggling to fill their schedules with something, that's why they love stuff like this.

Leo   And Spencer, you're turning back round and watching it when it's on.

Spencer   I'm not.

Leo   You are.

Spencer   I'm not!

Dean   Spencer, aren't you bored? Jesus.

Spencer   I'm thinking. (*Beat.*) A bit bored, yeah.

Russell   Here, you can read Miss Kirmani's notes, learn something.

He takes some pins and sticks up the sheets from the desk on to the wall in front of **Spencer***'s face.*

Spencer   Awh, thanks Russell, that's wicked.

Russell   I'll test you later.

Amid   Maybe that's what we should be doing now? Finishing our projects. So that when she comes back –

Zoe   No, forget it, doesn't matter, it's only Citizenship.

Leo   You don't need a grade in Citizenship to be a British citizen, it's bullshit, it's bollocks, man, I hate it. You can't learn that, they can't teach that.

Zoe   And no offence, and no disrespect, but Miss Kirmani isn't exactly the best person to be teaching it, either, is she?

Dean   What do you mean?

Shanti   What 'cause she's not white and English and / born in Wiltshire?

Zoe   That's not being racist, Shanti, that's just saying, she was born in a different country, she said so, that's all I'm saying. She might be from America, for all I care, or Belgium, or . . . you know, I don't know, anywhere. Holland. China, erm –

Russell   France.

Zoe   France. Exactly. I'm just saying what can a teacher *born* in Pakistan teach me about Britain. That's not being racist.

Shanti   India. She's Hindu, like me. Hindu is mainly India, not Pakistan.

Leo   Shanti, chill out, she's just saying she's a wank teacher.

Russell   She is pretty shit.

Amid   She's shit at everything, she's a supply teacher, supply teachers are meant to be shit. That's what they supply: they supply shit.

Rachel   I can't believe how badly she lost it.

Aimee   I don't think she's coming back ever. And it's lunchtime, I'm starving, I am literally starving. The rest of the school are gonna come back after they've seen the coffins go past and they're gonna find *us* dead.

Leo   Oy. Don't.

Aimee   Sorry. But –

Dean   You're not gonna die from starvation in an hour, Aimee.

Rachel (*looking through* **Leo***'s things from his bag*)   Leo, why have you got spray cans in your bag?

Leo   Art.

Rachel   What?

Kelly   Oh-oh, someone was gonna graffiti something, naughty.

Leo   I've got art, Lesson 5. It's an art project.

Kelly   Bollocks. You were gonna spray a wall or something, I know it.

Leo   You don't know – how do you know? You don't.

Kelly   Because I know.

Leo   Psh. You wish you knew me –

Kelly   What?

Leo   You wish you knew me.

Kelly   Urgh, dream on.

Leo (*taking a can*)   I might tag this wall. That'd show Miss Kirmani.

Kelly   Oh, whatever.

Spencer   Don't, Leo.

Kelly   He won't, don't worry.

Leo   A big fuck-off Union Jack. That can be my project. Citizenship. A-star, job done.

He takes the lid off and shakes the can, aims it at the wall . . .

Spencer/Dean/Graeme/Aimee/Rachel   Don't!

Pause. **Leo** *smiles and puts the top back on the can. Paces, swinging . . .*

Amid   What time is it? Do we really think Miss Kirmani won't be back until after lunch?

Rachel   Amid, if we knew that, then . . .

Amid   Well. I may have to pray here.

Leo   You what?

Spencer *starts to count something on the sheets.*

Amid   Noon prayer. *Dhuhr.* If people don't mind.

Jonathan   Of course no one minds, Amid.

Rachel   Spencer, what you counting?

Spencer   The wars.

Rachel   The what?

Spencer   Twelve. We had twelve wars. Britain.

Russell   Uh, I think we might have had a few more than that, Spence.

Jonathan   When does that timeline start from?

Spencer   Er. Oh yeah, 1900.

Russell (*laughs*)   Numpty.

Spencer   All right, twelve since the start of the century, then.

Joanne   Last century.

Spencer   What?

Joanne   That's last century.

Spencer   Whatever, it's still a lot.

Russell   It's not that many. All things considered.

Aimee   All what things considered?

Russell   I dunno, it's a saying, isn't it.

Zoe   Amid?

Amid   Yes.

Zoe   Can I ask you something?

Amid   Yes.

Zoe   Don't take it funnily.

Amid   Don't take it what? What?

Zoe   Does it bother you?

Amid   What?

Zoe   Being the only one?

Amid   The only . . . ?

Zoe   Muslim.

Amid   Uh, there's one or two more of us, actually. I saw some the other day on tele.

Russell (*laughs*)   Yes, Amid. Get in.

Zoe   You know what I mean, in the school.

Amid   No.

Joanne   Yeah, that's only this school, if we were in Reading or London or somewhere, we'd probably be / . . . you know, in the –

Rachel   Why would it bother him, gets special privileges, doesn't he?

Amid   What special privileges?

Rachel   You know. Nothing bad, just saying.

Zoe   Like getting to skip out of some lessons to pray and all that.

Shanti   It is a bit odd when you first come here and there's only like a handful of people who aren't white.

Leo   Well, what do you expect, that's not our fault.

Shanti   No, I know.

Leo   I can't help it that I'm white and I'm not sorry, either.

Shanti   Zoe was asking a question.

Leo   Yeah, to Amid, not you, about being a Muslim, not you.

Amid   Actually, Zoe, getting out of lessons means I just have to work harder, so no, they don't actually feel like privileges, actually.

Rachel   Are you gonna pray now then, Amid, or not?

Amid (*looking around, uncertain*)   In a second.

Shanti   How's your sponsored silence going, Lucy?

Lucy *gives thumbs up*.

Leo   Hey, Lucy –

Leo *jumps up behind her, making a noise, tying to make her jump, which she does a bit.* **Leo** *laughs, carrying on pacing around, swinging his bat.* **Lucy** *scowls.*

Rachel   Don't be a twat, Leo, she's doing really well. Trying to ruin it and make her speak.

Kelly   How long's it been now, Luce?

Rachel   Kelly!

Kelly   What?

Rachel   You're just as bad, stop tricking her.

Kelly   She can hold her fingers up can't she? I'm just asking how long.

Lucy *flashes ten fingers, then another ten . . . then thinks . . . then holds up six fingers.*

Spencer   What's she doing?

Joanne   Holding her fingers up.

Spencer   How many.

Rachel   Twenty-six.

Shanti   Twenty-six hours!

Russell   Well done, Lucy.

Amid   Well done, Lucy.

Kelly   I don't think I've been quiet for twenty-six hours altogether in my whole life.

Leo   Yeah, no shit.

Dean   What's she raising the money for?

Jonathan   Royal British Legion.

Aimee   Well done, Lucy.

Leo   Well done, Lucy. Sorry for being a dickhead, that's brilliant.

Kelly   Well done, Lucy.

Russell   It's the veterans who started the whole lining the High Street thing, wasn't it? When the first coffins went past.

Amid   He used to be the mayor. The man.

Leo   I was out there. The second time it happened. Soon as I heard what was happening, I was out there.

Joanne   My grandad's a veteran.

Aimee   Mine too.

Joanne   He's one of the people with the flags. When they lower them as the coffins pass. Outside the Cross Keys.

Jonathan   Will he be out there now?

Leo   They all will be. We should be. Course he's out there now. Proud.

Joanne   He doesn't like the clapping, though. Goes on about it all the time.

Russell   Why not?

Joanne   He just thinks the clapping is wrong.

Leo   It's not wrong. It's saying thank you.

Joanne   He just thinks there should be silence.

Leo   Jesus Christ, people clap all the time, at everything, things that don't deserve anything, people singing, or doing dancing with a dog or something on *Britain's Got Wankers* and all that. You've got to clap people who are fighting to protect us, they deserve it. Got to.

Aimee   Be better if they just came home alive, though, wouldn't it?

Zoe   What do you mean?

Aimee   Well. You know. (*Slight pause.*) 'Cause they can't . . . you know, they can't hear everyone clapping. Can they? When they're dead . . .

Leo   Doesn't mean we should bring them home, though, Aimee, they're out there fighting to protect us.

Aimee   I'm just saying I wish it could end so they could all come home.

Leo   I don't wish it could end, I want it to go on and on. I want it to go on until I can get out there.

He mimes being a soldier, holding a rifle, ducking, and scouting around.

Joanne   Leo, haven't we all had to watch enough coffins go down the High Street?

Rachel   I was in Worcester yesterday visiting my cousin – well, she's not really my cousin, but like my auntie's new husband's – anyway, she's like in her forties, or something, like old anyway, and her nan died the other week and she was saying she was nervous about going in because she'd never seen a coffin before and I was just like, 'Seriously? I'm, like, a kid and I've seen about a hundred, 'cause of living here.'

Leo   Yeah, it's because of seeing them that I wanna go out. So they didn't die for nothing.

Kelly   That doesn't even make any sense, Leo.

Leo   So. You don't make any sense. (*At* **Joanne**.) You don't make any sense. (*At* **Aimee**.) You don't make any sense. So . . .

Aimee   I'm just saying I don't know any more, that's all.

Leo   What don't you know, any more?

Aimee   It's just my opinion.

Leo   What's your opinion?

Aimee   I just don't know whether them being out there is protecting us, whether they're actually making a difference or not, I don't know.

Leo   Making a difference?

Russell   Oy, OK, let's not start a debate, it'll only end in tears.

Leo   Whether or not it's . . . You say that? On the day of a repat, on the day when one of our old pupils from the school flies back in a coffin –

Aimee   I'm not saying I'm not grateful –

Leo   It sounds pretty ungrateful.

Aimee   I'm not saying that I'm ungrateful –

Leo   Because it sounds pretty ungrateful.

Russell   Leo, mate.

Aimee   And it makes me sad when they die, and I'm grateful that they risk their lives, OK, all right, I'm just not sure what the point is any more.

Leo   Point is so they don't come over here and blow us up, that's the point.

Aimee   I'm –

Leo   That's the point, Aimee.

Amid   The 7/7 guys were from Leeds.

Leo   What?

Amid (*pause*)   The 7/7 guys. Who blew up the tubes. They were from this country, they were from Leeds.

Leo   And?

Amid   And I'm just saying.

Leo   What?

Amid   I'm just saying.

Leo   What are you saying?

Spencer   Oy.

Russell   All right, chillax, everyone, Jesus.

Amid   And they said that it was Iraq. Why they did it.
Because Britain was in Iraq.

Leo   So.

Spencer (*looking at his sheets*)   Actually, Britain's been in Iraq
before, lots of times. In fact we were the ones that invented it,
kind of. Drew its borders anyway, after the First World War.
Used to be called Meso – . . . Mesop – . . . po–ta–mia. Or
something. And then we invaded in 1991. With the Americans
again. So we've already done this war, once before! Did
anyone know that?

Russell   How would we know that, Spence; we weren't
even born.

Amid   So if we weren't there, there wouldn't have been any
bombs. Is all I'm saying.

Leo   So because we got bombed we should give in?

Amid   No.

Leo   Because we're scared?

Amid   No. I'm just offering up an alternative view. From
yours.

Leo   You don't think we should be there?

Amid   Like when all those images came out with the
Americans abusing the prisoners.

Jonathan   Abu Ghraib.

Kelly   Abu what?

Amid   The prison. Torturing the prisoners in the prison.

Russell (*scrambling on to a table*)   Oh yeah, have you seen that
one with the guy and a blanket over him, stood like that with
electrodes and shit on his fingers like a scarecrow.

He stands on the table, mimicking the image.

Amid   Photos of them stripping them down and being naked and pointing and laughing and getting them to pile on top of each other and touch each other and –

Leo   Yeah, but you just said it, that wasn't us, that was America.

Amid   – so I just don't necessarily think we've made ourselves safer by being there.

Leo   So you don't think we should be there, Amid, right? Am I right?

Amid   In Afghanistan we should maybe be there. Maybe. I don't know.

Leo   We are in Afghanistan, though.

Amid   I don't think we should have been in Iraq.

Leo   Oh?

Jonathan   I don't think we should have been in Iraq.

Leo   Oh. Lots of views. OK.

Kelly   I don't know the difference, sorry.

Leo   Well, this is interesting. This is interesting. On the day that Charlie is flown home, on the day of his repat, and on all those other days on all those other repats, when we've had, what is it now, over a hundred coffins go past us and we all stood and watched that –

Russell   Mate.

Leo   I'm just saying it's interesting, Russell, especially how many of us, as well, have relatives up at Lyneham or based elsewhere, army, navy, RAF, yeah? I'm jut saying it's interesting.

Amid   I can be grateful for the soldiers' sacrifice without agreeing with the reason that politicians sent them in the first place.

Leo   Can I ask you something?

Shanti   Can we all just maybe talk about something else instead?

Leo   You know them Islam4UK people, those people who were gonna march through Bassett in protest?

Amid   I know what you're going to say, don't.

Leo   What?

Spencer   Leo.

Joanne   Leo.

Zoe   No, maybe he should ask it, I'm interested.

Rachel   Zoe.

Amid   Don't.

Leo   Did you agree with them? Did you think they should have been allowed to march through Bassett holding fifty empty coffins?

Amid   Because I'm a Muslim?

Leo   Because of what you just said.

Amid   Because we're all the same?

Leo   Did I say that?

Amid   Because we all believe the same things?

Leo   Did I say that, Amid? I said, 'Do you agree with them?' I was asking, asking a question. Do you agree with them?

Amid   No.

Leo   No?

Amid   No. I'm going to pray now if that's OK.

Leo (*long pause, indicates the floor*)   Be my guest.

Pause. **Amid** *goes off on his own, and begins raising his hands up, before folding his arms across his chest, and eventually kneeling on the floor . . .*

Amid   (Allahu Akbar . . .)

Leo *continues to pace, swinging his bat. Some silence . . .*

Spencer   Does anyone know who started World War I. I can't make it out, even from this. We won it though.

The projector flickers on and off, projecting numbers on to the board.

Zoe   Is it working?

Graeme   Erm. Getting there, just . . .

Graeme *and* **Jonathan** *keep fiddling with the wires. Working on the laptop.*

Russell   I remember speaking to Charlie once, in Year 8, he was a prefect, he helped me. Some pricks had stolen my packed lunch box and were taking stuff out. They stamped on my sandwiches and just as they were about to stamp on my Mars bar, Charlie came along and sorted them out, pushed them away and snatched my Mars bar back. I don't even like Mars bars, but that's not the point.

Spencer   I love Mars bars.

Kelly   Awh yeah, me too.

Russell   I prefer a Twix.

Aimee   I like Bounties.

Russell   You're off your tits. Bounties? They're rank.

Shanti   I got an award from him once, for maths. He was Head Boy and he presented it to me in this, like, after-school assembly thing. A certificate. Still got it.

Leo   Remember beating Matravers once, football, three–two, Charlie was captain. I was subbed, second half, left back, we were like two–one down. What's-his-name's brother, ginger hair, got sent to prison, I chipped it down the line to him, about ten minutes to go and he scored, top right-hand corner, and then about three minutes to go, Charlie got fouled, just outside the box, everyone went forward for the free kick, including me, because it was all-or-nothing type of thing. Charlie takes the kick, and he could have gone for glory, everyone thought he was just going to blast it, swerve it round the defence, doing a Beckham, but he didn't care about glory, Charlie, never did, a team game, wanted the team to win, and instead he did this light little tap, to his right, to ginger thingy, and ginger thingy with a clear view of the goal, blasted it in, three–two, job done. Awesome.

Jonathan   I saw his passing-out parade.

Rachel   His what?

Jonathan   When you're a cadet, after training, before you go off for active duty. Get your green beret.

Leo   You saw him?

Jonathan   Brother was the same year as him, they went out to Afghanistan together. We were there to watch him, but Charlie was part of it as well. Stood behind him when they marched past.

Leo   Awh, that's wicked.

Joanne   Your brother's in Afghanistan?

Jonathan   Yeah.

Joanne   My uncle is.

Graeme   Jonathan's in the air cadets.

Leo   Are you?

Jonathan   Yes.

Leo   Do you do all the marching and that shit?

Jonathan   Yes.

Leo   Awh, that's wicked, show us.

Jonathan   Show you what?

Leo   Do some marching, show us.

Jonathan   No.

Russell   Yeah, go on, Johnno-boy.

Jonathan   You'll just take the piss.

Zoe   We won't.

Joanne   We won't, Jonathan.

Jonathan   Well, like what, I don't know what you mean.

Leo   When you march past and salute and all that.

Jonathan   What, like this?

He marches into the centre of the classroom, and stands fiercely to attention. Everyone cheers or whoops or goes 'whoow'.

Kelly   Whoow!!

Rachel   Alright, Jonathan, Jesus.

Russell   Bloody hell, you're like a proper soldier.

Leo   Show me.

Dean   I think a little bit of wee just came out, oh God.

Rachel   I want to do it as well.

Leo (*marching around*)   Is that it, just swinging your arms?

Jonathan   Well, if you're going to do it properly like at the air cadets, you have to start by standing in rows, like this, a line of two, next to each other. Leo, you at the front here, I'll be next to you.

Leo, **Russell**, **Rachel**, **Joanne** *and* **Lucy** *arrange themselves, organised by* **Jonathan**. **Amid** *is still praying in the corner.* **Graeme** *is working on the projector.*

Jonathan   So you swing your right arm forward as you step out with your left leg, keeping your arm really straight, counting one, two, one, two, to that rhythm. OK?

He joins **Leo** *at the front.*

Jonathan   So on my command. 'Quick. March.'

They begin to march around the room. The others watch, occasionally laughing, or clapping. Suddenly the BBC News Channel appears, projected on to the whiteboard from **Graeme***'s laptop. Everyone breaks off and looks.*

The High Street is getting ready for the coffins to pass through, the pavements lined with thousands of people.

Kelly   Oh wow.

Russell   Well done, Graeme, you bloody legend you.

Rachel   Jesus, how many people.

Aimee   That's more than normal.

Russell   Do you reckon?

Shanti   Are his mum and dad there?

Leo   Course they'll be there, idiot.

Spencer   They'll be by the post office, won't they? That's where they normally stand.

Kelly   Nothing's happening yet.

Jonathan   They won't even have left Lyneham yet.

Spencer   What's happening?

Russell   Nothing, get back to your wall.

Joanne   Awh, this is so sad.

Kelly   I'm gonna cry.

Leo   Shut up.

Joanne   I don't want to watch it, it doesn't feel right.

Aimee   Let's not have it on until it happens.

Leo   Keep it on.

Aimee   But the build-up and everything, there's no point, turn it off until they come.

Leo   Keep it on.

Russell (*going to the laptop*)   Let's go on YouTube, watch people falling over or something, that'll cheer us up.

Leo   We don't want cheering up! This isn't about cheering up!

Dean   That's it, I can't wait any more!

Dean *runs to near the desk and grabs a plastic bin, running with it to a corner of the room, and undoing his fly. Everyone screams.*

Kelly   Dean, what you doing, you munter?!

Rachel   No way! Don't piss in the bin!

Dean   I can't help it!

Aimee   Waaah!

Shanti   That's disgusting.

Russell   This is hilarious!

Spencer   What's he doing?!

Russell   Pissing in a bin.

Spencer   What?!

Dean *starts to wee, back turned to the class. More screaming and laughing from everyone. On the whiteboard, some new websites come up as* **Russell** *surfs the web on the laptop.*

Joanne   Oh my God!

Aimee   Urgh! What if it leaks.

Kelly   It's gonna smell.

Dean   Shut up, it won't.

Kelly   Aimee, dare you to go have a look.

Aimee   No!

Dean   No, don't!

Russell   Mate, have you thought what you're going to do with it after?

Dean   I've not thought anything except that I need a piss! Just leave me alone, will you, bit of privacy, God's sake.

A quick flash of some very soft porn suddenly gets projected on to the screen – **Russell** *laughs as some of the girls scream and turn away.*

Graeme   Oy, what are you doing?!

Rachel   Russell!

Spencer   What? What is it?! What's that noise?

Graeme   I'll get in trouble!

Leo   Russell!

Graeme   How did that get past the school filter?

Shanti   Russell, I don't want to see that, turn it off.

Leo   JUST TURN IT OFF, RUSSELL! NOW!

Russell *turns it off. The screen goes blank.*

Leo   We're not even meant to be here! We're meant to be out there! Watching Charlie come home and you're just messing around like knobheads.

Russell   All right, Leo, calm down.

Beat. **Leo** *goes to the desk where his spray cans are.*

Leo   Fuck this.

He shakes the cans – a red one and a blue one – and aims them at the wall.

Dean   Leo, don't.

Leo *begins spraying. Everyone watches.*

He sprays the red Cross of St George first. And then blue around it to create the Union Jack. He tosses the cans to one side and stands, assessing his work.

Kelly   Mate, you're a goner.

Leo   What? It's the best citizenship project Miss Kirmani will have ever seen, I bet. I know my flag, I like my flag, I'm proud of my country, A-star in Citizenship, surely? Done.

Russell   Fucking hell, mate, that . . . that's bad.

Spencer   What? What's he painted?

Russell   Mate, that's . . . what you gonna – what are we going to do? When she asks us?

Leo   Tell her.

Amid *finishes praying. He stands and sees the flag.*

Leo   What do you think, Amid? Like it? For Queen and Country?

He salutes, and then starts marching around the room again. Others watch.

Rachel (*looking at the flag*)   We do have the best flag, don't we?

Aimee   You what?

Rachel   I'm just saying. When you look at everyone else's flag, some of them are seriously minging, but ours, I think it's probably one of the best. Ours and America's.

Joanne   Yeah, except you're not really meant to have it around or anything, are you.

Zoe   What do you mean?

Joanne   I mean it . . . it means something, doesn't it. Sometimes. Means . . . you know . . .

Zoe   No.

Joanne   That you might be seen as a bit . . . racist.

Leo   No, what the fuck are you talking about, Joanne?
Racist.

Shanti   I know what she means.

Joanne   I just mean that people might *think* you are, because
other people have, like . . . what do you call it. Nicked it –
hijacked it, that's what I mean.

Shanti   Like the BNP.

Leo   Why is – this is what pisses me off, why is it racist to be
proud of where you're from?

Joanne   It's not, but –

Zoe   In America, nearly everyone has a flag in their back
gardens, and they salute it like once a day, and everyone
thinks they're great and nobody ever says they're racists.

Leo   Exactly, Zoe.

Amid   I think a lot of them are sometimes probably a bit
racist.

Zoe   Well . . .

Shanti   It's not racist to be proud to be British because
Britain is full of lots of different races, and they can be proud
of Britain as well, it's not racist, fine, but I think what Joanne
was saying is that when idiots and thugs and skinheads and
people have it in their window or tattooed on their arm or
whatever, they're normally like BNP or racists or something.

Joanne   Exactly, and I'm just saying that it's a shame,
because I like it, I like the flag.

Leo   Fine.

Joanne   I like the colours.

Leo   It's not about the colours.

Dean   There was that guy who stood as a BNP thingy, he
lives next to you, Joanne.

Joanne   Not me – Aimee.

Dean   Aimee, then.

Aimee   Yeah, so?

Kelly   Do you go round and have tea with him, Aimee?

Aimee   No, course not, I hardly even know him.

Dean   Does he have a swastika in his living room?

Aimee   I don't know, I hardly know him, just say hello now and again, that's all.

Shanti   You say hello? Why? Why are you nice to him?

Aimee   He's my neighbour, you have to be nice to your neighbour, don't you? Even Hitler was probably nice to his neighbours.

Spencer (*looking at his sheets on the wall*)   Depends what you mean by neighbours; if you mean Poland and Czechoslovakia then, no, he wasn't very nice to his neighbours.

Aimee   It doesn't mean anything, he's just a man, an old man who we say hello to.

The church bells ring in the distance. Everyone turns towards the sound.

Leo   It's starting, it's coming. Oy, put the news back on the thing!

Graeme *turns the footage back on so that it is projected on to the screen. An image of the High Street. Full now. The coffins are starting to arrive.*

Kelly   I've changed my mind, I don't want to see it.

Zoe   Kelly, don't.

Kelly   What? It's too painful for me.

Leo   Shut up, Kelly! Everyone stay quiet!

Rachel   No, I think she's right, I don't want to see it, it's too sad.

Zoe   Well then, just look away.

Leo   No! Everyone watch! The least you can do.

Rachel   I'm just a bit sick of it. This town. It being us all the time. I'll be glad when it ends. I'm sorry −

Kelly   I don't want to see his coffin. I don't −

Graeme   Maybe I should turn it off.

Leo   Graeme, you leave it.

Jonathan   It's Graeme's laptop.

Leo   No. Shut it!

Jonathan   He can do what he wants with it −

Leo   Oh you two, shut up will you, you pair of gays?

Rachel   Leo!

Aimee   Oy?

Jonathan   What? No.

Leo   Everyone knows what you two are, just no one ever says anything.

Graeme   That's not true.

Rachel   Stop it, Leo! That's really mean.

Leo   Even if you don't know what you are, I can tell, so just shut up and watch.

Jonathan   Leo, that's really not fair, I was only saying −

Leo   Shut up, you homo! All of you! Shut up and watch the screen!

Lucy (*breaking her silence*)   LEO, JUST STOP IT YOU EVIL LITTLE BASTARD!

Everyone gasps.

Rachel   Lucy!

Aimee   You broke your silence.

Lucy You bully. You hypocrite. You know what I'm talking about.

Russell Eh?

Kelly What, what you talking about?

Leo Nothing. Nothing, Lucy. Get back to being quiet, no one cares.

Lucy You're such a fucking bully.

Leo Get back to being quiet, I swear.

Kelly What you talking about, Lucy?

Lucy He knows.

Leo Haven't got a clue.

Lucy You have.

Leo I haven't.

Lucy You have.

Leo Tell everyone, then, if it's such an amazing secret, tell everyone.

Lucy You're such a nasty bully.

Leo Tell everyone.

Lucy Charlie.

Russell What?

Kelly What?

Lucy He knows.

Kelly WHAT?!

Lucy You're such a hypocrite, leave them alone. Leave everyone alone.

Kelly Him and Charlie what?

Lucy What I saw. In the changing rooms.

Rachel What?

Lucy   Year 8.

Aimee   Are you joking?

Lucy   After football.

Russell   What's she talking about?

Lucy   I was walking in to find Mr Hunt, after Hockey. Donna in sixth form needed the first-aid box.

Kelly   What?

Lucy   Charlie kissed Leo.

Russell/Kelly/Spencer/Dean/Rachel/Aimee/Shanti/Amid   WHAT?!

Lucy   So you're such a hypocrite, Leo. Leave them alone.

Russell   Charlie was gay?

Kelly   No he wasn't! I went out with him.

Dean   He was captain of all the teams, though!

Russell   That doesn't mean you can't be gay, you bell end.

Lucy   It was just one kiss, and Leo pulled away and Charlie said sorry and he said he'd never done anything like that before and Leo said that was OK, it didn't matter, he thought it was funny and they shook hands and that was that and the only reason I'm telling it now is because you shouldn't bully people all the time because we're all growing up and we all have questions and we're all really fucking confused most of the time so don't bully Jonathan or Graeme or anyone and just leave us all alone.

Silence.

I'm going back to being quiet now. If anyone tells anyone I broke the silence I'll rip your teeth out and bite you in the arse with them, OK?

Silence.

Spencer (*still facing the wall*)   We, we drew the borders of a couple of other, erm . . . countries as well. After wars. And that seems to have caused some trouble now and again too, but I think that we meant well. Pakistan in 1948, separating it from India. Huh, like you Shanti, and you Amid –

Kelly   Leo, I can't believe you kissed a boy.

Russell   Oy, a boy kissed him, *once*, there's a difference.

Spencer   And then Israel –

Rachel   Spence! Shut up.

Kelly   What about all those girls over the years. All that 'big man' shit you chat all the time, what's that about, eh?

Zoe   It doesn't mean he's gay, all right? Lucy said Charlie kissed *him*. Right Luce?

Lucy *points to her mouth to indicate her silence.* **Leo** *goes and stands in front of the whiteboard, watching the news images. The hearse has appeared on the High Street. Some people have started to throw flowers. People start to clap.*

Beat. **Russell** *looks around. He starts to clap. So do the others. Except* **Leo**. *Who just stares at the screen.*

They clap, and watch the images of the coffin coming to a stop on the High Street. **Leo** *walks close to the whiteboard. His face almost pressed against it, and the image.*

Leo *turns, grabs his baseball bat, and starts smashing the desk with it. Some of the others scream, others jump out of the way,* **Spencer** *stays facing the wall.*

Leo   WANKERS! ALL OF YOU! DISRESPECTFUL, UNGRATEFUL, IGNORANT WANKERS! Why did you have to ruin it, today! Him coming home! Why did you have to bring that up, Lucy?! He's dead, he's dead, he died protecting and serving you lot, you ungrateful bastards, and then you go and bring up something like that!

Russell   Mate . . .

Everyone stands around the edge of the room, scared. **Leo** *paces, swinging his bat. Stops. He's begun to cry . . .*

He sees **Amid**. *He points his bat at him . . .*

Leo   Come here.

Amid *doesn't move.*

Leo   Come here.

Pause. **Amid** *edges in to the centre of the room. Faces* **Leo**. *Pause.*

Leo   Get on the floor.

Amid (*pause*)   W . . . what?

Leo   On the floor! Bent over!

Russell   Mate.

Beat. He raises up his bat.

Leo   ON THE FLOOR!

Russell   Leo!

Amid   It's OK! It's . . .

He gets on to his knees. **Aimee**, **Shanti** *and* **Joanne** *have started to cry.*

Leo   Graeme, come here.

Graeme *comes over, nervously.*

Leo   Lie on top of him. Across, like that.

Graeme *stays still.* **Leo** *knocks him in the back with his bat, not too hard, but hard enough . . .*

Leo   On top of him.

Graeme *lies on top of* **Amid**.

Leo   Shanti.

Shanti *doesn't move.*

Leo   Shanti.

Shanti *comes forward.*

Leo   Lie on top.

Shanti *lies on top of them both.* **Leo** *steps back and takes a picture on his phone.*

Leo *looks around. Points at* **Kelly**.

Leo   You.

Kelly *shakes her head.*

Leo   You. You big . . . you . . . fucking . . . sl-slut. You. COME ON!

She doesn't move. **Leo** *raises his bat above her head. She flinches. She lies on top of the pile.* **Leo** *steps back and takes a photo with his phone.*

Jonathan   Leo, please.

Leo *(turning on him)*   You. You puff. On the table.

Jonathan   What?

Leo   ON THE TABLE NOW, SOLDIER!! Quick, march, quick, march, one, two, one, two!

Jonathan *gets up unsteadily on to the table.*

Leo   Trousers down. You . . . you big . . . gay.

Russell   Leo, mate . . .

Leo *raises his bat to* **Russell** *and he flinches. He swings his bat at* **Jonathan**.

Leo   TROUSERS DOWN! NOW!

Jonathan *undoes his belt, shaking, and lets his trousers fall down.* **Leo** *tosses him up a sports T-shirt from his bag.*

Leo   Put that over your head. Put your arms out.

Jonathan *puts the T-shirt over his head. He slowly raises his arms out to his side.* **Leo** *takes a picture on his phone. Then another of the pile of people. Exhausted. Crying. Rubbing his head. Unsure . . .*

Spencer (*still facing the wall*)   And erm . . . course in the
Second World War, I think . . . I think a lot of people forget
that we were the first ones to declare war. On Germany. Not
America or anyone. Or France. Or . . . which, you know, I
think . . . well, that's quite brave. Isn't it? Really. We didn't
want a war, says here, we were still a bit buggered from the last
one. But we saw someone doing something wrong to people.
Invading countries that didn't belong to them and doing bad
things to the people that lived there. And we thought . . . 'No,
that . . . that's not right.' And so we did something about it.
And Hitler made us an offer to stay out of it, which would have
meant a lot of our grandads and grandmas wouldn't have
died and we'd be really powerful, but we still said no. And by
the time they got to us, we were like completely alone. And
everyone thought we would lose. But we didn't. And then it
looks like America came along, and finished it up, and then
we owed them a lot of money because we'd been fighting for
so long on our own. And that meant we lost our empire and
have been shrinking and struggling a bit ever since, never quite
the same, but we knew that might happen and yet we still did
it. Because we thought we had a responsibility. And I think
that . . . you know. That's something that we should be, like,
proud of. A bit more. And something that we forget, when all
this other stuff is happening. Even when we get things wrong,
and make mistakes. That if it wasn't for us. On this island. Then,
like, the world and all that, it would be really quite bad right
now. Worse than it is. And so . . . you know . . . that's what I've
learnt, anyway. That we're better than we think we are. And
that we can do better, most of the time. If only we remembered
that. So I think we'll be all right, actually . . . you know, in
the . . . in the, like, long run. I do. I actually do . . .

Silence.

Leo *lowers his bat slowly. Quivering. Tired . . .*

From the other side of the door, the sound of keys.

The door is unlocked. It starts to open . . .

Blackout.

Bassett

An interview with James Graham, November 2010

What gave you the idea for your play in the first place?

I was just completely fascinated by the idea that 2011, the year of the Connections performances of my play, will be the tenth anniversary of the 9/11 attacks. Schoolchildren in their final year would hardly remember the events, being only five or six at the time. A 'pre-9/11 world' is unknown to them. I'd also been fascinated, touched and intrigued for some time by the 'Wootton Bassett phenomenon' – a completely random and idiosyncratically British way to mourn the war dead, in a quintessentially 'English' town. But where were all the young people, and what did they think? I decided to find out.

How did visiting the town and meeting the people shape your idea?

It totally shaped the idea – it was built upwards from that. I think my expectations were that, it being a fairly small rural town, the young people would be quite deferential and reserved. What I discovered was often the opposite – there was some anger, some very passionate, conflicting points of view – strong, even 'extreme' opinions. They were vocal, strong-willed, intelligent, and a little fierce. And I was more excited as a result.

What detailed research did you carry out once you'd got to know Wootton Bassett?

I sent the pupils who had helped us in Wootton Bassett a stream of endless questions about where they hung out, what they did with their spare time, to get a sense of their world, the culture, and the people within it. I also spoke to and did workshops with other young people outside Wootton Bassett about politics and their views, their fears about and hopes for the future. Even though this is a play very specific to a town and what goes on there, it contains wider themes and a more general exploration about a generation as a whole – I want it to resonate with all young people, and adults, everywhere.

From your research, were there any surprises which really brought the idea for your play into focus?

Mainly the level of passion, of care, and of articulacy that all the young people I worked with had regarding the issues that face them and the country. We're constantly told, mainly by the media, that the younger generation are ignorant and apathetic. I couldn't disagree more. My God, did they *care*; my God, did they have opinions, and a vested interest – *of course they do*. They're *inheriting* whatever we leave them with.

I think that's what the play began to focus on. How are we influencing the younger generation, and how well are we equipping them for the future? Imagine a whole town of young people forced to face the horrific consequence of the war on a weekly basis, not just watching it on the news. Combine that with the constant talk of 'terror' and of 'fear', of an onslaught of violent images, and of our own failure to lead the way in tolerance and understanding of different faiths, nationalities and backgrounds. I think, in this context, the difficulties, conflicts and confusions that Leo suffers from, resulting in his extreme outburst at the end, don't seem so unprovoked after all. It's fizzing away, under the surface . . .

Can you describe how you then took 'real life' and turned it into a work of fiction?

Having great themes and ideas are one thing – making a good piece of drama out of them is something completely different! I eventually settled on an ensemble piece of 'real-time' theatre. When you 'contain' your characters in a highly charged environment, with emotions running high, you can discover the most about them in a very short time. Just remember, this was an emotional day for a lot of our characters anyway, before we even meet them. Denying them the outlet for that emotion by not letting them go to the repatriation means it needs other outlets within the goldfish bowl of their 'prison'.

I wanted there to be a constant air of 'unpredictability' and 'threat'. There are, of course, lighter, funnier moments, deliberately placed, but I think this 'suspense' of when, if ever, a real explosion might happen between these characters (think every time Leo grabs his bat and starts wandering round, swinging it) is what sustains the play. The audience need to *feel* that we're always on the brink of descending into chaos.

Did you consciously write Bassett *in a way which conceals your own attitude to its content?*

It's a collection of different opinions and viewpoints expressed by different characters, and where possible I didn't want to impose a judgement value upon them. No doubt different audience members will find certain opinions disagreeable, even offensive, which is fine, good, great – the point is that these views *exist*, and so we *have* to present them in order to debate them.

What do you hope young actors will discover during the process of rehearsing the play?

I would love for the individual actors to take ownership of their characters, and enjoy the process of building them up in a rehearsal and then sustaining that character through 'real-time' action on stage, trying to take them on a journey over forty-five minutes during each performance they give. They have to find their characters and then stay honest, truthful and authentic to them.

I hope they relish the rhythm of the language – the lines are deliberately short, sharp and snappy. That doesn't mean they should *always* be delivered at a relentless pace – silences and pauses peppering the pace are just as important. If they can work together as a team to get the rhythm of the dialogue right, then I think they're halfway there.

What do you hope an audience will gain from receiving a performance of Bassett?

I want the audience to gain an insight into the legacy they're leaving the generation that comes next. I want them to be open-minded and brave about the different points of view expressed in the play. I want them to laugh, of course, and enjoy the experience, to revel in the musicality and the bouncy-ball rhythm of the dialogue, and in a way I suppose I do want to shock them into addressing, head on, how confused and conflicted and often angry a generation of young people are becoming, rather than pretending everything is fine.

From an interview with James Graham by Anthony Banks

Carl Grose

Gargantua

Characters

Gargantua (*a.k.a.* **Hugh Mungus**)
Mini Mungus, *his mum*
Marcus Mungus, *his dad*

The Prime Minister
Pippa Wellard, *Deputy Prime Minister*
Jeff Creams, *Treasury*
Robin Wilt, *Junior Minister*
General Malahyde, *an American Army General*
Professor Julian Swan, *Head of Janus Technologies*

Sally Butters, *a TV news reporter*
Arnie, *her cameraman*

Regina Buxley, *local businesswoman*
Lionel Buxley, *her husband*

Dr Lucky
Nurse One
Nurse Two

Gazette, *local reporter*
Morning News, *local reporter*
The Bugle, *local reporter*

Agent Allbright
Agent Starkhammer
Agent Blackstone

The Voice of the Door

People of Skankton Marsh
The Three Good Women
   of Skankton
Sandy the Haidresser
Skankton Girl

Skankton Boy
Constable Yapp
Preacher Pike
Headmistress Gunning
Brian Uber, *record producer*
Grannies Wintz, Curdle
   and **Hawkhumph**

Chorus
Citizens
Midwives
Hardhats
Soldiers
Nappy-Wearing Zealots

And featuring:
The Dummysuckers,
   a rock band

Darkness.

In the distance, an ominous sound:

Boom . . .

Smoke hangs thick. Civilians slowly pick themselves up from the rubble.

The sound, closer, more frequent now:

Boom . . . Boom . . .

TV news reporter **Sally Butters** *appears from the shadows.*

Sally   Hear that?

Boom.

Sally   Arnie? We keep filming. No matter what happens, we stand our ground and we keep filming. We'll cover this story to the end. Or my name isn't Sally Butters, TV news personality of the year. 2008. How's the hair?

Arnie, *her cameraman, gives her a thumbs-up.*

Sally (*to camera*)   As you can see from the devastation around me, the monster tore through this street only moments ago . . . People nearby pick themselves up from the rubble, shell-shocked, unsure of what has just hit them.

Boom.

We understand that the military will engage the creature and bring it down at all costs but so far we've seen nothing –

BOOM.

That was close.

BOOM!

He's coming back.

BOOM!!

Arnie, he's coming back!

Everything moves in slow motion. Jaws drop in utter disbelief.

BOOM!!!

Bodies shake —

BOOM!!!!

With the intensifying —

BOOOM!!!!!

Vibrations.

Necks craning, they all look up and point at the sight before them.

Civilian   Run!

The crowd scatter in all directions to reveal a two-hundred-foot giant baby.

This is **Gargantua**.

He brings his foot down hard with an earth-shattering —

BOOOOOOOOOOMMMMMMM!!!!!!!

Gargantua (*a monstrous echoing roar*)   Gaaaa-gaaaa-goooo-gooooo!

Tiny Sally   Keep filming, Arnie! Keep film—

Gargantua *crushes her underfoot like a grape.*

Tiny Arnie   *Sally!*

Gargantua   Haaaaa-haaaaa-haaaaaa!

A band, **The Dummysuckers**, *rock out:*

Singer
Gargantua! Gargantua!
You can try and out run him but you won't get far!
There's nothin' but to bow before his giant might
Cus man, this baby knows just how to win a fight!
Gargantua! Gargantua!

Tiny Army General (*through megaphone*)   Open fire! Open fire!

The sound of machine guns and heavy artillery.

Singer
> Armour-piercing bullets land like flakes of snow!
> Those laser-guided missiles dunno where to go!
> So this is how it ends? Well it just might be!
> Armageddon all thanks to a big baby!
> Gargantua! Gargantua!

The sound of twisting metal, explosions, buildings collapsing.

The **Chorus** *run for their lives in all directions.*

Singer
> And what of those who lead us? Well, they've all jumped ship!
> So much for politicians shooting from the hip!
> We're left holdin' the baby – the baby from hell!
> Will mankind survive? Guess only time will tell!
> Gargantua! Gargantua!
> Gaa! Gaa! Gaa! Gaa! Goo! Goo! Goo!
> Gargantua!

Gargantua, *in glorious slow motion, towering amidst smoke and fire, cries out a gurgling howl of triumph.*

Suddenly, he stops and looks to us.

Gargantua (*plummy English voice*)   Prime Minister? Prime Minister, are you alright?

Wellard   Prime Minister!

The **Prime Minister** *sits bolt upright.*

Prime Minister   Who's cooking onions?!

We're in an ante-chamber under 10 Downing Street.

At the back is a large metal door. To the side of it, a keypad.

Standing over the **Prime Minister** *are members of his cabinet –* **Jeff Creams** (*Treasury*), **Pippa Wellard** (*Deputy Prime Minister*) *and* **Robin Wilt** (*Junior Minister*). *There is also* **General Rex Malahyde** (*of Texas*) *and* **Professor Julian Swan** (*of Janus Technologies*).

They all look concerned.

Wilt   He's alive!

Creams   Well, that's something.

Malahyde   What's all this 'onions' talk?

Wellard   It's what he said just before he collapsed.

Prime Minister   Where am I?

Wilt   You had a funny turn, sir. Gently does it.

Prime Minister (*to* **Wilt**)   Doris? Is that you?

Wilt   It's Robin Wilt, sir. Junior Minister. But I can be Doris if you want me to be . . . ?

Wellard   Wilt!

Creams   You were about to punch in the entry code when you turned and said, 'Who's cooking onions?' Then your eyes rolled about in your head like this –

Wilt *demonstrates.*

Creams   And you collapsed! We need the entry code, John. And we need it now.

Prime Minister   Onions? *Who's* cooking onions?

Malahyde   No one's cookin' onions! Goddammit! What the hell is he talking about? Swan? You're a man of science. Enlighten us!

Swan (*steps forward*)   I believe the Prime Minister has suffered what is commonly known as . . . a mind melt.

Everyone   A mind melt?

Wilt   Think I had one of those in the canteen earlier.

Swan   The undue stress he's been under these past seven days has finally taken its toll.

Creams   But only *he* knows the entry code to get us through that door and safely underground before the nuclear missiles launch in –

Everyone (*they all look at their watches*)   Twenty-nine minutes!

Wellard   But he also has the power to call the launch off!

Swan   Let's not start this all over again.

Wellard   He should never have authorised a nuclear strike!

Malahyde   But he did.

Wellard   Only because you made him, Malahyde!

Wilt   He's the Prime Minister. He has a mind of his own.

Swan   Except when it's melted.

Malahyde   He had no choice but to retaliate what with that nappy-wearing fiend runnin' around up there!

Creams   The countdown's begun, Pippa. It can't be stopped.

Wellard   It can be stopped, Jeff. All he has to do is make the call. And we don't have to obliterate the whole damn country to stop Gargantua! Prime Minister? Make the call.

The **Prime Minister** *looks at* **Wellard**.

Creams   Prime Minister? You must remember the entry code!

The **Prime Minister** *looks at* **Creams**. *He then blows a raspberry and slaps his hands together like a seal.*

Swan   The Prime Minister has gone bye-bye.

Prime Minister (*to* **Wilt**)   It's so lovely to see you again, Doris.

Creams   It's finally happened.

Wellard   Can't we bring him round? Snap him out of it? Jog his memory?

Malahyde   I'll jog his goddamn memory –

Malahyde *hauls the* **Prime Minister** *to his feet and goes to slap him.*

Swan   Not that way, General Malahyde. His brain is in a state of flux. We must coerce his neural pathways back into operation gently.

Creams   How?

Swan   Remind him. Remind him of the past seven days, in as much detail as you can stand.

Creams   And then he'll remember the entry code?

Wellard   And then he'll stop the missile launch?

Wilt   And then he'll stop calling me Doris?

Swan   We can only hope.

Wellard   Prime Minister? Listen very carefully. We're going to tell you about what happened over these seven days . . .

Prime Minister   Why? What's happened? Anything I should know about?

They all look to each other. None of them quite knows how to start. They take a deep breath and –

Sally *and* **Arnie,** *seven days before we saw them last, are filming.*

Sally (*to camera*)   I'm here in the quiet village of Skankton Marsh. 'Where?' you might ask. Well, you'll be hard pressed to find it on any map, that's for sure. But today, all that is about to change. Because today sees the grand opening of the town's formidable new mega-mall, a vast construction more than two years in the making. And the visionary behind this monster is local businesswoman and mayonnaise magnate, Regina Buxley –

Enter **Regina Buxley** *before a crowd of Skankton Marshians.*

Regina   Hello, good people of Skankton Marsh! That's right. You know me. Reg Buxley. Go on. Take a look at that mega-mall! Massive in't it? It's the biggest in the world by three cubic centimetres! Eat that, America! Any questions? Yes, the *Skankton Evening Gazette*?

Gazette   Mrs Buxley, critics of the mega-mall say you've ruined an area of outstanding natural beauty?

Regina   You're telling me this palace of glass and steel in't as impressive as some rare breed of duck? Ruined it? Improved it, more like! Next question. Yes, Peter.

Morning News   Hello, Reg. Got to ask. Does Skankton Marsh really need a forty-nine screen cinema complex given that there are only forty-eight people living in the village?

Regina   Everybody gets a screen, Peter – you can't say fairer than that! Next?

Bugle   The *Skankton Bugle*. Mrs Buxley, where will the customers park?

Regina   Have you not seen? There's a multi-storey out back so big it'll make you want to puke! Listen up. Regina Buxley does not do things by halves. This masterpiece behind me took vision. And time. And craploads of money. But 'ere it is. Done. Dusted. And dropped right on your bloody doorstep.

A frail man with a neck brace and crutches stands beside her – **Lionel**.

Regina   Now, before I ask my beloved husband Lionel to cut the ribbon, I just want to say . . . those of you that fight your way to the front get a free jar of my delicious Buxley's Thick 'n' White Traditional Homemade Mayonnaise. One free jar – I'm not joking. And that's just a taster. So get in, spend your money and enjoy yourselves! This is my legacy to you. Scissors at the ready, Lionel. And so, without further ado, I now declare the Skankton Marsh Mega –

From the crowd, someone groans.

Nutter in the crowd. They'll be pleased to know the mall's got its own insane asylum. Oh, I've thought of everythin', me. Scissors, Lionel.

Lionel *does his damnedest to ready the scissors and balance on his crutches.*

Regina   I now declare the –

Another groan. The crowd parts to reveal **Marcus** *and* **Mini Mungus**, *a young couple very much in love.* **Mini** *is twenty-two months pregnant, and* massive. *She groans again and starts puffing.*

Regina   Uh, could you keep it down, love? I'm trying to open a mega-mall 'ere.

Marcus   Mini? Are you alright?

Mini   No, Marcus. I'm not. It's the baby . . .

Marcus   Eh?

Mini   I think the baby's coming!

Sally (*smelling a story*)   Arnie?

Arnie   Yup!

Arnie *films* **Mini**.

Mini   My waters are about to break . . . it's coming . . . it's coming . . . look out, love!

The Dummysuckers *kick off as* **Mini***'s waters break –*

Singer
    All of a sudden there's a tidal wave!
    Tell the lifeguard there's many lives to save!
    All of a sudden now the waters rise!
    This shock tsunami took us by surprise!

Mini *blasts the bystanders with a high-pressure force.*

Singer
> Someone call Noah, say we need his ark!
> This amniotic fluid gush is quite a lark!
> This girl's birth water is unstoppable!

A momentary stillness as the **People of Skankton** *float underwater.*

Then –

Singer
> Somebody get her to a hospital!

Mini *spins in on a gurney puffing and panting, her enormous belly bulging and rippling.* **Marcus** *holds her hand.*

Nurse One   How are the contractions?

Nurse Two   Like earthquakes!

Mini   Oooooooooohhhhh, here comes another!

Everything shakes and rattles.

Nurse One *and* **Two**   Dr Lucky?

Dr Lucky *bursts through a pair of swing doors. He hands his glass of Scotch to* **Nurse One** *and his bag of golf clubs to* **Nurse Two**.

Dr Lucky   Yowza! Is that for real?

Nurse One   Patient's name is Mini Mungus.

Nurse Two   Patient is very very very very pregnant.

Dr Lucky   How overdue is she?

Nurse One *and* **Two**   Two years?

Dr Lucky   Leaping lizards! That's a world record for longest pregnancy of all time! Is the husband/partner/lover/donor here?

Nurse One   Right there.

Dr Lucky   Where?

Nurse Two   He's the one holding her hand, Doctor.

Dr Lucky   *That's* the father? He looks like a kitchen utensil. What's your name, son?

Marcus   Marcus. Marcus Mungus.

*The two **Nurses** dress **Dr Lucky** in green surgeon's gown, mask and cap, rubber gloves.*

Dr Lucky   Well, Marcus Marcus Mungus, today you and your wife are in luck. Because I'm Dr Lucky.

Marcus   That puts my mind at ease.

Dr Lucky   Ultimately, it's just a name. It doesn't give me superpowers, son. But it does give me edge, and sometimes that edge is all the difference you need.

Marcus   Will she be alright, Doctor?

Dr Lucky   Do you love her, boy?

Marcus   More than anything!

Dr Lucky   Then why the hell didn't you bring her in after nine months? How could you let it get so big?

Marcus   She just . . . held it in.

Dr Lucky   She doesn't want the child?

Marcus   Oh, she does! She's just not keen on giving birth is all.

Dr Lucky   She's going to want her pelvic floor back at some point. Stay here, Marcus. And don't touch my golf clubs. (*Returns to* **Mini**.) Nurse. Close the door. Let's give this woman some dignity. She's about to give birth, for God's sakes!

Nurse One *draws a (mimed) curtain across.*

Dr Lucky   Now then, Mini, let's get this baby out, shall we?

He roughly hoiks her legs up in the air.

Mini   I don't want to give birth, Doctor.

Dr Lucky   Why ever not? It's the most natural thing on earth! Nurse, give her lots of drugs!

Nurse Two *jabs* **Mini** *with a large syringe.*

Mini   No, I . . . Ooooooooo . . .

Dr Lucky   Groovy, eh? What you're feeling is drugs. Delicious, pain-killing drugs. Forceps!

Nurse One *hands him forceps.*

Mini   Mmmmmmmmmm . . . (*Starts singing a song.*)

Dr Lucky   Now let's have a looky see. My, he is a big one. (*To* **Nurses**.) Hit her again. This is going to hurt.

Nurse Two *jabs her again.*

Mini   Ooooo, yes! That's lovely! More . . . more . . .

Dr Lucky   Plunger!

Marcus   Plunger?

Nurse One *hands him a plunger.*

Nurse One   Oh my God! Is that its *head*? That's its *head*!

Marcus *stares at her in horror. She smiles reassuringly, and slips back to work.*

Dr Lucky   Damn. Too bloody big! Can't squeeze the skull through the pelvis. I didn't want to do this but . . . I'm going in!

Nurse One *and* **Two**   You're going *in?*!

Marcus   He's going 'in'?!

Dr Lucky   It's what's commonly known as the Heineken Manoeuvre or the Kronenberg Technique. One of the two. I forget which. I'll see if I can't push the thing out from the back. Wish me luck, ladies. I may be some time.

Dr Lucky *climbs head-first up into* **Mini**.

Mini   What's going on . . . ?

Nurse One   Relax, Mrs Mungus. Doctor's just performing an impossibly dangerous birthing technique on you. Nothing to worry about.

Mini (*stoned*)   OK . . .

Nurse One   Look! It's coming!

Nurse   He's doing it! He's doing it!

An arm suddenly bursts out from **Mini***'s groin.*

Nurse One   Shit a brick!

Nurse Two (*to* **Marcus**)   We're gonna need a hand here, dude.

Nurse One   Push, Mrs Mungus! Push!

Nurse Two   Pull, Mr Mungus! Pull!

Mini *wails.*

Nurse One   What a day to be understaffed!

Nurse Two (*at the top of her lungs*)   Auxiliaries!

A squadron of **Midwives** *run circles around the birth, then charge in to help.*

Midwives   Push . . . (pull). Push . . . (pull). Push . . . (pull).

Singer
  Now comes the seminal moment in our story
  When he is born unto us in all his glory
  The prodigal son turns to greet the dawn
  Gargantua, the monstrous one . . .

Mini *screams. So does* **Marcus**.

Suddenly, POP!

Singer
  . . . is born!

Revealed in **Mini***'s arms is a huge, man-sized baby.*

Midwives   Woah, momma!

Nurse One   It's . . .

Nurse Two   It's . . .

Mini   A little baby boy!

Midwives   Little?

Mini   I'm going to call him Hugh. Hugh Mungus.

Marcus   Well done, love. You did it.

Mini   *We* did it. (*Thinks, then.*) No. Actually, you're right. *I* did it.

Nurse One   Shall I cut the umbilical cord?

She holds aloft a large pair of rusty shears.

Nurse Two   Oh. Before you do, could we have Dr Lucky back?

Mini   Yes, of course. Why? Where is he?

Dr Lucky (*emerging from* **Mini**)   Good work, everyone! It seems the delivery was a complete success!

Marcus *faints.*

Three Good Women of Skankton *sit and have their hair done by* **Sandy**, *who hovers and sculpts.*

Good Woman One   Is he as big as they say?

Good Woman Two   Bigger!

Good Woman Three   How did he get so big?

Good Woman One   Who knows? It's Nature's way!

Good Woman Two   What happens when he grows?

Good Woman Three   The cost of new clothes, they ain't cheap!

Good Woman One   Mini Mungus – mother of a modern miracle!

Good Woman Two   Or a monstrous abomination, you could say.

Good Woman Three   Either way, it beats traipsing round a mega-mall all day.

Regina *overhears this.* **Lionel** *hobbles beside her.*

Regina   I shan't forget this, Lionel. The day my dream was eclipsed by a bloody great baby. I shan't forget, and I shan't forgive. But in the meantime . . . I think I just want to go home.

She opens a jar of mayonnaise and spoons a wodge into her mouth.

Sally (*to camera*)   So it seems Skankton Marsh has had a busy day. A day where the world's biggest mall was overshadowed by the world's biggest baby.

Arnie *gives the thumbs-up, drops the camera.*

Sally   Arnie. We shouldn't leave. I smell Nobel Peace Prize for Journalism all over this sucker! Let's go see what the word on the street is.

Arnie *throws his camera on to:*

Skankton Girl   I just love him. I just want to wear nappies and hang out.

Then on to:

Skankton Boy   My girlfriend told me I was a big baby – I took it as a compliment, you know?

And so forth:

Constable Yapp   Oh, I saw them leave the hospital – they lashed him to the back of Wilf Canker's flatbed truck. It was quite something!

Sandy the Hairdresser   He's cute. Huge. But cute.

Preacher Pike   When something like this happens it happens for a reason . . .

Headmistress Gunning   I look forward to welcoming the boy to Skankton Primary. But he better mind his head. We have low ceilings.

Grannie Wintz   I'd give anything to nibble on his pudgy leg.

Grannie Curdle   It's the flesh, you see? Old women love baby flesh.

Grannie Hawkhumph   Well, there's certainly enough flesh to go round on this one.

Grannies (*imagining nibbling*)   Mmmmmmmmmm . . .

Preacher Pike   There are lots of visitors pouring in from all over. I suppose Skankton Marsh is like Bethlehem, isn't it? But without the camels.

Brian Uber (*record producer*)   It's refreshing to see an icon who's created such a stir who isn't connected to the music industry, who isn't a movie star or some overpaid sports personality, who is just pure individuality.

Sally   Might we hear a hit single from the Giant Baby some time soon?

Brian Uber   We've got him gurgling in the studio on Monday. It's gonna be *big*.

Preacher Pike   I might be speaking too soon but . . . this Gargantua could be the new messiah!

Swan   The specimen's physiology is fascinating. He seems possessed of an accelerated growth rate quite unlike anything I've ever seen. Hello, I'm Professor Julian Swan, head of Janus Technologies –

Malahyde   This *enfant terrible* is a walking ten-man army. If he could walk, that is. Right now, I believe he's just at the crawlin' stage. But when the world goes to hell, I want this drooling Gargantua on our side!

Sally   Prime Minister, one last thing. What's your view on Hugh Mungus?

Prime Minister   He'd get my vote, Sally!

The **Prime Minister** *winks.*

Sally   So there we have it. Even the Prime Minister has gone gaa-gaa for Gargantua.

Mini *shoos the final stragglers out of the garden.*

Mini   Alright! That's enough! Show's over! Come back tomorrer! Visiting hours two till four. It's his feeding time now. Thank you. Bye, bye!

Gargantua *sits there like Buddha, now the size of a house.* **Marcus** *is up a ladder feeding the ravenous* **Gargantua** *with a bucket.*

Marcus   Open wide, Hugh! Here comes a choo-choo train! Come on. Open up! Nice, look, mmmmm. Daddy likes it! Lovely cabbage purée!

Gargantua *opens his mouth.* **Marcus** *pours the bucket down his throat.*

Marcus   Good boy! More?

Gargantua (*flapping his arms excitedly*)   Maaaaahhhhhhh!!

Marcus *climbs down the ladder and fetches another bucket.*

Mini (*fondling a pair of woollen booties*)   It's a shame nothing I knitted him fits.

Marcus   He's a growing lad, aren't ya. Hugh?

Mini   You can say that again. Gor, he puts it away, doesn't he?

Marcus   He's like his mother in that respect.

Mini   Cheeky.

Marcus   Sling us another bucket, love.

Mini   There are no more.

Marcus   Check the cement mixer. I made up a fifty-cabbage batch.

Mini   It's empty, Marcus. He's had it all.

Marcus *climbs down the ladder.*

Marcus   And he's drunk the milk lorry dry!

Gargantua   Waaaaaaaaaaahhhhhhhhhh!!!!

The sound is deafening.

Mini   There, there, Hugh. Come on, you've had your fill for today.

She climbs up the ladder and sings:

'Hush little baby don't say a word
Mummy's gonna buy you a mockingbird . . .'

Gargantua *instantly falls asleep.*

Mini *and* **Marcus** *look at their boy, look to each other, smile, then collapse with exhaustion.*

Meanwhile, in a secret laboratory . . .

Swan   General Malahyde. Welcome to Janus Industries.

Malahyde   'Preciate the invite, Swan. Always wondered what you boys got up to down here.

Swan   Can you guess why I asked you here to my . . . secret underground laboratory?

Malahyde   Would a freakishly oversized baby have anything to do with it?

Swan *(smiles)*   Do you remember what we once discovered about each other that time on the shores of Lake Geneva?

Malahyde   Indeed I do. That we both have tattoos in unusual places.

Swan   No, the *other* thing we discovered about each other.

Malahyde   That we share a common ambition?

Swan   Bingo.

Malahyde   That we could . . .

Swan   Go on. Say it.

Malahyde   That we could control the world if we wanted.

Swan   Precisely. My brains. Your brawn. And our place in history sealed for ever.

Malahyde   It was an impossible dream, Professor!

Swan   Not so impossible now, my friend.

Malahyde   The baby?

Swan   Yes, General. The baby.

Malahyde   Whadda ya need from me?

Back to the Munguses' house.

From nowhere, three **Sinister Agents** *appear. They wear shades and black suits. They are* **Agents Allbright**, **Starkhammer** *and* **Blackstone**.

Agents   Mr and Mrs Mungus?

Marcus *and* **Mini** (*waking up*)   Yes?

Allbright   May we have a moment of your time?

Mini   Marcus, I've just got him off. Tell 'em.

Marcus   Listen, lads, it's been a long day –

Allbright   Oh, we're not salesman.

They all flash their badges.

Blackstone   Agent Blackstone.

Starkhammer   Starkhammer.

Allbright   Allbright.

Starkhammer   This really won't take a second, Mr and Mrs Mungus.

Blackstone   We'll jump straight to the point.

Allbright   The thing is, Mr and Mrs Mungus, the world is hanging by a thread.

Starkhammer   If the thread snaps, somebody needs to catch it.

Blackstone   And that somebody is your boy.

Mini   Who are you people?

Marcus   It's obvious, love. They're from the government.

Allbright   Not the government, Mr Mungus.

Starkhammer   A higher power than that.

Blackstone   Who we work for is classified information.

Allbright   That's right. We shouldn't even be here.

Starkhammer   The fact that we're even talking to you is anathema to our way of operation.

Blackstone   So we'll just cut to the chase –

Agents   We need your baby.

Mini   What?

The **Agents** *all put their fingers to their ears and vanish as –*

Regina *enters with* **Lionel***, on crutches.*

Regina   How do. You know me. Regina Buxley. Mega-mall *constructeur extraordinaire*!

Mini   We certainly do, Mrs Buxley.

Marcus   We buy your mayonnaise.

Mini   When we can afford it.

Regina   This frail piece of work is my husband, Lionel. Don't shake his hand. His bones are like glass!

Lionel *looks on pathetically as* **Regina** *admires* **Gargantua**.

Regina   So. You're the proud couple, eh? Got your hands full though, eh? Look at it, eh? A behemoth!

Mini   It's a 'he', actually. His name's Hugh.

Regina   Oh! Oh, yes! Very good! Hugh!

Mini *is confused.*

Marcus   Have you got any children, Mrs Buxley?

Regina (*re* **Lionel**)   What, with this cup of weak piss? Hardly.

Lionel *sighs heavily.*

Regina   You keep your baby in the front garden then?

Mini   We couldn't get him through the door.

Regina   What do you do when it rains?

Marcus   We've got a tarpaulin, and plenty of plastic sacks.

Regina   What do you feed him on?

Mini   Odds and sods. He's only three days old, so he's not that fussy.

Regina (*sniffs a bucket*)   Cabbage purée from a bucket?

Marcus   I can assure you everything's been properly sterilised.

Regina   I'm not Social Services, son. You don't have to justify anything to me. Feed him rat poison for all I care.

Mini   I beg your pardon.

Gargantua *stirs, yawns, stretches.*

Regina   There he is. My nemesis.

She squares up to **Gargantua**.

Gargantua   Maaaa-maaaaaa-maaaah-mahhhhhh . . .

Regina (*quietly*)   Don't you 'maaaaa-maaaaa-maaaah-maahhh' me. You stole my fire yesterday, son. I've been constructing that mega-mall for as long as you've been gestating. It's cost me a lotta dollar and I need to see some comeback. Now after what you did it's fair to say I could take an aggressive stance against ya. But I won't.

Gargantua   Oooooh?

Regina   No. So consider yerself blessed. Cus Regina Buxley is one loco bitch you do *not* want for an enemy.

Gargantua   Goooooooooommmm!

Regina (*back to* **Mini** *and* **Marcus**)   An understanding has been reached. I've got a proposition for ya, Mum and Dad. I want the Big Feller 'ere to open my mega-mall.

Mini *and* **Marcus**   Hugh?

Regina   The mall is the biggest of its kind on the planet. So's this leviathan. We could be rivals. However, I am offering the chance to join forces and become partners.

The **Agents** *appear from hiding places and watch intently.*

Marcus   Oh, Regina! That'd be wonderful!

Mini   No it wouldn't, Marcus. She's saying our Hugh becomes an advert for the Skankton Marsh Mega-Mall!

Marcus   Are ya?

Regina   I am.

Marcus   She is.

Mini   I know.

Marcus   But Mini –

Mini   I don't want Hugh advertising someone's business.

Regina   Just think of him as a living blimp!

Mini   Excuse me! My son is not a living blimp!

Regina   That's as maybe, sweetheart. But times are hard. Ten ton o' cabbage a day starts to add up. How long can you poor struggling sods keep the boy fed? You don't look like you're made of money.

Mini   You're right. We're not. But it's the principle of the thing.

Marcus   Mini, love, it could help us out.

Mini   Marcus!

Gargantua   Mmmmmaaaaaahhhhhhh!!

Marcus   All right, son, I know you're hungry.

Regina   It's simple business sense. I keep you in enough cabbages and milk to last a bloody lifetime, and your son advertises my mall. Tit for tat. Come on, people. Don't throw the baby out with the bathwater.

Mini   Look, Mrs Buxley –

Regina   Regina, please. Or better still, Reg. I know it's a little masculine but my father was a Reginald, and it makes me feel close to him, God rest his soul. He was a real man. Not like my Lionel over there. Oh, yes. I know what the townsfolk say – that Regina Buxley's more of a man than 'er husband ever was.

During this, **Lionel** *has shuffled round to see* **Gargantua**. *All of a sudden,* **Gargantua** *scoops up* **Lionel** *and eats him.*

Marcus *and* **Mini** *see this but cannot speak.* **Regina***, her back to the scene, is oblivious.*

Regina   Well, let 'em gas. Lionel is a funny sort. But his heart's in the right place, and when you want him you always know he'll be right –

She turns around but all that remains are **Lionel***'s crutches lying scattered right where he was standing.*

Gargantua *burps.*

Mini   Hugh!

Regina   Did your son just eat my Lionel?

Marcus   Mrs Buxley, I don't know what to say . . .

Regina (*as she picks up the crutches*)   That grotesque cannibalising freak! He swallowed my husband whole!

Marcus   No, he bit Lionel's head off first. It would've been quick.

Mini   Marcus!

Regina   Quick it may have been! But that does not change the fact that your child is a people-eater!

Marcus   Please, Mrs Buxley, if there's anything we can do . . .

Regina   Oh, there is! Your son. My mega-mall. The grand opening. This weekend. Say *no* and I'll have that baby thrown in jail for murder!

Gargantua   Ooooooooooooooo.

Regina   I'll be in touch.

She exits.

Pause.

Mini   Hugh, that was a very, very bad thing to do!

Gargantua   Waaaaahhhhhhhh!!

Mini   Are you just going to stand there gawping, Marcus? Tell him off or something!

Marcus   He was just hungry was all.

Mini   She's right, ya know. We haven't got the money to feed him. Not at the rate he eats. And he's just going to get bigger and bigger. He'll be too big for the garden in a few days. Then what'll we do?

Marcus   We'll manage, Min. We wouldn't have got him otherwise. He's our special boy.

Agents *appear again.*

Allbright   Oh, he's so much more than that, Mr and Mrs Mungus.

Mini   Not you again.

Starkhammer   That's why we've come to take him off your hands, Mr and Mrs Mungus.

Marcus   Over my dead body.

Blackstone   We knew you'd say that, Mr Mungus.

Mini   Then you've wasted a trip! Be off with ya!

Agents   Mr and Mrs Mungus . . .

Allbright   It's such a mouthful.

Starkhammer   Mr and Mrs Mungus? To save time, may we call you *The Mungi*?

Mini *and* **Marcus**   Eh?

Blackstone   *The Mungi* is much better.

Allbright   Not only is it better, it's much *quicker* to say.

Starkhammer   So, *The Mungi*?

Mini *and* **Marcus**   Yes?

Blackstone   We hereby inform you that we are requisitioning your child.

Mini   No!

Allbright   He will be taken to a secret but secure environment –

Starkhammer   Where, we assure you, he will be very well looked after.

Marcus   We look after him here!

Blackstone   But who's going to look after you?

Allbright   He just gobbled up an old man. Who knows who's next?

Mini   You aren't taking him!

Marcus   Please! He's our son!

Starkhammer   I know this must be hard but trust us – it's for the common good.

Blackstone   Where he's going, he'll get the treatment people like you could never hope to provide.

This hits a nerve with **Mini** *and* **Marcus***.*

A deep bass rumble, like thunder, rattles the land.

Allbright   What's that sound?

Marcus   It's his stomach.

Mini   He's hungry . . .

Mini *and* **Marcus** *look to each other and realise that the* **Agents** *are right.*

Mini   Could we come and visit . . . ?

Starkhammer   Of course. You can see him whenever you like.

Blackstone   Here. Take this card.

Allbright   Call this number. One of our guys will collect you, day or night.

Starkhammer   Easy-peazy. So, what's your decision, *The Mungi*?

The **Mungi** *both nod.*

Allbright (*whispers into his cufflink*)   That's a good-to-go.

The sound of helicopters approaching eventually drowns everything out. A team of **Hardhats** *encircle the area (*JANUS TECH *stencilled on the backs of their day-glo jackets) and flag the 'copters down around* **Gargantua**.

Confused and disturbed, he starts to cry and reaches out for his mum and dad.

Mini *and* **Marcus** *can't watch as* **Gargantua** *is lifted to the sky. The helicopters' downdraft sends everything into a whirl.*

Mini *and* **Marcus** *are left holding each other as the sound of helicopters fades.*

Mini   Oh Marcus, what have we done?

Sally (*to camera*)   Hugh Mungus-mania continues to spread across the globe, but it's here in Skankton Marsh where the phenomenon is in full effect. Behind me, hit rock band The Dummysuckers, are performing their number-one smash 'Potty Trained'!

The Dummysuckers *perform their hit before a seething mosh pit.*

Song
   I'm only happy in a nappy!
   I go so dotty on my potty!
   If I do something rather naughty!
   You better smack me on the botty!

We're in a vast underground silo.

Gargantua *howls and struggles against his restraints. He's now the size of a church.*

Swan *addresses the audience.*

Swan   Ladies and gentlemen, my name is Professor Julian Swan. I'm head of Janus Technologies, and I have a vision of the future I'd like to share with you all. Picture, if you will, this unique creature, cloned! Picture, if you will, an army of giant super-babies! The ultimate biological weapon! Ladies and gentlemen, I give you . . . Project Gargantua!

A burst of applause.

Wellard (*stands*)   I'm sorry, Professor Swan, but this is completely unethical! He's just a baby.

Swan   He is an anomaly of nature, perhaps the most wondrous we have ever seen! And his potential must be harnessed!

Wellard   Exploited, you mean?

Malahyde   We live in a fragile world, Ms Wellard. Don't you want our country protected?

Wellard   By an army of giant babies?

Swan   They would be controlled, trained, then dropped into war zones.

Malahyde   The Cute Factor alone would stun the enemy into submission.

Swan   This is the next revolutionary step in passive-aggressive warfare tactics.

Wellard   How many millions have you sold the genetic patent for, Professor Swan?

Swan   Ms Wellard, please –

Wellard   How many *billions*?

Malahyde   You're embarrassing yourself, missy. Now sit down.

Wellard   No, General Malahyde, I won't. Prime Minister, I move to block this insane motion –

Prime Minister   Sit down, Pippa.

Wellard   You aren't seriously considering this?

Prime Minister   Sit. Down.

Wellard, *stunned, sits.*

Prime Minister   What's the next step, Professor?

Swan   Bone marrow extraction, as well as blood typing, biopsy and skin-tissue samples –

Wellard (*to* **Gargantua**)   You poor baby.

Swan   Then we can get the cloning under way. We just need the go-ahead, Prime Minister.

Malahyde   The thumbs-up.

Swan   The green-light.

Malahyde   The A-OK.

Prime Minister   You have it. Do our country proud, Professor.

Swan   We'll do our best, Prime Minister. Let us begin the extraction process at once! Prepare the drills!

Wellard   Monsters!

Sally (*to camera*)   But where is the world's favourite giant baby? His sudden and conspicuous absence from Skankton Marsh is taking its toll on everyone.

Arnie *turns the camera to:*

Skankton Girl (*tearful*)   Someone's taken my baby away!

Skankton Boy   Baby? Come back!

Constable Yappy   Oh where oh where can my baby be?

Sandy the Hairdresser (*blubbing*)   Oh baby, baby! B-b-b-baby!

Sally   His parents were unavailable for comment.

Marcus (*on mobile*)   Yes, hello, I'm ringing about my son, Hugh? Hugh Mungus? No, it's not a joke. That's his name. We wanted to see him. Oh. Right. I see. Thank you.

He hangs up.

The card those agents gave us . . . it's for Dave's Pizza Delivery.

Mini (*cradling his feeding bucket*)   What have we done?

Enter **Regina** *from nowhere.*

Regina   Howdy, Munguses!

Mini *and* **Marcus**   'Lo Regina.

Regina   Where's the star of the show? The mall opens tomorrer. Now where is he? I want to get him painted up to look like an enormous jar of mayonnaise –

Mini   He's gone, Reg. They took him.

Regina   Who took him?

Marcus   A sinister trio of agents from Janus Technologies.

Regina   They took our baby against our wishes?

Mini   What do we do, Regina?

Regina   We get him back, love. We get him back.

Silo.

Gargantua *howls inconsolably. A dozen* **Soldiers** *surround and guard him.*

Soldier 1   Poor thing's been crying all night.

Soldier 2   I'm not surprised after all it's been through.

Soldier 3   I know what used to soothe me. A nice lullaby.

Soldier 4   Go on, then. Somebody sing to him.

Soldier 5   Timothy, you've got the voice of an angel.

Soldier 6   No I haven't.

Soldiers   You have. Sing to him.

Soldier 6
Hush little baby don't say a word
Momma's gonna buy you a mockingbird

Soldier 2 *joins in.*

And if that mockingbird don't sing
Momma's gonna buy you a diamond ring

And more. **Gargantua** *calms.*

And if that diamond ring turns brass
Momma's gonna buy you a looking glass . . .

Gargantua *is asleep.*

Soldier 1   Nice work, lads. Nice work.

Swan (*holds aloft a small glowing test tube*)   We have everything
we need, General Malahyde.

Malahyde   Giant baby DNA. Who the hell woulda thunk it?

Prime Minister (*appearing from shadows*)   This is a momentous
day, gentlemen.

Swan   It is indeed, John.

Prime Minister   To our chapter in history!

All   To our chapter in history.

Gargantua *farts, blowing several* **Soldiers** *across the floor.*

Malahyde   Sweet mother of God! Open the air vents!

Outside, there is a crowd of **Gargantua-worshipping Zealots**
*all dressed as babies. In nappies, in bonnets, you name it. At the head of
the pack are* **Mini**, **Marcus** *and* **Regina**.

Mini (*sniffs the air*)   That's my Hugh! He's let off a distress
signal! He's definitely in there somewhere! A mother knows!

Sally (*to camera*)   I'm standing outside the secret laboratories of Janus Technologies where, it is alleged, the giant baby Gargantua is being held captive. There are literally thousands of groupies, admirers, self-declared Hugh-worshippers, who have all caught wind of his whereabouts.

Zealots   Free the baby! Free the baby! Free the baby!

Regina   Charge!

Sally (*to camera*)   The fans are scaling the walls of the compound, pulling down fences –

Silo.

Swan   What's that noise?

Wellard   I tipped off the media to our whereabouts. It's the sound of your chapter in history going down the toilet. Gentlemen.

Soldier   Babies! Incoming!

Nappy-wearing Zealots *storm the space.*

Soldiers *flee.*

Gargantua *gurgles with delight as the* **Zealots** *bow to him.*

Zealots   Hugh . . . Hugh . . . Hugh . . .

Sally (*to camera*)   The swarming masses are overpowering military might! Soldiers are actually throwing down their rifles and donning nappies! The liberation of Gargantua has begun!

Gargantua *sees* **Tiny Mini** *and* **Marcus**. *He breaks his chains and stands triumphantly on two wobbly legs.*

Tiny Mini   There he is! There's our boy!

Tiny Marcus   My, he's grown! Again!

Tiny Mini   Look Marcus! He's standing!

Gargantua *scoops them up in his hand.*

Gargantua   Mmmmmm . . .

Tiny Mini   He's trying to say something!

Gargantua   Mmmmmmmmeeeee . . .

Marcus   His first word! His first word!

Gargantua   Mmmm-mega malll . . .

Regina   Oh, that's m'boy! Right. Let's get back to Skankton Marsh and get it bloody open! Onward!

Swan   Stop! This specimen is property of Janus Technologies!

Gargantua *eyes* **Swan**, *heaves, then projectile vomits all over him.*

Sally (*to camera*)   And yes, the giant baby has covered Professor Julian Swan in a biblical flood of thick milky baby puke!

Swan (*dripping*)   Noooooooo!!

Malahyde   That's a bad boy! Bring him down!

Soldier   Sir?

Malahyde   He's outta control! Tazer the brute! A thousand volts!

Soldier   I don't think I can, General.

Malahyde   What is your problem, soldier?

Soldier   I've grown rather fond of the fella. (*Punching the air.*) Free the baby! Free the baby!

Sally (*to camera*)   Hugh seems to be hitting his troublesome tantrum phase, and I think I know why! Yes, I . . . I can see it! His first tooth!

Indeed, **Gargantua** *reveals a huge single top tooth.*

Mini *and* **Marcus**   Oh, Hugh!

The world cheers.

Malahyde   What the hell is he doing now?

Swan   He's torn a hole in the waste container!

Malahyde   Is that bad?

Swan   It's worse than bad. It's where we dispose of his soiled nappies.

Malahyde   Oh. Shit.

Gargantua *throws down disgusting, soiled nappies, dropping them like giant pancakes on to the* **Tiny Soldiers** *below.*

Swan *gets splattered. Again.*

Everyone   Phhhhhooooorrrrrr!!

Sally   He seems to be forging a path through the maelstrom with his mother and father in the palm of his hand!

Ker-rashhhhh!!

And he's out through the wall, and off into the night!

Regina (*as she leaves*)   Never mess with us Skankton Marshians!

Malahyde   Son of a gun.

Soldier (*covered in baby crap*)   Orders, General Malahyde?

Malahyde   There's a monster on the loose, Timothy. He's a threat to civilisation as we know it! Hit him with everything we've got.

Soldier   But sir, he's just a baby.

Malahyde   Must I do everything myself? Mobilise all units! Ground-to-air! Air-to-air! Go! Go! Go!

Two hundred **Soldiers** *run past* **Malahyde***.*

The following scene is split between Skankton and the silo.

Gargantua *sets down his* **Tiny Mum** *and* **Dad** *on the roof of a building.*

Tiny Mini   We're so proud of you, Hugh.

Tiny Marcus   We're so sorry we ever gave you up.

Tiny Mini   We've got you back.

Tiny Marcus   And we'll never let you go again!

Tiny Regina   I now declare the Skankton Mega-Mall well and truly ohhh −

Malahyde (*in silo*)   Launch missiles! Roast that baby!

WOOOOOSSSSSSSSSHHHHH!!!!! (*Missiles.*)

Regina   Bugger.

A slo-mo moment − **Mini** *and* **Marcus** *see the missiles approaching, they look to* **Gargantua**. **Gargantua** *sees what's about to happen.*

Gargantua   Mamma dadda . . . ?

Mini *and* **Marcus**   He said our −

KAAAAA-BOOOOOMMMMM!!

Mini *and* **Marcus Mungus** *are no more!*

Malahyde   You vaporised the parents, you knuckle-heads!

Sally   That's not good.

Gargantua   WAAAHHHHHHHHHH!!

Tiny Regina   Steady now, young man! You mind my beloved mega-mall!

Gargantua *swats* **Regina** *like a fly, and roars with rage.*

He goes wild, and tears the mall apart.

Sally (*to camera*)   He's ripping through the mall. Pounding with his fists. Buckling metal. Shattering glass. Decimating the place flat. And who could blame him?

Gargantua *destroys everything he sees in glorious slow motion.*

Skankton Boy   What's he doing? He's smashing everything!

Preacher Pike   He's no messiah! He's the spawn of the Devil!

Skankton Girl   I just wish he'd never been born!

Sandy the Hairdresser   Run for your lives!

Grannies *(really slow)*   Mmmmmmmmmm . . .

Gargantua *scoops them up, chews them, and spits them out.*

Tiny Malahyde   Open fire! Open fire!

10 Downing Street.

The **Prime Minister** *and his cabinet* (**Wellard**, **Creams**, **Wilt**) *watch on in horror.*

Wellard   Congratulations, John. You're in the history books *now*.

Wilt   He's tearing up the world.

Creams   He's not a happy bunny.

Enter **Malahyde** *and* **Swan**.

Swan   Prime Minister? I regret to inform you that Project: Gargantua has suffered a temporary setback.

Malahyde   Setback? That creature's destroyed half the country! And he don't show no sign of quittin'!

Creams   He's headed straight for us.

Wellard   Of course he is. He wants revenge.

Creams   Then we should get below ground and hide. For a really long time.

Malahyde   Or, we stop the beast in its tracks good and proper.

Wellard   I thought you'd hit him with everything you've got.

Malahyde   Not yet. I still got an ace up my sleeve. I say we get out the Big Guns.

Everyone falls silent.

Prime Minister   That is the last possible option, General Malahyde.

Malahyde   It's the *only* option, Prime Minister. This little terror is hell-bent and will stop at nothing. He'll keep eating and growing and walking all over us with those oversized feet of his unless –

Wellard   Unless we nuke him and take half the northern hemisphere with us?

Malahyde   The decision is yours, Prime Minister.

Prime Minister   So be it.

Echoing the image from the first scene, standing amidst smoke and fire, **Gargantua** *howls to the heavens.*

Back to the ante-chamber.

They have all been frantically acting out the story for the **Prime Minister**, *and are exhausted.*

Wellard (*at top speed*)   You give the go-ahead for a nuclear strike. We arrive here, the door seals shut behind us. You're about to punch in the entry code when – who's cooking onions? You collapse clean away. Prime Minister? Prime Minister! You wake up. You've lost your memory! Forgotten the entry code along with the past seven days! We re-play the whole event. The birth of Gargantua. The secret cloning plan. Agents are deployed. The giant baby brought to Professor Swan. The people revolt. He escapes! *Raahh!* We attack! *Booshh!* We kill his parents. *Sorry.* He goes on the rampage! Bang! Crash! Impossible to stop! Stop! Prime Minister has no other choice! (Stop me!) We flee down here, to the safe house! Please somebody! (I can't stop!) You go to punch in the entry code! Hmm! Onions? *Bam!* Prime Minister? You come round! Lost your memory! No entry code! Re-play the past seven days! Again! And again! And again! And –

Wilt *gently slaps her.*

Wellard   Thank you, Robin. Prime Minister, the missiles launch in thirty seconds. Does any of this ring any bells?

The **Prime Minister** *stares at them.*

Swan   The entry code, man? Do you remember it?

Prime Minister   I don't deserve the safe house after what I've done . . .

Creams   Then just give it to us and you can stay here.

Prime Minister   None of us deserves it. We've brought this upon ourselves.

Wellard   Speak for yourself!

Malahyde   Twenty seconds.

Creams   What's the bloody number, John?

Prime Minister (*quietly*)   Who's cooking onions?

Everyone groans with despair.

Prime Minister   You know, one of my first memories was of an old lady named Doris. She used to cook onions every Thursday night. Fry them up. She was our neighbour. Lovely woman. So kind. I remember that smell as if it were yesterday.

Wilt   So *Doris* was cooking the onions!

Swan   I'm glad we got that cleared up.

Prime Minister   And, I'll never forget, she lived at Number 49.

The **Prime Minister** *punches in the numbers on the control panel.*

Prime Minister   Forty-nine.

And again.

Forty-nine.

And again.

Beat. Ping.

Voice   Access granted.

They all sigh with relief.

Prime Minister   Funny . . . the things you remember as a child.

He looks at them all, then opens the door to reveal –

A huge eyeball peering in at them.

The Dummysuckers *kick in:*

Singer   GARGANTUA!

Everyone screams. **Garantua** *emits a deafening roar. They slam the door closed.*

Boom! Boom! Boom! BOOM!

The door explodes inwards. They all fall back.

Singer   GARGANTUA!

Gargantua*'s huge hand reaches in and grabs the* **Prime Minister***, crushing him in his grip.*

Singer
   You can try and outrun him
   But you won't get far!

Gargantua *eats all of the politicians, sets his sights on* **Malahyde***, picks him up in his hand –*

Tiny Malahyde (*quietly*)   Ten . . . nine . . . eight . . . seven . . . six . . . five . . . four . . .

Gargantua *draws* **Malahyde** *into the unending darkness of his gigantic mouth –*

Tiny Malahyde   Three . . . two . . . one . . .

And like that –

Tiny Malahyde   . . . Boom.

We are consumed.

Darkness.

Gargantua

*Notes on rehearsal and staging, drawn from workshops
with the writer held at the National Theatre, November 2010*

Background: Influences on *Gargantua*

THE ORIGINAL NOVEL   Rabelais's enormous novel
Gargantua was an inspiration and jumping-off point, with the
title and the general feeling being drawn from it, rather than
Carl's play being a reworking of it.

FILMS   There are many films that were influences on Carl
Grose in the writing of *Gargantua*, and many more that came
to mind during the workshop, including: *Dawn of the Dead*,
Monty Python (particularly *The Life of Brian*), *Brazil*, *Ghost
Busters*, *The Simpsons*, *Potty Time*, *Delicatessen* and *Amelie*, *Little
Miss Sunshine*, *The League of Gentlemen*, *Godzilla* and *King Kong*,
Whoops Apocalypse, *Dr Strangelove*, *Cloudy with a Chance of
Meatballs*, *The Science of Sleep*, *Cloverfield*, *Edward Scissorhands*,
Belleville Rendez-Vous and *Mars Attacks!* B-movie references also
inspired a particular kind of strange, gone-wrong authority
figure, performed with some very good bad acting.

COMMEDIA DELL'ARTE   An Italian theatre form which
emerged in the mid-sixteenth century, with its archetypal and
sometimes grotesque characters.

Character Checklist

What do we know about the characters?

MINI
She's not well off, is very much in love with Marcus, and is
twenty-two months pregnant and terrified of giving birth. She
has principles, is caring of her child and not seduced by fame.
She has an innocence and naivety about her.

MARCUS
He is very much in love with Mini but is more pragmatic than
his wife. He is the provider, but isn't quite managing. He will

stand up for his son, though, and has a softness to him. Another character comments that he looks like a kitchen utensil. Whether Mini and Marcus are fat or thin is something to play with.

A thought from Carl on the parents: 'The parents are key. They need to be credible amongst the chaos around them. They are the most human characters in the play, and its emotional centre.'

Lu Kemp, workshop director: 'I would love to see a scene where Mini and Marcus meet for the first time.'

SALLY
Ambitious. She moves during the play from covering a shopping mall opening to covering the apocalypse. She keeps pursuing the story right until the end. There is a sense that she has missed her moment. She was 'TV news personality of the year 2008', so perhaps there is now a desperation from her, a sense that things are now going downhill.

MALAHYDE
A Texan. He is keen to launch a nuclear missile and this is his function in the story. He is heavy-handed, trigger-happy and into aggressive tactics. He is in on the genetic cloning plot. He believes in brute force.

PROFESSOR JULIAN SWAN
The head of Janus Technologies, a dubious corporation. He links to lots of filmic references, including Bond villains. He is the sinister English professor. A potential contrast to Malahyde, being all brain rather than physical brute. He is clinical, calling the baby a 'specimen'. Something of a mad scientist.

PRIME MINISTER
When we meet the PM he/she is vulnerable, but has previously been strong. He has fallen apart in the moment of crisis; a string has snapped. In the flashback, we see glimmers of when the PM was stronger.

PIPPA WELLARD
She is another credible, human character alongside the others. She retains some sanity and moral grounding. Her aim in the play is to stop the nuclear missile and to stop the DNA testing. She is the play's moral centre. She clearly sees Malahyde as a corrupting force on the Prime Minister.

JEFF CREAMS
Minister of the Treasury. Self-interested, a slimy politician. At the end he wants to be saved even if no one else is.

ROBIN WILT
Loves the PM. Is the youngest of the Cabinet bunch.

ARNIE
Very loyal to Sally. Put-upon in what he is asked to do. Quietly scared by it all.

REGINA BUXLEY
Northern industrialist. Trying to take on a posher accent. Could be played by a man – she says she is more man than her husband.

DR LUCKY
Thinks he has an amazing bedside manner. A sense that he is always checking his appearance in a mirror. He does cruel things kindly. He has echoes of the *commedia* archetype of the hero.

NURSES
They are controlling their scene, and are in charge of Dr Lucky. They have down-to-earth, colloquial speech. Like the soldiers, they fill the role of chorus leaders.

AGENTS
Have shades, flash badges and wear black suits. They work for a higher power than the government. There is a whole world of internal madness between the three of them – the whispering to each other, hand signals, etc. They are nimble, like cats. In their heightened world everything is extraordinary – wired-up, a bomb, aliens landing.

How to Start

Do a read-through/run-through of the play, encouraging everyone to go in at full pitch, to let the bad acting happen and enjoy the glory of the shambolic mess that will inevitably occur. Have the stage directions read in by one person, standing on a chair at the back so as to cut across the chaos!

Ideas from the Workshop Run-through

- Carl Grose believes that his play can take a rough handling and that there is potential for many different approaches.
- The band and Sally are both helpful devices to support scene changes, changes in energy and location.
- The potential for the chorus is exciting, with the swapping between different sets of choruses to shift location.
- The presence of the baby could be very clear without him actually being there; performers could give focus to an imagined place he exists in. This could allow the audience to imagine him for themselves.
- The mother–baby bond is key to putting the emotional heart of the piece in place.
- A challenge is keeping the tension and urgency in scenes where lots of people are doing nothing.
- It is useful to keep in mind the sense that there are twenty-nine minutes to go before a nuclear attack.
- The shifts in rhythm and location are as important for telling the story as achieving the more evident staging challenges.
- The invisible relationships between Lionel and others when Regina is not looking became clear. We have probably learnt more about him than is directly written by the time he gets eaten.
- Characters' responses to what happens in the scenes are as important as the staging in showing the chaos Gargantua is causing.
- The key to a good production is to keep everything simple.

Ideas for Staging

MINI'S WATERS BREAKING
Find a metaphor for them, such as a big sheet being the water, make it a slow-motion tidal wave with people swimming through it in flippers and snorkels, mime the water rising around you, use going from fast to slow motion to indicate a more extreme action taking place.

FOR POO AND VOMIT MOMENTS
Use sound to indicate these. Chocolate Ready Brek. A massive party popper.

STAGING AND THE USE OF THE BAND
The band helps to create the bigger epic quality of the piece. It's there to help shift scenes and move along the action. It could be a real band or something like a puppet band. They could play any style of music. It could be done Dennis Potter-style with characters jumping in and performing the songs. Could be a ukulele band. Different instruments could be grabbed by different actors, and unconventional instruments could be used; found objects could be played to create rhythm. The band could be present all the time, and also be used to create the sound effects. The band could potentially shift styles throughout (but bear in mind part of the band's function is to help lead the audience through the action and connect scenes up).

Carl, the writer, felt that it would be possible to also use some other pre-recorded music between the band's appearances. He felt that the key to the band is finding the most fun solution and working out the aesthetic – e.g., is it a band of the grannies?

MINI GIVING BIRTH
Four groups had a go at putting this scene on its feet. These were the different approaches they took:

- Mini is standing on a chair; in front of her, a group of bodies form a human vagina. Dr Lucky pushes through them to go up inside Mini. He pops back out with a telephone and a leg of lamb.

- Again Mini is on a chair. A group is linked in a circle around her, rising and falling, as if her breath or the contractions. Dr Lucky fights his way in. Mini is pulled down inside the group who part to reveal her sitting on the chair holding the human-sized baby.

- Mini lies on a table with her back to the audience. A scarf is held up over her middle. Her legs are the arms of another actor sitting at the upstage end of the table with his arms sticking out and boots on his hands. Dr Lucky, examining her, then hoiks her arm-legs back into an impossible and painful-looking position, making her scream. Dr Lucky then goes inside Mini by diving under the table.

- Mini is lifted up by two tall male members of the group. In a quick manoeuvre she is moved to be sitting on one of their shoulders with Dr Lucky's head between her legs, as if Gargantua's head has just appeared, enormous, and is about to be born.

GARGANTUA PICKING UP MUM AND DAD

A human chain represents a giant hand and 'scoops up' Mum and Dad by encircling them and transporting them across the stage. Mum and Dad actors drop down behind a box and Mum's hat and Dad's glasses appear above the box and are animated to represent them as if they are on top of a building.

GROWTH OF GARGANTUA

How do you show Gargantua growing? Here are some initial ideas from the workshop . . .

Use different sized stilts that get taller through the play and are covered by a baby grow that unravels to get longer and longer. • A huge mask animated by up to four performers. • Lots and lots of balloons filling up a giant babygrow – people are seen blowing them up and adding them throughout the play as Gargantua grows. • Backpacks worn by performers with carnival puppets on top or rod and stick puppets. • Three identical small houses in different sizes so as a baby figure moves past them he seems to get bigger and bigger. • A huge shadow of a baby on a sheet. • Using lots of sound. • The set becoming the baby as if it is consuming it. • The cast all become the baby throughout the play so there is more baby and less chorus as it goes on. • A human-sized actor plays Gargantua but with one massive hand and one massive foot.

SALLY BEING SQUASHED
A Sally-puppet made of a black jacket and part of a wig poking out the top moves along the floor. At the moment she is squashed by Gargantua's foot we don't see a foot but she drops to the ground flat (like the material falls), the jacket opens up and a red scarf is pulled out as blood. A crowd rush in, looking up as if seeing the giant baby.

LIONEL BEING EATEN
Lionel is an actor holding a jacket in shape above his head and a ball atop for the head, with a cap on top of it. During the scene Lionel follows baby sounds coming from offstage. At the point his head peers offstage the ball is whisked away as if Gargantua has bitten it off. For a moment the body staggers about on the stage.

DEMOLITION OF THE TOWN
Three performers with expressions of terror on their faces move forward in slow motion, rolling over each other and pushing each other out of the way. While this is happening Sally's report about the town being destroyed is delivered. An additional idea was that a live feed could be used to film this onstage action, but with arms and legs being zoomed in on, to emphasise fingers tearing and pulling. This camera could be held by Arnie so as to be part of the action.

Working with a Live Feed

The following are some possibilities that working with a live camera feed opened up:

- Actors doing the vox pops to camera, so they also appear on a screen. Could have just two actors doing these, but quickly changing hats to indicate each new character.

- Sally's interview with the Prime Minister with crowds surrounding him behind and trying to be seen on TV.

- The camera focused on a piece of paper filming kids'-style drawings being made as we hear of some action like the parents being put on the rooftop and the town being destroyed. Drawing the action with big felt tips or crayons, projected large.

- Drawing a face on a grape, the camera zooming in on it, and then seeing it squashed underfoot and juice spurting out, projected large. A doll-baby placed next to the grape-person. The camera zooming in on its hand or eye, then going blurry, and when it comes back into focus it is replaced with a larger, human-sized hand or eye.

- Close-up of a mouth and then zooming into the darkness inside the mouth.

Responses from the Writer

What should we be most careful of?

Find your convention and then go for it. One tricky thing is to be precise with moments of shift [in location] and making sure you let the audience know where you are. Simplicity is key. Finding the enjoyment of it for the audience.

What would you like the audience to feel after they see Gargantua?

To come away saying 'What the hell?', and feeling that they haven't seen anything like it on stage before. To feel full, like they've seen a total theatre experience.

Are you consciously taking a stand on the media and consumerism?

The play is what it is. It does hold metaphors in it, but there is a danger in pursuing them and not telling the story. It's all in there and an audience should pick up on that.

How do you want actors to approach the play?

They should be exaggerated and physical, but in the same way as Steve Pemberton is in *The League of Gentlemen* and *Psychoville*:

very truthful, you believe him. He is a real person as well as being grotesque. Mini and Marcus need to be grounded in emotional truth.

What's a silo?

It is a tower or pit used to store grain or silage. But it is also an underground chamber where a missile is stored ready for firing.

Why does Malahyde have the last word?

He is the most aggressive, the grandest and most hard-core character, and the last left standing. He is the archetypal villain behind it all.

From a workshop led by Lu Kemp,
with notes by Lucy Foster

Katori Hall

Children of Killers

Characters

Vincent, *eighteen years old, son of 'The Butcher'*
Innocent, *fifteen to eighteen years old, the peacemaker of the group*
Bosco, *fifteen to eighteen years old, charming and energetic, yet carries the seed of extremist hatred in his heart*
Mama, *Vincent's mother*
Félicité, *five to fourteen (very flexible with age), Vincent's young sister*
Esperance, *nineteen to twenty years old, a survivor of the 1994 genocide, the elder sister of Emmanuel*
Emmanuel, *fifteen years old, called 'a child of bad memories',* enfant mauvais souvenir, *a product of rape, is slowly dying of Aids, Esperance's younger brother*
The Gahahamuka, *the silenced (can be played with as few as three or as many as ten)*

'Gahahamuka' – the point of speaking where words cease to exist. It is where breath refuses to make syllables amounting to silence, and there is emotion instead.

Setting
Rwanda. Soon. The President of Rwanda is releasing the killers. Years after the Tutsi genocide, the perpetrators begin to trickle back into the countryside to be reunited with their villages. A trio of friends – born during the genocide's bloody aftermath – prepare to meet the men who gave them life. But as the day of homecoming draws closer, the young men are haunted by the sins of their fathers. Who can you become when violence is your inheritance?

Language
(/) indicates overlapping of dialogue
(–) indicates an interruption

Scene One

Rwanda. Soon. A field in a rural village. A fútbol *game. A group of boys playing barefoot.*

Innocent   Pass it! Pass it!

Bosco   Pass the bloody ball, Vincent!

Vincent   No! Hell, no!

Innocent   But you always get to score!

Vincent   This is World Cup, yo!

Bosco   The best players always pass! They know how to attack together.

Vincent   No, they don't. They take it to the goal.

Bosco   Bloody hell, just pass the bloody ball!

Vincent   Vincent the Invincible never passes!

He kicks the ball past the invisible goalie. He scores. **Vincent** *dances around and around in jubilation.*

Bosco   Awww, meean. You only score 'cause we don't have a goalie.

Innocent (*out of breath*)   I am too-too tired.

He falls out on the grass.

Vincent   Get up! Get up! Get up, Innocent. We not finished yet!

> *We gonna rock this field, like a niggah shoot to kill.*

Innocent ⎞   Oh, my God.

Vincent ⎠   *Rock it like a soldier and like no niggah will.*

Bosco   Been watching too many rap videos on YouTube?

Innocent   He thinks he's the Jay-Z of Africa.

Bosco   You think Jay-Z will ever come to Rwanda?

Innocent   Why would he need to come to here? He already has his Beyoncé. When will I get me my Beyoncé?

Vincent   When you get a new face!

Bosco   Ohhhh!

Innocent   Wha, wha! What are you talking about? I have a beautiful face.

He stands there showing his face in profile.

I could model. Rwanda's Next Top Model, yo.

Vincent   Modelling's for girls.

Innocent   That is what you think. I will be the next Djimon Honsou. Look at that face. Look at these abs. Could cut a diamond.

They laugh.

Bosco   Innocent, quit your dreaming and pass the bloody ball!

Innocent *passes it to* **Bosco**. **Bosco** *does a quick loop or figure of eight around the other boys.*

Vincent   Oh, look at that! He's on his World Cup grind!

Bosco   Next time the World Cup comes back to Africa, I'll be ready.

Vincent   You think you can bob and weave as good as me?

He lunges towards him and tries to swipe the ball away. **Bosco** *quickly dodges him.*

Bosco   Nope, better!

Innocent   Ahh ha ha ha ha! He schooled you. He schooled you.

Bosco   What'd you learn, Vincent, huh? What'd you learn?

He is running towards the other end of the field.

Look at the way I make love to this ball. Look how she do what I say? This ball's my bitch!

Innocent   He's been practising.

Vincent   I can see that.

Bosco   I'm World Cup bound!

Vincent   World Cup, my ass!

Bosco   World Cup, oh! I'll be ready for it next time. When they come back to Africa I'm gonna be World Cup, yo!

He scores! He plays to his imaginary audience.

(*Making crowd sounds*)   Ahhhhhhhhh! Ahhhhhhh!

He takes a bow. Then realises that he's stepped into a pile of cow dung.

Bosco   Awww, meeeean. Meeeean. Meeeean!

The other boys laugh.

Vincent   They say it is good luck to step in the shit of a cow.

Bosco   Who say this?

Vincent   The ancestors.

Bosco   Eh-eh! They never know what the hell they are talking about. (*He continues to inspect his feet.*) Meeeean. Meeeean!

Innocent   Whoever's cow made that was loved.

Bosco   Now I got to pick this shit out from between my toes. This is bloody disgusting.

Innocent   Be happy that you don't have to pick it out of your teeth.

Vincent *takes the ball and bounces it on his knees. The boys continue laughing.*

Vincent (*with a start*)   Eh-eh, what time is it?

Bosco *reaches into his pocket and pulls out an iPhone.* **Vincent** *runs to get something out of his backpack.*

Innocent   Eh – where did you get that iPhone?

Vincent   Knowing you, you must have stolen it.

Bosco   Ay, I'm not no pickpocket!

Innocent   Then how'd you get it?

Bosco   I took it out of that American's backpack. At the cabaret.

Innocent   So how you no pickpocket?

Bosco   I didn't pick it out his pocket, I picked it out his *bag*. Differences, my friend Innocent. Differences.

Innocent   You are a consummate thief.

Bosco   Well, a young man has to be good at something.

Vincent   'Cause you're certainly not good at *fútbol*.

He has taken out his transistor radio and is trying to get it to work.

Innocent (*playing with the ball*)   Vincent, we still have a score to settle!

Vincent   Time to hear the news.

Bosco   Ah, the 'old man' is trying to hear the news.

Vincent   Call me an 'old man' one more time, and I'll beat you like an old man should.

Bosco   Awwww, / meeeeean.

Innocent   You can't get the news out here. You can never get the radio to work up here.

For a moment the channel clears. A Beyoncé song pours through the speakers. **Bosco** *and* **Innocent** *start to grind it out.*

Bosco   Even in the most remote hills of Rwanda there is Beyoncé.

Innocent *starts to sing the song, but another song riding on the wind catches his attention. The village is wailing.* **Vincent** *turns off the radio.*

Bosco   Eh-eh, why you / turn it off!

Vincent   Shhh, be quiet, yo.

Bosco   Wha, wha?

There is singing coming from way off. Way off deep in the valley.

Why in the bloody hell are they singing?

Innocent   I don't know.

Bosco   What is it?

Innocent   If you would just quit your yapping for just a few seconds maybe we could hear.

Vincent   The song. Sounds familiar.

Bosco   It's the –

Vincent (*interrupting sharply*)   Shhhh . . . Listen!

The village continues to sing. A deep wail. Beat.

Innocent *and* **Vincent** *look at each other.*

Innocent   Could it be –

Bosco   True?

Vincent   I thought I would never hear that song.

Innocent   Never thought I'd hear it in my lifetime.

Bosco   It's the song of . . .

Vincent *and* **Innocent**   Machete season.

Emmanuel (*off*)   I got MTN credit! Zazu credit! Orange credit!

A young boy, **Emmanuel***, is selling cell phone credit. He is wearing a bright yellow jacket. He is of similar age to the young boys, but much* *slighter. He has the sickness.* **Emmanuel** *is out of breath from his climb to the top of the hill.*

Bosco ⎫ Eh-eh! Emmanuel! It true?

Innocent ⎭ Emmanuel!

Emmanuel   That what they say. The village is celebrating. We all heard it on the radio.

Innocent   We didn't.

Bosco   Your radio's for shit, Vincent.

Vincent   Fuck off, Bosco.

Bosco (*laughing*)   I gotta call my mama. Emmanuel, I need a sim card.

Vincent   iPhone take MTN SIM?

Bosco   I got it unlocked, yo.

Vincent   *Butter!*

Emmanuel   A thousand francs for a SIM. But for you, Bosco, I'll take fifteen hundred.

Bosco   Eh-eh! That not no steal.

Emmanuel   I know you got it.

Bosco   Eleven hundred.

Emmanuel   Thirteen hundred.

Bosco (*fast*)   Twelve fifty.

Emmanuel (*fast*)   Thirteen hundred.

Bosco (*faster*)   Twelve fifty-one.

Emmanuel (*even faster*)   Thirteen fifty!

Bosco *sucks his teeth and fishes for the francs. The wailing in the village gets louder.*

Bosco   You should be the president of Uganda as slick as you are.

He hands **Emmanuel** *the francs from his pocket.*

Innocent   My mama used to sing this when she rocked me to sleep. I was only this high. 'When they come home this will be riding on the wind.'

He sings the song coming out of the valley, he knows it well . . .

Isn't it the most beautiful song you ever heard, Vincent?

Vincent *is visibly shaking.*

Emmanuel   The President just announced it. They start the release on Friday.

Innocent   Friday?

Vincent   So soon?

Emmanuel   So soon. (*Acknowledging him.*) Vincent.

Vincent   Emmanuel. How's your sister?

Emmanuel   Esperance is cool.

Bosco *rolls his eyes.*

Bosco   What are you going to do when you meet your papa, Innocent?

Innocent   Man, I don't know. Maybe I'll –

Bosco   Hug him?

Innocent   No, I will let my sisters hug him. That is for the girls to do.

Bosco   Maybe you'll –

Innocent   Bring him out a Primus beer!

Bosco   Mama said that was my papa's favourite. Primus.

Innocent   Rwanda's favourite beer.

Vincent   It's Rwanda's *only* beer.

Innocent   Well, my auntie will make a jerrycan of banana beer to celebrate.

Bosco   Well, I'm coming over there!

Innocent   I can't believe it. I can't believe they are coming home!

Bosco   Our papas are finally coming home.

Innocent   No longer will we have to run the streets hungry.

Bosco   Or steal potatoes from other people's fields.

Innocent   Or raise our young brothers.

Bosco   Or give our sisters away at weddings.

Innocent   Or be the men of the house.

Emmanuel (*wryly*)   The killers are coming home.

Beat.

Bosco   Ah-ah, why you call them that? They're not that.

Innocent   Well, technically –

Bosco   Technically they *are* that, but you didn't have to *call* them that.

Emmanuel   Well, I'm a blunt boy.

Bosco   Blunt?

Emmanuel   I'm just saying.

Bosco   You're not *saying* anything –

Innocent (*interrupting*)   How many of them did your father kill, Bosco?

Bosco (*proudly puffing out his chest*)   They say my father killed 678.

The Boys (*without* **Vincent**)   *Whoa!*

Innocent   Well, they say *my* father killed 752.

The Boys (*without* **Vincent**)   *Whoa!*

Bosco   Well, no one has anything on Vincent's father. Isn't that right, Vincent?

Vincent (*weakly smiling, head bowed*)   That's what they say.

Bosco   Known around here for killing the most Tutsi. More than any Hutu man. That's who Vincent was named after.

Emmanuel   Really?

Bosco   Vincent the Invincible!

Innocent   Vincent the Invincible, Junior!

Bosco   Ah, oh!

Innocent   They say his father was so cold that he once made a man chop his own children to bits.

Bosco   They say he killed more than forty men in a single night.

Innocent   They say a man begged him to be shot with a bullet. But his father was soooo cold he chopped him to bits with the machete anyway.

Innocent *and* **Bosco**   Ooooo!

Bosco   No, no, no. Top this. They say, they say, *they say* he chopped off the head of a Tutsi woman and then made her children play *fútbol* with it.

Bosco *bounces the ball into the air playfully. They all stand there imagining . . .*

Innocent   Man, really, that's too *too* cold. Cold as ice. Cold as ice.

Emmanuel   So, you're the son of 'The Butcher'?

Beat. Head still bowed, **Vincent** *has grown remarkably uncomfortable.*

Vincent   Yeah, that's what they say.

Innocent *and* **Bosco** *look to* **Vincent** *with great pride,* **Emmanuel** *with great fear – and* **Vincent** *to himself with great shame.*

Bosco   Emmanuel, who is your father?

Silence. **Emmanuel** *looks around.*

Emmanuel   I don't have one.

Innocent   We all have a father.

Bosco   Yeah, we all have a father.

Emmanuel   I have no father.

Bosco   Impossible.

Emmanuel   Why is that impossible?

Bosco   It's biologically impossible for you *not* to have one.

Emmanuel   How do you know?

Bosco   'Cause I know about it. I read it in a book I stole.

Innocent ⎫   Goodness, gracious.

Vincent ⎭   Bosco!

Bosco   Wha? Wha? Nobody else was using it. I had to read up for the big moment.

Innocent   I've already had my big moment –

Bosco   Liar!

Innocent   I have. She said I was good!

Bosco   Liar!

Innocent   Whatever, Bosco.

Bosco   Go to bloody hell!

Innocent   No, you go! Come on, Emmanuel. Tell us who your father is.

Emmanuel   Like I said before, I have no father.

Bosco   As a seed you were spit out of the sword of life. Only a man can spit you out of his sword. (*He gestures.*)

Innocent   Bosco, did you read that biology book correctly?

Emmanuel   I have no father. My mother told me that I was conceived like Jesus.

Beat.

Innocent   Like Jesus?

Emmanuel   Yes, so help me God. I am a miracle child. Born during the genocide. Amongst the destruction and death, God blessed her with life, me, 'Immaculate Emmanuel'. I am the result of a 'virgin conception'.

Innocent and **Bosco** *take a look at each other.*

Bosco (*smiling*)   You?

Emmanuel   That's what she said. I am directly from God.

Bosco   Well, I certainly didn't read about that in no biology book.

Emmanuel   You should have stolen a Bible, then you'd know.

Innocent   Well, his mother's name *is* Mary.

Bosco *and* **Innocent** *laugh, while* **Vincent** *grows increasingly uncomfortable.*

Vincent   Leave him alone.

Bosco   So you think your mother was a virgin when she had you?

Emmanuel   Of course not. Esperance was born of man, but I, *I* was born of God. Like Jesus. I am a child of God.

Bosco (*laughing*)   Aren't we all.

Emmanuel   Not in the way you mean. I am special. I don't need a father.

Innocent   Nooo, I think I know your father.

Emmanuel   Yes, my father is God.

Bosco   No, I think your father is Claude.

Innocent   Or Alphonse

Bosco   His father could be Jean-Pierre.

Emmanuel ⎫   I was born like Jesus.
Innocent ⎭   Or Vianney.

Emmanuel ⎫   I have no father.
Bosco ⎭   Or François.

Innocent ⎫   Or Olivier.
Bosco ⎭   Or Jonas.

Innocent ⎫   Or Gazazi, his brother!
Vincent ⎭   Leave him alone.

Emmanuel   That's what my mother said! 'Immaculate Emmanuel!' That's who I am.

He runs away downhill as fast as his legs will carry him.

Vincent   LEAVE HIM ALONE!!

Bosco *and* **Innocent** *look after him and laugh.*

Innocent   Immaculate conception? That was a good one, eh?

Bosco   There is nothing immaculate about that poor boy. He skinny.

Innocent   That what the sickness do, yo. Disappear you.

Bosco   That's what his mama died of, too.

Innocent   Yeah . . .

Bosco   His mother wasn't no virgin. More like a whore. Can you believe he believed that story she told him? What a shame he doesn't know who his father is.

Vincent   His father might be yours.

They both stop chuckling.

Bosco   Wha?

Vincent   Maybe Emmanuel is your little brother.

Bosco   Impossible.

Vincent   You're so busy trying to name his father, you forgot to put yours in the mix.

Innocent   Hey . . .

Bosco   That's not fair.

Innocent   Heeey!!

Bosco   My father would never have done *that*. He did other things, but he would never ever do *that*.

Vincent   Why not?

Bosco   Because I *know* him.

Vincent   Oh, do you?

Bosco   Yes, I *know* my father wouldn't do that.

Vincent   Don't be so sure.

Innocent   Hey, guys, let's stop.

Bosco   Are you calling my father *that*?

Vincent   How else do you think Emmanuel came to be? He is a miracle child alright, but not that kind of miracle.

Bosco   My papa did not rape Mary. My papa did not do that. Plus they say – eh, eh – Emmanuel got the sickness. My papa don't got the Aids. They made the men with the Aids rape the women. My papa don't got the Aids.

Innocent   How you know?

Bosco   Does your papa got the Aids?

Innocent   Hell, no.

Bosco   Well, my papa don't either. My papa didn't have to force no women to be with him.

Vincent   Well, that's not what I heard.

Bosco   Well, there's a difference between what you hear and what you know. And, 'old man', why are you bringing up all this anyway? All this old shit! It's just rumours. Those down in the village don't know our papas. We do!

Vincent   We've never even met our fathers, Bosco. None of us! You don't *know* him.

Bosco   I know my father.

Vincent   Yeah, and what do you know about him?

Bosco *stands there in silence.*

Vincent   Emmanuel's right. They're killers.

Innocent   Look, the government made them do it.

Vincent   Do you really believe that, Innocent?

Innocent   That's what they said. That's what they said happened.

Vincent   Come on, Innocent. Think for yourself.

Innocent   Vincent, what's gotten into you?

Vincent   Do you really think that the government put a machete in your father's hand?

Bosco   That's what they said. So that's what we have to believe.

Innocent   Hey, that is what they are teaching in the schools?

Vincent   What if your papa just had it in him, just had it in him, and he wanted to go kill those women, those children –

Bosco   Eh-eh! My papa didn't kill no kids, *yours* did!

Vincent   The question is, do you know that *yours* did?

Bosco *stares at his friend. Beat.*

Bosco   I'm going home.

Innocent   Bosco –

Bosco *begins to trudge down the hill. He sharply turns.*

Bosco   Innocent, you coming?

Innocent *looks back to* **Vincent** *who stares back at him.*

Innocent (*foraging up a smile*)   Hey, guys, they're coming home. There's so much to celebrate. So much to be happy about . . .

Vincent   Yeah. They're coming home. No longer will we be the men of the house.

Innocent *follows* **Bosco** *down towards the bottom of the hill.*

Scene Two

Night time. **Vincent** *is lying in his bed. He is tossing and turning. A worn ball rolls from one side of the room.* **Vincent** *continues to sleep. A little girl emerges from the corner. She has on a slip. It is horribly distressed, caked with dried blood and vomit. She plays with the ball. She would have been a pro* fútbol *player. Would have been . . .*

Another girl comes from the other corner. Her clothes, too, are caked with blood.

Gahahamuka 1 *laughing.*

Gahahamuka 2   Shhhh! He's sleeping.

A young boy emerges from the shadows.

Gahahamuka 3   Not peacefully though.

Gahahamuka 1 *laughing.*

Gahahamuka 2   Why does she laugh so much?

Gahahamuka 3   Because they cut off her tongue.

Gahahamuka 1 *laughing.*

Gahahamuka 2   You're gonna wake him.

Gahahamuka 1 *laughing.*

Gahahamuka 2   Stop!

Gahahamuka 3   Be quiet both of you. Let's go to work.

The Gahahamuka *take their positions.*

Gahahamuka 1 *laughing.*

Gahahamuka 2 *and* **3**   *We are the gahahamuka.*

Gahahamuka 1 *laughing.*

Gahahamuka 2 *and* **3**   *We are the gahahamuka. Here to tell the tale if only you would listen.*

Gahahamuka 3   Listen.

Gahahamuka 1 *laughing.*

The young boy – **Gahahamuka 3** *– raises a machete above his head. He is about to take a slice. He raises the machete and with all his might he goes for Vincent's head.*

Félicité (*offstage*)   Vincent . . . Vincent . . .

Vincent *shoots straight up. He looks around himself.* **The Gahahamuka** *have vanished. His eyes adjust to the dark and he finally sees* **Félicité** *standing at the edge of the bed.*

Vincent   Why are you standing up there laughing at me?

Félicité   I'm not laughing at you.

Vincent   Yes, you were. I just heard you.

Félicité   It wasn't me, Vincent, I swear.

Vincent   What do you want?

Félicité   I need to take a piss.

Vincent   Piss in the bucket, Félicité.

Félicité   Unh, unh. I hate how it smells in the morning.

Vincent   So what you really have to do is go take a shit?

Beat.

Félicité   Guilty.

Vincent *sighs. He pulls the covers back and hops out of bed. Laughter rides on the wind.*

Vincent   What was that?

Félicité   What was what?

Vincent   That?

Félicité   What?

Vincent   That? Did you hear that?

Félicité   I didn't hear anything.

Vincent   Laughter.

Félicité *listens.*

Félicité   Maybe that was Mama.

Vincent   No, Mama doesn't laugh at night; she cries.

Crying and laughter ride the wind.

Shh! Listen, there it goes again.

Félicité *is shifting in her pants.*

Félicité   Vincent, I have to go shit. Bad!

Vincent   Alright. Alright.

Vincent *takes* **Félicité***'s hand and they walk out of the hut into the darkness of the night. Out of the shadows one of* **The Gahahamuka** *emerges. The ball she was holding has now been replaced with a skull.*

Scene Three

Next morning. The kitchen hut. **Vincent** *and his little sister,* **Félicité**, *around ten years old, sit at the table.* **Vincent** *is tuning in his transistor radio.*

Radio   The President's prisoner release programme is well under way. A wave of prisoners has been released from Gingkoro Prison in southwestern Rwanda.

Félicité   That's near us, Mama!

Mama   Shhh, Félicité!

Radio   Many prisoners have completed the national rehabilitation programme and are coming home. (*Voice of the President:*) 'The past is over and the future is now. Rwanda can only walk into the future with all of her children. We can co-exist peacefully in this society as neighbours. Gone are the days of the Hutu and Tutsi. In this Rwanda, the new Rwanda, we are one.'

Félicité *heads towards the stove.*

Mama   Eh, eh! Why you goin' for seconds?

Félicité   I'm a growing girl. Mama, let me eat.

Mama   Eh, eh, eh! We have to save that for later.

Vincent   Félicité always has to have seconds.

Félicité   Because Félicité is never satisfied.

Mama (*laughing*)   Yes, indeed that is true.

Vincent   I swear you have a tapeworm.

Félicité *sticks her tongue out at her brother.*

Félicité   Mama, can I please have seconds?

Mama   Eh! Eh!

Félicité   Mama, pleeeease . . .

Beat. **Mama** *sighs.*

Mama   Fine. But make sure you leave a little in the pot for the gods. Always have to have a little bit left over for them.

Félicité   Thank you, Mama!

Mama   Leave some for Vincent.

Vincent   Ugh, ugh, I don't want.

Mama   What, boy, you gotta eat. You don't want to look like a Tutsi now, do you?

Vincent *goes over to the stove. He fills his bowl with more porridge.*

Mama   Where are Innocent and Bosco? I do not hear those knotty-headed boys wrestling outside your window. I wonder why they are late.

Vincent   I – I – I told them I'd meet them down the road.

Mama   Good. Those two boys give me headaches.

She sits down in the kitchen and pulls out a tube of red lipstick. Her hands shake, but she applies it gingerly on to her pursed lips.

Félicité   Ooo, Mama! Why are you putting that on?

Mama   Mind your business, child.

Félicité   Can I put it on?

Mama   You don't need to practise.

Félicité   Practise what?

Mama   Being pretty. Because you already are. Unfortunately, your mama is out of practice.

Vincent   And who are you practising for?

Beat.

Mama   You know, Vincent.

Vincent   No, I don't know.

Mama   Don't be so silly, Vincent.

She picks up the rusted machete and continues applying the red lipstick.

Vincent   That stuff makes you look like a −

Mama   Vincent, you are not too *old* to get slapped.

Félicité *giggles.* **Vincent** *sulks at the table.* **Mama** *finishes her application. She looks up.*

Mama   How do I look? Do you think your papa will like this?

Vincent   If he likes a woman as beautiful as you, then indeed he will like this new look of yours.

Mama   I haven't worn red lipstick since . . . Almost forgot I had it.

She holds it close to her chest.

Félicité   Can I wear some, Mama?

Mama *stares at herself in the machete. She smiles at herself approvingly.*

Mama   Red was always his favourite colour.

Félicité *goes over to kiss her* **Mama** *on the lips.*

Félicité   There! I got some on my lips, too.

Félicité *looks at herself in the machete.*

Mama   Little girl, go by the bucket and wash that off your lips! And wash that millet from your hands while you're at it!

Félicité   Aww, meean.

Mama   Sa-sa! (*Clapping her hands.*) Child, and remember you are not too *young* to be slapped.

Félicité *trudges to the bucket in the corner.* **Mama** *continues to stare at herself in the shine of the machete.*

Vincent   What will he say about her? About Félicité?

Mama   Why, boy, what do you mean?

Vincent   Don't you think he's gonna be mad?

Mama (*laughing*)   What's he got to be mad about? I ploughed this land and made it bigger and better. When he left we had one cow, now we have three. We have a well on our land now, and why, my Vincent? I do think that it is because of me.

Vincent   And me.

Mama   Yes, so you pulled your weight, too. We had to. We all had to. Life goes on. Félicité is an example that life goes on.

Vincent   Yes, life goes on, but aren't you scared of him? What he will say –

Mama   Why would I be scared of your father? He is gentle as water rolling down a hill.

Vincent   He will know that you were not faithful –

She slaps him hard across the face.

Mama   What is 'faithful' when you are hungry? What is 'faithful' when you need somewhere to sleep? What is 'faithful' when someone must pay your school fees? I didn't hear you complaining about my 'faithfulness' then.

Vincent   I was a boy then; I'm a man now.

Mama   Let's see how much of a man you'll be when your papa comes home.

Félicité *stares at them from across the kitchen table.*

Mama   Time to go to work.

She looks back into the machete, admiring her face.

Scene Four

Bosco *is waiting by the well. He has a machete in his hand. He is about to start work out in the fields. A* **Gahahamuka** *runs by him.*

Gahahamuka 1 *laughing.*

Bosco *jumps.*

Bosco   Who's there?

Gahahamuka 1 *laughing.*

Bosco   What the bloody hell . . .

He lifts up his machete, hovering in a batting position.

Hey, Innocent, quit playing games.

Gahahamuka 1 *laughing.*

Bosco   Stop it, now. I'm not playing with you.

A ball is kicked towards him. **Bosco** *ducks. He runs to pick it up.*

Gahahamuka 1 *laughing.*

Bosco   Innocent! Stop playing you bloody –

Bosco *takes a look at the soccer ball. It is covered with blood. He drops it. And stares at his hands. He runs to the water pump to wash his hands. He keeps washing and washing and washing and washing and washing.* **Bosco** *turns around –*

Bosco   Aaaaahhhhh!

Innocent   Aaaaahhhhh!

Bosco   Why you playing around like that? You're always playing round!

Innocent   What you talking about? I called your name. You didn't hear me?

Bosco   When?

Innocent   Just then!

Bosco   Why you throw that ball at me man?

Innocent   What ball?

Bosco *looks to where the ball was. It's gone.*

Bosco   Right –

Innocent Where?

Bosco It was. Just. Right . . . there.

Innocent You going coo-coo.

Bosco *looks to his hands. He holds them up. They are no longer red.*

Bosco Must have been staring at the sun too long.

Innocent Something.

Bosco Seeing things . . .

Innocent You think he's mad we didn't stop by? To pick him up?

Bosco Who cares.

Innocent He's never been that way before. I wonder what's gotten into him.

Bosco 'Old man' just about had a heart attack.

Innocent He's only a few years older than us.

Bosco So what? He still bloody old.

Innocent Why you always saying 'bloody'?

Bosco *pauses and takes a look at his hands.*

Bosco It's every Rwandan's duty as newly minted members of the British Commonwealth to use the curse words of our fellow brethren.

Innocent I rather say 'fuck' like the Americans.

Bosco Bloody. Fuck. Whatever. You'd think he'd be happy. Our papas coming home, and there he goes bringing up all that – that history –

Innocent Just think, twenty years ago we all would have been speaking French.

Bosco French bloody sucks. I will thank the President every day for changing the national language to English.

Innocent   Why?

Bosco   So I can get me an American wife.

Innocent   Don't no American wanna marry you.

Bosco   An American see this fine African specimen, and she will keel over in delight and wanna make her a fine African-American.

They laugh. One of **The Gahahamuka** *runs behind them in the brush.*

Gahahamuka 1 *laughing.*

Bosco *jumps.*

Bosco   Innocent, did you see that?

Innocent   See what?

Bosco   There it is again. I saw something. Like . . . like . . . like a kid.

Innocent   You need to get out of the sun.

The **Gahahamuka** *runs past them again.*

Gahahamuka 1 *laughing.*

Bosco   There it is again. I know I heard something. Laughing. Something laughing . . .

Innocent (*he points*)   Maybe it's her, but I don't know what she got to laugh about.

A beautiful teenage girl walks down the hill. She balances a yellow jerrycan full of water on her head. She bears the marks of a survivor. Scars decorate her arms like bracelets. There is one that cuts across her head. (She may only have one arm.) But the slices of the machete were not able to cut her beauty away from her. She pauses when she sees the boys. She wonders whether or not she should continue. She decides to walk forward . . . carefully.

Bosco   Oooo, my God, it's hot.

He fans himself. **Innocent** *laughs.*

Innocent   Can we have some water?

She does not speak to them. They rib each other.

Bosco   We know you have a voice. A very pretty voice. That's what they say.

Innocent   Yeah, that's what they say.

Bosco   Don't be scared of us. We not gonna hurt you.

Innocent   At least *I'm* not.

She proceeds slowly.

Bosco   You wanna see my new phone?

Innocent   She don't wanna see that thing.

Bosco   I bet she do. Don't you want to see it?

She ignores them.

Innocent   *Inyenzi*, don't you hear us talking to you?

She whirls around and faces them.

Esperance   Do not call me that. That is not my name. You know my name is Esperance. Not *cockroach*.

Bosco   That's what we used to call you. During the war. That's what you are.

Innocent   Yeah, that's what you are.

Esperance   Have you looked in the mirror lately?

Innocent   Ooooo!

Bosco   She's a tough Tutsi. Haven't seen one of those before.

Innocent   She won't be so tough in a minute.

Esperance   You don't scare me.

Bosco   Oh, we don't?

He goes up to her and pushes the jerrycan from her head. As it falls water splatters all over the ground.

Ooops!

Esperance *picks up the jerrycan and throws the rest of the water at* **Bosco**.

Esperance   Leave me alone!

Innocent   Look! Look at her! The Tutsi who fights back!

Bosco   Hey, you got my iPhone wet! Grab her! Grab her!

Innocent *grabs* **Esperance**.

Esperance   Stop it! Stop it! Let go of me!

Esperance ⎱   Let go of me! Let GO!

Bosco ⎰   You got my iPhone wet!

He comes up to her and points his finger in her face.

Bosco   When my father comes home you better run. He will finish. He will finish what he started.

Esperance   Well, tell him to come. I may only have one arm, but the other can wield a machete just as wildly as any other man.

Bosco *raises his hand, but, suddenly, out of nowhere,* **Vincent** *barrels down the hill. He tackles* **Bosco** *to the ground.*

Bosco ⎱   What the bloody hell you doing?

Vincent ⎰   Get off of her!

He then rushes to **Innocent**, *who has her in his grip.*

Vincent   Let her go!

Innocent *is no match for the bigger* **Vincent** *and quickly lets her go.*

Esperance *takes off running down the hill away from the young men, leaving her jerrycan behind.*

Bosco   What you do that for, Vincent?

His nose is bloody.

Innocent   We were only playing.

Vincent   Playing?

Bosco   It was a joke. She was laughing. See, she was laughing.

Vincent   She was not laughing.

Innocent   Yes, she was.

Vincent   She was scared out of her mind. What were you trying to do to her?

Innocent   Nothing.

Vincent *pushes up close to* **Bosco**, *fire streaming from his eyes.*

Vincent   What were you trying to do to her?

Innocent   I said NOTHING!

Bosco   Why do you care so much about them, about her?

Vincent   I don't.

Bosco   You act like you love her.

Vincent   Fuck you!

Bosco   Is that it? Is it that you love the *inyenzi*? You a cockroach lover? Well, I tell you one thing, they don't love us. They would kill us Hutus if they could. Round us all up. They're out for revenge.

Vincent   That's not true.

Bosco   Remember how the Tutsi kids used to taunt us in primary. Huh, Vincent?

Innocent   They looked down on us.

Bosco   Because they had better clothes than us. Because everyone felt sorry for them. Everyone was giving them everything. 'Oh, the poor little orphans, they have no parents. Oh, the poor Tutsis.' Well, what about us, Vincent? What about us?

Innocent   They locked our papas away. Making *us* orphans.

Bosco   Called us children of killers.

Vincent   Well, can you blame them?

Bosco   We didn't do anything to them, Vincent! And we are the ones being punished.

Innocent   It's *inyenzi* like her that need to be punished.

Vincent   Punished for what?

Bosco   In case you don't remember, she is the main reason our fathers are behind bars. She is the one that pointed them out. At the trial?

Vincent   I don't believe that.

Bosco   Well, you better. My mother said that it was Esperance who pointed. She pointed her little finger and then my father was gone. Our fathers. Gone. If it wasn't for her . . . You know, all my life I've had to teach myself how to be a man. How to shave my beard. How to take a piss. How to hoe. How to sharpen a machete. How to chop firewood for the stove. How to make love to a woman. How to . . . She took my father away from me, Vincent. From *us*!

Vincent   She was just a child.

Bosco   *I wasn't even born!* I didn't even get to meet my father, Vincent. Not once. I've always wondered, do I have his nose? Do I have his hands? Do I have his moles? Do I have . . . I don't even know how he looks, Vincent. I don't even have one memory of him. I never got the chance. Because of her. Because of her little finger. Well, I wish they hadda chopped off her other hand.

Vincent ⎫   Are you hearing what you are saying?

Innocent ⎭   Hey, buddy, calm down. Calm down.

Bosco (*near tears*)   She was wrong. She was wrong. She was wrong. She was wrong. She was wrong. She was wrong.

Suddenly, the village begins to wail. They are singing the 'machete song'. There is a beat of the drum. A celebratory chant. It is louder and more aggressive than before. The young men stare at each other.

Innocent   They're here. Oh, my God, they're here.

Bosco   My papa . . . My papa's home.

He takes off running down the hill.

Innocent, you coming or what?

Innocent   I'll meet you. I'll meet you down there.

Bosco (*from the distance*)   Hurry! Hurry!!

He is gone.

Innocent   We weren't going to do anything to her, Vincent.

Vincent   People can get carried away.

Innocent   It wasn't like that.

Vincent   Yeah, that's what they say.

Innocent   I feel sorry for you.

Vincent   Yeah, well. I feel sorry for him.

Innocent   Why?

Vincent   Because he's just like his father.

Innocent   Well, you're nothing like yours.

He runs after his friend.

Vincent *picks up the jerrycan that* **Esperance** *left behind.*

Scene Five

The village is wailing the machete song.

Esperance *carries a basket of purple flowers. She sprinkles them on a soft patch of grass. She kneels down. While she speaks* **The Gahahamuka** *surround her and lay hands on her. To give her strength.*

Esperance   You told me that this day would never come.
You promised me. When you were in the hospice you said
that the worst was over. 'Don't worry, I am the last victim of
the genocide.' I remember you saying. 'I am the last.' You
hear that song? That sweet song that rings of murder? They
are coming home. They are coming home to finish what they
started. They can kill you fast, or they can kill you slow, but
at the end of the day they still kill you. They killed you slowly.
So slowly. I don't know why you wouldn't tell me. I knew.
I knew you had the sickness, Mama. I knew you took those
pills. But then you got worse. You got worse, Mama. Who
knew that Death would take so long, toying with you,
torturing you? You would have thought the rape would be
enough, but Death came right along to screw you until your
dying day. Filling your lungs until you could not breathe.
Ripping your skin with sores. Who knew one would rather
die at the stroke of the machete than of the slow tick-tock of
the Aids clock. Our little Emmanuel is . . . getting worse.
We try to get the money together every month, you know, for
his medicine . . . he's selling credit in the streets, I'm weaving
baskets and selling them by the roadside, it's barely enough . . .
I don't know what I'll do without him. If he goes then . . .
what am I going to do? I'll be the only one left. The only
one left of our family. They are singing in the streets. In
the cabarets. They are coming home. My neighbours, my
killers . . . I feel like I'm back beneath the dead bodies again.
I'm back to being smothered beneath the weight of the dead.
When they found me, they thought I was gone. Blood, blood
everywhere. Somehow I survived, but, Mama, I'm tired.
I don't think I can be a survivor any more.

Suddenly she can see **The Gahahamuka**. *They sing her a sweet
song that is a sharp contrast to the machete song. She is strengthened for
a moment and she sings along, and briefly the victims drown the machete
song out.* **Vincent** *emerges from the forest, carrying the jerrycan. He
watches her for a spell until she finishes her song.*

Vincent   Is this where your family is buried?

Esperance *looks up. Beat.* **The Gahahamuka** *have disappeared.*

Esperance   No, just my mother. I don't know where the rest are buried. Some say the mass grave up on the hill. Some say the mass grave down the hill. I do not know.

She begins to lift herself off the ground.

Vincent   Do you need any help up?

Esperance   No, I can do it on my own.

With one arm, she has trouble getting herself up.

Vincent   Here, let me help you.

Esperance   Look, I said I was fine.

Vincent   I just want to help.

Esperance   I don't need your help.

Vincent   Please let me help –

Esperance *takes a stumble. He catches her. He steadies her.*

Esperance   Thank you.

Vincent   You're welcome.

Esperance   I guess you want another thank you for before.

Vincent   No, I don't want anything from you.

She looks him up and down cautiously.

Esperance   Why aren't you down there with them? Singing.

Vincent   I'm not a good singer. You are, though. A beautiful singer.

Esperance   How long were you standing there?

Vincent   Just enough to be blessed by your concert.

She looks down and blushes. She notices the jerrycan in his hand.

Esperance   You filled my jerrycan for me.

Vincent   Yeah. Can I get a 'thank you' for that, too?

Esperance *smiles.*

Vincent   Lips like the sun, teeth like the stars.

Esperance *blushes. No one has told her that she's pretty before.*

Esperance   Thank you.

Vincent   You're welcome.

Beat. They hear the machete song in the distance.

Esperance   Are you happy your father is coming back?

Vincent   Yes.

Esperance   What are you going to say to him when you see him?

Vincent   I haven't thought about it.

Esperance   Come on, you have to have thought about it. You've had a whole lifetime to think about it.

Vincent   Really, I haven't thought about it.

Esperance   Think. If there was one thing you wanted to say, wanted to ask, what would it be?

Vincent   How does it feel to be like God?

Esperance *stares at him.*

Vincent   Sometimes I wonder. I wonder when he had the time . . . As he was roaming the countryside killing and maiming, taking an arm here, a nose there, a life here, a life there, he had enough time to give me life.

Esperance   Perhaps he wanted to put something into the world because he was so busy taking so much out.

Vincent   I understand the hatred in your heart.

Esperance   The hatred in my heart?

Vincent   Yes, I understand why you hate me.

Esperance   Why would I hate *you*?

Vincent   I'm Hutu.

Esperance   It's not that simple, Vincent.

Vincent   But – I want you to hate me.

Esperance   I'll never hate you, Vincent.

Vincent   Why not?

Esperance   Because you didn't do anything.

He looks at **Esperance** *softly. He takes in the scars adorning her body like tattoos. She stands there and lets him see them. Lets him see her. He takes his hand and slowly traces his finger along her past.*

Vincent   Who gave you these?

Esperance   Your father.

The Gahahamuka *stand in silence and witness.*

Vincent   I'm sorry.

Esperance   You are not who I want to hear sorry from.

Vincent   But I –

Esperance   You should go now. Go and meet your father. Go meet him now.

Vincent   I'm scared.

Esperance   But you are Vincent the Invincible, are you not?

Vincent *begins to walk away,* **Esperance** *looks after him. He looks back.*

Vincent   Thank you, Esperance.

Esperance   You're welcome, Vincent.

Esperance *picks up the jerrycan and places it on her head and walks away.*

Scene Six

A figure in a dark hoodie writes something on a wall. **The Gahahamuka** *stand there as witnesses. The machete song is getting louder and louder.*

Gahahamuka 1 *laughing.*

Gahahamuka 2   It is starting again.

Gahahamuka 3   He will be sorry.

Gahahamuka 2   A soul like that knows no contrition.

Gahahamuka 1 *laughing.*

Gahahamuka 2   He knows not what he does.

Gahahamuka 3   He knows exactly what he does.

Gahahamuka 1 *crying / laughing.*

Gahahamuka 2   Shhhh, don't cry. Don't cry, sisi.

Gahahamuka 1 *crying.*

Gahahamuka 2   Look, they've upset her.

Gahahamuka 3   It's upsetting. They haven't learned.

Scene Seven

Esperance *has arrived at her hut, her jerrycan delicately balanced on her head. She stands there looking up at her hut. It says 'Kill the Cockroaches' across one side. Horrifying graffiti.* **Esperance** *looks wildly about.*

Esperance   Emmanuel! Emmanuel! Are you in there?

Emmanuel *walks out of the hut with sleep in his eye.*

Esperance   Oh, my God. Thank God. Thank God you are alive. They didn't do anything to you, did they?

Emmanuel   No, no, what are you talking about?

Esperance *points.* **Emmanuel** *takes it all in. Silence. He looks at his sister.*

Emmanuel   What are we going to do?

Esperance *stands staring at the writing on the wall.*

Emmanuel *wobbles back inside the hut.*

Esperance *quickly takes the jerrycan full of water and heaves it at the wall. The water makes a splash against the stone. The words begin to slide like blood down the wall. She washes the hatred away.*

The machete song grows louder and louder until –

Scene Eight

Bright neon lights. Disco. **Innocent** *and* **Bosco** *are at the outdoor cabaret.* **Innocent** *is dancing, but* **Bosco** *is downing a beer in the corner.*

Innocent   This is cause for a celebration! A celebration, I say! Everyone raise your beer. Raise your beers! Our papas have come home!

He runs up to **Vincent** *and gives him a huge hug. They walk through the cabaret together.*

Vincent   Where are they?

Innocent   At home, getting washed up. They're on their way to the cabaret.

Vincent *notices* **Bosco** *in the corner.*

Vincent   I need to apologise to him.

Innocent   Hey, Vincent. Bosco's a bit –

Vincent   Tipsy? I can see that.

Innocent   Nooo. It's not just that.

Vincent   I know I've been acting crazy these past few days. I just want to –

Innocent   His father wasn't on the bus from the prison.

Beat.

Vincent   What, what do you mean? They said everyone from the village was coming home.

Innocent   That's what they said, but – bu—

Vincent   What happened?

Innocent   Something about him not expressing 'contrition'. Kept him. He got ten more years, they say.

Vincent   Why didn't he say he was sorry?

Innocent   I don't think he was.

Beat.

Vincent   Well, what about yours?

Innocent   Butter! The man is butter, yo! I see where I get this handsome face from.

He turns to show off his profile.

Rwanda's Next Top Model!

Vincent   You so silly.

Innocent   I know, man! This stuff make me silly. The papas are home! THE PAPAS ARE HOME!

He takes a huge celebratory swig from his beer.

Vincent   Innocent, did you see my papa?

Innocent   Yeah. I did.

Vincent *begins to shake.*

Innocent   You alright, Vincent?

Vincent   It just all of a sudden got a little chilly. Rainy season must be on its way.

Innocent   Rainy season would be a bit early if it's on its way.

Vincent   Maybe it is early. How did he look?

Innocent *gives him a look; he understands.*

Innocent   I don't think he's coming to the party tonight.

Vincent   I'ma go say 'hey' to Bosco, then head on home.

Innocent   Bosco's naturally . . . you know.

Vincent   Let me go talk to him.

Innocent   Just talk to him soft though. Talk to him soft.

Vincent *walks up to* **Bosco** *at the bar.* **Innocent** *watches carefully from the corner.*

Bosco (*to the bartender*)   Hey, can I get another Primus?

Vincent   I heard.

Bosco   What you hear?

Vincent   I'm sorry, man.

Bosco   No matter. He's a man. He stood by his values. What more could you ask for?

Vincent   Still, I'm sorry, man.

Bosco   Well, he's stubborn. I guess I see where I get it from.

Vincent   Like father, like son.

Bosco *pauses, his Primus in midair.*

Bosco   Yeah, like father, like son. Saw your father though – sa-sa . . .

Esperance *enters.*

Bosco   Well, look at that. The cockroach has joined us for the party.

Esperance *looks around the cabaret. The disco lights spin around the silence. Fire coming out of her eyes. As the following scene continues, one by one* **The Gahahamuka** *emerge from the shadows. Witnesses of the past, witnesses of the present. Everyone is oblivious to them though.*

Esperance   Who is the coward? Huh? I say, who is the coward in this room?

Bosco   So sad. She's gone crazy.

Esperance   You answer my anger in silence, eh? You cowards. You cowards. I spit at your feet.

She spits.

Esperance   I spit at you. If you wanna finish your work, then you do it. You DO IT!! But you do it in the light. I dare you to do it in the light!

Innocent *sweeps in and grabs* **Esperance**.

Innocent   You better leave before they come.

Esperance   They can come. I am waiting for them. I am waiting for them. I refuse. I refuse to leave.

Innocent   You need to leave, Esperance.

Esperance   I will not be leaving. Not before you show your face. Who did it? Who did it?

Bosco *begins laughing in the corner.*

Bosco   The Tutsi has gone mad. Look at her cockroach antennas shaking back and forth.

Esperance   So this is a joke to you, Bosco?

Bosco   You have gone mad. You are mad to be here. Get out before something happens to you.

Esperance   What will happen? Coward. You – you – you orphan!

Bosco   Vincent, you get her out of here before she says something she will regret.

Esperance   I will never regret anything. Never. Do not step one foot near my hut, Bosco! Or the anger of my ancestors will rain down upon this land. Step one foot near me and Emmanuel and I will kill you.

Bosco   Bitch, I don't know what you are talking about.

Esperance   You do! You were there tonight. You're so stupid you couldn't even spell cockroaches right.

Bosco   Can someone please tell me what the bloody hell she is talking about?

Esperance   He came to my hut!

Vincent   ⎫   Calm down, Esperance. Slow down.

Gahahamuka 1 ⎭   *laughing.*

Vincent *pulls* **Esperance** *outside. The others quickly follow.*

Bosco *can hear the laughter in his brain. The hollow echoes of the spirits. The reminder of the past.*

Esperance   He threatened me. Outside of my hut. I saw. I saw it. 'Kill the cockroaches.' Just like they used to say. It is a threat pure and simple.

Bosco   I didn't step anywhere near your hut, Esperance. I wouldn't step on Tutsi ground. It is evil.

Gahahamuka 1 *laughing.*

Bosco *grabs his head.*

Esperance   You step on Tutsi ground when you want to steal some potatoes to eat. You just take, take, take! Well, I refuse to let you take anything from me any more.

Bosco   ⎫   Hush up, Esperance.

Gahahamuka 2 ⎭   Hush up, Esperance.

Gahahamuka 3   Be silent.

Vincent   Yes, be quiet, Esperance.

Esperance   I will not be silent any more.

Gahahamuka 1 *crying laughter.*

Esperance   My back is already bent from carrying water from the well. You will not bend my back any more.

Gahahamuka 2 } Please, Esperance.

Vincent } Please, Esperance.

Bosco *holds his head.*

Bosco   Shut your mouth, Esperance, before I shut it up for you.

Gahahamuka 1 } *laughing.*

Esperance (*laughing*) } Are you that big and bold to threaten me out in the open like that?

Bosco   Stop the laughing. Stop laughing at me.

Esperance (*turning to everyone*) } Will you all just let him threaten me like that?

Gahahamuka 1 } *laughing.*

Gahahamuka 2 } His threats are promises.

Bosco } I do not make threats, Esperance, I make promises. Believe me, a threat that passes from my lips will be an order that is completed.

Esperance *goes up to* **Bosco** *and pushes him with her one arm.*

Bosco   Go home, Esperance.

Esperance   You think you can scare me? Well, I will not be scared. I will not! Your father did not scare me. And he is right where he belongs. Where I was.

Gahahamuka 2   In the bottom of the pit –

Gahahamuka 3   With a bloody lump –

Gahahamuka 1 *laughing.*

Bosco (*warning her*)   Esperance . . .

Esperance   Swimming amongst the piss.

Gahahamuka 1 } *crying.*
Gahahamuka 2 *and* **Gahahamuka 3** } And shit.

Esperance   Alone. With dead bodies being piled on top. And stones being thrown down.

Gahahamuka 1 ⎫ *laughing.*
Esperance ⎪ I hope he rots alone . . .
Gahahamuka 1 ⎬ *laughing.*
Vincent ⎭ Shhhh, Esperance . . .

Esperance   At the bottom of that jail where he belongs.

Beat. **The Gahahamuka** *tremble at her hatred.*

Bosco *lunges at her.*

Bosco   I will finish you! I will finish you off! I will finish you!

Vincent   Bosco, GET OFF OF HER !

But **Bosco** *is on top of her. Choking her with his bare hands.*

Gahahamuka 1 *crying.*

Gahahamuka 2   When will they learn?

Innocent   She's not worth it!

Gahahamuka 3   When will they stop?

Gahahamuka 2   It has begun again.

Vincent   LET HER GO!

Gahahamuka 3   Breathe, Esperance. Do not come to the other side. We are lost –

Gahahamuka 2   Floating in the piss –

Gahahamuka 3   And the shit –

Gahahamuka 2   Thrown into mass graves –

Gahahamuka 3   We are lost.

Gahahamuka 1 *crying and laughing and crying.*

The Gahahamuka *cry. The dead cannot help. They can only watch. Those that are alive could help, but they choose not to. They choose only to look on as history repeats itself. But* **Vincent** *does the unthinkable – he does something. He pushes* **Bosco** *off* **Esperance**. **Bosco** *lies on the ground.* **Vincent** *picks up a heavy stone. He towers over his friend.*

Bosco   Eh-eh! What are you doing?

Vincent   } Stop.

The Gahahamuka   Stop.

Bosco   Whose side are you on?

Vincent   } Stop.

The Gahahamuka   Stop.

Bosco   Are you sure your father was a Hutu?

Vincent   } Stop.

The Gahahamuka   Stop.

Innocent   Put that down, Vincent.

Vincent   I'm tired of this.

The Gahahamuka   Stop.

Vincent   I'm tired of you.

Innocent   } Put that down.

Bosco   What are you doing?

Vincent   I'm doing something. I'm doing something.

He raises the stone to his chest.

The Gahahamuka   Stop.

Innocent   Vincent, stop! Don't do it! He didn't do anything.

Vincent   He'll continue to terrorise her.

Innocent   Stop it!

The Gahahamuka   Stop.

Vincent   Did you do it, Bosco? Did you?

The Gahahamuka   Stop.

Bosco   Vincent! Vincent! Vincent!

The Gahahamuka   Stop. Stop. Stop.

Bosco *is backing into the corner, crawling away. He is in a vulnerable position.*

Bosco   What, now we are to kill each other? Other Hutus? But we are brothers, Vincent! We are brothers!

The Gahahamuka   Stop.

Innocent   It wasn't him!

The Gahahamuka   Stop.

Vincent *closes his eyes.*

Bosco   Vincent . . .

Vincent *lifts the stone above his head and –*

Blackout.

Scene Nine

In the darkness. The sound of water pouring on to the ground.

Vincent *is outside his hut. He is washing his hands at the pump. He is washing his hands. Washing his hands. Washing his hands.*

The hut door opens. **Mama** *stands at the door.*

Mama   Vincent . . . Vincent! Are you out there?

Vincent   Yeah. I'm out here, Mama.

Mama   Well, what are you waiting on, Vincent? Come on inside.

Vincent *walks through the door. His shirt is splattered with blood.*

Mama   You look like you've been slaughtering cows for the feast.

Vincent   I have.

He stands there and for the first time in his life he sees the man who fathered him.

Vincent Snr, *a withered man, sits at the table. Eating porridge. He is stooped over the bowl. He looks up. He has the face of the young* **Gahahamuka 3**.

Mama   Vincent, there he is. Your son.

Vincent Snr *stares at his son for the longest time. He stares. He does not get up from the table. Then he looks down again and begins eating.*

Vincent Snr   He's mine alright. Has my eyes. This one on the other hand . . .

He indicates **Félicité**. **Mama** *becomes nervous.*

Mama   Go in the back, Félicité.

Félicité   Why do I have to −

Mama   I said GO!

Félicité *takes her plate from the table. Not a child of 'The Butcher', she is forced to eat in the corner of the kitchen.* **Vincent Jr** *sits down and joins his father and mother at the kitchen table. He begins to eat. He eats with his left hand, the same as his father. They are mirror images of each other. The same.*

They sit and eat their dinner in silence and silence and silence.

Children of Killers

Notes on rehearsal and staging, drawn from workshops with the writer held at the National Theatre, November 2010

The Genesis of the Play

Over a hundred days in 1994 between 800,000 and 1,000,000 Rwandans (mostly Tutsi) were slaughtered. Playwright Katori Hall visited Rwanda for the first time in July 2009 to attend a Genocide Studies conference and returned there in January 2010. She wanted to write about the consequences of the genocide on Rwandan society now – sixteen years later – particularly its impact on the young people there.

Katori was struck by many positive signs of progress in the country – including the establishment of free education for children, the prevalence of women in government, employment possibilities beyond agriculture and the spread of technology (she noted a person carrying water on their head, but chatting on a mobile phone!) However, she also had the sense of a 'bandage being placed on the nation over a wound that has not yet healed' – that the country has not purged the events of the past, and that many tensions still existed.

After the genocide, special local *Gacaca* courts were set up to attempt to bring about speedy justice and reconciliation in order to allow the county to move forward (*Gacaca* means 'soft grass', referring to the symbolic meeting place where elders from the community would mediate and pass judgement on disputes). However, the confessions of some perpetrators, which reduced their sentence length, were not all thought to be true. With perpetrators now being released, there are also fears that violence will occur against those who identified them (as did Esperance in the play).

Some survivors in Rwanda now have to deal with the almost unimaginable experience of living next door to a released person who murdered their entire family. Katori found herself asking questions such as: Is forgiveness really possible? Can justice ever really be achieved? Is it possible to move on from the past? She witnessed government-encouraged acts of forgiveness and contrition that she felt didn't ring true; but she also heard of quite opposite cases, as where a survivor and a perpetrator have found love and married.

In her playwriting, Katori seeks to give a voice to those who are not heard. Here, she wanted to capture the complexity of the genocide's legacy and so chose to present her story from a Hutu young person's perspective. Also left fatherless by the genocide – with their fathers detained in jail – many Hutu children like Vincent, Bosco and Innocent have had to grow up knowing that they are the child of a killer. Katori has tried to explore the effect of this on the psyche and the soul.

Katori hopes that the stories she writes will speak as loudly as they can – and be vibrant, true and authentic.

Casting

Katori is very happy for actors of any ethnicity and accent to play the characters. She points out that by allowing anyone the opportunity to step into the shoes of these children, we see how close we are as human beings. There is no fundamental difference between us – culture, language and society may make us different, but we're truly all the same. She states there is 'no difference between a white boy and black girl, between a Hutu and Tutsi. We are all one. And that is what the play is attempting to show.'

On her trip, she found that there was really no way to tell by looking at a Rwandan whether they were a Hutu or a Tutsi. As these are now deeply stigmatised terms, people she spoke to would refuse to identify themselves, and generations of inter-breeding between the tribes have blurred any physical distinctions. Katori mentioned that during the genocide a rumour went round that 'Tutsis were tall' – which led to tall Hutus also being killed. This underlines that casting actors with physical distinctions to represent the Tutsi and Hutu characters in the play is also not necessary.

Approaching the Material

A huge amount of information is available about the Rwandan genocide, which can easily become overwhelming when conducting research. Some of it is particularly harrowing, so do be careful to manage young people's engagement with the subject matter. Katori's list of books and films which she found helpful when writing the play is included below.

Take care when researching and rehearsing this play not to immerse yourself in so much of the material that the results of your work seem indulgent: ensure that the story, the characters and their intentions are paramount and clear at all times.

You may also want to structure rehearsals so that participants have the opportunity to release tension built up working on this material. Including activities such as singing, and physical warm-ups and warm-downs may be helpful in achieving this.

Approaching the Text

Deciding what the main event in the play is, and how you interpret it, will really affect how you direct your production and what the audience take from it. The main event is the event at the heart of the play – what the play builds towards. Considering the weight Katori gives to some moments in her stage directions may help you identify it (*'silence and silence and silence'*). Each scene will have an important event leading to the main event too.

You will also need to make interpretive choices about ambiguous moments in the text. These choices will affect how various characters play a scene. For example: Why is Mama's hand shaking when she applies her lipstick? (Is it just that she is unpractised, or is she frightened, despite what she says?) Who is the hooded person that graffitis Esperance's house? Note at the end of Scene Eight how sure Innocent seems to be that it was not Bosco; is he as innocent as his name suggests? What happens after Vincent raises the stone in the blackout? Do you believe Vincent has been slaughtering cows like he says in Scene Nine?

The Production Language

Katori's text presents a number of staging challenges. In planning your production, you may want to create a 'shopping list' of these moments that need to be resolved (these might include staging the football match, the use of blood and water, the graffiti, the fluid transitions between locations, etc.). By coming up with as many different options as possible for each moment on your list, you may discover a set of choices that will also suggest which props, set and costume are needed (if any), what they might look like, and how they will be used.

Katori has deliberately left open music choices throughout the play, so that you can make decisions that fit your production. The 'machete song' was originally sung by Hutu to pump themselves up before they went out killing. It was an aggressive song (in the Kinyarwanda language), which would have been terrifying for Tutsi to hear. Your version may or may not have words, or incorporate instruments etc.

In attempting to dramatise events relating to the genocide, Katori has chosen to include expressionistic and metaphorical devices. For this reason, you may not want to represent literally things like Esperance's disfigurement. The power of suggestion may prove to be more powerful and evocative.

The Gahahamuka

The role of the Gahahamuka (pronounced *Ga-ha-ha-moo-ka*) changes throughout the piece – sometimes they are powerless observers, at other times witnesses or embodiments of guilt or psychoses felt by the characters. They represent the ever-present reality of the past; a constant reminder of the scale of the suffering that took place and which continues to haunt Rwandan society.

Again, choices can be made about the number of people used and their role and presence through the piece.

Katori's Suggested Reading List

Daillaire, Romeo, *Shake Hands with the Devil.*

Gourevitch, Philip, *We Wish To Inform You That Tomorrow We Will Be Killed With Our Families.*

Hatzfield, Jean, *The Antelope's Strategy.*

Hatzfield, Jean, *Machete Season: The Killers in Rwanda Speak.*

Hatzfield, Jean, *Life Laid Bare: The Survivors in Rwanda Speak.*

Koff, Clea, *The Bone Woman.*

Mamdani, Mahmood, *When Victims Become Killers: Colonialism, Nativism and the Genocide in Rwanda.*

Katori's Suggested Viewing List

Hotel Rwanda, 2009 (directed by Terry George).

Sometimes in April, 2005 (directed by Raoul Peck).

Shooting Dogs, 2005 (directed by Michael Caton-Jones; also released under the title *Beyond the Gates*).

My Neighbour, My Killer, 2009 (documentary, directed by Anne Aghion).

*From a workshop by James Macdonald,
with notes by Michael Longhurst*

Nell Leyshon

The Beauty Manifesto

Characters
the minimum required

Ambassadors:
Jasmine
Chloe
Rachel
Paloma
Hannah
David

Birthday People:
Silas
Sam
Ella
Alexis

The world of *The Beauty Manifesto* is set in the near future, but also in the present. These events are already happening around us.

The **Ambassadors** represent the companies which desire total adherence to the notion of beauty duty. The **Birthday People** are reaching sixteen, the age of transformation.

The clinic. Cool, antiseptic.

Scene One

The **Ambassadors** *enter, their movement coordinated, crisp.*

Jasmine *follows. She pulls out her sister,* **Chloe**.

Jasmine   Chloe?

Chloe   Yes.

Jasmine   Welcome. Lift your chin up.

Chloe   Like this?

Jasmine   That's better. Are you happy to be here?

Chloe   Excited.

Jasmine   So am I. Have you brushed your hair?

Chloe   I was in a hurry.

Jasmine *smoothes* **Chloe***'s hair.*

Jasmine   That's better.

She walks around **Chloe**, *inspects her. She brushes down her top, adjusts her clothing.*

Jasmine   Keep your chin up. You don't want that fat there.

Chloe *feels her own face.*

Chloe   Here?

Jasmine   Yes.

Chloe   Is there fat?

Jasmine   It'll be got rid of.

Chloe   Mum never said anything.

Jasmine   I'm saying it. It's important to be honest. We have a duty to be as beautiful as we can. I'm just helping you, that's all.

Chloe   Thanks.

Jasmine   It's what sisters are for.

She takes a step back and speaks to the **Ambassadors** *who line up,* **Chloe** *with them.*

Jasmine   Congratulations to our other new people.

Hannah/David   Thank you.

Jasmine   Many other teenagers applied to the company, but you are the chosen ones. You will be our youth ambassadors.

We all mention the Beauty Manifesto and the company to our peers, both online and face to face, and we reinforce the core values at all times. In return you will be incentivised by money and training.

Questions? (*Waits.*) Good.

Your first task is to collect the Birthday People.

Hannah   Do they know we're coming?

Rachel   It's their birthdays.

Hannah   I know, but what do we do if they won't come with us?

Paloma   Why wouldn't they?

Rachel   They've been prepared. They've had their faults pointed out. Everyone wants to look beautiful, don't they?

Hannah   Yes.

Paloma   Of course.

Jasmine   Just remember what we believe and you can help the company transform society and all its people.

Line one?

They all speak in unison.

All   The Beauty Manifesto will be applied to all. There are no exceptions.

Jasmine   Perfect. Good luck.

Jasmine *retreats.*

Rachel   Are we ready?

Hannah   I think so.

Rachel   You?

Chloe   I think so.

Rachel   You?

David   I am.

Rachel   Let's get the first.

The **Ambassadors** *collect* **Sam**.

Scene Two

The clinic. **Sam** *enters in a confused state. The* **Ambassadors** *greet him.*

Rachel   Happy birthday.

Ambassadors   Happy birthday, Sam.

Sam   Who are you?

Rachel   You know who we are.

David   We work for the company.

Rachel   We're here to help you.

Sam   I don't need help.

David   Course you do. He does, doesn't he?

Hannah   Of course.

David *takes one arm.* **Hannah** *takes the other.*

Sam   Let me go. Don't. I haven't said goodbye to my mum.

Rachel   He wants to say goodbye to his mum. How sweet.

Hannah   That is so sweet.

Rachel (*cold*)   Sugar is sweet. Your mother's paid for this for you. She's handed over money. Good money.

Paloma   Come on.

They place **Sam** *in the clinic waiting room.*

Rachel   Line two?

Sam   I don't know.

Rachel   You do know.

Paloma   Difference is unacceptable.

Rachel   Are you different?

Sam   I don't know.

Rachel   Have you looked at yourself?

David   Have you seen your chin?

Hannah   Have you seen your chest?

Paloma   Your stomach is soft. Feel.

She pushes his stomach.

Chloe   Difference is unacceptable.

Rachel   You want to look like this for ever?

Sam   No.

David   You don't have to.

Rachel   The Beauty Manifesto will be applied to all. There are no exceptions.

Sam   There are no exceptions.

Rachel   You are to wait here overnight. We're locking the door for your own safety and you'll be collected in the morning. You understand?

Sam   Yes.

Rachel   Wait here.

David   Wait.

The **Ambassadors** *leave.*

Sam *is alone. He feels his chin and examines his stomach, feels if it is soft.*

The **Ambassadors** *bring in a reluctant and angry* **Silas**.

Alexis *follows willingly.*

Silas *struggles to get free.*

Silas   Get off. Let me go.

They place **Silas** *with* **Sam**. **Alexis** *joins them. The* **Ambassadors** *leave.*

Silas   Where are you going? You can't do that.

There is no response as they leave. **Silas** *looks around, sees* **Sam**.

Silas   Where are we?

Sam   I don't know.

Silas *looks for a way out.*

Silas   Is that the only way out?

Sam   I think so.

Silas   They locked it?

Sam   Yeah.

Silas   They can't do that.

Sam   It's for our safety.

Silas   Is it your birthday too?

Sam   Yeah.

Silas   And yours?

Alexis   Sixteen today.

Silas   Happy birthday all of us, then.

Alexis   Thanks. I've been waiting years for this.

Ella *enters, escorted by the* **Ambassadors**.

Silas *approaches them, grabs* **Hannah**.

Silas   Let me out.

The **Ambassadors** *help pull* **Silas** *off* **Hannah**.

Silas   You can't force people. You have to let me out.

Rachel   We're not forcing you. We're helping you make the right decision.

The **Ambassadors** *leave.*

Silas *recovers.*

Sam   You OK?

Silas   Yeah.

Ella   You sure?

Silas   Yeah. (*Nods.*) Happy birthday?

Ella   Thanks.

Sam   What happens now?

Alexis   What do you think?

Sam   I don't know.

Alexis   You must know why you're here.

Sam   Not really.

Alexis   You know what you're having done?

Sam   No.

Alexis (*to* **Silas**)   Do you know?

Silas   I know what they want us to have. I'm not having it.

Alexis   How can you say that?

Silas   Like this. Watch. I don't want – you see how I move my mouth and the words come out – anything done. Clever, aren't I?

Alexis   But the manifesto.

Silas   What manifesto?

Alexis (*shocked*)   You haven't heard it?

Silas   Of course I have.

Alexis   Then why did you say that?

Silas   I was teasing you. You know, saying something not true, laughing at you. At your expense.

Alexis   I don't understand. You're odd.

Silas   Am I?

Alexis   He is, isn't he?

No one responds.

Difference is unacceptable.

Silas   Is it?

Alexis   You don't want to be different.

Silas   Maybe I do. Maybe I don't want to look perfect.

Alexis   We all want to.

Silas   Do we?

Alexis   I don't understand you.

She looks at **Ella**.

You're pretty. What are you having done?

Ella   They haven't said.

Silas   What do you think you need doing?

Ella   It doesn't matter what I think.

Silas   It could.

Ella   I don't understand.

Silas   Nothing.

Ella (*to* **Alexis**)   Do you think it'll hurt?

Silas   Of course it'll hurt.

Alexis   All beauty hurts.

Ella   Line three.

Alexis   Line three.

Jasmine *and* **Chloe** *enter.*

Jasmine   Happy birthday.

Alexis   Thank you.

Jasmine   The surgery's scheduled for the morning.

You'll be asked to undress and they'll mark up your bodies for the procedures.

Sam   What procedures?

Jasmine   They'll tell you what you need.

Ella   Do we have to be naked?

Jasmine   Of course.

Ella   I don't want them to see me naked. I won't stand there. I won't.

Jasmine   You will.

Alexis   They have to, to see what you need doing.

She steps forward, looks at **Jasmine**.

Alexis   Do you mind?

Jasmine   No.

Alexis   You had a great surgeon.

Jasmine   There is no excuse for imperfection.

Alexis   Line four. My favourite.

Ella   Did it hurt?

Jasmine   You'll be anaesthetised. If you're worried, think of how you'll look after.

Jasmine *inspects* **Ella**.

Ella   I've been told my skin is the wrong colour. My nose is crooked. My chin is weak. And my teeth aren't straight.

Is it that bad?

Jasmine   It won't be after tomorrow. Get some sleep and it'll be your turn.

Ella   I don't think I'll be able to sleep.

Jasmine   Try. Chloe's staying here with you for the night.

Silas   Why?

Jasmine   To ensure you don't eat.

Silas   To ensure we don't try and escape.

Jasmine   What did you say?

Silas   Nothing.

Jasmine   No one is forced to have the procedures. You know that.

Silas   You are locking us in.

Jasmine   So you can think it through carefully. You understand?

Silas   I understand what you say.

Jasmine   Line one?

All   The Beauty Manifesto will be applied to all. There are no exceptions.

Jasmine   Good. You're all nil by mouth. OK? You'll be collected in the morning.

She leaves.

Ella   Who was she?

Alexis   She's the main ambassador. She's beautiful.

Chloe   She's my sister.

Alexis   Your sister is the main ambassador?

Chloe   Our father is the top surgeon.

Alexis   Oh. I didn't know. Really? Your father?

Chloe   Yes.

Alexis   That's amazing. But you haven't had surgery yet.

Chloe   My birthday's next week.

Alexis   Oh, you really are lucky.

Silas   Why is she?

Alexis   Because her father is doing her procedures. He's an artist.

Silas   An artist? (*To* **Chloe**.) Do you think your dad's an artist?

Chloe   I don't think anything.

Sam   What are the procedures?

Chloe   Whatever they think you need to make you look acceptable.

Sam   What like?

Chloe   Did you not learn?

Sam   Please tell me.

Chloe   Your face. Your body. Whatever isn't right.

Sam   Will I look the same?

Chloe   The idea is you don't. Didn't your mother tell you?

Sam No.

Chloe Your friends?

Sam I don't really have friends. I learned a bit from school.

Chloe You'll be fine. Get some rest and it'll be done soon.

They settle.

Ella I can't sleep.

Chloe Try.

Ella I'm hungry.

Chloe She said nil by mouth. No food. No water.

Silas Chloe, do you think you're lucky?

Chloe That's enough talking.

They are quiet again.

Silas Did your dad operate on your mum as well?

Chloe If you carry on talking I'll call for them.

Silas What will they do? Stitch my mouth closed?

Chloe Please. Stop talking.

Alexis Yeah, stop. Don't ruin it. I want the operation. I want to be acceptable. I want to be beautiful like the women in the magazines. I want a smooth face. I want perfect teeth. Difference is not acceptable.

They curl up, sleep.

Scene Three

Hannah *and* **Jasmine** *enter and see the sleeping people. They creep around them, then step forward.*

Jasmine You said you really wanted to be an ambassador.

Hannah   I do.

Jasmine   You want to earn money and help transform society.

Hannah   Of course.

Jasmine   You want to carry out the tasks we set?

Hannah   You know I do.

Jasmine   When you came to see us, we asked you if you had any secrets.

Pause.

Hannah   I know what I said.

Jasmine   You told us you had none.

Hannah   I know.

Jasmine   An ambassador is a role model. Everything an ambassador does is important.

Hannah   Of course.

Jasmine   People talk.

Hannah   I don't know what you mean.

Jasmine   You do.

If I was able to find out, others could know.

Hannah   How do you know?

Jasmine   I did some checking.

Hannah   She doesn't live with me.

Jasmine   But she was born when you were underage.

Hannah   No one knows. I didn't live here then.

Jasmine   But they could know.

Hannah   I made sure she wasn't near here. I found a couple to look after her.

Jasmine   I know. I visited them.

Hannah   When?

Jasmine   When I found out.

Hannah   Did you see her?

Jasmine   Yes.

Hannah   How was she?

Jasmine   I don't want to get drawn into all that.

Hannah   All that? She's my daughter.

Jasmine   They weren't showing her any images or magazines. I left materials so they can introduce her to the manifesto.

Hannah   She's only six months old.

Jasmine   It is never too early to understand your flaws.

Hannah   But not that early.

Jasmine   You knew she would have to learn. It's the way it is now.

Hannah   I wanted to protect her for a bit.

Jasmine   Then you shouldn't have had her.

Hannah   I love her.

Jasmine   Love is a weakness. You need to forget her.

Hannah   I can't.

Jasmine   Do you want to be an ambassador?

Hannah   Of course I do. I want a career. I want a life.

Jasmine   Then you need to put it behind you.

Hannah   I don't think I can.

Jasmine   You have to.

Hannah   Will you tell them?

Nell Leyshon

Jasmine I don't know.

Hannah Please don't. I won't let you down. I'll be the best ambassador.

Jasmine I'll see.

Hannah Please. I'll work so hard.

Jasmine I said I'll see.

Hannah Thank you.

Jasmine You collected all the birthday people?

Hannah Yes. They're all here.

Jasmine Any problems?

Hannah Nothing we couldn't solve.

Jasmine *nods.*

Hannah Please don't tell.

Jasmine You've made your case. Come on. We need to go and prepare for the morning.

Hannah Thank you. Thank you.

Jasmine *checks the birthday people are still asleep, then they leave.*

Scene Four

Silas *wakes, stands, looks around him. He taps* **Chloe***, who wakes. They move away from the sleeping people.*

Silas Chloe. I want to talk to you.

Chloe Shhh. You'll wake them.

Silas I don't care.

Chloe You need to get up early. You need some sleep.

Silas I don't want to sleep.

Chloe   I do.

Silas   You don't.

Chloe   Please stop talking.

Silas   Why do you keep trying to stop me talking?

Chloe   You know why.

Silas   Because you're scared you'll listen.

Chloe   Listen to what? You saying you don't want to sleep?

Silas   No. You're scared I'll say something you agree with.

Chloe   I don't know what you're talking about.

Silas   You do.

Chloe.

I don't want the surgery.

Chloe   You can't say that.

Silas   I can. Chloe. I don't want the surgery.

Chloe   Shhhh.

Silas   I can say it as loud as I like. I don't want the surgery. I don't want the surgery.

Chloe   Stop it. It's for your own good. It'll make you successful.

Silas   I don't want to be successful. I want to be happy.

Chloe   Happy?

Silas   Yes. You think you have no choice, don't you? You do. We are free to say no.

Chloe   But I don't want to be different.

Silas   Your dad did the operation on your sister.

Chloe   Of course he did.

Silas   And he'll do yours.

Chloe   Yes.

Silas   And he did your mum?

Chloe   She's really beautiful.

Silas   In which way?

Chloe   She's perfect. Her face. She doesn't look like me.

Silas   What do you think you look like?

Chloe   I'm ugly.

Silas   Who told you?

Chloe   Everyone. Look at this fat here.

Silas   You don't have fat there.

Chloe   My nose is too big.

Silas   You can still breathe through it.

Chloe   Don't be stupid.

Silas   My mum hasn't had surgery.

Chloe   Really?

Silas   She hasn't had anything.

Chloe   Do people stare at her?

Silas   Of course.

Chloe   She's brave.

Silas   She's happy.

Chloe   I don't know how she can be.

Silas   Because she did what she wanted.

Chloe   I haven't heard of anyone doing that.

Silas   Only because of how your family live. There was a time when no one had it.

Chloe   When they were all ugly.

Silas   I don't think they were.

Chloe   But everyone says they were.

Silas   That doesn't mean they were.

Chloe.

Chloe   What?

Silas   Tell me something about you.

Chloe   There's nothing to say. Stop it. Stop talking. Stop trying to get me to talk.

They are silent for a moment.

Silas   Tell me a secret.

Chloe   You know we can't have secrets.

Silas   I have them. I have small secrets. I have things I think and do.

Silence again, then:

I have this one.

I was young and in the garden and I found a caterpillar. I put it in my bedroom in a box with netting over it. One night I heard a noise. I turned on the light and the sound was the beating of wings against the net. I woke my mum and we took it outside and let it go, and its wings were white in the dark. We waited until it had gone. She said I had to always remember that the moth had done that all by itself, with no help. It had done what it was supposed to do. What was intended.

Chloe.

Chloe   Stop.

She moves quickly. **Silas** *grabs her.*

Chloe   Get off. Stop it.

Silas   No. I know you're different.

Chloe   You have to stop. Don't say anything else. Please.

Silas   Nothing?

Chloe   Nothing.

They are silent for a moment, then,

Silas   I am unacceptable. All beauty hurts but nothing hurts as much as an unacceptable body.

My difference needs to be eradicated.

I need to be the same as all the others.

Is that better?

Is it?

He steps back and curls up to sleep with the birthday people.

Scene Five

*The **Ambassadors** in the clinic, preparing for the operations:* **Jasmine**, **Rachel**, **David**, **Paloma** *and* **Hannah**.

Jasmine   Scalpel?

David   Sharp.

Jasmine   Needles?

Rachel   Threaded.

Jasmine   Thread? I said thread.

Hannah   Sorry. Waxed.

Jasmine   Black pens?

Paloma   There's a new box in the cupboard.

Jasmine   Surfaces?

David   Sterilised.

Jasmine   Surgeons' gowns?

Hannah   Clean.

Jasmine   My father's gown?

Rachel   I did that one. It wasn't quite clean.

She didn't get some stains out. The last operation was messy.

Jasmine   Hannah?

Hannah   The patient bled too much.

Jasmine   You should have cleaned it properly.

Rachel   She doesn't pull her weight.

Hannah   I do.

Jasmine   We are named ambassadors for a reason. We set an example to our peers. We are here to show people how they can be.

Rachel   We have to be perfect. There is no excuse for imperfection.

Hannah   I'm trying.

Jasmine   Trying is not enough. You need to be succeeding.

We have some time, so get some rest before we go and get the birthday people.

They leave. **Jasmine** *remains, then* **Paloma** *returns.*

Paloma   Jasmine? I need to ask you something. I want you to do something for me. I have a problem here.

She indicates underneath her breasts.

It doesn't feel like it did. There's scar tissue building up. And it's not even. It's not what they said it would be.

Jasmine   Maybe it needs more time to settle.

Paloma   I've given it time. Can you talk to your father? Will you ask him to see me?

Jasmine   You've had your surgery.

Paloma   I don't think it worked.

Jasmine   Of course it worked. Would you want to return to how you were?

Paloma   That's not what I was saying. I'd like him to look to see if there's anything he can do to improve this.

Jasmine   He's a busy man.

Paloma   But he would listen to you.

Jasmine   I'll see, but he wouldn't do it for nothing.

Paloma   I thought if you were an ambassador, you got it free.

Jasmine   You only get one procedure for nothing. You'd have to find some money.

Paloma   I don't have any.

Jasmine   Your parents?

Paloma   They don't have any. My mother would have to sell something.

Jasmine   Then that's what she'll have to do. So you want me to ask him?

Paloma   Yes please.

Jasmine   If he says no, there's nothing more I can do.

Paloma   Thank you. Thank you.

Jasmine *starts to leave.*

Paloma   It means so much.

Scene Six

The birthday people sleep.

Chloe *wakes up. She looks around, approaches* **Silas**. *She wakes him.*

Silas   Is it morning?

Chloe   No.

I can't sleep. I've been thinking.

Silas   Thinking is dangerous.

Chloe   How did you know?

Silas   What do I know?

Chloe   That I'm different. Did you recognise something?

Silas   Yes.

Chloe   I'm sixteen next week.

I keep thinking of him cutting me open. Smashing my nose and rebuilding it.

Silas   You don't have to let him do it.

Chloe   He says I'm ugly.

Silas   You're not ugly.

Chloe   I am.

Silas   Ugly is just a word. Someone ugly now might have been beautiful a hundred years ago. Ugly means nothing.

Chloe   But if I have the operation, it'll make him love me more. He loves my sister now. He said when I have it, he'll put his arms around me.

Silas   Come here.

He holds her, lets go.

I like the way you look now.

Chloe   You can't.

Silas   I do. I like your nose.

Chloe   No one's ever said that before.

Silas   It's different.

Chloe   I don't want to be different.

Silas   I do. I know you do.

Chloe   You say things I haven't heard before.

Silas   I want to get out of here.

Chloe   You can't.

Silas   If I could, what would you do?

Chloe   I'd come with you.

Sam *wakes up.*

Sam   Is it morning?

Chloe   Not yet.

Sam *moves closer to them.*

Sam   I want to go home.

Silas   So do I. (*To* **Chloe**.) You're the only person who can help us. Can you do something?

Chloe   They come to check on us.

Ella *has overheard. She sees them and comes closer, waking* **Alexis**.

Ella   Are you going to try and leave?

Sam   Yes.

Ella   You can't do that.

Sam   We're going to.

Silas   You can come with us.

Ella   I don't know.

Alexis *approaches.*

Silas   We have to get away from it all.

Alexis   What are you talking about?

Sam   All this. The system.

Alexis *moves closer.*

Alexis   What do you mean, *system*?

Chloe   All of this. The procedures, the manifesto.

Alexis   It's life, isn't it? It's just how it is.

Silas   And we have no choice?

Alexis   People have to look at us. We have a duty to be beautiful for them.

Silas   But why do we all feel ugly?

You've been made to. That's how the system works. The companies create thoughts which creep in your mind and infect you, until you feel so bad about yourself you have to have the procedures. The procedures create jobs and pay salaries. They make profits. That's how her dad lives. That's how they all live. They're getting rich on your misery.

Alexis   I won't be miserable when I have the procedures.

Silas   They won't make you happy.

Alexis   They will.

Silas   Happiness can't be bought.

Alexis   The companies sell it.

Silas   You're going to make a great ambassador.

Alexis   Thank you.

Ella   I don't think it's a compliment.

Chloe   I believed it all.

Silas   You don't have to. No one has to have any operation. We can all choose not to.

Alexis   And live an inferior life?

Silas   Live a natural life.

Alexis   You're so ungrateful, all of you. (*To* **Chloe**.) Especially you. Your dad's the top surgeon.

Chloe   But he wasn't always. He wanted to be a real doctor. In a hospital. He had ambitions to help people. But when he qualified he was offered this. He got paid so much he couldn't stop.

Each slice into skin, each drop of blood, he gets richer.

Alexis   You're only saying that to stop me.

Chloe   I'm not going to even try and stop you. I'm trying to stop myself.

Ella   Don't you want it?

Chloe   I don't think I do. I don't think I need it. Look at you. You don't need anything, do you? You know you don't.

Ella   I don't know.

Chloe   You don't.

Ella   No.

Chloe   Are you with us?

Ella   I think I am.

Alexis   What are you doing?

What are you planning?

Don't ignore me.

Hannah *enters.*

Hannah   You should all be asleep.

Chloe   I need the door unlocked. Some of us want to get out.

Hannah   It's not time yet. They'll come for you in the morning.

Chloe   It's not for that.

Hannah   You need something?

Alexis   They're planning to leave. They say they won't have the surgery. You have to do something.

Chloe   Don't do anything. Listen to us.

Alexis   You have to stop them.

Hannah   Chloe, you're an ambassador.

Chloe   I know, but I have to do this.

Hannah   I have to ask for help. You know that.

Chloe   I ask you not to. Give us the keys and no one will know.

You could come with us.

Hannah   I'd lose my position. I need the money.

Chloe   You can find something else.

Hannah   Sorry.

She leaves to fetch help.

Silas *takes* **Chloe***'s arm.*

Silas   No one can force us.

Chloe   No.

Alexis   You know the manifesto. You know what you should do.

Silas   I know the law. I know I can say no. She can say no. He can say no. We can all say no.

Jasmine *enters with* **Hannah**.

Jasmine   What is it?

Chloe *steps forward.*

Jasmine   Chloe?

Chloe   It was me. I asked her to unlock the doors.

Jasmine   Why?

Chloe   I want to leave.

Jasmine   Leave?

Chloe   I don't want the procedures.

Jasmine   You're not having them till next week. Are you nervous?

Chloe   It's not that.

Jasmine   It'll be Dad doing it anyway.

Chloe   Jasmine. I don't ever want the procedures.

Jasmine (*laughs*)   Of course you do.

Chloe   I don't. I want to stay like this. Like I am now.

Jasmine   Of course you don't.

Silas   Don't tell her what she wants.

Jasmine   This is not to do with you.

Silas   It's to do with us all.

Jasmine   Chloe. Look at me. Let go of him.

Chloe *drops* **Silas***'s hand.*

Jasmine   Come here.

Chloe *steps forward.*

Jasmine   You don't want to be gross. Wild. Untamed. You don't want to be an animal.

Chloe   I am an animal.

Sam/Ella   I am an animal.

Silas   We are all animals.

Jasmine   You were born to be an ambassador with me, to transform people.

Chloe   I know.

Jasmine   Then stop all this.

Chloe   I can't.

Jasmine   Of course you can.

Chloe   I don't want the surgery. I don't agree with it.

Jasmine   Do you want to be ugly?

Chloe   If this is ugly, yes. It's how I am supposed to be. How nature made me.

Jasmine   With a fat chin. A too-big nose. Misshapen nostrils. You're ugly. Ugly. Ugly.

Ella   Leave her alone.

Sam   Yeah, stop it.

Jasmine (*to* **Chloe**)   You know what this'll mean for me? The shame for Mum and Dad?

Chloe   You mean for the company?

Jasmine   The company, yes.

Chloe   Is that what matters?

Jasmine   Yes. Yes, that is what matters.

Chloe   Money.

Jasmine   There's nothing without money.

Chloe   There's love. Happiness.

Jasmine   Everything has its cost.

Chloe   And being sisters? Does that mean nothing?

Jasmine   No.

Chloe   So it means something?

Jasmine   Of course.

Chloe   What?

Jasmine   I've always done things for you.

Chloe   Like tell me how ugly I am.

Jasmine   It's for your own good. For you.

She holds out her arms.

Come here.

Chloe   No.

Jasmine   Please. Come on.

Chloe   No.

Jasmine   You are my sister.

Chloe   Am I?

Jasmine   Come back home with me. We can talk. I'll be there with you.

I'll help you. They'll listen to me.

Chloe   I don't want to talk to them.

Jasmine   Then what do I say?

Chloe   Tell them what I told you. Tell them I am making my own choice. Tell them I've gone.

She goes to leave.

Jasmine   Where are you going?

Silas   She's coming with me.

Jasmine   Don't go.

Chloe   Ella? Sam?

Ella *and* **Sam** *step forward.*

Chloe   Hannah?

Hannah   I need the money.

Chloe   It's your choice.

Hannah   I can't. I really can't.

She moves towards **Jasmine**.

Silas   Alexis?

Alexis *turns away.*

They leave. **Jasmine** *and* **Hannah** *are alone with* **Alexis**.

The other **Ambassadors** *enter. They circle.*

During the following, the **Ambassadors** *help remove* **Alexis**'s *shoes and socks, and some of her clothes. They draw on her with black pen, dress her in the gown.*

Alexis   I want to be an ambassador like you.

I am ugly. I am unacceptable.

I have had nil by mouth and I am ready for whatever the surgeon thinks I need.

I want to be beautiful.

The **Ambassadors** *lead her off.*

Scene Seven

Chloe *and* **Silas** *are alone.*

Chloe   Happy birthday.

Silas   Thank you.

Chloe   Sixteen.

Silas   Sixteen and still myself.

Chloe   That's what I want to be. Myself. As I am.

I want to thank you.

Silas   I only said what you already thought.

Chloe   Was beginning to think.

Silas   Every thought has a beginning.

Chloe. I have to go home.

Chloe   Of course you do. You go.

Silas   Maybe you should go home.

Chloe   No.

Silas   You could try and talk to them.

Chloe   They won't listen.

Silas   Have you ever tried?

Chloe   Of course not.

Silas   Then you don't know.

Chloe   It's everything my father stands for.

Silas   But you said he wasn't always like that.

Chloe   He wasn't.

Silas   Why don't you tell him what you think?

Chloe   I don't know.

Silas   Tell him what you believe.

Chloe   Maybe. Maybe.

Silas, I'm not ready to do that now.

I need to know my own mind before I can change his. And I need to just be me. I can't be persuaded that I have to be changed. I have to be stronger. You understand that?

Silas   Yes.

Where will you go?

Chloe   I have a bed in a hostel. It's somewhere to stay.

Silas   You sure?

Chloe   Completely.

Silas   OK. You can come and get me, if you need me.

Chloe   I will.

Silas   Any time.

Chloe   Even at night?

Silas   Even at night.

Chloe   When you're watching your moths.

Silas (*correcting her*)   Watching my *caterpillars*.

Chloe   Caterpillars.

Silas   You could watch them with me. We could wait till they're ready to hatch.

Silas   We could pick them up. Hold them.

Chloe   And watch them crawl out, and dry themselves.

Silas   And we could hold up our hands and watch them fly off into the night.

Chloe   Their wings white.

Silas   Their wings white.

Chloe   Against the dark of the night.

Lights down.

The Beauty Manifesto

*Notes on rehearsal and staging, drawn from workshops
with the writer held at the National Theatre, November 2010*

Background

Nell developed the idea behind *The Beauty Manifesto* with the
Young Company at the Plymouth Theatre Royal, a group of
young people with limited previous involvement in theatre.
Nell was also interested in finding a youth piece that didn't
involve swearing but tackled a serious and sensitive issue.

The initial impetus for the play came from a real story: her
neighbour's daughter decided to have breast-enlargement
surgery. All the girl's family tried to persuade her not to have
the operation, but she was adamant, having spent much time
feeling insecure about her body. At seven a.m. one morning,
a car picked up the girl in the south of England and drove her
to the clinic in the Midlands, picking up five other young
women on the way. The girl's operation was due for nine p.m.
that night, and the following morning, after the operation, all
six of the girls were driven back in the same car, being dropped
off one by one, all groggy and alone, feeling ill from the pain
of the operation. Nell thought, 'Something is very wrong here,
I have to do something to address this.'

At the start of the week's workshop in Plymouth, Nell asked
the sixteen young participants which of them would want
some form of cosmetic surgery. Twelve responded that they
would – and not just the girls but some of the boys too. By
the end of the week, after confronting the themes of cosmetic
surgery, peer pressure, body image and identity, and developing
characters and scenes, Nell asked the same question and only
four out of the sixteen replied that they would still like to have
surgery.

Nell wanted to write a play that offered choices and opened up
possibilities for young people.

Ensemble Exercises

EXERCISE 1

• Ask a group of about fifteen to find a space in the room and stand.

• With no prompting, eye contact or discussion, one person decides to walk around the space and then come to a stop.

• Again with no eye contact or discussion, two people will then begin to walk around the space and then come to a stop.

• This continues with three, then four people, and then goes back down each step to one person.

The key to this powerful and rewarding exercise is not to get into a panic and rush the game. Encourage the participants to take their time and embrace the moments of stillness in between people walking. The aim is not to plan ahead but to let the movement grow organically. If more than the required number of people start walking, it is up to the individuals to correct themselves, again without discussion. It is fine if some people do not walk or if others walk more than once.

This exercise encourages people to work as a group, building an organic, intuitive ensemble feeling. When done regularly, a company can witness their growth and will get to a point where they are truly listening to each other. It is also very inclusive as a game that part of the larger group can participate in, and the rest of the group observe.

EXERCISE 2

This is a continuation of Exercise 1.

• This time, ask the participants to 'colour' their movement, to bring a different energy to how they walk.

• Be conscious that movement can have atmosphere. It is in this exercise that the spaces in between the walking are very important, because if the groups run on too quickly from each other they can find themselves 'infected' by the energy of the preceding group. When used in the context of a rehearsal process, characters and relationship dynamics from the play can often subconsciously infuse the exercise.

EXERCISE 3

• Ask each partner to tell the other about a moment in which they felt self-conscious. This can be as shallow or momentous a moment as they like; however, the moment will be shared with the group, so make sure the participants are aware of this before they start.

• Once the stories have been shared, position a certain number of the group (for instance six) to present to the rest of the group. Two of the group might be sitting on chairs, someone else could be leaning against a wall – it is a random picture created purely for this exercise.

• One by one, each of the participants must tell the story they have just been told but as if it is their own. However, as with the earlier exercises, they should not discuss what order they tell the stories in, and should embrace the moments of silence in between.

In this exercise, we see how stories or memories can become someone else's. It is an interesting way to open a group up to sharing experiences and their own moments of vulnerability, but in a theatrical context. The simple and random 'staging' further distances the story from its origin and also shows how an audience will begin to read a picture before anyone has even started to move or speak. The moments of silence frame the stories and create tension and anticipation. Some young people might choose to play their story for laughs, and this could be an area to examine more closely. Participants could also be eager to work out which story belongs to which person, so make sure from the start that the participants are aware that their story will be looked at by the entire group.

EXERCISE 4

• On small pieces of paper, write random relationships (e.g. 'false friend', 'mother', 'judge', 'ex-lover' etc.).

- Ask one person to sit in a chair with their back to the audience (the group not taking part).

- Give each of the other participants one of the pieces of paper and ask them to enter the space one by one and position themselves in relation to the person sitting in the chair, based on the relationship they have on their piece of paper, to create a still image.

- Once everyone is in the image, ask the group watching to suggest what narrative the image is suggesting – who are these characters and what has happened? Ask for titles for the image.

- Play with the narrative by asking everyone in the image to change their focus of attention on to a specific person.

This exercise is a great way to start to create relationships through spatial dynamics. It can help a group to embody status. It is also a good exercise in showing the importance of focus – who people are looking at is very important, and in *The Beauty Manifesto* non-speaking roles can be just as powerful in terms of their focus and physical presence.

Character Exercise

- Ask an actor to come into the centre of the space and find a comfortable position.

- Give the actor a physical reality for their character, e,g.:

    'You are Chloe. It is midnight and you are in your bedroom after a night out with your friends, two weeks before the action of the play.'

- Give the actor the facts that are known about their character from the text:

    'You are the only one in your family left with physical imperfections.'

    'You will soon be having the surgery,' etc.

- Anyone from the group can come into the space and create a short scene from any point in Chloe's life, for example:

    A teacher telling her off in primary school.

    A friend playing with dolls at age ten.

Mum coming in with a letter from the Tooth Fairy.

• The actor must engage and improvise the scene with the person coming in, so the person coming in needs to help the actor with clues as to who they are and when this is happening.

• People coming into the scene should also be respectful of keeping the character's history as we know it intact, so don't come in as a police officer saying 'Your mum has died in a car accident' if we know that the mother is alive in the text. The actor should return to his/her given physical reality (the bedroom at midnight) in between the scenes. This reality becomes a 'neutral space' that allows the actor to stay in character throughout the exercise.

• People do not have to physically enter the space if they do not want to – they can send a 'letter' or leave a 'voicemail' or 'phone' into the space.

This exercise is a great way to explore, in a relatively short period of time, a character's history on many levels. It creates a shared history that the group has devised together, and makes things only referred to more concrete. It can help an actor have a physical memory that they can then take into a scene.

Movement and Stylisation

The stage directions describe the Ambassadors as moving in a 'co-ordinated, crisp' way. Be careful not to make them too robotic. These characters are *us* and are not completely alien to who we are.

Try playing with repetition and synchronised movement as a physical tool. This can be highly effective yet very easy to choreograph.

EXERCISE I

Take several gestures from a 'waiting room' context:

• Look ahead.
• Look at your watch on your left wrist.

- Look ahead.
- Look over your right shoulder.
- Look at the door.
- Make a rash decision to leave.
- Take three steps and then return to your chair.

Start with a single person running through this sequence of gestures. Then, with any number of actors, layer, repeat and coincide these actions. With very simple movements and gestures, you can create a stylised physical choreography that unites a group without becoming too mechanical.

EXERCISE 2

Split a group into smaller groups of about five or six and ask them to create a sequence of about four or five images that show shifts in perspective or power:

- A group of five people in a single line facing in one direction.
- Four of the group turn their heads to look at the one in the middle.

This is a shift in power through the use of a very simple physical change. What happens if one person from the line walks forward two steps? How does this change the perspective or power play?

Design/Music/Lighting

There are many choices when it comes to the design, and these should support your production rather than get in the way. Remember that the set is there to serve the play and the actors.

Be careful with music – try to avoid being overly manipulative with your music choices, or cluttering up the pace of the play.

Also be careful when choosing songs that contain lyrics – these have not been written by Nell, and may interfere with the language of the play which she has chosen very carefully.

Some Additional Suggestions

• Gender-swapping of roles is completely possible.

• Address notions of race, gender and sexual orientation; however, be aware that the casting of this play will make a statement. Discuss this with your group – how will you choose the Ambassadors? What are you saying with this choice?

• Create a safe environment in which discussions about beauty and peer pressure can be entered into.

• Allow people to participate in theatrical games or not – give them a choice.

• Identify the group's pressure and try to take it off them – people are most productive when they feel safe.

• Stick to the sixteenth birthday as the date for surgery, as this is the gateway to adulthood.

• This play opens up possibilities for young actors who want to participate but don't want a speaking role.

• The manifesto could be used for chorus vocal work.

• Be aware of the difference between plastic and cosmetic surgery – this is a play about cosmetic surgery. This is a useful distinction to discuss with your group.

• The manifesto was extrapolated from current advertising.

• In the context of the play, the manifesto is not a law but a social pressure.

• Nell wanted to leave an impression of hope at the end – the last two characters are the most self-confident. However, there is also loneliness and sadness.

• Young people today can be tempted to judge themselves on their looks because they are aware of the commercial value of their appearance. Their role models can be fabricated constructs with hair extensions and false eyelashes. The crucial horror of this play is that the Ambassadors are not other people – they are people we know.

From a workshop led by Deborah Bruce,
with notes by Luke Kernaghan

Douglas Maxwell

Too Fast

Characters

DD
Spoke's Brother
Amee
Sean
Marcy
Nadia
Young Jean Brown (YJB)
Callum Hunt
Laila
Frankie
Jake Spence
Ali

The play is set — for the most part — in the side room of a church. At the moment the room is being used for storage.

It's a dusty, unloved place: crammed with broken statues, unwanted crosses, dated Jesus paintings, wonky baptismal fonts, stacks of hard seats, mammoth candlesticks — and a group of very uncomfortable-looking young people in school uniform.

There's a door at the back which opens out on to the congregation and another less obvious entrance/exit which is curtained off and leads down a corridor.

It's a cold room and there's a thin-ice, backstage, pre-show atmosphere.

To one side is **Spoke's Brother***. He's not with the others — they can't be doing with him. He's a bit younger than them too, maybe thirteen or fourteen. And he's talking. He knows no other way.*

All the others in the room are between fourteen and sixteen years old and part of 'Sensation Nation', a choir/singing group led by **DD***. 'Sensation Nation' is* **DD***'s baby and when* Britain's Got Talent *comes back, she swears to God they're going to be huge, man. She's nervous though. This will be their debut, and it's a different kind of gig altogether.*

They're here to sing at a funeral.

Amee *has the best voice in 'Sensation Nation'. She's not officially second in command, but something about her (the accent?) means that her opinion carries a bit of weight. For all that though, she's not really too bothered about 'Sensation Nation'.*

Sean *is stealing looks at* **Amee** *while pretending to fiddle with his phone. He's a bit confused. It's all bit vague exactly how* **Sean** *ended up in 'Sensation Nation'. Or how he ended up with* **DD** *and not* **Amee***. Or how they ended up at this girl's funeral singing in front of the whole school — the whole world it seems like. Or how . . . yeah, everything's a bit vague and confusing for* **Sean***.*

Marcy *keeps a lookout at the door. She's providing an excited commentary on who's in the pews. God, it's going to be huge, this. Everyone's here. Mind you, the dead girl was only young. People love that.*

Nadia *is* **DD***'s biggest fan. She's* **DD***'s shadow – her Mini-Me-Rottweiler. She's working hard to get her moves down: the turned-up face and folded arms, the tuts, the struts, the hair-flicks. She's a good bit younger than* **DD** *but she's working on that too.*

In fact **Nadia***'s in the same year as* **Young Jean Brown***, a small, almost silent girl who looks mouse-like and insular. When* **Young Jean Brown** *speaks she tends to get a reaction.*

Later on we'll meet some older pupils. They will be between sixteen and eighteen. They're friends of the girl who died.

We'll meet **Callum Hunt***, an intimidating guy who has taken it upon himself to ensure that this day will be a fitting and respectable tribute, even if he has to break a few heads to make it happen.*

We'll meet **Laila***,* **DD***'s big sister – bursting bubbles in that delighted, older sibling's way.*

And we'll meet **Frankie***, the dead girl's best pal and a school celebrity (a goddess,* **DD** *would say) after an unsuccessful appearance on* X-Factor. *She's only just recovered from that debacle, and now this.*

They will be looking for **Jake Spence***. Keeping an eye out.* **Jake***'s not welcome here. The dead girl's mum and dad said that if he dared show his face . . .*

Why? Didn't you hear? See, when the ambulance got to the crash and found her body trapped in that mangled can of a car . . . they didn't find **Jake***.*

Because **Jake** *ran away.* **Jake** *left her. He left his girlfriend there to die.*

Poor **Ali***. We'll meet her later too.*

But that's to come. Right now it's just the members of 'Sensation Nation', and **Spoke's Brother***. And he's still talking. It looks like they've been listening to him talk for a long, long time . . .*

Spoke's Brother   I'll tell you another children's programme that's all about death. I said I'll tell you another children's programme that's all about death.

Nothing.

Spoke's Brother *In the Night Garden.* Yup. *In the Night Garden* is all about death.

Sean What's *In the Night Garden?*

DD Sean!

Sean What?

DD What did I just say?

Sean When?

DD Just there. Don't engage with him.

Nadia She's only just said it there, Sean!

Sean I'm not engaging with him, I'm asking him a question.

DD That's engaging.

Nadia That's what engaging *is*, Sean. God's sake.

DD Just keep focused. Right? Everyone. It's enough we have to listen to Young Jean Brown here constantly spouting filth every single minute of the day without him distracting us with all his CBeebies death-show stuff. This is too important to . . . *(deep breath).* Focus on your parts, focus on your breathing and before we know it . . . we'll be . . . Just everybody focus! (*To* **Marcy**.) Anything?

Marcy No. The front ones are still empty. But there's about a million people crammed in down the sides. Can't be long now. It's so quiet. All you can hear is Callum Hunt telling people where to sit and even that's a whisper.

Sean I hate Callum Hunt.

Marcy (*not listening*) He's so mature isn't he? All those little nods and telling people where to sit. He's like a real live proper person. He's better at this than the teachers. Old Blades was crying, right, and Callum what-do-you-ma-call-him . . . rectified him. Right there in front of everybody. It was very impressive.

Amee   Yeah, I'm not sure rectified is the right word, Marcy.

Marcy   Well he put his arm round him and everything.

Amee   Yeah but . . .

Sean   I hate Callum Hunt.

Marcy   You wouldn't say that if he was telling you where to sit, Sean. You would be very impressed.

Sean   I'd be impressed if he apologised, but that's never going to happen.

Amee   Apologised for what?

Sean   I can't talk about it, Amee. (*Beat.*) Once, like, for no reason, he grabbed me from a swing, rubbed my head in nettles and then tied my shoes to the tail of a stunt kite. For no reason.

Amee   Aaaaw.

Sean   I know. I remember thinking at the time, 'Oh my God.'

DD   Right, that's another thing, we can't cry. That's very important, everyone? OK? No crying. If *we* cry *they* won't – and we want them to cry. That's a vote-winner.

Nadia   No crying.

DD   Just remember . . .

Nadia   She was going too fast, it was her own fault.

Pause.

DD gives **Nadia** *a Sergeant Major's glare before continuing* . . .

DD   Just remember . . . let the song do the work. That's what Simon Cowell says and I for one listen to Simon after everything he's achieved in the industry. I give Simon a lot of respect. And could everybody please, *please* just . . . focus. No more talking. I don't want to boss people about, but that is actually an order.

Pause. They go back to doing whatever it was they were . . .

Sean   What's *In the Night Garden*?

Amee   It's like *Teletubbies*. My little sister is addicted to it. All babies are. It's like baby heroin. And OK, it might be a bit freaky, but it's not about death. It's all teddies and toys, all like totally hugging in a forest and stuff.

Sean   I don't get it.

Amee (*teasing*)   Yeah it's a bit complicated for you, Sean. If you like I can get one of my sister's picture books and we can work on it a page at a time and . . .

Sean (*pretending to be offended, but really delighted*)   Hey, that's not what I . . . I mean. I don't get how it's all about . . . Oh my God, I can't believe you would . . . cheek man . . . !

He playfully punches **Amee**, *who squeals a bit. They toy-fight a little.* **DD** (*and* **Nadia**) *are not amused . . .*

DD   Excuse me. Excuse me!

Nadia (*viciously*)   Excuse me!

Sean *and* **Amee** *stop.*

Nadia (*disgusted*)   For God's sake.

DD   I'm sorry, Sean, if this isn't important to you, but you know what I mean?

Sean   Sorry, DD.

DD   Maybe you don't want to be in Sensation Nation any more, is that it?

Sean   Well . . . no, it's . . .

DD   Maybe you don't want to have the honour of performing a poor dead girl's favourite song in front of the whole school and be a total legend, is that it?

Sean   Well . . . no, it's . . .

DD   Or maybe you don't want to be my life partner any more then. Is that it?

Sean   . . .

DD   You and 'Amee' now is it? Maybe you and 'Amee' would rather just watch Sensation Nation win next year's *Britain's Got Talent* from the comfort of your own home? Is that what this is? Is that what you would both prefer?

Em . . . yes.

Nadia   No! That's preposterous.

Sean   No, I was only . . . sort of . . . Sorry, DD.

Amee   Sorry, DD.

DD   Whatever. Can I just ask a question? And this is for everyone . . .

Spoke's Brother   Me too?

DD   No, just them. Who is it that runs Sensation Nation? Who actually *is* Sensation Nation?

General mumbles from the group. **Nadia** *helps out by pointing at* **DD**.

DD   Pardon?

Nadia   Pardon?

Everyone responds now: 'You,' 'DD,' 'You are,' etc.

DD   That's right. It's a collective. We're doing this for each other. We need to work together, guys. Come on. (*Pointedly at* **Amee**.) As the saying goes: this is no time to drive wedges between life partners just so you get to do more solos. Know what I mean?

Marcy (*back at the door, peeking out*)   Aw. He's ruffling their hair now. He's ruffling their hair and they're loving it. It's cheering them right up. Aw. Bless.

Amee   He's ruffling the teachers' hair?

Marcy   No, the little kids. There's a whole class of little kids coming in. Don't know who they are. Why would someone bring little kids to this?

Amee   It'll be her brother's class. Her brother's only six.

Marcy   Still. It's a bit brazen.

Amee   Brazen?

Marcy (*snippy*)   Yes, Amee. Brazen. This isn't your old school, you know. We don't play Quidditch and wear hats here. We speak normal us, so desist it up.

Sean   He's ruffling hair now, but just watch: in five minutes' time he'll have their shoes on the tail of a stunt kite doing loop the loops. Then the shoes will fall into a garden and there'll be a big dog in that garden and they'll have to walk home in their socks and they'll get into bad, bad trouble. God, I hate Callum Hunt.

Spoke's Brother *has his hand up.* **Nadia** *points this out to* **DD**. *Reluctantly . . .*

DD   Yes?

Spoke's Brother   Children need to know about death. It's what separates us from the animals. Even blue whales think they're immortal. That's what's so great about *In the Night Garden*. It might look like toys cuddling in a forest but what it's really saying is that everyone has to face up to death some day. Everyone. Little kids *should* be here.

DD   We're not talking about this now, thank you.

Amee (*to* **Spoke's Brother**)   Yeah, but *In the Night Garden* isn't about any of that.

DD   We're not talking about this now, Amee.

Amee   Just a minute . . .

She holds her finger up to **DD**.

Nadia *gasps at the outrageous insubordination.* **DD** *keeps up appearances for the benefit of the group with a tolerating smile.*

Amee   It's not about death – that's absurd. It's toys in a forest going goo-goo ga-ga. It's for babies. Trust me, I've seen it a million times, man.

Spoke's Brother   Well then, you'll know it starts with Iggle Piggle lost at sea. 'In a boat, no bigger than my hand, out on the ocean, far away from land.' Right? And what does he do? 'He takes his little sail down.' Down! Iggle Piggle is ready to die, when, above him, all the stars in the sky turn into flowers and suddenly he's in a garden. And yes, there are toys there, and yes, he does play – one last time. But soon they all go to sleep – Upsy Daisy, The Tombliboos, The Pontipines: they all sleep. All of them *except* Iggle Piggle. Because Iggle Piggle has to live. And do you remember what the last line is? 'Don't worry, Iggle Piggle, it's time to go.' It's time to *go*! Not sleep, not die, but *go*. To accept death and live! Living, fighting, trying! And so he does – he leaves the garden and goes back to his ship, sailing from sight, forward on the tide, into the now.

Young Jean Brown (YJB)   Fuck *off* !

DD (*raging*)   Hey! What did I say!? What did I say about swearing?! We could get pulled from the gig if the church people hear that. Church people go ballisto at swearing. Swearing is the worst thing anyone can do at this moment in time. Sometimes I think you're a saboteur, Young Jean Brown. Know that? See if I find out you're trying to destroy Sensation Nation from within then . . . oh . . . know what I mean?

Nadia (*right into* **YJB**'s *face*)   I will fight you.

Another pause.

Amee   What's he doing here anyway?

Sean   That's Spoke's Brother.

DD   He's doing the reading. Don't engage.

Amee (*to* **Spoke's Brother**)   You're doing the reading?
How'd you swing that?

Spoke's Brother (*different*)   I knew her.

*

A little time has passed.

'Sensation Nation' are all crowded round the door, trying to get a glimpse of what's going on in the congregation. **Amee** *is stuck right at the back and can't see anything.* **Spoke's Brother** *is where he was before.*

Amee   What's happening?

Marcy   Callum Hunt shook their hands and hugged the mum. It was amazing and now they're all kind of . . . walking down to their seats in clutches. There's a troop of them. Cousins must be. Her dad's still at the back though. He's not moving. Oh – he is now. He's like, gripping on to the seats though. It's like he's on a boat or . . . like he's going to fall down. No. Don't fall down. Don't fall, man, please. They've got him. No. He's shrugged them off. It's just him again. He wants to do it on his own I think. And now he's . . . just . . . kind of . . . just . . . just . . . disintegrating.

Amee   I don't think you mean disintegrating.

The crowd parts to let her see for herself.

No. Disintegrating was right.

Soon they don't want to look at that any more. They go back to their places.

After ages . . .

DD   Right. Em. We need to put that out of our minds. Focus. Breathe. It won't be long now. Talk about something else.

Nothing springs to mind.

Talk about something else, I said.

This seems to be directed at **Nadia**, *who struggles a bit. Then . . .*

Nadia   Em . . . what's *Postman Pat* all about?

DD   What?

Nadia   What's *Postman Pat* about? You know. Is it about dying or something? I wonder.

DD   Nadia, *Postman Pat* is about a postman. Called Pat.

Nadia   Oh yeah. So it is. Good point, DD.

Spoke's Brother   It's not, actually.

DD   I swear to God, man . . .

Spoke's Brother   There's a postman in it, and he is called Pat but that's not what it's about.

Amee   No no no. You can't get us on this one. We've *all* seen *Postman Pat* and we all know it's definitely nothing to do with death.

Spoke's Brother   Didn't say it was about death. *Postman Pat* is about how everyone has to tell themselves that they're happy even if they're not. You've got to put on a show, find a happy song to sing, or how can anything change?

Amee   Where are you getting this crap from?

Spoke's Brother   It's all in the song. 'Pat thinks he's a really happy man.' He's not *actually* happy – he just 'thinks' he is. He has to tell himself all's well every day or he'll notice that his life is a humdrum shambles and he'll fall apart.

Sean   Shut up! Pat's life is not a shambles!

Spoke's Brother   Well, everything's a mess underneath innit? I don't see why Pat should be any different. People are always saying that in a village with only one ginger-haired man, there are a great many ginger-haired children running about. So it could be that.

Sean   No, this isn't right.

DD   Sean, do not engage with –

Sean   It's not 'Pat thinks he's a really happy man'. It's 'Pat *feels* he's a really happy man'.

Spoke's Brother   That's the same thing.

Sean   Thinking and feeling is not the same.

Spoke's Brother   In this case there's very little difference in the words.

Sean   They're opposites.

Spoke's Brother   They sound like opposites but the ultimate meaning is the same. Like em . . . like . . .

YJB   Like a guy who's a dick but at the same time is also a fanny?

Spoke's Brother   Yeah. Pardon?

DD (*to* **YJB**)   One more from you! One more!

Nadia (*to* **YJB**)   One more I swear to God!

Sean   Nah. I'm not having this. He's a lovely guy Postman Pat. A really lovely guy. And I hate it when people say his life is a shambles and he's got loads of other kids. Because sometimes, right, when I'm in on my own I watch *Postman Pat*. I don't care. Nah, I don't care. And yeah, it's for little ones but it's wonderful and everything. I like the colours. The colours sort of remind me of when it wasn't shit and stuff. Know what I mean? When it wasn't all pressure and . . . shit. And for that ten minutes I'm back again. When it was alright. You know? And I sing the song. I do, I sing it. And even when I'm not watching it, sometimes I sing it. If things are turning wrong and my guts are all tight and sore, I sing it. Know what I mean? And for as long as the song lasts I'm alright. So leave him alone. Yeah? He's not like all the others. And I am telling you, it is, definitely, one hundred per cent, 'Pat *feels* he's a very happy man.' I'm singing it in my head now. 'Feels.'

There's a long pause.

Someone – who I wonder? – starts to hum the Postman Pat *theme. After a bit, some others join in.*

It does actually help. They're feeling better.

Soon they're all humming. Even **DD**.

It gets louder and louder. They hum a couple of verses and the middle bit.

They're having fun. The next time the verse comes round they start to sing. **Marcy** *has moved away from the door to join in.*

They feel good. They feel like children. They sing . . .

All
Postman Pat
Postman Pat
Postman Pat and his black and white cat.

Early in the morning
Just as day is dawning
Pat thinks/feels . . .

Callum Hunt *explodes through the door in a fury. Everyone jumps and stops singing, except* **Sean**, *who has his back to the door and carries on happily with 'He's a really happy man!' until . . .*

Callum *grabs him and wrestles him to the floor.*

This has happened in seconds and the shock of it has everyone else frozen and staring.

Sean, *in a panic, tries to kick* **Callum** *off, but* **Callum** *grabs his foot and roughly removes his shoe.*

Sean   Not the shoes! Oh my God! Not the shoes!

Callum *gets the other one off and after battering* **Sean** *with them a couple of times he throws them into the corner of the room over by the curtained exit, goes to the main door and shuts it, then rounds on the rest in a terrifying stage whisper . . .*

Callum   This . . . is . . . a . . . funeral! Have . . . some . . . fucking . . . *respect*!

Sean (*from the floor*)   I don't believe it. It's my worst nightmare come true. Again!

Callum   Is he in charge? Is this the leader?

Spoke's Brother   It's a collective.

Callum   I beg your pardon, ballbag?

Nadia   I'm the leader. It's my shoes you want.

DD   No. It's not. She's not. And neither's he. I'm the leader. Although technically it *is* actually a collective but I organise the –

Callum   Then you're coming with me, girl. Right now! You're bloody lucky Keith got carted off to get some holy water splashed on his face and missed your little flashback singalong or you'd be in even worse trouble. But everyone else caught it. So you're coming with me to apologise to the whole church. Now!

DD   What? But we were just . . .

Amee (*simultaneously*)   Warming up . . .

DD (*simultaneously*)   Nervous.

Amee   And anyway, how is our singing any worse than you battering people with shoes?

Nadia   And swearing. We're not swearing. Swearing is the worst thing anyone can do at this moment in time.

DD   Nadia just . . .

Callum   'Worst thing anyone can do'? Oh yeah. Right. OK then, when you're out there grovelling why don't you ask Ali's mum and dad and all those weeping teachers what the worst thing anyone can do is? Do you think they'll say 'swearing'? Or 'slapping some dunce with a shoe'? Do you? I don't.

Nadia   Church people really hate swearing though.

Callum   Worse than killing someone?

Nadia   Worse than singing 'Postman Pat'.

Spoke's Brother   He didn't kill her, though.

A couple of big beats.

Well. He didn't.

Callum *shifts his gaze to* **Spoke's Brother**, *who immediately realises that he's made a mistake . . .*

Callum   Who says he didn't? Who says?

Spoke's Brother   She . . . she was killed . . . in the crash. Immediately.

Callum   You know that for a fact, do you? Well do you? You were in the car with her when she left the party, were you? Hey, I said were you?

Spoke's Brother   No.

Callum   No. But who was? Who was?

Spoke's Brother   Jake Spence.

Callum   And who was in the car with her when she lost control and skidded off the road?

Spoke's Brother   Jake Spence.

Callum   And who was in the car when the ambulance arrived and found her dead at the wheel?

Spoke's Brother   Jake Spe—

Callum   Wrong! Wrong. Jake Spence was *not* with her when the ambulance arrived because Jake Spence had bolted. Jake Spence had run a mile. He left her there to save himself. His own girlfriend. We know *that* for a fact and the police know it. And the papers know it. Everyone out there knows it. But what we don't know is exactly when she died. Because no one was there to see it. And that's a crime as bad as killing in my eyes. The worst thing anyone could do. End of.

Pause.

Marcy   God, you're so impressive, Callum.

Callum   What?

Marcy   Nothing. I'm just saying you're like, really impressive. The way you speak, the way you behave out there. The nods, the whispers . . .

YJB   The beatings.

Marcy   If ever you like, want to . . . ?

Callum   What?

Marcy   Well. I dunno. Anything. With me. I would. I don't mean . . . I'm talking about ice-skating really. Or playing something on the Wii. Just hang out. I mean . . . you probably don't. Want to. You definitely don't. Sorry. Just. For God sake I'm only joking!

Callum *laughs in her face. Shakes his head in disbelief.* **Marcy** *shrinks away to nothing.*

Callum   You bloody babies. (*To* **DD**.) Right – c'mon.

DD   Where?

Callum   Out there. People need to see justice.

DD   What, apologise? Seriously? To . . . what, to everyone?

Callum   Today.

DD *doesn't move.*

Amee   You're in no position to demand apologies. You owe Sean an apology and look at him: still waiting. And anyway who says you're in charge?

Callum   Keith. The dad. In their kitchen two days ago. 'You're a good lad, Callum. Any trouble at the funeral, you know what to do.' Exact quote from the dad. *Postman Pat* was trouble, he was the principal Pat singer, I knew what to do: shoe justice to the chest and arms. End of. No apology needed.

Amee   I'm not talking about Pat. I'm talking about the stunt kite incident. You tied his shoes to a stunt kite and you've never even said sorry. Not once.

Callum   What? When was this?

Amee   When was this, Sean?

Sean (*sheepishly*)   Oh, I dunno. I can't really remember, Amee. My birthday, I think. May the second, 2001 or something. About three o'clock or something. I dunno. Quarter past three. Or something. I dunno.

Amee   May the second, 2001. Three-ish.

Callum   I'm not apologising for something I'm meant to've done on May the fucking second, 2001. Christ I was only . . . what, nine?

Sean   Yeah, I was six. I always remember it was my sixth birthday cos that was the birthday I got my shoes eaten by a big dog.

Amee   If you apologise we'll apologise. That's justice.

Callum   Nah, nah, nah. That's out of order. No one blames kids for the stupid shit they done when they were kids. That's the rule. Kids do stupid shit but then one day they stop doing stupid shit, all is forgiven, and that's us grown up. That's life in a nutshell. No apology necessary. Justice does not apply. And anyway how can you fly a stunt kite with a six-year-old moron tied to it? It's just not believable.

Sean   No, I wasn't wearing the shoes at the time. They'd been yanked off.

Callum   You're yanking me off right now, son. This is bullshit.

DD (*faking confidence*)   Look . . . We're still singing the song. You can't stop us.

Callum   What song?

DD   We're Sensation Nation.

Spoke's Brother   I'm not.

DD   He's not. The rest of us are, though. We're singing her favourite song as the coffin gets carried out. Miss Ronson said we were all to wait here until we heard the cue. We're still doing it. Aren't we? Apology or no apology. You can't stop us. Actually. It's all arranged and everything.

Callum   Well, tough luck, girl, cos I'm going to unarrange it just as soon as . . . wait a minute. Hold on. *Postman Pat* was Ali's favourite song?

DD   No.

Spoke's Brother (*pointing at* **Sean**)   It's his favourite song.

Sean   No, it's not.

Callum   Why you singing his favourite song as the coffin gets carried out? He's a little pussy.

Sean   It's not my favourite song.

Callum   What's he even got to do with it? He didn't even know her.

DD   We're not singing his favourite song . . .

Sean   It's *one* of my favourite songs . . .

DD   We're singing this.

She hands over a lyric sheet.

Callum   This isn't her favourite song either. Nah, you should've asked me. I'd've told you. This'll be shit.

Nadia (*snatching it back*)   No it won't. We've practised it. DD's done the arrangement and it's beautiful and everyone'll cry cos it's beautiful and we do this really cool thing.

Callum   Should've got some of us older ones to do it. Frankie Tear should've done it. She's been on *X Factor* and everything, what've you ever done? OK, she was shit, but at least she was Ali's real mate – wouldn't be barging in on it like all you lambs.

Amee   We didn't barge in on it.

Callum   Well, you weren't invited. I know who was invited. How come you're doing the song if you didn't even know her and weren't invited?

Good point. The rest of 'Sensation Nation' hadn't thought about that. Their gaze slowly turns to **DD**, *who's avoiding eyes.*

DD   What? (*Beat.*) We were invited. We were. (*Beat.*) Eventually. Kind of.

Amee   DD . . .

DD   Look, we got the gig, didn't we? This is our debut, it's been decided and it's perfect. This is the sad story we spring from – they'll show us wiping away tears in slow motion if we get to the semis. Springing from a sad story is the ultimate vote-winner. No one can say this isn't a total opportunity.

Amee   Yeah, but how did we get invited if we didn't . . . ?

DD   As the saying goes, 'Sometimes, in order for good things to happen, some people have to tell some other people lies.' End of.

Callum   You lied to Keith? Ooooooh. This is trouble. Justice is coming.

Amee   DD! Did you lie to Keith?

DD   No! I lied to my sister and she lied to Keith. But she didn't know she was lying so there's really no need to tell her. Laila's weird, she gets angry about stuff like that. Look, all I said was that Ali was a member of Sensation Nation and one of her last wishes was to hear us sing. Which is a *white* lie really, cos I have actually made her an honorary member since she died.

Sean   Since she died? What, like a ghost?

DD   Sean . . .

Amee   Oh my God, we've totally crashed this.

DD   The whole world's crashed it, Amee. You think every weeper out there knew Ali Monroe? No way. But they're all here, aren't they? All dressed up and gawping. Well, we're contributing. That's the difference. We're helping, know what I mean? We're offering her something. Something good.

Spoke's Brother   She's right. You are doing something nice for Ali. She loved music, she would've loved this. It *is* good.

Amee   It's based on a lie, though.

DD   So what? If it ends in something beautiful so what? This isn't a random thing, you know – I've worked at this, planned it out. You don't understand how these programmes work, I do. When we go on the show it's all about layers and storylines. New things have to crop up to keep the voters interested week by week or we're dead. It's not all about singing. For some people, who, you know, can't sing as well as you, it can't be about singing at all. That's why I've layered our story. Why do you think I picked this particular group of people for Sensation Nation? Singing skills? Yeah, right. We can learn that. No. There are other reasons. Believe me.

Pause.

Callum   What other reasons?

DD   What's it to you?

Callum   Dunno. Interested.

Amee   So am I. What other reasons, DD?

DD   Well. Look, you're a really good singer. And we need a really good singer. I'm a really good leader and we need a really good leader. Know what I mean?

Marcy   What am I, then? Why did you pick me?

DD (*this is all difficult*)   You're . . . well . . . you know . . . (*Sigh.*) Remember the time when we were at that Geography conference and the seats caught fire and you said to me that you totally hated Amee? Well, I thought . . . if you fell out during the heats it wouldn't be the worst thing in the world. Tension is a vote-winner and so is someone walking out.

Don't make the face, Marcy, everyone has a role. Young Jean Brown is the rotten-looking one that they can make over and who'll get better and better as the series goes on. That's her role and she's not complaining.

Sean   Oh no. Don't tell me. Don't tell me you only picked me cos we're going out? Did you? DD? Is that the only reason I'm here? Kissing ability? Is it?

DD   No. Of course that's not the only reason, Sean. You've also got learning difficulties. And after Susan Boyle, that's more important than ever. So that's two reasons.

Sean   Oh my God!

DD   I'm sorry, Sean. But it doesn't change the fact that I really love you or whatever.

Sean   I don't have learning difficulties, DD.

DD   Oh come on, Sean, you do.

Sean   I don't though.

DD   Yes, Sean, you do.

Nadia   DD? DD? Can I, em . . . ask? Why, em . . . why me? What's my role? I wonder.

DD   Well. Well. You're poor, aren't you?

Nadia (*devastated*)   Oh. Yeah. Yeah. OK.

DD   I don't think I've done anything wrong. I really don't.

Pause. The room disagrees.

Sean   Hands up who thinks I've got learning difficulties.

Callum *puts his hand up. No one else does.*

From outside the door the organ plays.

Spoke's Brother   It's starting.

The door opens and **Laila** *and* **Frankie** *come in.* **Laila** *looks all keyed up and* **Frankie** *looks terrible – the shadow of her former self.*

Callum (*straightening his tie*)   I know. I'm coming, I'm coming. (*Threatening the others.*) Later.

Laila   Jake's back.

Callum   What?

Laila   Jake. Frankie saw him, didn't you, Frankie?

Frankie   He was running round the side of the church . . . He was . . . he was hiding, but yeah, it was definitely him.

Laila   Callum . . . Jake Spence is here.

*

Some more time has passed.

We can hear the drone of the service next door. For the first time we can see that the wall and ceiling of this room is covered in a faded mural. From what we can make out behind the piles of cluttered and damaged church stuff, it's of the moon and the stars – the heavens I suppose. The style is ancient, ornate, though the details are lost, the paint faded.

'Sensation Nation' – apart from **Sean***, who's over in the corner looking for his shoes – are gathered in a huddle. Very, very quietly they're warming up.* **DD** *hums a note and the others match it, then harmonise.*

It doesn't last – fizzles out. The group's heart isn't in it. They feel used and sad. They wish they weren't here. **DD** *probably knows that 'Sensation Nation' is over.*

Spoke's Brother, **Callum**, **Laila** *and* **Frankie** *aren't here.*

After a moment . . .

DD (*without her previous authority*)   We have to warm up.

Amee   Why?

DD   If we want to be good . . .

Marcy   Who says we want to be good?

DD   The whole school is . . . We have to do the song. It's a funeral. We don't have a choice. Imagine if we don't sing?

Marcy   I imagine you'd be desolated. Is that the right word, Amee?

Amee (*not malicious*)   Yeah. I think it is, Marcy.

Sean   How can shoes just disappear man? They're nowhere! It's like, if Derren Brown worked in a shoe shop this is what would happen. Absolutely no work would get done. Can someone please help me look?

He gets no response.

DD   We've got to sing. It doesn't matter about *Britain's Got Talent* or anything, but we've got to sing today.

Marcy   Maybe you should sing on your own then, DD? I'm sure everyone will be moved by your beautiful leadership skills.

DD   I can't sing on my own.

Marcy   Why not?

DD   I'm not . . . I'm not good enough.

Marcy   Well, that's a shame.

Sean   They have just simply vanished. They were here one minute then that arsehole Hunt has somehow lobbed them into a parallel universe. I need shoes, man. I'm just not myself without shoes on. Help me look, someone! I can't see the shoes for the trees here, man!

The door opens and **Spoke's Brother** *comes in. He's just done his reading. He goes to close the door but* **Frankie** *bustles in after him, followed by* **Laila**. **Frankie** *is upset and finds some space away from the others.* **Laila** *comforts her a bit.*

Frankie   I'm alright. I was just, you know . . . Drowning a bit. (*About* **Spoke's Brother**.) I saw him come in and . . .

Laila   It's OK.

Frankie   I thought it'd be another world in here or something. God. Sorry.

Laila   It's OK. It's just my little sister and that. They don't know anything about anything.

Spoke's Brother   Wait a minute. What the hell am I doing back in here? I was supposed to go and sit with my mum and dad! Sake. Oh well. Would you all like to know how it went? Would it be useful if I describe, in detail, my recent experiences? To give you, you know, an idea of what awaits you on the other side?

Beat.

Amee   Maybe we should help Sean look for his shoes?

Yeah, the group agree that they'd rather do that than listen to **Spoke's Brother***. He doesn't seem to mind the fact that they all turn away and start a halfhearted hunt through the room. He continues as if they were rapt . . .*

Spoke's Brother   Yeah, it went OK, actually. Nervous though, see. (*His hands are shaking.*) I was alright until I looked up. They're even standing outside, all the way up the gravel to the graveyard. And there's speakers out there so everyone can hear. But a stand must've broken or something because Mr Gibbons is up on a plastic chair, holding a speaker in both hands, like this. I thought, God, whatever I say next will vibrate in his arms. It'll go all the way back to the graves. And when I looked back down at the reading I couldn't make out the words any more. I could see them, but as, like, marks on paper, not as real words with meanings. I heard someone say 'Poor kid'. But I wasn't upset. Well, not until then. Cos then, after that, the meanings kind of came into focus. And now it *did* seem sad. Sad that all these words – every word from now on in – will vibrate nowhere near Ali. And I thought 'Poor kid'. But I just read it. Without thinking or feeling or meaning or anything. And got off. I concentrated on not tripping and anyway, it went OK apart from, you know, coming back in here.

Pause. During his speech, one by one they stopped looking for **Sean***'s shoes and started to listen to what he was saying. After a bit . . .*

Marcy   What about Jake Spence?

Spoke's Brother   Dunno.

Laila   He won't show. No way. He knows what would happen.

Spoke's Brother   Callum Hunt and all them – they're going in and out, down the aisles, watching at the door. It'll be all their birthdays if he does show.

Laila   It makes no sense for him to show.

Marcy   Yeah, but maybe he's drunk? Or on drugs. I heard he's a mess. Everyone says he was on drugs the night they crashed. That's *why* they crashed my mum says.

Frankie   He wasn't on drugs. Neither was Ali. She'd never done anything. And now she never will, so tell your mum to relax.

Laila   Don't let them get to you, Frankie, they're just little kids.

Frankie   Must be nice. To be a little kid again. I didn't know how good it was, did you? It was gone so quick. I remember the day right, the exact day it went. I was in the garden, playing with this doll I had, my favourite one and I just . . . couldn't do it any more. I felt dumb. Watched. It was gone.

Laila   Do you want me to get my mum?

DD   Is Mum here?

Laila   Everyone's here.

DD   Is Dad here?

Laila   Of course not. Frankie, do you want me to get my mum?

Frankie   What are you all doing? Why are you all here?

Laila   It's DD's little singing thing. They're doing a song. It's nothing. You don't need to go back to Ali's house if you don't want to. I'll tell them you're not feeling well.

Frankie (*to* **DD**)   You're going to sing?

DD   Well. We were going to, but it all got kind of . . .

YJB   Fucked.

DD   Yeah. Would you like to sing, Frankie? You know the song. You'd be amazing.

DD *hands her the lyric sheet.*

Frankie   This is her favourite. Was. Is.

DD   You'd be amazing.

Frankie   No I wouldn't.

DD   That's why I'm, know what I mean. Doing it. Cos of you on *X Factor*. I couldn't believe it.

Frankie   Right.

DD   Cos no one in this place ever does anything. None of them. They just sit back and jeer and do nothing. But you did. You showed them. Didn't you?

Frankie   Yeah. I showed them. Showed them how shit and desperate and scared someone could be. And the funny thing is I asked for it too, didn't I? Queued up and begged for it. I was at my worst. And now everything I touch . . . absolutely everything is exactly as bad as I was that night. And always will be.

DD   No, you were great. Wasn't she? She was amazing, wasn't she?

No one responds. Until . . .

Nadia   Yeah. I thought you were amazing.

DD   The very next day I decided, 'Right, I'm getting a group together.' If Frankie Tear can do it, I can. You were my inspiration. That's why I'm doing this.

Laila   I thought you were doing this so Dad could see you on TV?

DD   No.

Laila   DD thinks just cos Dad met his girlfriend at Glastonbury that means he's in the record industry.

DD   He *is* in the record industry.

Laila   You know what, DD, think what you want, I don't care. It's not important. But in my opinion people Dad's age shouldn't even be going to Glastonbury. They should leave that to us. But people like Dad and all his friends, they can't. He can't just let us be young and him be old, he has to get in on it and have the music and the clothes and the games and the phones and I think it's pathetic. He'd rather do all that than . . . it's pathetic. I wish they would just admit that they're not young and we are. Dress like an adult! Talk like an adult! Apologise and help us! Then maybe we could . . . Look, this isn't important, OK? Sing your little song. I'm going to take Frankie back to ours, right?

They go to leave.

DD   Laila. I told you a lie. About Ali being in Sensation Nation. I told a lie and I'm sorry.

Laila   Yeah, I know. Of course I know. She was my friend.

DD   Then why did you . . . ?

Laila   I was doing something nice for my sister. You got a problem with that? Good luck.

She leaves. **Frankie** *hands the lyric sheet back to* **DD**, *shakes her head apologetically and exits through the door after* **Laila**.

Pause.

YJB   Those bastards said that if I just joined in I'd get better. So I did this. Heard you talking in the corridor and joined right in. Did it quickly too, not really, you know, thinking about it or whatever. Unbelievable, really. Joined in. They were right. For once. I think. So I'll sing with you if you want. I can't be this . . . terrified . . . for nothing. There needs to be a point to feeling like this. Or else . . . nothing's changed. Know what I mean?

Marcy   Oh well, DD, it's a duet now. Things are looking up.

Sean *has been out of sight in the far corner of the room looking for his shoes again. He pops up, shoe in hand.*

Sean   Yeesss!! Found one. It was under this curtain. And guess what? There's a door here! Check it out, look. There's a kind of door here or something – with a curtain. That's where they went. I knew they couldn't've gone into a parallel universe. There'd've been lightning flashes and thunder noises and stuff, wouldn't there? Nah, it was just a normal door with nothing behind it but . . .

He opens the door to reveal **Jake Spence**. *He immediately shuts the door again.*

Sean   Ghosts.

Reactions from the others.

Sean   Oh my actual God.

He slowly opens the door again.

Jake   Please don't . . . Please. I just wanted to . . . I dunno.

Amee   How long have you been back there?

Jake   Since *In the Night Garden*. There's a window down there, I climbed in, I'm not hurting anyone . . .

Marcy   I'm going to get Callum.

Jake   No! Please. I'm not hurting anyone. I just want to say . . . No, I just want to listen. Why can't I just stay here and listen? This is the last time. This is the last chance I have. Why can't I be here?

Spoke's Brother   Because you left. You left her once, you left for ever.

Jake   But. No. You said. You said I've done nothing wrong. I heard you.

Spoke's Brother   I said you didn't kill her. Cos you didn't. But you did do something wrong. You left her.

Jake   I couldn't . . . I couldn't help it. I was thrown from the car, man, and when I opened my eyes, I was running. Like a little kid. Running that way you used to. Full pelt. So fast. Too fast. I couldn't stop. No one could.

Spoke's Brother   I could. Because, see, the difference between you and me is that I loved her. So I couldn't've ran. You're just a guy who was there and this'll be you and her tangled together for good. You got lucky. You and her are like a tattoo now. So what? It doesn't mean you love her. Not like me. Cos I've known her since I was a kid. Her dad and my dad went to school together. This school. And I loved her. I loved her when she used to come to my house for Christmas and I loved her when we played in her garden and once it was really raining and we didn't go in. Well. I loved her then the most. They called for us to go in but we didn't. She held me back. It was raining so hard and it was all ours – this rain-world. Every night I've thought about her. Every single night. And when I got rid of . . . rid of . . . fucking . . . THIS! She would've loved me back. Oh yes she would. Oh yes she would.

Spoke's Brother *meant his body, when he said 'this'. He meant when he grows up. He punched himself in the chest when he said it. He screamed the word. He tears at himself a bit. Then he stops.*

Jake   I loved her too.

Pause.

Spoke's Brother   Whatever. Nothing matters. I'm going to find my family.

Jake   Are you going to tell them? Are you?

Spoke's Brother *doesn't answer. He exits.*

There's a big pause. The organ plays again.

DD   That's the cue.

YJB   I'm ready.

Marcy You're doing it?

DD It's either that or we run.

Nadia I'll do it. Too. For me, I mean. If you want?

DD Yeah. I do. I really do. Thank you, Nadia. And I'm
sorry. Everyone. I am. Sean, if you want to go out with Amee
I don't mind. Well, I mind, but . . . you know what I mean?
I can't stop it. (*To* **YJB** *and* **Nadia**.) Ready?

They look terrified. Deep breaths.

Jake What song are you going to sing?

Nobody responds.

DD See you on the other side.

DD, **YJB** *and* **Nadia** *exit like soldiers going into battle.*

Amee I'm going too. Sean?

Sean Oh my God, Amee. I . . .

Amee Sean. No.

Sean Right. Good.

They scuttle off, **Sean** *desperately putting his shoe on as he goes.*

Marcy (*as they go*) But why? But why?

They're gone. It's just **Marcy** *left from 'Sensation Nation' now. After a
quick beat, and a glance at* **Jake**, *she goes after the others.*

Jake But why?

She turns, shrugs and exits.

It's just **Jake** *now. Just* **Jake** *and the candles and the crosses and the
stars above him.*

*But when the song starts, that changes. Everything changes when the song
starts . . .*

*

I have no idea what song 'Sensation Nation' sing. I really couldn't say what an eighteen-year-old girl's favourite song would be.

But you know don't you?

Think about it. Talk about it. And you'll know what's right.

Although 'Sensation Nation' are in the main church, away from this room, I think we should see them somewhere, as they line up, ready – scared. Brave.

The cool thing they do, the thing **Nadia** *mentioned earlier, is that seconds before they sing, they link hands.*

And she was right. It is beautiful.

And it changes everything.

Jake, *when he hears the song begin and realises what it is, slowly folds up, down upon his knees, head wrapped up in his arms, crying hard for himself, like a baby.*

All the junk in this room, all these relics and paraphernalia, these weird wooden icons . . . they go. They disappear. We don't need them now.

We have the song.

Above us, the stars and the moon which were faded and flaking before, glow. They glow and then they blossom.

The stars turn into white flowers. Flowers fall, flowers burst through every dusty and dank corner on the stage. White flowers . . . everywhere.

Then, all at once, the petals clear and **Jake** *is exactly as he was, but is no longer in some side room at a service.*

He's in a garden.

And the song continues . . .

The grass here is green and perfect. The sky is childhood blue. There are long, fake-looking daisies here and there. Strong trees let dappled summer-morning light pulse kindly on the lawn. It feels like a garden we were in once before. Years and years ago maybe. A perfect garden for children.

Jake *opens his eyes.*

There's a bridge. Painted white and twinkling with tiny lights.

And standing on that bridge is **Ali**.

The music continues throughout, underneath this. But they aren't singing right now . . .

Ali   Alright, mate?

Jake   Ali?

Ali   You alright?

Jake   This is your favourite song?

Ali   I fucking *love* this song.

Jake   I didn't know that.

Ali   Well. It's not important.

Jake   I think . . . I think it's important.

Ali   I'm telling you, mate, it's not.

Jake   I'm . . . I'm . . . oh God, Ali, I am so sorry. I am. I really am so fucking . . .

He cries.

Ali   I know, man. Yeah, I know you are. But it's OK.

Jake   I'm going to kill myself or something, Ali.

Ali   Nah. You're not.

Jake   Why not? There's no reason now.

Ali   Yes there is. I'm asking you not to. It wasn't your fault, man. I was driving, the other guy was overtaking in a crazy place . . .

Jake   But I ran. They're right, I ran! And that's going to be *on* me for the rest of my life. What can I do now that's not running? Nothing.

Ali   Something will happen. Something good. Just wait.

Jake   It's like I know what I'm going to be, though. And it's not fair. I have to be the bad guy now. Everything I do. Imagine that. Imagine having no choice when it comes to that.

Ali   You're not a bad guy. I'm not into bad guys. I liked you cos you were funny in Physics and you were sweet to my little brother and your jeans look great. You're not bad. And anyway there's no rule, I don't think. Everyone can change. If you want it bad enough.

Jake   That sounds like it's from *Hollyoaks*.

Ali   It *is* from *Hollyoaks*! Oh my God! That's something else I like about you, you're totally into *Hollyoaks* even though it's desperate and sad.

Pause. They smile.

Jake   What . . . what's it like?

Ali   Amazing. There's another world right underneath. Like a vibration or something. Hey, see when the car flipped? Did time kind of . . .

Jake   Slow . . .

Ali   Yeah! Like, totally slow down. Well, that's what it's like.

Jake   What do you mean?

Ali   It's only when you get things at real-time speed – at this speed – that you realise everything's been going too fast. Too fast to see. I think we knew it was there, felt it was there, this other world, but we just couldn't see it. It was zooming by – right in front of our noses. Even photographs are travelling at the speed of light, Jake, so what chance do we have? You can feel it though, like a vibration, but you can't see it. You can't see anything except the vapour trails of stuff that's long gone. Well, when the car flipped we got to see the world as it really is. Didn't we? And where I am now I see it all the time. And it's simple and it's beautiful and . . . yeah, I'm fine. And I'm there under everything, inside everything. I'm not gone, Jake. You're just moving too fast to see me.

Jake   I want to stay here. I'll never leave you again, Ali. I swear to God. I'll never leave you.

Ali   Mate, you're going to leave me now.

Jake   No.

Ali   Yeah.

Jake   Why?

Ali   Because it's time to go.

Ali *kisses* **Jake** *and walks over the bridge.*

'Sensation Nation' start singing again. The last chorus.

Ali *waves goodbye.*

Jake *waves back.*

When she's gone the garden goes with her.

Jake *is back in the room again. The door to the congregation right in front of him.*

The song finishes. 'Sensation Nation' let go of each other's hands and go into darkness.

Jake *gets to his feet, takes a deep breath and walks through the door: forward on the tide, into the now.*

Too Fast

*Notes on rehearsal and staging, drawn from workshops
with the writer held at the National Theatre, November 2010*

Douglas has set you a challenge of imagination, inspiration and detail – finding the balance between using your imagination and getting answers from the text. At the very start write a list of adjectives, images, thoughts and feelings from your first reading of the play. Your first reading is your most important connection to the play. The audience will be seeing it for the first time – your job is to recreate the excitement you had when first reading it. Douglas actually writes down the idea of why he's writing the play at the very start so that he can refer back to it and keep on track.

How the Play Came About

Douglas wanted to make the play an emotionally affecting piece – to be driven on an emotional rather than political or social level. His father was a teacher, and at his funeral a group of his students sang – an odd moment which made him consider the lack of emotional connection the kids must have to his father's death, yet how the power of the performance itself acquired meaning because of its setting. Where Douglas grew up there were frequent car crashes, and everyone knew a teenager who had died. At his own school that teenager was the school genius, a talented musician whom he knew in passing. He wanted to explore the generation gap between thirteen-year-olds and sixteen-year-olds – the crushes you have on older kids in school who aren't even aware of your existence, how it's difficult and frustrating being fifteen, and how at fifteen you can already feel nostalgic about your own childhood. The play was constructed to allow a range of young actors to contribute relative to their age. Older characters aren't on stage as much but they have harder things to do.

Aspects of the Play

THE START

The awkwardness of the situation at the start needs to be
tangible. Sensation Nation almost *want* the nervous, pre-show,
backstage atmosphere because it legitimises them being there –
Spoke's Brother is spoiling that. You might improvise the
scene just before the written action of the play starts. Spoke's
Brother has been *talking* for some time. How has that created
the atmosphere the audience need to be hit with? How can
you instantly place images of the characters and their
relationships and status? What differences are there between
what the characters know and what the audience know? Not
knowing we're at a funeral for a few pages makes the audience
active in their attempts to figure it out.

THE SONG

The song is the crucial moment in the play – it makes the
other world possible. That world is there all the time, we're
just going too fast to see it. The song slows time, it takes you
out of the physical. It has a similar effect to *Postman Pat* – it
allows the group safety and childhood, and allows them into
another world. There are also rules of literal storytelling – it is
Ali's favourite song from before the start of the play; the song
needs to be suitable to be played at a funeral; her parents have
approved it. The singing has to be good in order to achieve
the transformative function of the song. It requires open-
heartedness and a lack of cynicism.

Therefore the choice of song to use is absolutely integral to the
style of the production. The group need to choose what the
song is; they should engage in pitching what they think the
song should be and testing that as a company of actors.

A Possible Exercise

Each member of the group brings in their favourite song. Why
is it your favourite song? There will be emotional and rational
reasons. Are they equally important? Why? What feeling does
the song give you? How can you explain that to someone else
without describing it? Each group member has to create an

exercise or experience or situation to help the rest of the group
understand why that song is important to them, and give
the group a shared understanding of the feeling the song
gives them. For example, in the workshop an experience of
sitting in the dark and being pushed around and shouted at
gave a shared understanding of 'Where Is My Mind?' by the
Pixies; being firmly held back and at a given point being let
go and running as far and as fast as possible gave a shared
understanding of 'Born To Run' by Bruce Springsteen;
starting as low and as small as possible and gradually getting
as high and big as possible gave a shared understanding of
'The World's Greatest' by R. Kelly. The group could then try
this with what they think would be Ali's favourite song.

You might approach the song from the lyrics like teenagers
do, poring over every possible meaning – what action might
come from that? You might explore the power of the voice
itself and think about the meaning later. You might want the
group to find their own equivalent of *Postman Pat* – a trigger
song which can make the group nostalgic for their own
childhood. What physical action and sensation might help
communicate that? Is there a way of incorporating a similar
physicality in the staging of that moment of the play?

The group should discover the song in different ways, each of
them could improvise so they have a memory of rehearsing in
character. Perhaps there's a memory of a terrible rehearsal,
so when the tension rises they have the fear of known failure.
They should surprise themselves with the performance they
actually give at the end: it's a leap of faith, and this time the act
of holding hands has real meaning – it's not just a gimmick.
DD's ideas of performance are right: 'If *we* cry *they* won't.'

THE NIGHT GARDEN

In fact, the song may well be the key to getting us into the
Night Garden. As the plays shifts into magic, there are a series
of theatrical moments – Sensation Nation holding hands, the
group singing, the song disappearing, the Night Garden
appearing, the dead girl appearing – each of which needs to
be clear, and individually thrilling. The overall moment needs

to be delivered with the magic described in the stage directions, regardless of your budget, resources and what you can achieve technically. Whose transformation is it? The audience's? Sensation Nation's? Jake's? And what is the mechanism to get us there? Ali's world has always been there, we've just not noticed it. Can what has already been on stage be transformed? Can this be done by using different lighting? The song is the catalyst, so could Sensation Nation orchestrate the change?

It's a challenge for every production, but crucially it's about the gesture that the moment creates. Therefore it's almost certainly the right approach to design the Night Garden first, then work backwards into the room. What visual vocabulary does the production have? How realistic/inventive/playful is it? How can the company meet the challenge with any number of low-tech solutions? What does the room literally *need*? What are the images? Just two doors, with one covered by a curtain? How simply can you create the room?

Characters

For each character, find a line in the play which best describes how they would like to be seen, and a line which best describes who they actually are.

Some thoughts about some of the characters which it might be worth considering:

SPOKE'S BROTHER is only known in relation to others (i.e. to his brother, Ali). Does the actor need to know his actual name? Possibly, but it should be owned by that actor, and not known by others. He is effortlessly comfortable with lecturing his philosophy but incapable of giving his reading – what change does he go through?

YOUNG JEAN BROWN's name has been given to her. She needs to look as if she's the last person in the world who would ever swear.

NADIA is like a football manager's deputy – she says everything DD says a bit later and a lot rougher. The actress playing her needs to find that urge to jump in.

MARCY wants to grow up fast and sometimes offends other characters with suggestions that they don't. She's prickly. She loves the sound of words in her own mouth (even if she gets them wrong).

AMEE's intelligence means she doesn't have to get involved. She's from a privately schooled background. DD needs her because she's the only really talented singer. Light is shone at her through Sean.

DD thinks her dad and Simon Cowell are in the same industry.

Finding the Units

Making units means breaking the play up into manageable chunks. A unit is a narrative arc from A to B to C, a bit of story, an emotional moment. A new unit starts when something has changed, a thought has ended. Each time a new unit starts you should find a new energy to push it forward. One unit doesn't fade and a new one fill its place – a new unit overtakes an old one. Unit breaks (/) in the first act might be:

DD   Just everybody focus! / (*To* **Marcy**.) Anything?
(p. 487)

Sean   I remember thinking at the time, 'Oh my God.' /
DD   Right that's another thing, we can't cry.   (p. 488)

Nadia   She was going too fast, it was her own fault. /
Pause.   (p. 488)

DD   I don't want to boss people about, but that is actually an order. /
Pause. They go back to doing whatever it was they were . . . (p. 488–9)

DD   Whatever. / Can I just ask a question . . .   (p. 490)

DD   Know what I mean? /
Marcy (*back at the door, peeking out*)   Aw. He's ruffling their hair now.   (p. 490)

Sean   God, I hate Callum Hunt. /
Spoke's Brother *has his hand up.* **Nadia** *points this out to* **DD**. *Reluctantly* . . .   (p. 491)

Nadia (*right into* **YJB**'s *face*)   I will fight you. /
Another pause.

(p. 492)

Once you've broken up your units you could describe them so
that you know what that unit needs to do (e.g. 'Chaos', 'We
see Amee and Sean's relationship', 'DD taking control'). You
could also consider what each character wants to do for the
duration of the unit, and what journey the audience needs to
see them taking.

Acting Style

The awkwardness of being a teenager is expressed by the action
of the play, it's not articulated. Therefore the acting style needs
to be front-footed, open and without a ponderous subtext. The
subtext is seen in the action not the dialogue, so the actors
need to get on with saying the line, not thinking about it.

A Possible Exercise

Set up a space for the scene which has no bearing on reality or
the set – it's just a neutral space. The actors play the scene
physically, demonstrating what they're doing to each other –
not literally or realistically, just finding the clearest way of
physically expressing their psychological action. Who do you
want to be near, avoid, intimidate or support? What do the
actors notice about how they feel towards others? This exercise
can uncover instincts and impulses which you might otherwise
not notice. We looked at the following section on page 488:

DD   Right, that's another thing, we can't cry. That's very
important, everyone? Okay? No crying. If *we* cry *they* won't
– and we want them to cry. That's a vote-winner.

Nadia   No crying.

DD   Just remember . . .

Nadia   She was going too fast, it was her own fault.

Pause. **DD** *gives* **Nadia** *a Sergeant Major's glare before continuing.*

DD   Just remember . . . let the song do the work.

The actors and people watching noticed several things: Nadia
wants to order people about whilst maintaining her second

place status; Spoke's Brother wants both to avoid DD and to punch her; Sean is trying to be obedient to DD but also be his own person; DD is like a Sergeant Major, but wants to give everyone individual attention.

This exercise encourages everyone to listen, especially when they're not talking. It allows everybody to discover the dynamic of the scene together, and it becomes learned in the room. Play the scene again, but with no wandering – every movement must relate specifically to the line being said, the moment occurring. You can continue to keep playing the scene, noting what feels surprising, what the spatial physicality reveals about relationships, and refining each time – sharpening each decision an actor makes, tightening each beat of action or dialogue, highlighting interesting moments that you might use in the actual staging. Because it takes away the pressure of 'performing' (particularly to an audience) and worrying about where you need to be, you can find out the underlying shape of a scene, which can then be adjusted on to the set in a way that makes much more psychological sense and, crucially, has been found by the actors.

Some Additional Thoughts

- Stage directions should be seen as inspirations for the performers. In traditional and everyday storytelling the tense freely changes and jumps around – allow that imagination to be the vocabulary of the rehearsal.

- Don't get stuck in literalness – there are rules in the play, but you will need to be fluid and imaginative.

- The action has to go at a certain pace: you and the company have to believe where it's going and that it's going to work.

- There can't be extra characters/actors in that room, but that doesn't mean that other actors can't be involved – there is another room.

- 'How do we stage this?' is the wrong question – if you unpack the play fully, it will provide answers.

- Create your own exercises – decide on the areas/themes you're interested in (i.e. nostalgia, funerals, social ranking), and get small groups to devise an exercise that explores that idea. This can also be used to troubleshoot specific moments in rehearsal.

- Be technical and strict about hitting the starts of lines – don't allow 'Um . . . ' and 'Look . . . ' and so on.

- The actors should know what their characters are like outside the situation depicted in the play.

- The rhythm of the play is essential. It's like a piece of music: you need to mark the stage directions as clearly as spoken lines so that the unarticulated moments between characters are captured.

- There are several catchphrases throughout the play ('As the saying goes', 'Know what I mean', 'End of') – find them and makes sure actors have an awareness of them. Discover the habit of the catchphrases.

- Important storylines are buried within the dialogue. You don't need to signpost them, but the company are collectively and collaboratively responsible for knowing where the important lines are so they're not lost. Make sure you land the clues, references and objects which thread through the play, so that we have a sense of the magic which is achieved by the end.

- In describing the offstage action the company need to excite the audience and get them up to date. The desire to communicate needs to be stronger than the 'seeing' of the offstage action.

- It is notable and important that the characters don't talk about death in terms of their own feelings about it, therefore make sure that the tone of the production isn't dour and reflective.

- There is not much physical action in the play, it's a play of waiting – how can you keep that fluid? What is the social make-up of the characters? What do they wear? How do they move? Find answers from their characters not their age. Make a video of the group in a relaxed situation so they can see how active they are when unaware. Can you create a physical vocabulary for the play which has a similar vibrancy?

• The play's jumps in time allow a greater amount of space and time in a story which is otherwise pretty relentless. How do you make the transition from the end of one act to the start of the next? Literalness is probably not that useful. Could you use these moments to set up a stage vocabulary which leads to the ending?

From a workshop led by Vicky Featherstone,
with notes by Dan Bird

Participating Companies

Aberconwy
Academy of Creative Training
Act One Theatre School
Ad Lib Theatre Company
Antidote Youth Theatre
Artemis Studios
artsdepot
Astor College for the Arts
Barnwell School
Barnwood Park Arts College
Bedford College
Berzerk Productions
Biddenham Upper School
Bilimankhwe Young Company
Birmingham Metropolitan
    College
Black Box Theatre School
Blue Elephant Theatre
The Blue Coat C of E School
Bodmin College
Bradfield College
Brewery Youth Theatre
Bridgend College
Brigshaw High School
Bristol Old Vic
Bryanston School
Burntwood School
Caerphilly County Youth Theatre
Callington Community College
Cardinal Wiseman RC High
    School
CAST Ensemble Youth Theatre
Castle Youth Theatre
Castleford High School
Cathedral School
Chesterton Community College
Chichester Festival Theatre
Chichester High School for Girls
Chislehurst and Sidcup Grammar

Chorlton High School
City Academy Bristol
City Academy Norwich
City College Plymouth
Colbury and Ashurst Theatrical
    Society Youth Theatre
Colchester Royal Grammar
    School
Coleg Sir Gar
Coombe Boys' School
Coombeshead College
Cotton Shed Theatre Company
Coulsdon College
Court Fields Community School
Craigholme School
The Crestwood School
Croydon Clocktower
The Customs House Trust Ltd
Deafinitely Theatre
Debden Park High School
Duck Egg Theatre
Dukes Theatre
Dumont High School
Easy Street Theatre Company
Epsom and Ewell High School
Everyman Youth Theatre
EXIT 25 Theatre Group
Falkirk Children's and Youth
    Theatre
Flying High Expressive Arts
    Company
Fowey Community College
The Garage
George Green's School
Grand Youth Theatre Company
Graveney Theatre Company
Griese Youth Theatre
Group 64 Youth Theatre
The Hazeley School

Hertfordshire County Youth Theatre

Hertswood School

High Jinks Drama Group

Highly Sprung Performance Co.

Hope Valley College

Impatient Vagrant

Institute of Contemporary Interdisciplinary Arts (ICIA), University of Bath

Ipswich High School

Islington Community Theatre

Jigsaw Youth Theatre Company (North London)

Junk Shop Theatre Company

Key Youth Theatre

Kildare Youth Theatre

The King's School, Ely

Kingsley School, Drama Department

Kirklees College Huddersfield Centre

Lammas School and Sports College

The Latimer Arts College

Little Actors Youth Theatre

The Little Angel Theatre

Llanelli Youth Theatre

Lodestar Tuition

LOST Youth Theatre Company

Lowton High School

Lyceum Youth Theatre

Lyme Youth Theatre

Macrobert Young Company

Marple Hall School

The Manor School

Masquerade

Millfield School

Monaro High School

More House School, Drama Department

Moulton Theatre

The Mountbatten School

Move Youth Theatre

Newcastle College

Newquay Tretherras School

NIDA

Norden Farm Centre for the Arts

North Walsham High School

NSW Public Schools Drama Company

Oceantide Entertainments

Odd Productions

Off the Ground Youth Theatre

Ormskirk School

Oslo International School

Oundle School

Outwood Grange Academy

The Oxford Actors Company with Wheatley Park School

The Park Players

Perfect Circle Theatre Company

The Phoenix

Platform Performance (Glasgow East Arts Company)

The Playing Space

The Priory City of Lincoln Academy

Priory School

Pump House CYT

Questors Youth Theatre

Ralph Thoresby School

RAW Academy

REDMAN Youth Theatre

Royal & Derngate Youth Theatre

Saffron Walden County High School

Sandwell College

SAVVY Theatre Young Company

Scarborough Youth Theatre

Shenfield High School

Shetland Youth Theatre

Southwark College